# CHAOTIC JUSTICE

JOHN ERNEST

# CHAOTIC
# Justice

RETHINKING

AFRICAN AMERICAN

LITERARY HISTORY

The University of North Carolina Press
CHAPEL HILL

Designed by Courtney Leigh Baker
Set in Whitman and Futura by Rebecca Evans
Manufactured in the United States of America

The paper in this book meets the guidelines for permanence
and durability of the Committee on Production Guidelines for
Book Longevity of the Council on Library Resources.

The University of North Carolina Press has been a
member of the Green Press Initiative since 2003.

Library of Congress Cataloging-in-Publication Data
Ernest, John.
Chaotic justice : rethinking African American
literary history / John Ernest.
p. cm.
Includes bibliographical references and index.
ISBN 978-0-8078-3337-7 (cloth : alk. paper)
ISBN 978-0-8078-5983-4 (pbk. : alk. paper)
1. American literature—African American authors—History and
criticism—Theory, etc. 2. American literature—African American
authors—History and criticism. 3. African Americans—Intellectual life.
4. African Americans in literature. 5. Criticism—Unitted States. I. Title.
PS153.N5E75 2009
810.9′896073—dc22
2009019735

*Portions of this book have appeared previously, in somewhat
different form. For details regarding the publications
involved, see the end of the Acknowledgments.*

cloth   13  12  11  10  09   5  4  3  2  1
paper   13  12  11  10  09   5  4  3  2  1

FOR ALL THOSE CROSSING THE BRIDGE

# CONTENTS

# ACKNOWLEDGMENTS

A number of people have been especially helpful to me as I thought through the ideas and the readings that led to *Chaotic Justice*. In many ways, I have been working on this book for a number of years, but I finally set out to write it on the suggestion of Robert Levine, to whom I am greatly indebted for his initial advice and his ongoing encouragement. From the beginning, I could not have found my way without the intellectual and ethical compass provided by my great colleague at West Virginia University, Katy Ryan. I am grateful as well to Donald Pease for his encouragement—both at the Futures of American Studies Institute and in a later reading of the first chapter—and to Michael Lackey, who also read an early version of that chapter.

When I completed an early draft, I was aided considerably by the astoundingly generous Dana Nelson, who offered not only cogent suggestions for revision but also efficient and thoughtful readings of the revised chapters. While I remain solely responsible for any shortcomings in the chapters that follow, I have to say that this a much better book than it would have been without Dana's sound advice. I am grateful to the anonymous reader for the University of North Carolina Press, whose astute commentary on a draft of the manuscript helped me find my focus as I worked through the revisions.

For continuing inspiration, along with useful conversations about portions of this book or about nineteenth-century African American literature more broadly, I am indebted to William Andrews, Brigitte Bailey, JerriAnne Boggis, Leonard Cassuto, R. J. Ellis, Audrey Fisch, P. Gabrielle Foreman, Frances Smith Foster, Eric Gardner, Henry Louis Gates Jr., Kathy Glass, Gordon Hutner, Maurice Lee, Lisa Long, Koritha Mitchell, Joycelyn Moody, Samuel Otter, Eve Allegra Raimon, Hollis Robbins, Xiomara Santamarina, Rhondda R. Thomas, David Watters, Stefan Wheelock, and Barbara White. I'm grateful also to Rebecca Mays Ernest for our many conversations about this book at the Hammer and the Beanery.

I have explored various aspects of this book's argument in other forums, and my thinking has developed considerably through exchanges
with various editors, readers, and audiences. I am grateful to the editors
of and readers for the following books and journals: *The Cambridge History
of African American Literature, Modern Language Studies, Frederick Douglass and Herman Melville: Essays in Relation, Southern Quarterly, Harriet
Wilson's New England: Race, Writing, and Region, The Cambridge Companion
to African American Slave Narratives, Arizona Quarterly, African American
Review, American Literature,* PMLA, *White Scholars/African American Texts,*
and *Literature on the Move: Comparing Diasporic Ethnicities in Europe and
the Americas.* I have delivered versions of some of this material in various talks and am grateful for the encouragement offered by audiences
at the Third Annual Black New England Conference (2008), American
Literature Association Annual Conference (2008, 2006, 2004, and 1999),
NEMLA Annual Convention (2008 and 2007), College Language Association Annual Convention (2008 and 2007), American Studies Association
Annual Meeting (2007 and 2006), MLA Convention (2006), Society
for the Study of American Women Writers Conference (2006), Society for the Advancement of American Philosophy (2006), National Association of African American Studies (2006), European American Studies
Association Conference (2002), MELUS-Europe Conference (2000), and
Nineteenth-Century Studies Association (1999). For their invitations to
present the material on chaos and race before thoughtful audiences, I am
indebted to Kathy Glass at Duquesne University and Donald Pease at the
Dartmouth College American Studies Institute.

Sian Hunter, my editor at the University of North Carolina Press, has
been characteristically supportive and knowledgeable throughout the
writing and revising of this book. I have deeply appreciated her quiet and
wise guidance through the more difficult stages of the argument and for
her encouraging reading of the opening chapters. I am grateful to Beth
Lassiter for keeping me informed and on track throughout the process. I
thank the editorial, production, and marketing staff at the Press—particularly Ron Maner for his thoughtful and attentive work as project editor.
Stevie Champion was an exemplary copyeditor, both in her attention to
detail and in her thoughtful suggestions on style. This is a much stronger,
more focused book because of her work.

It would be difficult to overstate my debt to my colleagues at West
Virginia University. The core argument in this book began as a talk I presented during my interview at WVU, and since then many individuals have

provided warm encouragement, intellectual inspiration, and informed advice. I am fortunate to be associated with so many great scholars (and writers) of American literature, including Tim Adams, Mark Brazaitis, Gwen Bergner, Cari Carpenter, Anna Elfenbein, Michael Germana, Emily Mitchell, Kevin Oderman, Katy Ryan, Mary Ann Samyn, Ethel Smith, and Timothy Sweet. I have also learned much from my participation in the Faculty Research Group of the Department of English organized each year by the energetic and supportive Donald Hall. For their assistance on specific aspects of this project, I sincerely thank Kirk Hazen and Adam Komisaruk. For their encouragement and interest in this work, I am particularly grateful to Dennis Allen and Katy Ryan, and to my colleagues in the Department of History—among them, Robert Blobaum, Peter Carmichael, and Kenneth Fones-Wolf. For giving me the time I needed to concentrate on this project, I am indebted to the Department of English and the Eberly College of Arts and Sciences of West Virginia University.

PORTIONS OF THIS book have appeared previously, in somewhat different form, in the following publications:

"Economies of Identity: Harriet E. Wilson's *Our Nig*," PMLA 109 (1994): 424–38. Reprinted by permission of the copyright owner, Modern Language Association of America.

"The Family of Man: Traumatic Theology in the *Narrative of the Life of Henry Box Brown, Written by Himself*," *African American Review* 41, no. 1 (Spring 2007): 19–31.

"The Floating Icon and the Fluid Text: Rereading the *Narrative of Sojourner Truth*," *American Literature* 78, no. 3 (September 2006): 459–86. Reprinted by permission of the copyright owner, Duke University Press.

"Fugitive Performances: William Wells Brown's *Three Years in Europe* and Harriet Martineau's *Society in America*," in *Literature on the Move: Comparing Diasporic Ethnicities in Europe and the Americas*, ed. Dominique Marçais, Mark Niemeyer, Bernard Vincent, Cathy Waegner, 159–68 (Heidelberg: Universitätsverlag C. Winter, 2002). Used by permission of the publisher.

"Losing Equilibrium: Harriet E. Wilson, Frado, and Me," in *Harriet Wilson's New England: Race, Writing, and Region*, ed. JerriAnne Boggis, Eve Allegra Raimon, and Barbara A. White, 203–11 (Hanover, N.H.: University Press of New England, 2007). Reprinted with permission.

"Outside the Box: Henry Box Brown and the Politics of Antislavery

Agency," *Arizona Quarterly* 63, no. 4 (Winter 2007): 1–24. Reprinted by permission of the Arizona Board of Regents.

"Representing Chaos: William Craft's *Running a Thousand Miles for Freedom*," PMLA 121 (2006): 469–83. Reprinted by permission of the copyright owner, Modern Language Association of America.

"William Wells Brown Maps the South in *My Southern Home: or, The South and Its People*," *Southern Quarterly* 45 (Spring 2008): 88–107. © 2008 The University of Southern Mississippi. Reproduced by permission.

# Loosed Canons

## The Race for Literary History

People who are looking for "a lot of interesting ideas," and hope to
dabble here for little more, offend the author and degrade themselves.
They would do well to stop right now. Those who read in order to take action
on their consequent beliefs—these are the only readers I respect or look for.
Atrocities, real and repeated, proliferate within this social order. The deepest of all lies in our will not to respond to what we see before us.
—JONATHAN KOZOL, *The Night Is Dark and I Am Far from Home*

This book has been inspired by numerous conversations, conferences, articles, and books over the years, but basically it was sparked by my initial
experience of reading and trying to understand Frances E. W. Harper's
*Iola Leroy* (1892). Intrigued by the names of the characters in Harper's
novel, I started to do some very elementary research on such names as
Iola, Delaney, Latimer, Latrobe, and Gresham, and in so doing found my
way to Ida B. Wells, Lucille Delaney, George Latimer, John Hazlehurst
Boneval Latrobe, and Gresham's Law, among many other entrances to the
complexities of nineteenth-century American history and culture.[1] Since
then, I have had many occasions for realizing anew that I did not know
nearly enough about the literary and cultural history on which, according
to my doctorate and professional experience, I was supposed to be an ex-
pert. As I read and taught numerous narratives, novels, poems, pamphlets,
orations, and other pieces, and as I immersed myself in the relevant and
even peripheral scholarship on African American literature, culture, and
history, I found myself increasingly convinced that we cannot appreciate
American literary and cultural history without a deep understanding of
nineteenth-century African American literature. I found myself focused
on a single though admittedly broad question: What are the requirements

for this field? Why is it that so many conversations, conference sessions, articles, and books about American literary history seem to require so much translation, adaptation, qualification, or simply patience to those who come to questions about the field by way of a broad and deep involvement in African American literature? What constitutes a *just* approach to nineteenth-century African American literature, and what does justice in literary studies have to do with the broader realm of justice so central to Black Studies?

Perhaps another way to put this is to say that this book is devoted to a very simple question: What is African American about African American literature, and why should we identify this as a distinct tradition? If we take African American literature to be literature written by African Americans, then a great number of nineteenth-century texts cannot be considered part of this tradition—the *Narrative of Sojourner Truth* (1884), for example, or any number of slave narratives written by a white amanuensis. If we take it to be literature *about* African Americans, then we will face the specter of such texts as Harriet Beecher Stowe's *Uncle Tom's Cabin* (1852), Joel Chandler Harris's "Uncle Remus" tales (1881–1910), and William Styron's *The Confessions of Nat Turner* (1967). We can, of course, dismiss the question altogether and merely note that it matters little how we identify some of these texts as long as we read them. But the insistent reality of African American history, the literary traditions that have been influenced by that history, and the scholarly traditions that have developed in turn will not be so easily decategorized, and the presence of black caricatures, stereotypes, or even feminist icons in the works of white writers only highlight the cultural dynamics that have made *African American* a significant ideological and cultural marker, one still very much needed. In this book, I will have occasion to talk about the various Uncle Toms, Uncle Remuses, Nat Turners, and "Ar'n't I a woman" icons that play an important and sometimes defining role in African American literary history. My goal, though, will be to address a more complex network of authors, texts, narratives, tropes, and rhetorical maneuvers, the deeply intertextual and multivocal world of nineteenth-century African American literature.[2]

Even without such historical work, questions about the significance or even the necessity of the term "African American" have been matters of familiar but increasingly serious and pressing debates. Various versions of such questions have been regular features of conservative commentary on the dangers of identity politics. But such questions are implicit as well in the work of prominent commentators on race who understand and appreciate the difficult history out of which this literary tradition emerged—Paul Gilroy and Anthony Appiah, for instance, who have argued for the need to work "against race" and toward a new "ethics of identity."[3] Although such approaches have been variously denounced or ignored by many scholars, one could easily argue that conventional approaches to both American and African American literary history actually support and even justify the presentation of "race" as a conceptual category that can be simply developed, abandoned, or otherwise transcended to meet the needs of a complex social world. Too often, that is, the role of race in literary history is limited to a feature of identity, a problematic identifier for cultural traditions, or a theme in literature—even to the point of making it a significant revelation to observe that sometimes African Americans do not write explicitly about race. More historically grounded and rigorous race theory—the work of David Theo Goldberg or Saidiya Hartman, for example—is applied selectively in literary scholarship but has had little discernible effect on approaches to American and African American literary history, as if the history of and theories about race are important topics to cover but luxuries we cannot afford when faced with the chronological demands of anthologies, the narrative demands of literary history, or simply the capitalist demands governing the play of new ideas, fashionable frameworks, and intellectual capital central to scholarship. Such approaches to and avoidances of the complexities of racial history, I suggest, threaten to reduce African American literary history to the dynamics of a familiar and facile multiculturalism, the story of heroic struggles against the odds, a history of a body of literature that is an important part of America's larger story, a dramatic story of the evolutionary process that takes us from Harriet Wilson to Toni Morrison.

At the same time, African American literature as a field of study has become increasingly institutionalized—always problematic for any field of study, but certainly not a bad development. Anthologies of African American literature have been published throughout the twentieth century, and major press anthologies are now a well-established presence in classrooms. The story of African American literary history has been constructed as well in scholarship published throughout the twentieth century and in recent years. This story has been raised to a new level of authority by valuable literary histories, including most prominently Blyden Jackson's *A History of Afro-American Literature* (1989), Dickson Bruce's *Black American Writing from the Nadir: The Evolution of a Literary*

*Tradition, 1877–1915* (1989) and *The Origins of African American Literature, 1680–1865* (2001), and Bernard Bell's *The Afro-American Novel and Its Tradition* (1987) and *The Contemporary African American Novel: Its Folk Roots and Modern Literary Branches* (2004). *The Cambridge History of African American Literature*, still under way as I write this introduction, promises to be an especially important and innovative attempt to relate the history of African American expressive culture on its own terms. Significant, too, are the major considerations of specific genres of African American literature that are beginning to appear, such as *The Cambridge Companion to the African American Novel* (2004) and *The Cambridge Companion to the Slave Narrative* (2007). If not yet a familiar story to most readers, African American literary history has become an increasingly established one.

This is, though, a history in danger of becoming a *settled* story, even as it continues to develop; it is also a history in danger of becoming *unsettled*, its fundamental terms theorized beyond the point of stability, before it has a chance to fully establish its authority. Of course, African American literature surveys will still be taught, and there will still be a vital community of African Americanists who will gather at conferences and in publications for the purpose of exploring the literature of those identified as African Americans. African American literary history will continue to exist in roughly the way that African American history exists during Black History Month—sometimes a sophisticated story, more often a simple one, frequently an inspiring one, but almost never one in any danger of keeping anyone up at night.[4] The field will remain marginalized, a somewhat suspect area of specialization, but not one to which scholars interested in broader, more encompassing fields need to attend to scrupulously when writing about black authors in other contexts. Like the numerous histories of "America" that sequester African American history into a chapter or a series of scattered paragraphs, or the many biographies of white Americans that make no mention of race, American literary history will continue to variously account for and ignore the larger significance of African American experience and aesthetics. African American literary history will continue to carry the burden of representing the discredited but lingering social category of race.

My approach in this book follows the usual framing of African American literature by emphasizing the importance of U.S. racial history in the creation, distribution, and reception of this literature, though from a different angle.[5] Specifically, it accounts more fully for the complexity of U.S. racial history, as well as for the central importance of black scholarly and activist history in shaping the tradition of African American expressive culture. The developing interest in African American literature over the past few decades has demonstrated, I believe, that it is all too possible to isolate or contain African American literature, distancing it from the broader concerns of Black Studies. Often, it either is contextualized within established notions of the literary tradition and approaches to literature or is placed in "conversation" with various literary traditions in the service of an idealized multiculturalism, bringing to mind the justice of Charles Mills's observation that "the recent advent of discussions of 'multiculturalism' is welcome, but what needs to be appreciated is that there are issues of political *power*, not just mutual misconceptions resulting from the clash of cultures" (125). Race is a presence in the literature, or a quality or identifier of the author, or one among many social topics, rather than a social order that writers work to represent, or to which writers respond, or within the particular contingencies of which writers develop an approach to the art of what can be said against the force of the unspeakable. A generalized and flexible understanding of race becomes the entrance to or identifier of literature produced by nonwhite writers, while literature by white writers still largely remains racially neutral—accomplished, in part, by identifying certain works or moments in texts as racist, so as to distinguish these racial moments from the "nonracial" mainstream of the text as a whole, of the author's work generally, or of the larger tradition in which the author is viewed. Such racial moments can be seen as a blemish, an unfortunate part of an author's perspective, a troubling stream of thought in the cultural landscape, but they are in little danger of inspiring a consideration of American literary history with Black Studies at its center, and certainly not a wholesale reconsideration of the terms and goals of literary study. There is, after all, much to support Robert E. Washington's argument that, in the twentieth century, "the liberal-left white intelligentsia both fostered and culturally subjugated the dominant black literary schools" (330). Often, African American literature is kept so busy *representing* race in scholarship and in the curriculum that it is not given the opportunity to represent the race that extends beyond blackness and to retheorize the cultural order that constitutes race.

In this book, I insist that a complex understanding of racial history—with an emphasis on the deep structures of the social order that "race" has both defined and justified historically and on the communal networks that have formed over those deep structures—is central to the cultural history that produced nineteenth-century American literature, and that this is the framework within which nineteenth-century African American literature and aesthetics can be most fully appreciated. This might seem like a basic enough claim, given the nature of the struggles of African Americans throughout the nineteenth century. But I make this claim in the face of a long history of scholars who address race largely as a matter of embodiment or by way of generalized accounts of the discredited sciences and social politics of the past. I also make this claim in the face of an academy that sometimes seems rather impatient with the subject of race and determined to get beyond it by rejecting "race" (often, in such studies, a floating and rather slippery signifier) as a useful category for literary and cultural analysis. This is not to say that I am unsympathetic to Paul Gilroy's view "that there is something worthwhile to be gained from a deliberate renunciation of 'race' as the basis for belonging to one another and acting in concert" (*Against Race* 12), though I am afraid that many will be only too happy to get on this particular bandwagon. Nor do I want to miss what Gilroy says is "a chance to break away from the dangerous and destructive patterns that were established when the rational absurdity of 'race' was elevated into an essential concept and endowed with a unique power to both determine history and explain its selective unfolding" (*Against Race* 14). I am, however, left with that history that has been determined, unfolded, and explained. How do we revise a history narrated according to the imperatives of "the rational absurdit[ies] of 'race'" if we do not attend to the realities of the manifestations and effects of a social order that race *is*? What do we do with the sites of memory we encounter daily—the movies, music, textbooks, indexes of books—that continually lead us back into the matrix of race, reminding us that however much we might want to avoid dwelling in the past, we cannot avoid the multifarious ways in which the past dwells in and around us? Even if we can give up "race relations" or racial group identities as a way of categorizing and understanding social behavior and envisioning possible worlds of understanding, we should be careful about dismissing "race" as a category for understanding the cultural geography of the economic, political, and historical orders.

In applying this rationale to the study of literature, it is important to recognize that renouncing race will have no effect on how most practitioners teach and write about white literature. But it will seriously affect the ways in which we read, react to, and utilize the lessons of African American literature—making much of that literature a response to a category of thought that no longer has currency and leading us to lose the ways in which that literature responds to a matrix of concerns, a historical/ systemic order, that remains all too current. After all, we are still more likely to encounter an essay, or a pedagogical approach, that "complicates" the category of race in the study of, say, Zora Neale Hurston's work than to find complicated racial dynamics in the novels of Ernest Hemingway. Similarly, in anthologies and classrooms, "units" devoted to race focus more on the Hurstons of the literary world than on the Hemingways. In other words, the project of rejecting race as a category of thought is complicated by the fact that white culture has long renounced or repressed race as a category of thought for many of its writers—to the extent that it is still rare to encounter specialists in Hemingway or in other authors who consider race to be a pressing research concern. It is rarer still that such scholars will identify themselves as specialists in white national literature. Aside from those conducting "race studies," many literary theorists will be satisfied to enter and exit the subject of race with a good (mis)reading of Gilroy and a few others. Many, in fact, will be satisfied if the rest of us renounce race and send the message up to the head office.

In this book, I argue that such perspectives rely on dangerously naive concepts of race, superficial conceptions of African American literary history, and simplistic understandings of how scholarship and intellectual commentary function in social space and time.

With such concerns in the background—and often in the foreground— of the chapters that follow, *Chaotic Justice* is about the demands, the pleasures, the challenges, and the occasional misdirections involved in reading nineteenth-century African American literature. To get at a just approach to this body of literature, I argue, we will need to learn to look at the race that extends beyond the identity or social position of authors, the race that is manifest in the literature and in the web of connections that both lead to and follow from the literature. Nineteenth-century African American writers stand out in their approach to the concerns addressed throughout this book precisely because they understood that they had no stable narrative of history or community capable of either shutting out or representing the force of historical experience. These writers, I believe, provide us with the most useful of maps—not the kind that charts a course to the future, but rather the kind that enables us to determine our present orientation in the currents of history.

Too often, this body of literature is identified simply as the beginnings of a literary tradition that eventually discovers its force in the Harlem Renaissance and is fully realized in the unprecedented authority that some of the most prominent African American writers enjoy today. However, I do not seek merely a new conception of the origins of African American literature, the new beginnings of a familiar story that we can now adjust accordingly. Indeed, I reject a chronological construction of African American literary history. The story I mean to tell has to do with the activist roots of African American literary history and therefore an understanding of literature devoted to interrogating the social order, constructing community, and promoting concepts of justice beyond those imagined by most white sympathizers. These are roots that branch out in several directions; they are not just the source of the imagined first fruits of black aesthetic achievements in the twentieth century. Thus, these are roots that should complicate our understanding of African American (and American) literary history—its construction, its significance, and its demands upon those who invoke it. At a time when the great majority of scholarship on African American literature focuses on the twentieth century (with essays on Toni Morrison being submitted to journals virtually every week), it is essential to explain the importance of the relations among politics, aesthetics, and social order negotiated by nineteenth-century African American writers.

While I admire the work of Morrison and the many other contemporary African American writers deserving of serious attention both in scholarship and in the classroom, I think that we are not in a position to understand them, or the world they address, unless we attend with equal care to the many texts produced throughout the nineteenth century, a time often represented by a virtual handful of narratives, poems, novels, and speeches by a few of the most prominent writers. It is, of course, significant that in the face of almost unimaginable injustice, and often against all odds, many African Americans of that era turned to literature. Although a version of my argument could be constructed from any historical period, I focus on the nineteenth century in this book because its cultural pressures (the system of slavery, the development of racial science, the social, political, and economic practices governed by a white supremacist culture) and the major historical moments of the century (the Civil War, Reconstruction, and important legislation and Supreme Court decisions) highlight the multidimensional locale, the intricate inequities, and the racist policies central to the development of African American literature and central, too, to the social, political, legal, and literary systems in which we still live and work. Moreover, the historical distance of the nineteenth century to many readers today is itself significant (as amply demonstrated by both classroom experiences and the studies produced by those relatively unversed in African American history), for twenty-first-century readers of these texts engage in a layered cultural performance as they negotiate not only the cultural dynamics that produced the texts but also the dynamic cultural processes that have shaped the critical reception of these texts today.

The artistic merits of early African American literature have long been a subject of considerable debate. Scholars have regularly pronounced, sometimes in print and often in conversation, William Wells Brown's *Clotel* (1853) a bad novel or Harriet E. Wilson's *Our Nig* (1859) a subliterary text, and some have felt obligated to ask of Harper's *Iola Leroy* and other texts, "Is it good enough to read?"[6] For many readers even of those texts that have been accepted into the canon, what makes the early writers representative of African Americans generally are the conditions under which they lived—and what makes them remarkable is that they have reached a level of achievement that meets the standards even of those who have enjoyed the benefits of education and a privileged life. As John Reilly observed long ago, "Despite other variety, the most prevalent assumption among those who think about Afro-American literary history—whether in articles, books, or classroom presentations—is that the success of literature can be discerned in its utility as social documentation, an assumption to which is sometimes joined severe judgment of works composed, it is presumed, before Afro-American authors had the option to choose art over combative writing. In other words, works of literature are dissolved into their referents" (89). One result has been an approach to African American literary history that has focused on the development of literary talent as measured by increasingly recognizable achievements in established genres, a romantic narrative of African American writers who endured considerable oppression but still persevered in their literary ambitions until their achievements were established beyond all reasonable doubt. Another result has been an approach that has focused on an imagined progression from necessarily political writing in the nineteenth century (antislavery publications, for example) to increasingly more "universal" themes grounded in black history and experience. After all, it is hardly surprising that early anthologies of African American literature offered only a brief sampling of nineteenth-century publications, that the percentage of African American writers in American anthologies today increases as the volume nears the present, or even that anthologies of African American literature struggle to represent, in their subdivisions

and other organizational schema, the difficult tension between the political and the aesthetic that has been the hallmark of African American
literature.

Of course, it is possible to define this tension in ways that favor a nar-
row understanding of the political, but to do so is to misrepresent both
African American history and the literature it has produced. African
American writers have long been aware of the dangers of identification
with the stereotypical condition of oppression, that all there is to African
American life is the experience of degrading conditions. Understandably,
then, many writers and scholars have worked over the years to prevent
African American literature from being viewed simply as sociological—
that is, an unremitting comment on the injustices that have defined the
contours of black communities in the United States.

I argue that this defense undermines the power of African American
literature. As Robert Washington asserts, "Most scholars writing about
black literary works simply assume those works have been socially consequential but fail to explain how they operate—sociologically speaking—in
cultural space" (10). There are a number of reasons for this failure to explain, not the least of which are concepts of cultural space that rely on
naive understandings of the concept of race and of the history of race
in the United States. Drawing on chaos theory, I will explore the shifting instabilities of racial identity and cultural performance during the
nineteenth century, and the ways in which African American literature
produced throughout that century reveals various pressures that have
directed the guiding currents of U.S. history. Because they have been, of
necessity, so directly, consistently, and profoundly engaged in the multifarious contradictions of American history and culture, African American
writers have created a body of literature capable of explaining a nation
that often appears profoundly inexplicable. Variously excluded from the
national story or reduced to a supporting role in it, African American
writers have long been engaged in the challenge of representing the
complexity veiled by the nation's convenient fictions. The terms of that
engagement are the subject of Chaotic Justice.

What is African American about African American literary history?
Toni Morrison has spoken of her desire to "develop a way of writing that
was irrevocably black," noting that "if it was truly black literature, it would
not be black because I was, it would not even be black because of its subject matter. It would be something intrinsic, indigenous, something in
the way it was put together—the sentences, the structure, texture and

tone—so that anyone who read it would realize" (qtd. in Gilroy, *Small Acts*, 181). Here, Morrison emphasizes the role of the reader, the one capable of a significant realization. A great deal of teaching and scholarship inspired by African American literature has been devoted to trying to encourage and guide such realizations—that is, that understanding that extends beyond complacent or even celebratory responses to black literature. And involved in those realizations would necessarily be some understanding of the shifting dynamics of a white supremacist culture, the unstable terms of which even the most intrinsic blackness must struggle with and against. It is not incidental that so much of African American culture focuses on the performative, the improvisational, the dynamic. John Bryant has rightly observed that "our culture is a fluid text, but we want to read it as a fixed thing, never seeking to find the dynamics of its changing but always to discover the authority of its imagined fixity, its nonexistent past purity" (174). In this book I consider what it might mean to imagine African American literary history not only as something other than "a fixed thing," but also as something other than a single or linear narrative. In other words, I contemplate a literary history defined not simply by authorship or subject matter—and how it is put together by an imagined master narrative connecting authors and subjects—but rather by the way that it functions within an unstable culture, the way that it is considered in its component and dynamic parts, and the way that it is *read* by readers always and at once both prepared and unprepared to understand it.

## Links of a Chain

In 1985 the Black Classic Press republished Drusilla Dunjee Houston's *Wonderful Ethiopians of the Ancient Cushite Empire*, a book originally brought out by the Universal Publishing Company of Oklahoma City in 1926. In a commentary written for the 1985 edition, James G. Spady tells the story of his discovery of the book and its journey back into print. Spady asks, "How did we learn of her?"—and he answers: "First of all being in Philadelphia and surrounded by a rich culture and oral history, the names and deeds of our progenitors were ever present. One of the great oral historians of our era was Thomas W. Harvey, president of the Universal Improvement Association and a close associate of Marcus Garvey. Among the many experiences he shared with us in a typical Saturday session was this dynamic Black author of *Wonderful Ethiopians of the Ancient Cushite Empire*" (v). Spady's story is instructive, involving communities, oral history, black political organizations, and regular gatherings where black history could be introduced, shared, preserved, and extended. Having heard of the book through those networks, Spady looked for it at university libraries, but without success. So he turned to a prominent black bookstore, Sheikh Muhammad's in Philadelphia, and then another, Lewis Michaux's, both of which he identifies by location and by the prominent patrons sometimes encountered there. Of the bookstore owners, archivists, and local historians devoted to the collection and preservation of texts by black authors, Spady pauses to say that scholars claiming great discoveries today "must begin to give credit to the Sheikh Muhammad's, the Lewis Michaux's and of course the F. H. Hammurabi's" (vi). Eventually a copy was obtained and republished by the Black Classic Press, though even in that edition Spady and W. Paul Coates disagree over Houston's birthplace. Coates notes that there is evidence that the other volumes that Houston planned to follow the first book were completed and revised but never published.

African American literary history is—in this regard as in others, and very much like other aspects of African American history—maintained and recorded through both collective and individual efforts, largely missing from or only sporadically mentioned in the standard reference sources and indexes, always in a process of rediscovery, and often located in cultural centers beyond the mainstream scholarly or even bookish maps. Frederick Douglass opens his novella *The Heroic Slave* with the narrator promising his readers a history constructed of mere "glimpses" into a subject "covered with mystery" and "enveloped in darkness. . . . Speaking of marks, traces, possibles, and probabilities, we come before our readers" (*Heroic Slave* 474). Commenting on the politics of historical documentation, the narrator declares that some are celebrated in "American annals" while a man like Madison Washington "lives now only in the chattel records of his native State" (473–74). African American literature has been affected by the same politics. Many of the texts rediscovered and republished over the years speak of a history constructed of "glimpses," "covered with mystery," and "enveloped in darkness." Harriet Wilson's *Our Nig*, like so many other early texts, is now available to us only through the zealous efforts of Henry Louis Gates Jr., and ongoing phases of new biographical research have altered the way we view that text and the questions raised by Wilson's life. Gates is similarly responsible for the original publication of a nineteenth-century manuscript, Hannah Crafts's *The Bondwoman's Narrative*; although he was able to provide us with an extensively researched framework for biographical and textual scholarship, a great deal of work remains. Richard Newman, Patrick Rael, and

Philip Lapsansky have returned to print Robert Alexander Young's pamphlet *Ethiopian Manifesto* (1829), which is not to say that we know exactly where it came from or what to make of it. Every published text, it seems, only emphasizes how much we do not know.[7]

It is revealing that African American history has been so often gathered, preserved, and presented by way of fractal processes and fragmented narratives. Histories have been organized according to region, with significant African American challenges and achievements located in various historical and cultural settings. In the nineteenth century, William Cooper Nell felt compelled to organize by individual states his pioneering study *The Colored Patriots of the American Revolution* (1855), and George Washington Williams organized by colony much of the first volume of his *History of the Negro Race in America from 1619 to 1880* (1883). It is revealing, too, that African American history has been represented so often by way of collective biographies that address both well-known and relatively obscure individuals. From William Wells Brown's *The Black Man: His Antecedents, His Genius, and His Achievements* (1863) to such recent works as Kareem Abdul-Jabbar's *Black Profiles in Courage: A Legacy of African American Achievement* (1997), collective biographies have been a staple of African American publishing. Black history was always deeply enveloped, complexly contextualized by other histories, other communities; often the history presented has been the product of an activist determination, both individual and collective, to resist the pressures of the defining contexts and surrounding communities. Today, that tradition is most evident in the many histories painstakingly constructed by amateur historians and activists (both black and white) in the service of local or regional communities—for instance, Mark J. Sammons and Valerie Cunningham's *Black Portsmouth: Three Centuries of African-American Heritage* (2004) or H. H. Price and Gerald E. Talbot's *Maine's Visible Black History: The First Chronicle of Its People* (2006). Such histories often lack an overarching or connecting narrative, beyond the overwhelming evidence of communities, lives, and events not accounted for elsewhere, and their guiding narrative almost always involves the painstaking attempt to gather and preserve the isolated people and events so as to indicate a broader collective story not yet told and perhaps even unrecoverable as a single, coherent narrative. Like the Black Heritage Trails that are often associated with these texts, reading African American history can involve a more-or-less charted pilgrimage through a cultural landscape of important alliances across both space and time, sometimes a pilgrimage negotiated against the pressures and competing narratives of a nearly successful historical erasure.

The collection, preservation, and distribution of African American literary history has followed much the same route. Early notices of African American literary production, by white writers as well as black, often were designed to counter claims of African inferiority—among them, Henri Grégoire's *De la littérature des nègres, ou Recherches sur leurs facultés intellectuelles, leurs qualités morales et leur littérature; suivies de Notices sur la vie et les ouvrages des Nègres qui se sont distingués dans les Sciences, les Lettres et les Arts* (Concerning the Literature of Negroes, or Research on Their Intellectual Faculties, Their Moral Qualities, and Their Writings; Followed by Accounts of the Life and Works of Negroes Who Have Distinguished Themselves in the Sciences, Letters, and Arts) (1808), translated in 1996 by Thomas Cassirer and Jean-François Brière under the title *On the Cultural Achievements of Negroes*. The connecting narrative thread in these accounts involves the identity of the authors, a connection that has as much to do with attacks on a perceived collective quality or essence as it does with the collective evidence presented in refutation of such attacks. African American literary history has similarly relied heavily on local activists and community organizations—among them, the collective efforts of nineteenth-century literary groups so brilliantly presented in Elizabeth McHenry's *Forgotten Readers: Recovering the Lost History of African American Literary Societies* (2002). No doubt, we could trace a winding path connecting such societies, and the library collections of antislavery reading rooms, to the important work of early book collectors like Robert Mara Adger of Philadelphia or Arthur Alfonso Schomburg of New York, among many others. Many of those collections became significant research archives, helping to make possible the publishing boom in Black Studies during the 1960s and 1970s—by way of the Arno Press and the New York Times books, the various publications by the Negro Universities Press, the Ebony Classics of the Johnson Publishing Company, the Books for Libraries Press, and other publishing houses and initiatives.

Early African American literary history, in short, has been collected by way of a series of labyrinthine paths directed by many different centers of activity—and this work has been preserved in numerous editions, encyclopedias, and collections. Behind the heroic labors of Dorothy Porter Wesley have been numerous individuals searching for, collecting, researching, or simply recording in written and oral histories books and rumors of books, the stories of authors long gone and the stories inspiring a search for authors nearly forgotten. Behind the epochal publishing ventures of Henry Louis Gates Jr., without whom much of the scholarship and teaching on nineteenth-century African American literature might still be waiting for a brighter day, is a complex tradition of individuals and collectives working to preserve and publish the archives of a largely forgotten and often misrecorded past. Gates has recently looked back on his early career and his regular conversations with John W. Blassingame. At Naples Pizza, an unassuming restaurant in New Haven, Connecticut, the two men and many others would gather for breakfast; "and it was at Naples," Gates reports, "that he [Blassingame] and I would plot—fantasize, actually—about the future of the fledgling field of African American studies in the decades ahead" (Foreword, x). Significantly, Gates notes, "Upon one thing we agreed early on: we had to find a way to map the field with reference works, sophisticated reference works such as biographical dictionaries, encyclopedias of history and culture; scholarly editions of texts; collected works of authors who had published essays primarily in periodicals; collected papers for canonical figures . . .; bibliographies; concordances—in short, all foundational reference works that, taken together, make a field of study, well, scholarly" (x). So successful have Gates and others been in creating this "textual legacy of memory," that Gates can refer to a generation of students "who now take reference works such as these for granted" (x).

It is important to both remember and continue these efforts, but it is important as well to look beyond the comprehensive and voluminous information and the impressive bookshelves of reprinted texts to see the fragmented histories, the partial recoveries, the forgotten strands of history, the still-unprinted and even undiscovered texts and manuscripts that have always been a part of the living memory of African American history. The African American history and literary tradition continues to be distinguished by "marks, traces, possibles, and probabilities," and historical narratives that attract centers of authority, interest, and need. For example, one can learn a great deal about the challenges and responsibilities of preserving the African American literary tradition, as well as about the challenge of connecting books to lived experiences and texts to histories, from the essays collected in Elinor Des Verney Sinnette, W. Paul Coates, and Thomas G. Battle's *Black Bibliophiles and Collectors: Preservers of Black History* (1990).

In all of the efforts to recover African American publications through the years, the interest has never been limited solely to texts written and published by African Americans. Collectors have gathered a wide range of texts and ephemera related to black history, including a great many racist works that indicate the insistent cultural context within which African American history and literature necessarily functioned. These scholars have recognized that all of these texts are essential to an understanding of African American history, and that the cultural currents such texts represent flow in the background and between the lines of African American literature. This understanding was, in fact, a part of the great publishing efforts of the sixties and seventies. In addition to works by William Wells Brown, for example, the Negro Universities Press published in 1864 the Reverend Hollis Read's *The Negro Problem Solved; or, Africa as She Was, as She Is, and as She Shall Be*, in which Read quotes favorably, and at length, from Brown's *The Black Man*, which appeared in 1863. As its subtitle suggests, *The Black Man: His Antecedents, His Genius, and His Achievements* is a historical survey of the African diaspora (with a particular but not exclusive focus on the United States) from its origins, but the major part of the book is a collective biography, composed of sketches of a wide range of people of African origins, including but extending far beyond African Americans. Read draws liberally from these sketches to support his argument that, "notwithstanding the crushing pressure of ages, men of the crisped hair and thick lips have become statesmen, scholars, soldiers; brave, accomplished, successful; men of science; writers, poets, novelists, dramatists; men of business and wealth; men of good social position; and Christians, illustrating, in an eminent degree, the religion pure and undefiled—the spirit of the meek and lowly One" (180). If traces of what had, by Brown's time, been identified as the Uncle Tom school of Christianity (discussed in Chapter 2) can be apprehended here, Read's main point is that black men (and he follows Brown in focusing primarily on men) have distinguished themselves in virtually all professions and all walks of life. Read seems sincere when he states, "We mean to claim for them capabilities of competing with white races"—and when he concludes that "Africa still produces *men*" (179–80).

But Read's high praise for the black history and black lives that Brown records only underscores the difficulties that Brown or any of his biographical subjects would face in attempting to claim as home the land, the region, or the town of their birth—for Read's point is that people of African origins are quite capable of thriving in Africa and are almost morally bound to look to Africa for their future. "In the following pages," Read explains in his preface, "colonization is advocated . . . as a boon to the colored man, a privilege to every one who is fitted to profit by it, and the most suitable and hopeful agency by which to raise Africa from her present debasement, and to assign her an honorable place among the nations" (v–vi). Anticipating objections to his argument, he emphasizes that he is not saying that African Americans have no place in the land of their birth. Indeed, Read asserts, "We would most distinctly concede the *right* of the negro to remain in this country. It is *his* country as well as ours. Yet, we would not the less earnestly and kindly urge on him his *privilege* to go" (v–vi). African Americans willing to take advantage of this privilege, he argues, "even if it be at a personal sacrifice," can look forward to not only the strong possibility of immense personal success, but also the satisfaction of being "the only agents that can rescue a continent from the low depths of social, civil, and moral debasement" (vi). Success in the United States will be long in coming if "success" is taken to mean social equality and equal opportunity—achievements that will depend on "time, events, changes, revolutions, which wait the sure, though often mysterious movements of Providence" (vi). In Africa, however, there will be no wait, for one can be sure of "connecting the highest and best destiny of the colored man with his fatherland," an opportunity like that of "Israel of old" to "quit the land of his captivity, and return to the land of his fathers and the land marked out by Heaven for his habitation" (vi). Those who remain in the United States, Read seems to suggest throughout his biblically based argument, have chosen the lesser path of moral responsibility and therefore have no right to complain of the slow movement of Providence.

Even when less direct, such exchanges and such reminders of the complex contingencies of African American literary production in a white supremacist culture were a standard presence in the earliest and most significant efforts to preserve not only African American history but also the African American literary tradition. But an awareness of such contingencies can be easily lost in the neat contours of an anthology of African American literature, a biographical dictionary, or a literary companion. Such publications, such momentous achievements, are to be celebrated and deeply appreciated, but this would not be the first time that scholars and teachers would have reason to learn the lesson that with success comes another set of problems. Today, when independent bookstores are struggling for their existence and when the preservation and presentation of African American literary history is increasingly centered in educational institutions, it can be easy to miss the usefully messier education available in local bookstores patronized by the community and leading activists. What is lost is not simply the experience of oral history, of rare finds, or of nonlinear accounts of a tradition of writing. Also lost is a vital part of history itself, the experience of a history constructed of "glimpses" into a subject "covered with mystery" and "enveloped in darkness," the unique arrangements of available texts and local priorities, the effects of different centers of organization and of different attractors influencing the trajectory of the narrative line. In his prominent study *Impossible Witnesses: Truth, Abolitionism, and Slave Testimony* (2001), Dwight A. McBride notes that he has examined "literary texts, political pamphlets, speeches, essays, newspaper articles, historical and scholarly treatises on both the institution and the morality of slavery, and, of course, slave narratives" (2). "This broad-ranging approach to understanding abolitionism," McBride asserts, "rather than assuming a hierarchy among these forms, is concerned with the production of meaning that is possible when one considers the interplay of these forms taken together in the terrain that is abolitionist discourse" (2–3). I would add that "this broad-ranging approach" is also characteristic of what I identify as early versions of African American literary history—the various collections of texts and documents, the bookstores and archives that developed locally and eventually found national and international readers, the attempts to republish texts connected only by the racial ideologies that have been a major part of African American historical experience. This is the archive largely lost in anthologies of African American literature, as well as in many considerations (deliberated or assumed) of African American literary history.

I focus on the nineteenth century, then, in part because it has become a crucial site for conceptualizing the challenge of recovering, interpreting, and publishing (in reprint editions, in scholarship, in historical narratives, in classrooms, at conferences) the story or stories of an essential and formative time in African American literary history. A great deal changed after the Civil War, Reconstruction, and the turn of the century that complicates a sustained narrative of this history—indeed, that encouraged Alain Locke and others to envision a fundamentally new phase of African American locales as important sites of global black history, inspiring new approaches to and hopes for literature. Moreover, the publication, distribution, and even reception of African American literature changed dramatically from the early years to the middle of the twentieth century. That literature was increasingly and variously contextualized, highlighted, and marginalized by a developing profession of American literary studies and by aggressive and influential new phases in the writing and publication of literary histories devoted to "American" literature.[8] It was only years later that sustained efforts to recover early African American authors and texts began in earnest, efforts brought to great new levels by Dorothy Porter Wesley, Henry Louis Gates Jr., William Andrews, Frances Smith Foster, and others. With the benefit of the Schomburg Library of Nineteenth-Century Black Women Writers, the numerous texts included in the Documenting the American South website, the many lives addressed in the *African American National Biography* (each one an invitation to deeper research), important anthologies (of narratives, pamphlets, poetry, and orations), and often amply introduced and annotated editions of texts, we have an unprecedented perspective on nineteenth-century African American literary production, and we have developing literary histories accounting for that rich field of publications. Accordingly, it is more important than ever that we think carefully about the responsibilities presented to us by that field, and that we do not confuse the recovery of texts with a self-evident literary history.

It is essential, then, to return to, learn from, and extend the work of those who have played principal roles in focusing our attention on the questions raised by the concept of an African American literary history. The title of this introduction refers to two influential and contested commentaries on constructions of and approaches to African American literary history: Henry Louis Gates Jr.'s *Loose Canons: Notes on the Culture Wars* (1992) and Barbara Christian's "The Race for Theory" (1987). Gates's book is an important consideration of the settings, the contexts, and the goals of Black Studies, and offers a perspective on multicultural studies generally. In three major sections—Literature, The Profession, and Society—he presents arguments for and defenses of the priorities of African American literary studies and of Black Studies as a whole, along the way clarifying, correcting, and resituating a great deal of the discourse, academic and political, on the rise of Black Studies (with Gates's own work for the *Norton Anthology of African American Literature* [2004] variously providing an explicit or implicit centerpiece for his engagement in these debates). Christian's essay, although sometimes viewed as a complaint against what she terms "the movement to exalt theory" (354), is a particularly thoughtful consideration of the responsibilities of those who study literature that falls beyond the pale of the traditional Western canon. "People of color," she argues, "have always theorized—but in forms quite different from the Western form of abstract logic" (349). Her essay is a consideration of that theoretical tradition as it both pertains to and emerges in lived experienced and literary art.

Although the full range of Gates's analysis is important to the work I do in this book, I am especially interested in his comments on the construction of a canon in the form of a literary anthology. Emphasizing that he is "not unaware of the politics and ironies of canon formation," Gates borrows "a leaf from the right, which is exemplarily aware of the role of education in the reproduction of values" (*Loose Canons* 32, 35). "The teaching of literature," he agrees, "*is* the teaching of values; not inherently, no, but contingently, yes; it is—it has become—the teaching of an aesthetic and political order, in which no women or people of color were ever able to discover the reflection or representation of their images, or hear the resonances of their cultural voices" (35). Accordingly, "just as we can and must cite a black text within the larger American tradition, we can and must cite it within its own tradition, a tradition not defined by a pseudoscience of racial biology, or a mystically shared essence called blackness, but by the repetition and revision of shared themes, topoi, and tropes, a process that binds the signal texts of the black tradition into a canon just as surely as separate links bind together into a chain" (39). Among the results of this perspective—indeed, its primary product—is the *Norton Anthology of African American Literature*, which has revealed possibilities in the curriculum, in and of itself and by helping to open the door for a number of competing anthologies. I have profited greatly from all of those anthologies. Although my purpose in this book is to complicate our understanding of African American literary history, I am decidedly not presenting these views to suggest that the drawbacks of a defined canon (drawbacks that Gates both acknowledges and comments on) outweigh the considerable benefits of offering a focused introduction to African American literature, one that indicates the "repetition and revision of shared themes, topoi" that have shaped the tradition. Rather, I am interested in the steps that must follow this introduction, "the history we need to teach" that proceeds from the basic introduction to or overview of a potential field of study.

Gates argues for "a process that binds the signal texts of the black tradition into a canon," and Christian explains and defends that process. "The race for theory," she asserts,

> with its linguistic jargon, its emphasis on quoting its prophets,
> its tendency towards "Biblical" exegesis, its refusal even to

mention specific works of creative writers, far less contemporary ones, its preoccupations with mechanical analyses of language, graphs, algebraic equations, its gross generalizations about culture, has silenced many of us to the extent that some of us feel we can no longer discuss our own literature, while others have developed intense writing blocks and are puzzled by the incomprehensibility of the language set adrift in literary circles. (350)

As the author of a book that draws from chaos theory and talks about fractal lines and strange attractors, I am naturally concerned that my work might violate the principles of someone who has been, for me, a major inspiration and guide. But I am also concerned about getting at the rich complexity of the tradition and the historical process that Christian seeks to promote. "I consider it presumptuous of me to invent a theory of how we *ought* to read," Christian states, and I am not interested in trying to present such a theory in this book (350). But I *am* interested in identifying the process that constitutes the tradition we are trying to read.[9]

That process, I will argue, is less like links of a chain than like elements of a complex design—like a Mandelbrot set, a world of fractals in which, as Alice Fulton has usefully explained, "each part of a fractal form replicates the form of the entire structure. Increasing detail is revealed with increasing magnification, and each smaller part looks like the entire structure, turned around or tilted a bit" (55). This is, I maintain, the process of "repetition and revision" vital to African American literary history—a process that, as Gates and Christian emphasize, involves readers as much as writers, as well as the cultural and even institutional settings in which readings are discussed, disseminated, and applied to individual and collective life. "I think we need to read the works of our writers in our various ways," Christian remarks, "and remain open to the intricacies of the intersection of language, class, race, and gender in the literature. And it would help if we share our process, that is, our practice, as much as possible since, finally, our work is a collective endeavor" (350). In *Chaotic Justice*, I am interested in the way this interactive process (sometimes characterized more by tension and conflict than by the collaboration of a coherent collective) has influenced the currents of the tradition, and I am interested in exploring the overlapping processes and practices that constitute nineteenth-century African American literary history.

Both Gates and Christian have done much to press toward the ongoing rediscovery of the literary past, and both have reminded us that we are hardly in a position to talk about African American literary history unless we continue to recover, reprint, and actually *read* the texts produced in the past, the links of the chain we claim as the binding force of a literary tradition. I have mentioned Gates and Blassingame's early fantasy—"to map the field with reference works"—which has largely been realized both in reference rooms and online. "We were determined," Gates explains, "that we would be part of the generation that eliminated forever the curse of scholars of African American studies: that each successive generation was forced to reinvent the proverbial wheel, repeating research undertaken by previous scholars of which we remained painfully unaware" (Foreword x). That goal has been largely accomplished, though the resources continue to be underutilized. Perhaps it would not be too much to say that the enduring problem is captured in the phrase "scholars of African American studies." African American literature is now a presence on the literary scene. It is increasingly rare that anyone would write an article or a book or teach a class claiming to cover "American literature" without including works by African American authors. But while Black Studies as a field—as a framework, in this case, for the examination of literature—is flourishing in the imagined communities of scholarship, it is still struggling in individual educational institutions, in the provision of mentorship for young scholars, or in its demands of those practitioners who write about or teach African American literature but who define themselves either in broader or simply different terms. It is still eminently possible to approach individual texts and to conceptualize "African American literature" in ways that can be easily marginalized, appropriated, or deconstructed—links of a chain, indeed.

Among the texts in need of recovery, then, are the various critical and theoretical analyses by scholars of African American history, culture, and literature who have responded to earlier versions of this sort of appropriation and marginalization. Some of the most consequential pronouncements regarding the priorities of Black Studies, the responsibilities of African American literary scholarship, and the challenges of teaching individual African American writers have been published over the years in response to misrepresentations, exclusions, and selective engagements by scholars who lacked sufficient grounding in African American history and culture. As African American literary history becomes increasingly established, it is necessary to return to, reconsider, and resituate those earlier critiques and challenges. This is another archive that is important to this work—and, like literature, it is an archive that has been partly recovered and collected in such influential publications as Beverly Guy-Sheftall's *Words of Fire: An Anthology of African-American Feminist Thought* (1995), Hazel Arnett Ervin's *African-American Literary Criticism, 1773–2000* (1999), Winston Napier's *African American Literary Theory: A Reader* (2000), and Angelyn Mitchell's *Within the Circle: An Anthology of African American Literary Criticism from the Harlem Renaissance to the Present* (2002). We can trace in these and other collections something approaching a canon of African American literary criticism, but how we narrate the history suggested by that canon is a significant question. Is it the story of a developing sophistication enabled by the increasingly established presence of African American literature and the expanded institutional settings in which African American literary study is encouraged and supported? Well, certainly, scholars have learned from one another and benefited from the increased interest in the field. Nevertheless, by reading many of the essays gathered in these volumes and in the pages of many still-marginalized journals, we can see that much has been lost, or that much is still waiting to be realized. Recognizing that "an essential, unmistakable characteristic of African-American literary criticism is the heavy influence of Euro-American aesthetic standards," Joyce Ann Joyce observed that in the 1960s and 1970s such scholars as Larry Neal, Amiri Baraka, Stephen Henderson, and Addison Gayle "attempted to distill and codify those aspects of African-American literature that make it distinctly different from the literature of the mainstream," but that by 1994, the year Joyce published this comment, "less than a handful of scholars attempt to continue that practice" (*Warriors* 22).

In our own time, one might say that few scholars demonstrate any awareness that there have been such attempts, and fewer still seem inclined to credit these attempts as having much value. It has become all too easy to ignore, dismiss, or even denounce the work of the Black Arts movement, or the concept of Black Aesthetics, or the scholarship associated with a generalized Afrocentrism, or even important essays published in journals rarely read or in issues too old to be deemed relevant. In 1997 Nellie Y. McKay was asked to draft an essay for PMLA on preparing scholars, black and white, to teach African American literature. Since some read the piece as a challenge to white authority in the teaching of African American literature, the essay inspired quite a response, both in print and in hallways, and eventually led to a collection of essays published by Rutgers University Press. In other words, McKay wrote a good essay, one that was provocative, challenging, and influential. Many such essays have appeared over the years, though not in PMLA—for example, Trudier Harris's "Miss-Trained or Untrained? Jackleg Critics and African American Literature (Or, Some of My Adventures in Academia)" and Mae G. Henderson's "'Where, by the Way, Is This Train Going?': A Case for Black (Cultural) Studies"—but other than the scholars and teachers who read them in connection with their participation in journals and conferences involving Black Studies, those essays have been met with oblivious silence rather than charged debate.

Beyond such scholarship is the large body of work from various disciplines that pertains to African American history and culture. The history of slavery is itself a complex study marked by cultural politics, white supremacist assumptions, problematic counterassumptions, questions about source material, and geographical and temporal variations on the same historical moments and sites. The history and cultural politics of antislavery movements are similarly challenging, as indicated by the extent to which terms like "abolitionist" can refer to white reform efforts, the center from which to locate black abolitionist contributions to the cause—and this in a historical field that can speak of the South and the North when commenting only on white communities, politics, and culture. The history of Reconstruction, and the even more difficult years that followed, is perhaps more complex still, as emphasized by W. E. B. Du Bois in his own survey of scholarship in his time. The scholarship on race, moreover, includes traditional historical accounts as well as a wide variety of theoretical and interdisciplinary approaches that together fail to add up to a coherent field of study, making it a field open enough for multiple entrances, isolated encampments, and sometimes strategic maneuvers and avoidances of the issues at hand. Race, then, a term that is still used more often than not to refer to nonwhite literature and history, often becomes simply the starting point or one locating point from which an author responds to various challenges. African American literary studies, in short, both encompass and are encompassed by a broad interdisciplinary realm of activity characterized by premises that sometimes are not shared or even examined, approaches that sometimes work either in isolation from one another or at cross-purposes, and by educational contexts that sometimes frame these studies as overly basic (devoted, as they often are, to fundamental work of textual and biographical recovery), or as examples of disciplinary identity politics focused on the creation of boutique courses in literature.

To be sure, those most responsible for envisioning and constructing

African American literary anthologies and histories are familiar with the fullness and the complexity of the literary and scholarly foreground to their efforts, but it remains relatively easy for that foreground to be moved to the background by those less invested in the ongoing and collective *process* of representing and serving the field. African American literary history too often operates as a floating and sometimes even suspect signifier, a loose assumption—literary history by default. Such operating assumptions on the part of those who engage selectively in the study of African American literary texts do not emanate from the scholarship or the history of the preservation of this imagined tradition—beyond, maybe, what they glean from the recovery of individual texts. Often, this default-mode literary history is author-based—African American literature as literature produced by African Americans—and so it does not deal with race as a cultural, environmental, economic, political, theological, regional, or legal construction and subsequent process. These various concerns rarely influence how we locate a text; instead, they are brought to the text that is listed according to the isolated racial identity of the author, often in a restricted chronology for anthologies governed by other concerns.

In this book, then, I focus on the challenge of locating, understanding the dynamics of, and working with nineteenth-century African American literary history. In doing so, I have tried to be attentive to the complex process that did not simply produce or influence this tradition but was, in fact, a principal dynamic of the tradition. In a 1979 interview, Amiri Baraka discussed his "Restaging Langston Hughes' *Scottsboro Limited*," which led him to reflect on black literary and theater history. "The history of Afro-American literature, of Afro-American drama," he observed, "is still not clearly outlined according to its own traditions. Black theatre history is always told in terms of its relationship to antithetical forms." Thinking about how one might tell a more accurate or just story, he suggested that "in Afro-American literature, there is a revolutionary tradition and a tradition of capitulation and liberalism. Both of these traditions exist at the same time. The crucial issue is how do you differentiate between the two. If you cannot recognize the difference between these two traditions, then it's impossible to teach the literature correctly." To understand these traditions, one needs a comprehensive familiarity with the literary past, without which—again—"it is impossible to teach Afro-American literature correctly." But such "a thorough/all-sided/encompassing analysis of the history and development of Afro-American literature and Afro-American theatre is very difficult to do," Baraka asserted, "because the materials are

25

scattered. Therefore, the history, as it is told, remains discontinuous with so many gaps and holes in it." As for individual texts, there is a great deal of history for which one must account. "If you don't deal with the entire social parameters of a play's existence, then the play is meaningless. But that's the way literature is taught to us, in a meaningless context so that we don't see what it really is" (68).

In many ways, this book follows the outline of concerns that Baraka presented in that interview. I am interested in identifying the ways in which this history is related to forms or frameworks that misrepresent the literary past. I am interested in various traditions of African American literature, and the ways in which they have overlapped, interacted, and influenced one another. Moreover, I am interested in the scattered materials, the gaps, the holes that are also a vital presence in this literary tradition. In *Liberation Historiography*, I examined William C. Nell's reconstruction of a black community torn apart by the shells of the government's military force. "Many were crushed by the falling earth and timbers," Nell writes, and "many were entirely buried in the ruins. Some were horribly mangled by the fragments of timber and the explosion of charged shells that were in the magazine. Limbs were torn from the bodies to which they had been attached; mothers and babes lay beside each other, wrapped in that sleep which knows no waking" (261). This physical fragmentation, I noted, is an apt image for the larger fragmentation of the African American community, a fragmentation mentioned again and again in the publications of the time. As the narrative progresses, Nell's image picks up biblical echoes: "Their bones have been bleached in the sun for thirty-seven years, and may yet be seen scattered among the ruins of that ancient fortification" (262). Breathing life into those bones is for Nell the task of the historian, the scholar who finds the bones, in effect, displaced in the nation's archives: "These facts are all found scattered among the various public documents which repose in the alcoves of our national library. But no historian has been willing to collect and publish them, in consequence of the deep disgrace which they reflect upon the American arms, and upon those who then controlled the government" (263). In short, Nell connects metaphorically and methodologically the scattered bones of an embattled community and the scattered documents in the library of a nation formed by the false consciousness inherent in the system of slavery and the ideology of white supremacy. In *Chaotic Justice*, I similarly look to the scattered documents of the past for a story that calls for a just but challenging telling.

## An Overview

I approach the interrelated issues of race, identity, literary scholarship, and literary history in separate chapters, although the chapters are intended to supplement one another in various ways. When I first laid out my plans for this book, a friendly reader summarized my overall goals: "I understand him to be looking for a model that accounts for the local contingencies and shifting tensions and bases of micro- and macro-racial relations at any given moment, and the interplay between historical accounting, and the political and professional contingencies and desires of particular representational moments in the development of our account of African American literature." Well, that is it exactly—but it is also a mouthful, and some packaging might be useful. In the following chapters, then, I try to focus on key issues in this overall model without losing sight of the dynamic interplay among them.

I begin by offering a framework for interpreting the dynamic process of racial history in the first chapter, "Representing Chaos and Reading Race." Basically, I draw from chaos theory to argue against a simply ideological understanding of racial history and to explain the "fractal dimensions" of nineteenth-century African American approaches to narrative, but the chapter prepares me as well for the challenges of constructing a narrative history of that literature. I am particularly interested in African American experiences and conceptualizations of racial history, though my principal assumption is that all racial history in the United States has emerged from attempts to define and promote a white supremacist social order. African Americans, quite insightful about those attempts, found themselves charting different racial paths involving different understandings and appropriations of racial culture. Following their lead, I suggest that we have barely begun to map the racial past, that doing so is a major challenge to any approach to African American history, literary or otherwise, and that chaos theory offers a useful framework for constructing such maps.

Central to my argument are two applications of chaos theory. The first is my contention that the history of race is not neatly ideological; rather, it is a complex series of contingent events and cultural currents both directing and directed by shifting racist ideologies. "Racism," Alexander Saxton has written, "is a theory of history" (14). I would add that it is a theory that leads not only to a narrative of progress but also to the importance of process, the attempt to identify and negotiate, constantly again, the active manifestations of a history of race marked by recurring patterns and shifting contingencies. My second application of chaos theory relates to the attempt to *represent* racial history in nineteenth-century African American literature. Ultimately, I draw from chaos theory to examine an early African American poetics informed by the need to represent over-whelming complexity, a poetics that resembles efforts in chaos theory to represent a world (both natural and social) that escapes the clean lines of Euclidian approaches. African Americans understood that the racial dynamics shaping virtually every area of their collective lives were irre-ducible to a simple theory of racial prejudice or racism. In other words, they recognized that claims and views about the embodiment of race were merely the most visible aspects of the broader racial problems they faced. In this way, they became intimately involved in the more famil-iar understanding of chaos, what Clifford Geertz had in mind when he observed that "there are at least three points where chaos—a tumult of events which lack not just interpretations but interpretability—threatens to break in upon man: at the limits of his analytic capacities, at the limits of his powers of endurance, and at the limits of his moral insight" (100). African Americans had sustained experience with all three points, and they would have understood well Geertz's following point: "Bafflement, suffering, and a sense of untractable ethical paradox are all, if they be-come intense enough or are sustained long enough, radial challenges to the proposition that life is comprehensible and that we can, by taking thought, orient ourselves effectively within it" (100). However, African American expressive culture is eloquent testimony to the fact that many *did* find ways to orient themselves within a comprehensible life, if only by creating a body of thought and expression capable of dealing with the limits of understanding and the shifting contingencies of life. They did so, in part, by finding ways to represent the larger realities of race—that is, the race inscribed in social institutions, practices, and processes, the racial dynamics that made life unpredictable in its specifics but broadly predictable (within certain realms of possibility and probability) in its ever-emerging and recurring patterns. They became, in effect, theorists of chaotic dynamics and process.

The racial dynamics that framed and influenced African American experience leads to the second chapter, "Truth Stranger than Fiction: African American Identity and (Auto)Biography." What were the chal-lenges of representing African American lives in the nineteenth century, and how should an awareness of those challenges direct our readings of slave narratives and other autobiographical and biographical texts? Here I explore those challenges as they pertain to the dynamics of African

American identity and to the frameworks for moral agency in promoting reform through the story of one's life. I consider as well the importance of the sheer variety of autobiographical texts: the fact that multiple versions of some narratives were produced, that almost every narrative raises significant questions about points of departure and points of arrival, that some were written by white authors, and that some are challenging hybrid narratives—novelized autobiographies, as William Andrews has argued.[10] Locating African American autobiographies—ideologically, generically, or even geographically (from Elizabeth Keckley's White House, for example, to Louis Hughes's Milwaukee)—is itself a challenge. The main purpose of this chapter is to explore the complexity of self- or biographical representation—that is, the attempt to represent the African American lives central to any understanding of African American literature. How did the chaotic constructions of race shape individual lives, and what are the implications of these constructions for writers and readers of African American autobiographies and biographies? African American writers (and the subjects of narratives by others) faced the challenge of representing a life defined by race, resisting that definition while also cultivating community, negotiating the cultural politics of readership and of occasions for publication, and redirecting the trajectory of possibilities of and settings for African American identity. Addressing these many hurdles led many writers not only to novelize their narratives but also to fictionalize their lives and their worlds so as to get at the realities of a world defined by race that was barely apprehended by white writers and readers. How, then, does the complexity of African American life writing both complicate and direct our approach to African American literary history?

The consideration of African American life writing and biography naturally raises questions about how we locate these lives and the texts they produced, both culturally and in scholarship. This is the subject of the third chapter, "The Shortest Point between Two Lines: Writing African Americans into American Literary History." With the increasing accessibility of affordable editions of many nineteenth-century African American texts supporting ongoing developments in scholarship, many practitioners who pursue the broader field of American literary and cultural studies are naturally interested in placing African American writers "in conversation with" other writers. Nevertheless, despite the increased scholarly attention to nineteenth-century African American writers over the past two decades, studies still turn on a largely familiar story about the nature and significance of African American literature and about its place in American literary history. We have yet to fully confront Eric Sundquist's sense of "the challenge of revising the contours of literary tradition," nor have we come to terms with "the necessity of living with the paradox that 'American' literature is both a single tradition of many parts *and* a series of winding, sometimes parallel traditions that have perforce been built in good part from their inherent conflicts" (19, 18). In this chapter, I observe that the winding paths of those traditions remain largely uncharted, and I discuss the dangers of assuming that African American and white writers can easily be brought into conversation with one another. In the absence of a radical reconsideration not only of literary history but also of the cultural work of literature in the face of the instabilities of cultural identity, placing black and white authors together, or even categorizing different African American writers according to established historical paradigms, amounts to a ritualized reenactment of the protocols of U.S. racial history. I argue, then, that such conversations need to be negotiated among different cultural spaces and different historical continuums, and that such negotiations return our attention to a concept of African American literature that includes but extends beyond the identity of its authors.

Those continuums were shaped in part by the laws, both juridical and social, restricting or otherwise directing the lives of African Americans in the nineteenth century. These laws are the focus of the fourth chapter, "Choreographing Chaos: African American Literature in Time and Space," which examines the ways in which African American experience in the nineteenth century was shaped by laws of time, laws of mobility, and laws of affiliation. The negotiation of such laws plays a double role in many African American texts in their approaches to history, in the perspectives afforded by both domestic and international travel, and in their attempts to envision the terms of a stable ideological and political community. This double role is seen at the level of experience and at the level of literary representation, which I identify as the attempt to choreograph African American experience as it functions in social space and time. In each case, a legal code regulating African American lives defines the environment that African American writers attempted to address. The chapter concludes with a prominent example of a doubled negotiation of social forces and possibilities, the story of William and Ellen Craft's escape from slavery and William's subsequent representation of that journey in *Running a Thousand Miles for Freedom*.

The fifth chapter, "The Story at the End of the Story: African American

Literature and the Civil War," follows these negotiations to the dramatic cultural shift that characterized life during and after Reconstruction. Here I apply the arguments of the previous chapters to a case study of African American literary history. The Civil War was, among other things, a conflict of various narratives—national, regional, religious, and racial. Its influence on American literature was profound, as various studies have demonstrated. It was also a time when the significance and centrality of race in the United States was variously exposed and veiled, and in the wake of that conflict the course of racial history was altered in significant ways. Following the Civil War, the racial presence in literature by white Americans became increasingly pronounced, regional and national narratives were newly intertwined, and the forums for constructing and presenting national and literary history were becoming increasingly institutionalized. For African Americans, the Civil War was both the fulfillment of a collective narrative of liberation and justice and, following Reconstruction, a forceful reminder of the limitations of a linear, progressive narrative of history. African American autobiography changed dramatically after the Civil War, because it now operated both outside of an antislavery context and within a newly threatening and profoundly complex racial environment. And as conceptions of the possibilities for self-representation changed, so did African American approaches to literature generally.

But this was not simply a historical break separating antebellum and postbellum writers, for some of the most prominent African American authors of the nineteenth century—Frederick Douglass, William Wells Brown, Frances Harper, and Martin Delany, among others—wrote and published both before and after the Civil War and Reconstruction, highlighting the difficult transition into a newly chaotic narrative landscape. Anthologies typically struggle to represent this transition, usually placing these writers in the antebellum period, and literary histories generally follow the national narrative in defining the significant periods of African American literary production. In this chapter, then, I argue that the literature produced before and after the Civil War forces us to reenvision the course and terms of African American literary history by returning our attention to the historical contingencies that frame and continually reframe African American identity. Ultimately, African American writers of this time are rarely read as African Americans (that is, as members of a broader network of associations, inhabitants of an identifiable historical continuum), understanding the contingencies of African American identity remains important, and such readings involve a disruption of the usual approaches to historical context and interpretation.

What follows the end of the end of the story? In a brief conclusion, I review the historical demands upon African American authors and the demands upon readers of African American literature, emphasizing the contingencies of authorship, readership, and social action. The question is not whether African American literature will continue to be read, for all signs indicate its continued popularity. Rather, the question is how this literature will be changed by its readers, and whether the readings will justify any mention of an African American literary tradition. In short, will we draw from this chaotic literature to address injustice or avoid it? Considered here as well are the implications of my argument that racial history cannot be ignored or transcended and that African American literature is uniquely capable of charting a course through that historical terrain in ways that can enable us to reconceptualize current political and ideological debates.

The stakes, it seems to me, are high, especially in a time when even prominent advocates of the political left are talking about the trouble with diversity and using simplistic and largely ahistorical concepts of race to argue for the priorities of an equally simplistic concept of social class. In *To Wake the Nations* (1993), Eric Sundquist reminds us that "value . . . is not solely an aesthetic criterion," and that it "cannot be severed from justice and, therefore, from politics." For his concept of justice, he turns to Patricia Williams's useful formulation. "Justice," she contends, "is a continual balancing of competing visions, plural viewpoints, shifting histories, interests, and allegiances. To acknowledge that level of complexity is to require, to seek, and to value a multiplicity of knowledge systems, in pursuit of a more complete sense of the world in which we all live" (121). Joining Sundquist with Williams, I would add that justice cannot be ahistorical and we cannot afford to think of it as a goal for the future. Justice is not the *result* of the "continual balancing of competing visions" and "shifting histories" that Williams speaks of; justice is a measure of how we manage that balancing process.

In 1855 Frederick Douglass, assessing the force of white supremacist assumptions within the antislavery movement, complained about the "self-appointed generals of the Anti-Slavery host, the Euclids who are *theoretically* working out the almost insoluble problem of our future destiny" ("Self-Elevation" 362). These many years later, we cannot afford to leave either literary history or social justice in the hands of those who favor Euclidian models of social process. We will need to attend carefully to what is a central concept in the chapters that follow, Saidiya Hartman's formulation of "the 'community' or the networks of affiliation constructed in practice"—communities that are to be understood, Hartman argues, not by a simple narrative of race but rather "in terms of the possibilities of resistance conditioned by relations of power and the very purposeful and self-conscious effort to build community" (59). To do this, we will need to bear in mind the complex dynamics of African American literature in social space and time. In short, we will need to account for a chaotic history if we are to have any hope of envisioning and working toward the realization of what I am calling "chaotic justice," a historically informed, ongoing negotiation of the overwhelming complexity and vicissitudes of a society shaped by the ideologies of race. The work ahead involves not the celebration but the application—indeed, the activation—of the documents "bequeathed us by history," documents capable of guiding us to the future by guiding us through the past.[11]

## CHAPTER ONE

# Representing Chaos and Reading Race

Out of a chaos of elements no orderly creation can arise
but by the operation of a sound principle: and sound principle here,
there is none.—HARRIET MARTINEAU, *Society in America*

In *The Souls of Black Folk*, W. E. B. Du Bois famously asserts that "the problem of the Twentieth Century is the problem of the color line" (359). We are now past the twentieth century, and many scholars and other cultural commentators have argued that it is time for us to be past or get beyond or just get over the concept of race. I think that such arguments are ahistorical, or possibly more deeply historical than their proponents appreciate. Many examinations of race in the present are haunted, troubled, and tainted by the philosophical traces, the absurd frameworks, the overdetermined discourse, the studied avoidances, and the rhetorical hat tricks of the past—and not just by the obvious, easily dismissed examples of overt racism, pseudoscience (now called), or time-bound political commentary. Although practitioners have done much to define the intertwined social, legal, ideological, and linguistic forces that combine to give daily significance to what we call "race,"[1] many and perhaps even most literary scholars and historians avoid that complexity. Rather, they see race simply as an ideological imperative that can be, depending on one's politics, either promoted, dismissed, transcended, or transformed—a pliable concept receptive to the ministrations of those who are theoretically sharp or politically determined enough to announce the end of the problem of the twentieth century so as to work toward the promise of the twenty-first. But the problem of the twenty-first century is that the problem of the twentieth century was even more complex than we imagined, and we have barely begun to understand that complexity.

While I disagree with a great deal of recent work on race, I also appreciate its intent—so I do not mean to simplify or undervalue the importance of scholarship that focuses on race as a set of ideological assumptions and priorities that can be reformulated by way of informed intellectual exchange. Rather, I am emphasizing the requirement to map the historical and cultural dynamics within which all commentaries on race must necessarily function in order to more accurately locate the sites at which and the terms by which such commentaries can be most effectively directed. Ideological critique, I suggest, is always in creative tension with the sheer messiness of history; it usually involves the presentation of a reasonably coherent and summarizable history of racial theory and racist practices so as to envision a postracial or postracist future. Ideological critiques of racial constructions usually are devoted to an imagined ideal of the future. They often involve what David Theo Goldberg has identified as "the common contemporary call, at least as the first-level commitment, the causal condition, to erase race from our conceptual apparatus and frame of reference, from all state characterization and concern" (*Racial State* 243). Too often, as Goldberg observes, social progress relating to race is considered to be an approach toward an imagined horizon by which either the color line gradually disappears or an imagined multiculturalist ideal emerges—an escape, in effect, from a social world largely constructed by and long devoted to racial theories and racist practices. In fact, the concept of race cannot be so easily controlled. It certainly cannot be erased so long as the formidable manifestations of history continue to define various and interconnected cultural, economic, and political landscapes.

In this chapter, I argue that race is a dynamic system and that to understand race it is useful to be guided by chaos theory, a theory devoted to the patterns created by complex and seemingly irregular systems.[2] "An important turning point in the science of chaos," N. Katherine Hayles has noted, "occurred when complex systems were conceptualized as systems rich in information rather than poor in order" (Introduction 6), and the science has proved an able descriptor in numerous fields, from physical forms to complex social interactions. Chaos theory focuses on "extreme sensitivity to . . . initial conditions"—as, for example, in the divergence of the path of two leaves in a running stream that demonstrates the significant difference of their initial positions in the water's complex currents (Briggs 18). The underlying patterns of those paths of development are what Benoit Mandelbrot has identified as "the fractal geometry of nature." As John Briggs puts it, "Chaos theory tells the story of the wild things that happen to dynamical systems as they evolve over time; fractal geometry records the images of their movement in space" (22). "Fractals," Briggs explains, "are images of the way things fold and unfold, feeding back into each other and themselves" (23). According to James Gleick, Mandelbrot's great achievement was that he "specified ways of calculating the fractional dimension of real objects, given some technique of constructing a shape or given some data, and he allowed his geometry to make a claim about the irregular patterns he studied in nature. The claim was that the degree of irregularity remains constant over different scales" (98). The claim was sufficiently trustworthy to describe a wide range of complex systems. As Gleick has written, "Mandelbrot glided matter-of-factly from pulmonary and vascular trees to real botanical trees, trees that need to capture sun and resist wind, with fractal branches and fractal leaves" (110). Indeed, Mandelbrot and others have extended the application of fractal geometry to account not only for natural forms but also for the arrangements and technologies of social systems, ranging from economic practices to literary dynamics.[3]

I have turned to this theory because I believe that it is important to understand that what we call race involves both the process and the effects of cultures that legally, economically, socially, educationally, and at times even theologically define and distinguish between different groups of people.[4] Cultures group individuals; individuals and collectives respond to such groupings; those responses often lead to new cultural concepts and manifestations of racial definition and control; and new or slightly different cultural dynamics inspire improvisations on established strategies for dominance, resistance, or survival. What we commonly call race, in other words, cannot be limited to physical features or mapped by DNA, for it encompasses the complex processes by which individuals are positioned, both socially and geographically, sometimes delimiting and sometimes extending privileges, options, mobility, and ideological flexibility. And after all these years, we have barely begun to study this dynamic process.

In this chapter I will plot out a cultural landscape that is overwhelming in its complexity, but I also want to draw attention to the dynamic principles and historical processes that formed this landscape—something like looking at a mountain range and seeing the evidence of glaciers long gone, of still powerful rivers, and of the gradual workings of shifting wind patterns. An understanding of race, I will argue, requires consideration of the entire system of events—ideological, social, biological, and historical—involved in its formation. In other words, race cannot be separated from the dynamic process of its construction, for the formation of race *is* race.

If we think about race not as product but as process, our map of the cultural landscape unfolds to reveal not a Euclidian delineation of social space—a color line, a problem in need of a solution—but rather a social terrain characterized by fractal patterns. Mandelbrot's concept of fractal geometry emerged in part from his attempt to account for those "mathematical structures," as F. J. Dyson explains, discovered through the years "that did not fit the patterns of Euclid and Newton" and thus challenged established models of order and measurement (qtd. in Mandelbrot 3).[5] Mandelbrot begins his seminal book *The Fractal Geometry of Nature* with a simple question: "Why is geometry often described as 'cold' and 'dry'?" He answers: "One reason lies in its inability to describe the shape of a cloud, a mountain, a coastline, or a tree. Clouds are not spheres, mountains are not cones, coastlines are not circles, and bark is not smooth, nor does lightning travel in a straight line" (1). Similarly, race cannot be defined by color or other physical features, nor can it be reduced to a set of essential features or practices, political positions or allegiances. And yet the history of race, or the cultural processes shaped by the turbulent currents of history, are everywhere evident in cultural life, with patterns of the racial eruptions that regularly punctuate the news familiar enough to be identified and ridiculed, defended and dismissed. I take it as a given, then, that no simple "color line" is adequate to describe the complex racial landscape in which we live, but I argue as well that our lives are, in fact, defined by color lines that are both irregular and definitive.[6]

To appreciate this fact of American history and culture, we need only consult the history of laws and practices by which race has been defined, redefined, and associated with cultural privilege and access—such as the various laws, court decisions, and treaties that decided, from time to time and place to place, who would count as white. We might begin by scrutinizing the 1790 Naturalization Act, which limited naturalization to "free white persons." Certainly, we would need to delve into the complex legal, economic, and political system of slavery, as well as explore the ways in which the 1850 Fugitive Slave Law made life very insecure for free African Americans living in the North. We would need to consider the *Dred Scott* decision of the Supreme Court in 1857, when Chief Justice Roger B. Taney, speaking for the majority, declared that African Americans had "no rights which the white man was bound to respect." Probably, we would want to study the process by which the Irish and other social groups were gathered into the pale of whiteness and granted more flexible though often still controlled privileges. And, of course, we would have to consider the reality that at various times throughout our history it has been possible to be legally black in one state but not in another, or to be white in one decade and nonwhite in the next, as Louisiana ruled in the case of Chinese Americans in 1860 and 1870. Also in this category was the ruling of a 1909 U.S. Circuit Court that rendered Armenians white and the 1923 Supreme Court decision that Asian Indians were nonwhite. The list goes on—from the local to the federal level, from one region to the next, and even from one neighborhood and one school district to the next. These are laws that supported economic practices and social and political opportunities, laws that led to social arrangements that inspired new laws, the one consistent concern being the definition and protection of sometimes highly flexible understandings of white privilege and opportunity.[7]

These ongoing and complex constructions, the highly contingent dynamics by which racial identity is formed and sustained over time, were especially contorted in serving the system of slavery. Accounting for these dynamics, however, takes us into chaotic territory, for beyond observing the obvious fact that the color line increasingly could not be definitively tested by actual distinctions of color, following the social geometry of race in the nineteenth century requires us to explore the complex interrelation of laws pertaining to the system of slavery and laws restricting the rights of nominally free African Americans. Such an exploration involves recognition of what William W. Fisher has called "the remarkable degree of inconsistency and instability in the law of slavery" and the process by which "the vocabularies, images, and arguments developed in Southern fiction, political economy, formal defenses of slavery, and popular political debate provided judges and legislators the materials and analytical tools from which they fashioned the rules that regulated the relations of masters and servants" (66). As Fisher suggests, even if we were to focus only on the legal apparatus by which the white supremacist social system was defined, justified, and maintained, we would quickly enter into the realm of popular culture and literary representations, and other modes of social interaction—a world of practices, discourses, and assumptions in dynamic interaction. This dynamic process shaped legal practices, which redirected the process in turn as numerous legal decisions, large and small, not only verified or supported an existing racial distinction but also redefined what it meant to be white or black, often building on or veering from previous redefinitions.

These overlapping and contradictory laws established to define and maintain "the color line" shaped the experience and the performance of social identity. To say this, of course, is to assert what has become a commonplace of scholarship—that race is a systemic, historical construction, and that race is also the developing and dynamic response to that complex construction, the traditions, the rhetorical maneuvers, and the ideological methodologies of survival, resistance, and collective self-definition that operate in the fields of the racial state. But the insistent presence of *the* color line was and is marked by many color lines—the possibility of being legally black in one state but not in another, or of being white in one decade and nonwhite in the next, or of becoming differently raced by moving from one region or even one situation to another. This chaotic configuration of racializing forces, relations, and institutions has ensured not only that a person's experience would be bound to his or her racial identity but also that racial identity would be a highly contextualized, contingent, and always unstable entity. Quite simply, we can no more avoid the effects of the racial past than we can avoid the lingering effects of carbon dioxide produced in the past by declaring it irrelevant in the present or future. Institutional race has encouraged cultural race which has shaped cultural practices and new systemic formations, all of which position and shape individuals born into the culture, sometimes inspiring new manifestations of racial affiliations.

In America's long history of legally controlling access to social power and economic opportunity, many lines of relations have been established, a sort of genealogy of connections that are central to just about anyone's understanding of cultural process. Some might say that, in talking about race, we should not dwell on the past, but people who inherit money rarely refuse it on the grounds that the social conditions of the past, when the money was acquired, should have no relevance in the present. And those who benefit from a relative or a friend in getting a job or getting a loan or getting a second chance rarely refuse that help on the grounds that we should leave the historically developed lines of influence behind us and insist on an absolute model of individual access, ability, and merit. Since the processes of race position people economically, geographically, and historically, it would be difficult to show that the world shaped by race is now inoperable, that race has played no role in forming both the connections we enjoy and our understanding of how those connections might function. I agree, then, with Thomas M. Shapiro, who has argued that "the real story of the meaning of race in modern America . . . must include a serious consideration of how one generation passes advantage and disadvantage to the next—how individuals' starting points are determined" (8). In his study of "wealth accumulation and utilization," Shapiro demonstrates that common distinctions between race and class are just too simple to explain the historical effects of the dynamic system of race. "Deeply embedded policies," he observes, "such as those underlying the Federal Housing Administration and locally funded schools, and market incentives, such as property values, shape how we think about neighborhoods, what we mean by integration, and how we think about educational prospects in ways that reward discrimination" (14). Throughout our lives, we acknowledge in ways large and small, collectively and individually, that the order of the past has a lot to do with the opportunities of the present, yet that admission is largely absent from a great many discussions of race. As Shapiro argues, "Without attending to how equal opportunity or even equal achievement does not lead to equal results—especially concerning wealth—we will continue to repeat the deep and disturbing patterns of racial inequality and conflict that plague our republic" (204).

What is white about white people, then, is not the color of their skin (which is not, after all, white) but rather the historical situation that has made "white" bodies such able predictors of experience, understanding, and access to privilege and cultural authority—a whiteness, in other words, that cannot be transcended merely by good intentions or by the reach of an individual's consciousness. To attend to the historical process by which race has been constructed is, after all, to recognize that instead of race being *somewhere*, in individuals, race is, in fact, *everywhere*: in the way we live, the images we encounter in popular culture, the way wealth and access to power are passed on from one generation to the next, the way that schools are funded, and the ways in which justice has been defined in different places and at different times throughout our nation's history. To talk of white people, then, is not to talk about *who they are*, but rather to address *who, where, when*, and perhaps even *why they have been*, people living in a culture in which that most significant of legal and economic identifiers, whiteness, has had and continues to exert considerable force over individual experience and identity formation. It is important, I think, to acknowledge the obvious fact that we live in a culture that neither requires nor encourages those who are "white" to think seriously about race. Indeed, too often white Americans are not even in a position to engage others in a reasoned and informed dialogue or debate about the issues of the day or about the realities of the past.

Thus, they fall back either on arguments drawn from their chosen race representative or on the prepackaged race discourse that stands in for serious conversation in the public forum—predictable complaints about affirmative action, platitudes about diversity, and the like. In conversations about most other subjects, people might be embarrassed about having so little to offer, but in conversations about race they can be grandly unaware of what more there might be to bring to the subject. Plainly, the great majority of white Americans lack the historical understanding and the cultural self-awareness that identify the need for a complex set of experiences, a detailed body of information, and a sophisticated and practiced vocabulary.

This is not the case for many others. The great majority of black Americans, for example, cannot avoid thinking about race at various times in their lives—not because they embrace the subject, but because they cannot avoid it. This is not to say that black Americans always approach racial concerns with knowledge and wisdom and that white Americans never do. It is only to echo and endorse Charles W. Mills's observation that "the Racial Contract," the Lockean concept he uses to address the terms and dynamics of white supremacist ideology and society, "prescribes for its signatories an inverted epistemology, an epistemology of ignorance, a particular pattern of localized and global cognitive dysfunctions (which are psychologically and socially functional), producing the ironic outcome that whites will in general be unable to understand the world they themselves have made" (18). One result, as Mills notes, is that "nonwhites . . . find that race is, paradoxically, both everywhere and nowhere, structuring their lives but not formally recognized in political/ moral theory. But in a racially structured polity, the only people who can find it psychologically possible to deny the centrality of race are those who are racially privileged, for whom race is invisible precisely because the world is structured around them, whiteness as the ground against which the figures of other races—those who, unlike us, are raced—appear" (76). It is small wonder that those who find race everywhere also find themselves looking for ways to articulate, represent, analyze, and understand what they see—and small wonder, too, that they will have trouble drawing a clear line between "racial" questions and other issues. One result of "a racially structured polity" is interpretive instability. On the one hand, we have developed an awareness of and an ability to analyze racial situations; on the other hand, we cannot always be sure that we are dealing with an intentional or even implicit racial situation. It can be argued that race is in the very structure of the situation, but in everyday experiences, how do we explain this to people who see race only in isolated contexts?

In fact, race has everything to do with the cultural practices and institutions that govern our interactions today, for conditions of the past do not change merely because new laws are passed or old ones are overturned. Our nation's history is burdened by the weight of laws defining and controlling whiteness, but it reflects as well various attempts to support and justify those laws. From the beginning, the most absurd concepts of race defined by law have been supported by popular culture—such as blackface minstrel shows, arguably the most prominent and influential form of entertainment in American history, or other caricatures of black identity pervading the popular media. We grow up surrounded by certain images, certain stories, certain ways of envisioning the world and the people around us. Stephen Greenblatt has stated that all cultures are devoted to two central concepts, "*constraint* and *mobility*"—that is, "beliefs and practices" that determine the "set of limits within which social behavior must be contained," or models of identity to which individuals are expected to conform (225). Other scholars have called these models and expectations cultural roles or cultural scripts, which refer to the ways in which we are given a sense of our place in this world, a sense of what counts as success and of what kind of behavior is valued. The limits on our behavior, Greenblatt observes, "need not be narrow—in certain societies, such as that of the United States, they can seem quite vast—but they are not infinite, and the consequences for straying beyond them can be severe" (225). Indeed, for serious offenders, these consequences can be severe, including "exile, imprisonment in an insane asylum, penal servitude, or execution." Yet the most powerful cultural practices that encourage some behaviors and discourage others can be the smallest gesture—for example, "a condescending smile, laughter poised between the genial and the sarcastic, a small dose of indulgent pity laced with contempt, cool silence." "And we should add," Greenblatt goes on to say, that "a culture's boundaries are enforced more positively as well: through the system of rewards that range again from the spectacular (grand public honors, glittering prizes) to the apparently modest (a gaze of admiration, a respectful nod, a few words of gratitude)" (226).

This is where we most consciously encounter the complex history of race, and this is how we are most likely to recognize it in our daily lives. That complex history that dwells within us regardless of whether we care to dwell in the past, that cultural history that has shaped our understanding even beyond our awareness, will make itself felt in daily human interactions. Marcyliena Morgan has noted that we will be conscious of this history most frequently in conversation, in our observation of different patterns and habits of speech, for language, Morgan reminds us, "reflects social class, region, urban area, gender, generation, education, age, cultural background and speech community. Because language use reflects all of these things, interactions include shifts and switches that are often seamless, sometimes abrupt and awkward but always a reflection of social context, social standing and social face" (134). In other words, the language around us signals the history around us. We are likely to respond to the recognition of that history with a discomforting combination of an awareness of difference, an inability to understand the source or significance of that difference, and a certain self-consciousness that such differences have played a major, unjust, sometimes violent, and even murderous role in our nation's history.[8] One of the most frequent results of that combination of responses is defensiveness, a defensiveness that often leads many Americans to replicate the history of whiteness by attempting to assert control over their environment, either by direct intimidation and exclusion or by more subtle means.

The primary divisions at the foundations of U.S. racial history have, in short, bifurcated many times over to produce large-scale interpretive instability. This instability has led to recurring events (the beating of Rodney King; the Duke Lacrosse controversy; the reaction to the Reverend Jeremiah A. Wright Jr., Barack Obama's former pastor) in which the media reports that many are shocked, *shocked*, to discover yet again that black and white Americans can read the same events so differently. Indeed, through the prism of the interpretive instability that is both a condition and a consequence of U.S. racial history, interventions into systemic injustice can be read as both critiques and realizations of American political mythology, to the point where individual achievements (African Americans, for example, in the Supreme Court, on Capitol Hill, or in the White House) are read not merely as evidence of progress but as manifest signs that the national history of racial oppression has ended. U.S. racial history is what made it possible for Martin Luther King Jr. to deliver his most famous speech on the steps of the Lincoln Memorial in 1963; it is also the reason why that speech was necessary. U.S. racial history is the reason why most white Americans remember only the last third of that speech, in which King declared "I have a dream." And it is the reason why many white Americans continue to live in realities not far removed from those that King described in the first third of his speech. U.S. racial history is the reason why most white Americans can quote King's admonition to judge a person not by the color of her skin but by the content of her character. But that history is also the reason why most white Americans have no memory of King's declaration, in the same speech, that America had defaulted on its "promissory note" to its citizens of color, that it had failed to honor its sacred obligations, that it cannot afford the "tranquilizing drug of gradualism," or that "now is the time to make real the promises of democracy" (107). The culture formed by U.S. racial history thus can be both productive and destructive, open and restrictive, at the same time; it can be committed to grand ideals in practical and concrete ways and at the same time violate those very ideals; it can promote opportunities for some and at the same time limit opportunities for others; it can champion justice and at the same time render invisible even the most obvious injustices around us.

## Troubling Race

There should be nothing new or provocative in anything I have said thus far. Yet there is a need to say it, for *race* remains such a generalized, floating, and flexible concept that it is easily simplified, isolated, contained, and applied in what can appear to be very reasonable arguments—often, arguments *against* the need to continue using such a generalized, floating, and flexible concept in scholarship, in public discourse and policy, or in philosophy. Consider, for example, Walter Benn Michaels's book *The Trouble with Diversity: How We Learned to Love Identity and Ignore Inequality* (2006). As the title indicates, Michaels thinks that the concept of diversity has kept us from attending to the more pressing problem of economic inequality. One of his book's major goals is to shift "our focus from cultural diversity to economic equality" and in this way "to alter the political terrain of contemporary American intellectual life" (7). Certainly, it is not a bad thing to focus on economic equality, though I hope (as do some of the book's critics) that we can manage to deal with more than one issue at a time. I would agree as well that there is reason to explore the problem with diversity. Like many people, I have come to distrust the term "diversity," which has become a cultural code word that signals not a complex social and historical environment, and not a dynamic paradigm for maintaining the stability of collective principles over time, but rather a set of social concerns, superficially considered, that can be identified and isolated in the same breath. Like multiculturalism before it, diversity too often is a way of referring to a generalized otherness, of announcing a kind of cultural fair that requires only our attendance and heartfelt expression of interest, a kind of politically correct comfort food. This is not exactly Michaels's argument, but I approached the book feeling open to a critique of approaches to "diversity," and to the diversity industry, in the academic, political, business, and social spheres.

The trouble with *The Trouble with Diversity*, though, is that some might take it to be a book about race. It is not. Yet even the author seems to think so. To be sure, Michaels begins this work by distinguishing between race and diversity, noting the ways that many practitioners have come to use the terms interchangeably. But then he quickly embraces the association—as if those who have made the turn from race to diversity were actually *right*. In "its simplest form," he tells us, his argument is "that we love race—we love identity—because we don't love class" (6). By *race*, Michaels means an assumed aspect of identity, something that enables individuals sharing that aspect to identify themselves as groups. For him, class is largely a function of economic differences and therefore much more solid. It might be problematic to identify yourself as black or white, but you certainly know whether you are relatively rich or poor.

But the concept of race is not that simple; it is more than something we carry around. It can be understood more fully as something that awaits us as we move from place to place, something we bump into, something that often influences deeply, historically, how and (even today) where we live. Michaels accounts for this to some extent when he says that people are now expected to recognize (in certain public venues and forums) that "racism is a bad thing (which of course it is)" (5). The problem is his apparent confusion between the discourse and practices gathered under the heading of diversity and the systemic operations that should be assembled under the heading of race, along with his assumption that the concept of race is and has been limited to now-discredited biological theories. "Our enthusiasm for racial identity," he asserts, "has been utterly undiminished by scientific skepticism about whether there is any such thing" (5). What follows from this pronouncement is a conventional commentary on race, focused on the epiphany that there is no such thing—the subject of his first chapter, "The Trouble with Race." Michaels naturally turns to the *Plessy v. Ferguson* case of 1892. Noting that "Homer Plessy looked like the other people on the whites-only coach" (23), he joins Plessy's suit with a "twentieth-century story" (22) about Susie Guillory Phipps, who, after believing all of her life that she was white, discovered that her birth certificate identified her as "colored." She contested the documentation but, like Plessy, lost her case. This leads inevitably to the point that race is, at best, an unstable category of identity, followed by a brief review of racist and racial history, including the legal, scientific, and philosophical errors of those who have tried to define race in social or interrelational terms.

Of course, one point of Michaels's argument should be that the 1892 Supreme Court insisted on the existence of race, as did the Louisiana Court of Appeals in the case of Susie Phipps. Such decisions, especially those of the Supreme Court, have some effect—regardless of whether it can be determined that the individual being identified belongs to the group in question. Race as a biological entity did not exist in 1892 any more than it does now, though the Supreme Court decided that race did exist then, as well as in 1857, when it ruled against Dred Scott, and in any number of legal opinions handed down since the country was founded. The effects of those decisions were both obvious (segregation) and more complex—for example, how individuals understood their position and opportunities, and how they thought about those around them, of whatever complexion. No doubt some people were inspired to declare racial solidarity on the basis of court decisions; others might have turned in other directions. The point is not that all white people or all African Americans or all of any putatively racial group thought alike or shared the same perspectives, interests, or values. Rather, it is that the law positioned people differently, or had the potential to position them differently, and this shaped the complex processes of society in ways both large and small. In 1977 Susie Guillory Phipps was still determined to change her birth certificate when she found that she was identified as "colored." The point is that if race does not exist scientifically, then it did not exist in the past, even when scientists argued that it did. What race was in 1892 was not a biological condition but actually a social or ideological one: it was a framework for reading human life, for organizing society, for directing the principles of social, economic, educational, and political exchange.

Toni Morrison has written that for quite some time "every academic discipline, including theology, history, and natural science, insisted 'race' was *the* determining factor in human development" ("Unspeakable" 370). It is rather too easy to pass lightly over this institutional history and focus on the embodiment that was its primary concern. As Goldberg has observed, "Studies of racism have tended to divide methodologically between those assuming an individually oriented and those accepting

a structural approach. Taking individual beliefs and actions as analyti-
cally basic tends to commit one to viewing racism in terms of personal
prejudice. Structural methodology, by contrast, sees racism embedded in,
determined by, or emanating directly, even necessarily, from the prevailing constitution of social formation" (92). Studies of race that address individual beliefs and actions, or even studies based on the recognition that
monolithic racial identifications fail to account for the complex genealogy of actual lives, more often than not fail to account for the systemic
institutionalization and process of the shifting racial order in U.S. history.
This process along with the complex but still-influential historical record,
the multitudinous traces of that process, remain the primary forces to be
accounted for in any discussion of race.

Michaels's point really is that we are now in a position to create new
frameworks, new constitutions of social formation, that can provide new
ways to read human life, new ways to direct public policy, new ways to
understand and negotiate social interactions. The problem is, those frameworks would require a rather significant revolution—and after the revolution we would still be constantly trying to declare our independence from
the past, a process that has not worked out well for the United States in
its own ongoing declarations of historical independence and uniqueness.
In short, frameworks that do not employ the concept of race do not come
to much when we try to explain the past, and they seem to gesture toward
a future in which the past either is irrelevant or is open to dramatic re-
interpretation. However much we might want to endorse Michaels's call
for more focused attention to social class, we are still forced to attend
to the realities of racial history. As Matthew Frye Jacobson points out,
race and class are deeply intertwined, for one can hardly understand the
history of class without understanding the complexities of race. Given
that Michaels devotes a book to separating these concerns, it is worth the
disruption of a long quotation to consider the broad outlines of Jacobson's
explanation of the necessity of considering class and race together:

> First, republican notions of "independence" had both racial and
> economic valences; the white men's movement for "Free Labor,
> Free Soil, and Free Men" was but the flipside of certain racial no-
> tions such as a belief in the Indian's innate "dependency." Second,
> racial stereotypes like inborn "laziness," as applied to Mexicans
> or Indians, were economic assessments that had economic conse-
> quences (in the form, typically, of dispossession). Third, race has

been central to American conceptions of property (who can own property and who can *be* property, for example), and property in its turn is central to republican notions of self-possession and the "stake in society" necessary for democratic participation. Fourth, political standing, doled out on racial terms (such as the naturalization code limiting citizenship to "free white persons"), translates immediately into economic realities such as property rights or labor-market segmentation. And fifth, in cases in American political culture ranging from the Mexican population of Old California to the immigrant Jews of New York's Lower East Side, class markers have often been read as inborn racial characteristics: members of the working class in these groups have been viewed in more sharply racial terms than have their upper-class compatriots. (*Whiteness* 20–21)

What Jacobson offers here, of course, is merely a sketch or a broad outline. But even from this broad outline, with an eye toward the extensive research projects it suggests, we can see that an argument that asks us to turn away from race (presented as identity politics) is merely a continuation of, not a departure from, the policies and practices of the past.

Kwame Anthony Appiah, who is also interested in changing the frameworks by which we read our lives, is more persuasive about the value of this change and what it might entail. Although Appiah would certainly agree with Michaels that "racism is a bad thing," his work demonstrates a much sharper, more detailed, and more fervent awareness of the prevalence of racism and the challenges of dealing with it effectively. He has expressed his desire "to make sure that here in America we do not have discussions about race in which racism disappears from view" (*Color* 82). Moreover, Appiah's approach to the problem of the racial past as a presence in current attempts to understand race is more sophisticated than Michaels's. In his contribution to the coauthored (with Amy Gutmann) *Color Conscious*, Appiah observes that the

> current ways of talking about race are the residue, the detritus, so to speak, of earlier ways of thinking about race; so that it turns out to be easiest to understand contemporary talk about "race" as the pale reflection of a more full-blooded race discourse that flourished in the last [nineteenth] century. The ideational theory can thus be combined with a historical approach; we can explore the ideational structures of which our present talk is, so to speak, the shadow,

and then see contemporary uses of the term as drawing from various different structures, sometimes in ways that are not exactly coherent. (38)

Appiah's historically informed approach seems, at least in principle, more rigorous than Michaels's selective snapshots of the past, particularly in that Appiah emphasizes the influence of "various different structures" that have led to current uses of the term *race*, "sometimes in ways that are not exactly coherent." For his argument Appiah has three primary goals:

> First, I want to explain why American social distinctions cannot be understood in terms of the concept of race: the only human race in the United States, I shall argue, is *the* human race. Second, I want to show that replacing the notion of race with the notion of culture is not helpful: the American social distinctions that are marked using racial vocabulary do not correspond to cultural groups, either. And third, I want to propose that, for analytical purposes, we should use instead the notion of a racial identity, which I will try to explore and explain. (*Color* 32)

Appiah, in short, writes with a great awareness about the historical and philosophical complexity of race.

But he is, as he says, really concerned with a single race, "*the* human race," and is therefore devoted to isolating the all-too-flexible concept of race—certainly, a worthy goal. In pursuit of this goal, he proposes "the idea of racial identity," which he defines (roughly, he acknowledges) as follows: "A label, R, associated with *ascriptions* by most people (where ascription involves descriptive criteria for applying the label); and *identifications* by those that fall under it (where identification implies a shaping role for the label in the intentional acts of the possessors, so that they sometimes act *as an R*), where there is a history of associating possessors of the label with an inherited racial essence (even if some who use the label no longer believe in racial essences)" (*Color* 81–82). Allowing for this calculus of racial identity, Appiah is then free to emphasize that the overall calculus of identity is actually much more complex, and that no single formula should be allowed precedence over the others. "In policing this imperialism of identity—an imperialism as visible in racial identities as anywhere else—it is crucial," he argues,

> to remember always that we are not simply black or white or yellow or brown, gay or straight or bisexual, Jewish, Christian, Moslem,

Buddhist, or Confucian but that we are also brothers and sisters; parents and children; liberals, conservatives, and leftists; teachers and lawyers and auto-makers and gardeners; fans of the Padres and the Bruins; amateurs of grunge rock and lovers of Wagner; movie buffs; MTV-holics, mystery-readers; surfers and singers; poets and pet-lovers; students and teachers; friends and lovers. Racial identity can be the basis of resistance to racism; but even as we struggle against racism—and though we have made great progress, we have further still to go—let us not let our racial identities subject us to new tyrannies. (*Color* 103)

This observation is at the heart of much of Appiah's work, prompting him to gesture "beyond identities" in his recognition of the "potential for conflict between individual freedom and the politics of identity" (*Color* 99). More recently, this has led to Appiah's meditations on "the ethics of identity" and to his concept of a "rooted cosmopolitanism"—that is, not "a form of humanism that requires us to put our differences aside," but rather one in which "the cosmopolitan believes . . . that sometimes it is the differences we bring to the table that make it rewarding to interact at all" (*Ethics* 271).

In practical terms, much of Appiah's argument comes down to individual reason and choice—indeed, to the determination to practice freedom and resist tyranny in the *performance* of identity. "So here are my positive proposals," he offers in *Color Conscious*: "Live with fractured identities; engage in identity play; find solidarity, yes, but recognize contingency, and, above all, practice irony. In short, I have only the proposals of a banal 'postmodernism'" (104).[9] But we must wonder what happened to Appiah's careful sense of history in this postmodern offering. Those whose lives, and the lives of their loved ones, their community, their ancestors, were deeply affected and complexly *positioned* by race can now "engage in identity play." Why didn't someone think of this sooner? The answer, of course, is that someone did, for historically identity play has been a matter of basic survival for many African Americans—in the workplace, on the street, on the stage, in the shadows. Appiah's list of the many aspects of our identities is deceptive. Historically, some have not been allowed to marry, and some have been restricted in their choices. Some who have children have had to negotiate with the institutional and legal aspects of "parents and children" differently from heterosexual couples or from white couples. Some who are students discover that historical textbooks, films, and classroom lessons do not account for people who look like they do, or for the challenges they face, or for the sense of local, state, national, and international community that they experience. Too often, such historical reminders and lessons fail entirely to account for the world they find themselves living in, as if their neighborhoods and their lives are somehow inexplicable, unaccountable. Some, in fact, find the most intimate form of history—genealogy—much more challenging and inaccessible than others do. Some movie buffs encounter a world that requires translation—stories of people whose lives do not quite correspond to or answer their own, but might with a bit of adjustment here and there. Some encounter on MTV an implicit history of entertainment scripts and roles for black identity, so that certain forms of music—say, hip-hop—seem to be rather complexly and often disparagingly "about" them, but in ways that we are not taught to decipher. Other forms of music—such as country music—are assumed to be about other groups, a product of other cultural histories, at least for those who know little about the history of country music. Some are lawyers and find themselves grappling with seemingly clear discrepancies concerning those who are disciplined through the legal system, discrepancies for which there is a racial history. Again, some people have always been forced to "engage in identity play," which they have found to be a very high-stakes game.

Appiah's isolation of racial identity as a concept that accounts for the manifest traces of a now-discredited belief in the existence of race enables him to propose a new framework, a rooted cosmopolitanism, for reading our lives and for directing social interactions. But his rooted cosmopolitan—acknowledging differences, engaging us in conversation, and promoting rewarding interactions—is just a bit too reminiscent of the cosmopolitan in Herman Melville's *The Confidence-Man*: very good at conversation, quite aware of differences, devoted to rewarding interactions, and a master at exposing the private character behind the public persona. There is some value in such interactions, though the devil is in the details; such interactions might not lead us much further beyond where Appiah says that race has led us: still working with "various different structures" inherited from the past and "sometimes in ways that are not exactly coherent."

Again, though, my main concern is that Appiah confuses the effects of race with the source. Race as a biological presence never existed, so if we are simply trying to get beyond racial identity, then we are focused on the wrong thing. Race was, in the past, not in the body but in the frameworks through which the body was read, and those frameworks were never re-ducible to easily replaced philosophical abstractions. They followed from practice and were used to justify systemic assumptions and operations; they were frameworks that acquired legal authority, and in various other ways they were institutionalized and operationalized in social, economic, political, legal, and educational policies and practices; they were part of—indeed, a dynamic principle in—the machinery, the process, of culture. Moreover, these frameworks took on a life of their own as laws and estab-lished practices influenced legal decisions, as policies shaped other poli-cies, as institutional or economic trajectories veered in various directions when confronting or capitalizing on minor and major shifts in the cultural process or disruptions in the always-developing historical narrative. It is in this way that race has shaped lives by creating and enforcing/reinforcing racial identities, either overt or implicit, conspicuous or assumed, and people have responded to that shaping influence in various ways, some-times in ways that have led to new fluctuations in the frameworks.

In many ways, Appiah's definition of racial identity makes great sense, but it is important to be aware that he simplifies a dynamic process by leading to an end point: racial identities. Consider again his formula for defining racial identities: "A label, R, associated with *ascriptions* by most people (where ascription involves descriptive criteria for applying the label); and *identifications* by those that fall under it (where identification implies a shaping role for the label in the intentional acts of the possess-ors, so that they sometimes act *as an R*), where there is a history of associ-ating possessors of the label with an inherited racial essence (even if some who use the label no longer believe in racial essences)." One assumption here is that of conscious identification—that is, those who "sometimes act *as an R*" are conscious of doing so and perhaps have even chosen to do so. But how well does this apply to the racial group whose interests have dominated virtually all of the laws, social practices, and institutional frameworks associated with the history of race in the United States—that is, white people, those who often "act *as an R*" but who can be bewildered, even offended, if this racial identification is pointed out to them? More seriously, though, Appiah fails to account for the ways in which the results of his formula feed back into the formula in successive iterations over a great span of time and space. Racial identity simply cannot be isolated in such a way as to restrict it to individual choice; it functions within a world of contingencies that feed back to create new manifestations of racial identity, new configurations of ongoing contingencies.

A similar problem appears in any commentary on race that takes as its end point a simple or static (or ahistorical) concept of racial identities. In *Against Race: Imagining Political Culture beyond the Color Line*, Paul Gilroy offers a persuasively sophisticated and historically informed analysis of the limitations of the concept of race—specifically, "the relationship between 'race' and fascism" (2). Whereas in many ways Michaels and Appiah direct themselves to a U.S. readership, Gilroy approaches the topic from other shores and provides an international historical perspective. His goal is to "engage the pressures and demands of multicultural social and political life, in which . . . the old, modern idea of 'race' can have no ethically defensible place" (6). The book leads, in its closing sentence, to an admirable vision, even a call to action: "Our challenge should now be to bring even more powerful visions of planetary humanity from the future into the present and to reconnect them with democratic and cosmopolitan traditions that have been all but expunged from today's black political imaginary" (356). We can only appreciate Gilroy's attempt to release his readers from the tradition of a brighter day ahead so they can realize the brighter day in the here and now. In this way Gilroy, like Michaels and Appiah, calls for new frameworks to replace the old. My argument, on the other hand, is decidedly less visionary: any analysis of the world as it could be needs to be grounded in an analysis of the world as it is. Identity and the complex social institutions that regulate, direct, and provide for the sustenance, the security, and even the perspectives central to identity have always been transnational, and the modern nation-state has never functioned purely within geographical or even political boundaries. This state of affairs has led to various visions of cosmopolitanism over time, though such visions generally have not accomplished much in terms of social organization and the possibilities for individual freedom beyond the lives of a small percentage of people.

Still, Gilroy's vision is both admirable and desirable, but the problem of its implementation remains, a problem exacerbated by his focus on willful racial identities as the end point of racial history. In regard to "people who have been subordinated by race-thinking and its distinctive social structures (not all of which come tidily color-coded)," Gilroy observes that "under the most difficult of conditions and from imperfect materials that they surely would not have selected if they had been able to choose, these oppressed groups have built complex traditions of politics, ethics, identity, and culture" (*Against Race* 12). These traditions "have involved elaborate, improvised constructions that have the primary function of absorbing and deflecting abuse." The difficulty is that "they have gone far beyond merely affording protection and reversed the polarities of insult, brutality, and contempt, which are unexpectedly turned into important sources of solidarity, joy, and collective strength." In this way, Gilroy does in fact account for the dynamic process, the feedback loops, of racial identity. Yet he notes as well that this dynamic process complicates the means to realize his vision. "When ideas of racial particularity are inverted in this defensive manner so that they provide sources of pride rather than shame and humiliation, they become difficult to relinquish. For many racialized populations, 'race' and the hard-won, oppositional identities it supports are not to be lightly or prematurely given up." But how can this problem be overcome? Gilroy, whose credentials as a race theorist and proponent of social justice are impeccable, does not take lightly this reluctance to relinquish the established terms of social and political solidarity, the improvisational strategies for negotiating oppressed groups through a threatening world. He hardly believes that the world has become less threatening, though he does view the present strategies as both outdated and dangerously limiting. How, then, can we proceed toward the realization of a new framework? "These groups," Gilroy answers, "will need to be persuaded very carefully that there is something worthwhile to be gained from a deliberate renunciation of 'race' as the basis for belonging to one another and acting in concert" (12). To be sure, Gilroy wrote *Against Race* as a step in that direction, but certainly he knows that the book's message will not reach everyone in "these groups." And how might one envision the moment of "deliberate renunciation of 'race'"? Perhaps as a gathering in a great hall and a vote—but one would need to account for those who voted against the proposal.

My point is that any attempt to deal with the history of race, and the ongoing effects of that history, needs to look beyond purely discursive or ideological remnants—"the residue," in Appiah's approach, "the detritus . . . of earlier ways of thinking about race." In applying our understanding that there is no such thing as a biological race, we should not be too quick to conclude that there is no such thing as race. Yet a focus on racial identity as the end point of our analysis runs the risk of encouraging just such an assumption. This calls to mind James Boswell's description (in his *Life of Johnson*) of his 1763 conversation with Samuel Johnson about Bishop George Berkeley's theories. "After we came out of the church," Boswell reports, "we stood talking for some time together of Bishop Berkeley's ingenious sophistry to prove the non-existence of matter, and that every thing in the universe is merely ideal. I observed, that though we are satisfied his doctrine is not true, it is impossible to refute it. I never shall forget the alacrity with which Johnson answered, striking his foot with mighty force against a large stone, till he rebounded from it, 'I refute it *thus*'" (333). In touring any American city or traveling through rural areas, or in surveying the American political, economic, and social landscape, one will stumble over a great many large stones and rocks—what Appiah terms the "obstacles created by sexism, racism, homophobia" (*Color* 104). Such obstinate rocks have long been a central presence in the creation, distribution, and reception of that body of work gathered under the heading of African American literature. For that reason it is useful to come to an understanding of the concept of race that includes not just the people who live in those urban neighborhoods and rural areas but also the large stones and rocks that dot and define the landscape.

What is strange is that, while a great deal of work remains, we do not lack for studies of these "obstacles"—that is, studies that attend to both institutionalized racial frameworks and the identities of those affected and effected by those frameworks. Some of the classic historical studies are still relevant, especially George M. Fredrickson's *The Black Image in the White Mind: The Debate on Afro-American Character and Destiny, 1817–1914* (1971) and Thomas F. Gossett's *Race: The History of an Idea in America* (1963). Supplementing these histories are any number of more recent historical studies—for example, Matthew Frye Jacobson's *Whiteness of a Different Color: European Immigrants and the Alchemy of Race* (1998) and *Barbarian Virtues: The United States Encounters Foreign Peoples at Home and Abroad, 1876–1917* (2000), or Bruce Dain's *A Hideous Monster of the Mind: American Race Theory in the Early Republic* (2002). Among the excellent studies of African Americans or of race generally in the U.S. legal system are John Hope Franklin and Genna Rae McNeil's collection, *African Americans and the Living Constitution* (1995); A. Leon Higginbotham Jr.'s *In the Matter of Color: Race and the American Legal Process: The Colonial Period* (1978) and *Shades of Freedom: Racial Politics and Presumptions of the American Legal Process* (1996); and Mark S. Weiner's *Black Trials: Citizenship from the Beginnings of Slavery to the End of Caste* (2004). The economic and social dimensions of race are explored in Michael K. Brown, Martin Carnoy, Elliott Currie, Troy Duster, David B. Oppenheimer, Marjorie M. Shultz, and David Wellman's *Whitewashing Race: The Myth of a Color-Blind Society* (2003); Thomas M. Shapiro's *The Hidden Cost of Being African American: How Wealth Perpetuates Inequality* (2004); and Rodney E. Hero's *Racial*

*Diversity and Social Capital: Equality and Community in America* (2007). Important theoretical and ideological studies include David Theo Goldberg's *Racist Culture: Philosophy and the Politics of Meaning* (1993) and *The Racial State* (2002); Charles W. Mills's *The Racial Contract* (1997); Karim Murji's and John Solomos's collection *Racialization: Studies in Theory and Practice* (2005); Maria Krysan and Amanda E. Lewis's collection *The Changing Terrain of Race and Ethnicity* (2004); and Shannon Sullivan's *Revealing Whiteness: The Unconscious Habits of Racial Privilege* (2006). Moreover, there is a great deal to be learned from more popular works—among them, James W. Loewen's *Sundown Towns: A Hidden Dimension of American Racism* (2005). Finally, one can follow recent bifurcations and iterations of racial history by examining such studies as Lisa Nakamura's *Cybertypes: Race, Ethnicity, and Identity on the Internet* (2002) or the various essays collected in *Race in Cyberspace* (2000), edited by Beth E. Kolko, Nakamura, and Gilbert B. Rodman.

This is a highly selective list, but while we can often detect the influence of some partial configuration of this varied and detailed body of scholarship in studies of African American literature, these works are rarely mentioned in studies of white American authors. Often, references to these studies do not appear where we would most expect them. They play no role in Michaels's book, for example, and Appiah provides no sustained discussion of the issues they raise in his work. Generally, we have little sense of, or perhaps little regard for, the need to construct a sound and comprehensive approach to the subject of race, and few attempts have been made to apply this complex body of scholarship to the concerns of American literary history beyond discussions of cultural wars, identity politics, or the superficialities of the concept of race. Part of the reason for such omissions—beyond the assumption that race history and theory have little to do with white American literature—is that "race" is usually considered to be a kind of floating concept with some historical baggage attached rather than an ongoing historical and social dynamic in and of U.S. culture. There is no need to give a progress report of what we know so far and where we might go from here. Thus one can easily reference the concept of race-as-embodiment and locate it historically so as to discredit race as a valid subject for rigorous philosophical discourse.[10]

Of course, one could argue that the overwhelming complexity of the historical process of race makes any stable or coherent approach to the subject virtually impossible. Certainly, this is a problem acknowledged by Goldberg, who has pieced together, in his several studies, the most rigorous, systematic, and detailed account of racism available. "Paul Gilroy," Goldberg notes, "has argued that because racisms vary so widely and are by nature historically specific, no general theory of '*race relations* and race and politics' can be sustained. Gilroy's criticism is primarily directed at a specific tradition that has prevailed in social theorizing about race and racism, namely, the race relations industry, though the criticism potentially applies to any attempted analysis of racial phenomena" (*Racist Culture* 41). Goldberg's response to Gilroy's argument is instructive:

> One direction to explore in responding to Gilroy's challenge and in accounting for the ways in which racisms become normalized involves developing a general but open-ended theory concerning race and racism. The theory would have to account for historical alterations and discontinuities in the modes of racial formation, in the disparate phenomena commonly expressed in racial terms, as well as in those expressions properly considered racist. It must also enable and encourage opposition to racist expression, for ultimately the efficacy of a theory about race and racism is to be assessed in terms of the ways in which it renders possible resistance to racisms. Moreover, architectural safeguards against the theoretical imperative to closure must be built into this framework so that it will be open to identifying and theorizing continuities or new additions to transforming racialized discourse, as well as discontinuities and aberrant expressions. (*Racist Culture* 41)[11]

This, I suggest, is the approach we need to get at the dynamic complexity of U.S. racial history.

Indeed, we might say that Goldberg is looking for a model that will bring a useful complexity to the various categories of Appiah's formula for defining racial identity, as well as a model that accounts for the recursive, nonlinear, and iterative development of "modes of racial formation." In *Racist Culture* Goldberg lays out his own calculus, one that accounts for a more dynamic and iterative historical and cultural *process* than that outlined by Appiah:

> So whether any social group—Arabs or Aborigenes [*sic*], say, American Indians or Irish, Blacks or Hispanics, Japanese or Jews, Polish or Gypsies—is identifiable as a race at any spatiotemporal conjuncture turns on the prevailing weight of interacting formative considerations. These considerations include (a) a history

of being so named; (b) the processes and criteria of their boundary construction; (c) the rhetoric of their genesis; (d) the sorts
of contestational and exclusionary relations the group so circumscribed has with other groups at the time; and (e) the terms of self-
identification and self-ascription, given (a) through (d). (76–77)

These challenges are considerable, for behind every key concept is a complex and often nonlinear historical process and set of contingencies that
limit the terms of this explanation of group identification, especially since
the formula assumes a conceptually stable group identity in the form of
collective self-identifications and self-ascriptions.

## Chaotic Race and Affiliated Networks

Ultimately, I will argue that what Gilroy recognizes as a "profound and urgent theoretical and political challenge" is amply met in African American
literature. But before turning to that contention, I want to suggest that
there exists a framework for gathering together the dynamic properties of
racial history and identity. Let us begin with that problematic concept, the
African American community. The blended self-consciousness and self-
awareness that follows from individual but interrelated cultural positions,
joined with the unavoidable necessity of addressing issues of race, social
justice, and cultural incoherence, are the most prominent characteristics
of anything that might be termed the African American community. But
the dynamics here trouble the potential comforts of group designation.
As Saidiya Hartman has asserted, we need to look beyond the usual racial
logic supported by the usual historical narratives to recognize the more
complex communities lost to the narration of the past, what she terms
"the networks of affiliation enacted in performance." These networks,
Hartman explains,

> sometimes referred to as the "community among ourselves," are
> defined not by the centrality of racial identity or the selfsameness
> or transparency of blackness nor merely by the condition of enslave-
> ment but by the connections forged in the context of disrupted af-
> filiations, socially amid the constant threat of separation, and shift-
> ing sets of identification particular to site, location, and action. In
> other words, the "community" or the networks of affiliation con-
> structed in practice are not reducible to race—as if race a priori
> gave meaning to community or as if community was the expres-
> sion of race—but are to be understood in terms of the possibilities

of resistance conditioned by relations of power and the very purposeful and self-conscious effort to build community. (59)

Hartman's concept of a nonhomogeneous community that is constantly in flux and "conditioned by relations of power" is a particularly apt description of the complexity of what is often more simply referred to as the African American or black community, a complexity that those thus affiliated will readily recognize. This imagined but fragmented community, and this difficult recognition, constituted, in fact, the defining framework within which most nineteenth-century African American political activism (including literary activism) functioned.[12]

Eddie S. Glaude Jr., a scholar who has attended carefully to that framework, understands that central to any work devoted to the lives and rights of this imagined community must be the attempt to theorize both African American history and the concepts of agency, moral responsibility, identity, and community that have been shaped by that history. Glaude appropriately looks for an approach that does not rely on essentialist notions of black identity, on the one hand, or that does not theorize black history, experience, and identity beyond the reach of recognition and relevant social action, on the other. "How we think about black identity," Glaude argues, "how we imagine black history, and how we conceive of black agency can be rendered in ways that escape bad racial reasoning—reasoning that assumes a tendentious unity among African Americans simply because they are black, or that short-circuits imaginative responses to problems confronting *actual* black people" (*In a Shade* x). Glaude is obviously responding to numerous approaches to African American history, identity, and community that rely on what he calls bad racial reasoning. As he notes:

> Black history, for some, constitutes a reservoir of meaning that predetermines our orientation to problems, irrespective of their particulars, and black agency is imagined from the start as bound up with an emancipatory politics. When identity is determined by way of reference to a fixed racial self, the complexity of African American life is denied. Moreover, the actual moral dilemmas African Americans face are reduced to a crude racial calculus in which the answers are somehow genetically or culturally encoded. (8–9)

I share Glaude's concern about a fixed racial self, as well as his search for something beyond a "crude racial calculus."

By what calculus can we define the contours and follow the trajectory of the history that has shaped African American identities and experiences in order to determine the solutions we need to the problems that are so statistically obvious? This question is largely unaddressed by those who, like Walter Benn Michaels, rightly identify the problem with the diversity industry and with the bad racial reasoning that supports it but who use that analysis to return to the comforting calculus of a politics or an ideological position based on the assumption that it is possible to transcend, get beyond, or otherwise evade the racial past. In his own search for an approach to these concerns, Glaude turns to the philosophical promise of pragmatism. "History," he observes,

> should not be invoked to fortify our actions with the supposed certainty of past doings and sufferings. Instead, to use Emerson's wonderfully rich formulation, we draw circles around our inheritance, with history providing the instrumentalities to invade the future with a little more than luck. We understand more fully why certain features of our lives have lapsed into incoherence, how varying and competing approaches impact our form of life, and how the choices, beliefs, and actions of our fellows, as well as impinging events, turn us around and cast us off in new directions. We stand not as servants to History but as historically conditioned organisms transacting with environments, for weal or woe, in the hope of securing a better life. (*In a Shade* 82–83)

I agree with this formulation, though I must observe that History here operates as a rather unproblematic category—a world of information to marshal for a strategic invasion of the future. We will need a more complex understanding of history if we are to understand ourselves as "historically conditioned organisms transacting with environments," and we will need concepts of race and community that are capable of defining the terms by which the overwhelming data of history can be accessed and applied. But at the core of these complex interactions remains the difficult reality of African American experience—that "African Americans were forced to create themselves amid the absurdity of a nation committed, at once, to freedom and unfreedom" (*In a Shade* 48). "Theirs was a blue note," Glaude tells us, "an unstable chord that called attention to the unbridled chaos at the heart of American democracy" (48).

In attempting to account for the history and effects of the concept of race, then, we need to trace the constantly varying course of this "unbridled chaos." We might approach this challenge merely by turning again to existing attempts to account for this complexity, now listening for the hint of those features of social interaction and historical process so familiar to those involved in the study of chaotic phenomena and complexity. Consider, for example, Charles Mills's notion of the Racial Contract: "a visible or hidden operator that restricts and modifies the scope of its prescriptions" (72). As Mills sees it, "There is both synchronic and diachronic variation" in the Racial Contract, "many different versions or local instantiations" that "evolve over time, so that the effective force of the social contract itself changes, and the kind of cognitive dissonance between the two alters" (72). Goldberg similarly defines racist culture as "fluid," something that "grows and ebbs" (*Racist Culture* 222, 8). "Its transforming natures," he observes, "are deeply connected as cause and manifestation to reconstructed and restructured identities, to changing conditions in social structure and organization, as well as to anxieties about impending changes" (222). Accordingly, his task is to immerse himself in and chart the course of that fluidity—that is, "to account for the emergence, transformation, and extension, in a word, the (continuing re-)invention of racist culture, and for the varying kinds of discursive expression that it prompts and supports" (8). Gilroy looks beyond the tides that ebb and flow to note that "the pressure to associate [with a group identity], like the desires to remember or forget, may vary with changes in the economic and political atmosphere. Unlike the tides, the weather cannot be predicted accurately" (*Against Race* 126). In exploring such complex and unpredictable associations that "trouble" any concept of group identity, Gilroy suggests a turn to "the celebrated 'butterfly effect' in which tiny, almost insignificant forces can, in defiance of conventional expectations, precipitate unpredictable, larger changes in other locations" (126).

Since the *rhetoric* of dynamic systems is already being applied to the study of race, there is some value in stepping back and drawing from chaos theory to consider the implications, and the possibilities, of the rhetorical models we find ourselves using. In commentary by Mills, Goldberg, Gilroy, and others on the history and *process* of race, we can see references to the operation of what Mark S. Mosko has termed the six "interrelated characteristics" that are widely accepted as basic to "chaotic phenomena": "(1) sensitive dependence on initial conditions, (2) complex, unstable relations among variables, (3) fractal or self-similar patterning on different scales, (4) dynamical transformations in accordance with nonlinear (rather than linear) equations, (5) self-organization or 'dissipative structures,' and (6) universality or previously undetected numerical constants" (7). There is no doubt that these characteristics are inherent in the process by which the concept of race has been and is applied, developed, and transformed in U.S. culture. Suffice it to say, as argued in this chapter, that an understanding of universality in human life does not require a transcendence of race or a theoretical turn to cosmopolitanism, for such gestures, in my view, reduce the vital element of history, of *process* and *time*, in the above categories. Universality can be found in the ways that humans create and are shaped by systems of social organization, the ways in which this interactive process organizes humans into groups, and the ways in which they self-organize or otherwise respond to these conceptual frameworks and institutional pressures, individuality interacting with collectivity.

This is not to say that this process produces stable categories of identity in relation to the dynamic structures of racial ideology—indeed, quite the opposite. As Jack Morava has observed, chaos theory offers instead the opportunity "to speculate in principled ways about mechanistic models for social phenomena, without chaining those models to notions of determinism." "The hostility to determinism in the humanistic sciences is so strong," Morava rightly notes, "that it naturally leads to the repudiation of mechanistic models in general. Chaos theory offers *mechanistic* but not *deterministic* models to social scientists" (62). In discussions of race, in which the repudiation of any assumption of an inevitable or essential set of characteristics is so often and so aptly emphasized, chaos theory offers a useful approach to a cultural process that follows general patterns without leading to absolute or unchanging results—that is, patterns of identifiable configurations of specifically unpredictable results known as strange attractors, "the fractal form embedded in any nonlinear feedback process" (F. Turner xxiv).

Although my turn to chaos theory might seem unusual or even contrived, it hardly requires a great leap to suggest that this approach can lead us to a better understanding of the nonlinear processes, the recurrent patterns, and generally the dynamic and chaotic phenomena involved in the social history of race. Jeffery A. Bell, in considering the ways in which Gilles Deleuze's philosophy of difference functions "at the edge of chaos," believes that his own application of dynamic systems theory to philosophical method does not constitute a significant change from the usual process by which one might "set forth points of instability (i.e., definitions) which may lead to further work and 'thinking' in other areas (possible bifurcations)." "This," Bell says, "is doing philosophy" (209). Stuart

Kauffman similarly observes that "historians do not think of themselves as merely recounting the record, but as looking for the web of influences that kaleidoscopically interact with one another to create the patterns that unfold" (300). Noting that "we lack a theory of how the elements of our public lives link into webs of elements that act on one another and transform one another," Kauffman adds simply, "We call these transformations 'history'" (299). Certainly, it is no great innovation, then, to suggest that the cultural history of race involves an interactive web of elements—a dynamic central to the concept of emergence in both science and philosophy. The value of drawing from chaos or complexity theory is that it enables us—indeed, given the nature of many discussions about race, it *forces* us—to account for an overwhelmingly complex process of interactions and iterations. As Frederick Turner has written, if we can recognize that we are "probably dealing with a certain type of iterative process in a highly communicative system," then "we can begin to ask the right questions about it" (xxii). "Chaos," as Raymond Eve, Sara Horsfall, and Mary Lee maintain, "is not a static theory, but a dynamic one that captures movement and change, and as such, represents a powerful ally to more traditional theories of social phenomena" (xxxi).

The use of chaos theory thus permits us to turn from a simple notion of race—be it biological destiny, cultural affiliation, or a floating signifier in critical discourse—and consider race as a dynamic system obfuscated by an overabundance of information. Born into this systemic racial complex, individuals and groups reveal their sensitivity to initial conditions, their positionality in social time and space. The racial system can be characterized as a system rich in feedback, regularly folding in on itself as various eruptions resituate the racial landscape or redirect the cultural current, as apparently isolated or local or otherwise self-contained "racial incidents"—a local act of violence, or an apparently localized or limited interpretation of law—lead to seemingly disproportionate effects. In science, it is through the examination of fractal dimensions that one is able to see the regularity of what might appear to be chaotic, a regularity not only of surface features but also of scale, a "recursive symmetry" at various magnifications of the object of study (Hayles, Introduction 10). In nineteenth-century African American history, as A. Leon Higginbotham Jr. has noted, this regularity appears in "the mechanisms of control through judicial decisions and statutes" that "span the sanctioning of slavery and the special limitations imposed on free blacks, to the prohibitions against interracial marriage and sexual activity, to the eliminating of the legal significance of blacks' 'conversions to Christianity,' to generally restricting any activities or aspirations of blacks that might threaten the groups in control" (*Shades of Freedom* 14). Therefore, to map the historical construction (and reconstructions) of race in various regions and through various times, we would need to trace a complex process of recursion—that is, "a sort of feedback loop, with the end result of one stage brought back as the starting point for the next" (Eglash 8).

This feedback loop is evident even in the nation's foundational concepts. As Edmund Morgan, Kathleen Brown, and other scholars have demonstrated, from colonial times liberty was based on a racial concept, and as Eva Sheppard Wolf explains in her study of Virginia through the early national period, this concept necessarily shifted to accommodate significant changes in the social landscape. As Wolf argues:

> The construction of liberty in Virginia as white occurred not at a single moment but repeatedly and with extra vigor when political and social changes made possible some new arrangement. In part, the problems inherent in racializing liberty . . . necessitated the repetitive process. White Virginians also found it necessary to insist repeatedly on the privilege of whites over blacks because over time more and more people of African descent came to resemble free white Virginians in status, manners, and even appearance. (xiv)

Here Wolf points to the central dynamic of the phenomena of race: the ongoing and mutually modifying tension between race as embodiment and race as a systemic principle. As the concept of race as embodiment becomes less stable or more ambiguous or porous, the systemic controls for race become more pronounced and more complex—various manifestations, we might say, of the laws devoted to increasingly refined and absurd increments of racial affiliation, from the early politics of miscegenation to the one-drop rule.[13] Race, as I see it, refers to the always-shifting and contingent relationship between race as embodiment and race as systemic, and I am suggesting that chaos theory offers a means for studying the operations and patterns of this relationship. The patterns that follow from the repetitive processes central to the racialization of liberty, equality, and opportunity constitute "the changing same" of American history, and it is important that we not overlook or underestimate these patterns in our desire to get beyond the equally predictable instantiations of racial politics.[14]

As the studies of American foundational ideals indicate, perhaps the most obvious characteristic of racial experience is sensitivity to initial conditions. Quite simply, in terms of race, it matters where and when an individual was born, just as it matters in terms of class and gender. Environment and early experiences, along with the acculturated guidance of those around you, will influence how you understand certain aspects of your identity, how you understand and experience your relationship to the historical narratives you encounter, and how you perform or find yourself performing as an individual associated (alone or with others, through interpersonal relations or through legal identifications) with certain racial, economic, class, or gender classifications. This is not to say that you are bound and determined by your initial position in life, but only that there is a reason why political polls and sociological statistical analyses are fairly (within identifiable limits) trustworthy as predictors of human behavior. In some areas of U.S. culture, this fact of life seems particularly and tragically obvious. As the authors of *Whitewashing Race: The Myth of a Color-Blind Society* have found: "It is abundantly clear . . . that race still helps to determine who will enter the formal justice system in the first place and thus powerfully shapes what will happen thereafter. And what the research shows clearly is how persistent racial stereotyping meshes with the effect of long-term structural disadvantages to ensure that blacks wind up more often in the criminal justice system" (Brown et al. 152). Sensitivity to initial conditions applies as well to institutional recognition of race over space and time—the effects of initially isolating some racial groups and denying them, by law, social and economic mobility or professional opportunity. This led to a historical process of gradual, sometimes indirect access to such rights that is different from the historical process of assumed access experienced by others. One might say that there is a reason why affirmative action and preferential treatment are phrases that have applied to some groups but almost never have applied to the long history of legal and social facilitation available to certain classes of white men.

Central to the process I am describing are "complex, unstable relations among variables." Since a fundamental dynamic in U.S. culture has been an invented category of human identity, and since individuals in U.S. culture variously revealed their commitment to a false ideology with porous boundaries, the category or categories of race quickly multiplied and eventually extended to absurd and unstable distinctions. This instability and the multiple relations it produced became part of the social and legal environment through which racial identity is both experienced and comprehended.

Also central to this process—indeed, central to the institutionalization of race and racism—is ongoing feedback. William F. Stroup's explanation of this practice and its effects is useful here. As he puts it, "System process becomes structure under feedback or iteration. . . . Feedback simply refers to the fact that a portion of model, machine, or system output returns to be used again as input" (126–27). When considered in this light, the legal history of race might well be understood in terms of feedback or iteration. The *Dred Scott* case, for example, was the result of regional variations in laws on enslavement. In its decision, the Supreme Court drew from operating assumptions concerning race and established these assumptions as a ruling framework for law—that black Americans had no rights that white Americans were obligated to respect. But this institutionalization of operating assumptions created a fundamentally different, if not new, set of conditions for black Americans, as did the Court's ruling in *Plessy v. Ferguson* later in the century. Nothing was changed but everything was changed when white supremacist assumptions and practices were, in effect, used as input to the national legal machine. And that legal machine itself promoted an ongoing iterative process that both drew from and created various configurations of a racialized process. If, in studying this legal history, we limit our understanding of race to a false identifier of the individuals involved, then we will miss the complex and multiple variables interacting here, all of which should be understood as the results and producers of racial process.

It is beyond the purpose of this chapter, and beyond my current abilities, to identify and apply the variables by which chaos theory might offer a useful explanation of specific events in American cultural history. As Jacobson has said, "The vicissitudes of race represent glacial, nonlinear cultural movements" (*Whiteness* 7). Many scholars seem to agree, for they often find themselves writing about shifting foundations, redirected currents, and layered landscapes when looking back on the racial past. Mapping that past will require a labyrinthine narrative that brings together and considers numerous configurations of relations, contingencies, and shifts. To account for this complexity, one needs to account for a complex social process. Chaos theory is a useful and, I believe, methodologically appropriate way to approach this challenge. Through chaos theory, we might reimagine progress as infinite possibility within a social world bounded by the effects of a racialized past, a progress that involves most fundamentally the ongoing attempt to accurately describe how the manifestations of racial history position individuals, create highly variable concepts of identity, and organize variable standards of social justice. Although I want to approach the possibilities with care, I still cautiously share David Byrne's view of "the profoundly optimistic implication of the possibility of the understanding of the domain of complexity as character- ized by robust chaos. We can come to see what makes the difference. And if we can see what makes the difference, then we can make the differ- ence" (41–42). This, I think, is the challenge that awaits us, the problem of the twenty-first century, the fractal color line that has drawn us into the world of both awesome complexity and infinite possibility.

Much more can be said about complexity and possibility, but I will conclude here with a comment on the construction of the social or insti- tutional manifestations of racial ideology that facilitate the *process* that I identify as crucial to race—indeed, the process that *is* race. In her impor- tant study of the role of analogy in science, Nancy Leys Stepan nicely cap- tures the interactive process by which assumptions about human nature, character, and cultural position developed into institutional frameworks that promoted new configurations of established views and practices. The following paragraph summarizes the process that is central to Stepan's analysis, different configurations of which she describes in greater detail throughout her essay:

> When scientists in the nineteenth century . . . proposed an analogy
> between racial and sexual differences, or between racial and class
> differences, and began to generate new data on the basis of such
> analogies, their interpretations of human difference and similarity
> were widely accepted, partly because of their fundamental con-
> gruence with cultural expectations. In this particular science, the
> metaphors and analogies were not strikingly new but old, if un-
> examined and diffuse. The scientists' contribution was to elevate
> hitherto unconsciously held analogies into self-conscious theory,
> to extend the meanings attached to the analogies, to expand their
> range through new observations and comparisons, and to give them
> precision through specialized vocabularies and new technologies.
> Another result was that the analogies became "naturalized" in the
> language of science, and their metaphorical nature disguised. (42)

The process that Stepan depicts should not be new to anyone who has studied the history of race, though her analysis of that history is ex- emplary. Still, I would suggest that too often we fall into a largely linear model of historical understanding. We see the effects of the process, but we fail to appreciate the concept itself or we place it at the periphery of our discussions. My purpose in emphasizing the chaotic nature of this history is to underscore that the racial process itself—our primary subject—cannot be understood in terms of a simple or neatly linear cause-and-effect model.

## Old Guidebooks and New Maps

It is tempting to say that trying to examine race is akin to the experience of Melville's young protagonist in *Redburn*. With a revered copy of his father's guidebook, *The Picture of Liverpool*, in hand, Redburn wanders through the English city looking in vain for landmarks. He eventually comes to the inevitable conclusion that his "precious book," "full of fine old family associations," is "next to useless. . . . The thing that had guided the father could not guide the son." Redburn sits for a moment to take in the lesson: "This world, my boy, is a moving world; . . . it never stands still; and its sands are forever shifting. This very harbor of Liverpool is gradually filling up, they say; and who knows what your son (if you ever have one) may behold, when he comes to visit Liverpool, as long after you as you come after his grandfather. . . . Guide-books, Wellingborough, are the least reliable books in all literature; and nearly all literature, in one sense, is made up of guide-books" (157). The lesson, one could say, still applies, and those who learn it would do well to throw away the guidebooks of the past and trust the ones of the present. But we might want to think twice before doing so. Unlike an out-of-date directory to a changing city, modern commentary on race is designed more often than not to help us find our way around a promising present and a brighter future built on the imagined foundations of a generally stable past. Indeed, the attraction of turning away from race as a viable critical or political category is precisely that it rejects the father's guidebook. The problem is that the guidebook still works, though it leads not to recognizable edifices but rather to ongoing foundations, and we discard that book at our peril.

Discard it, though, we do. Viewed on a larger scale, the lack of correspondence between guidebook and landscape that Redburn discovers characterizes the nation's tenuous acknowledgment of its heritage of slavery and racial control. Increasingly, the complex social, economic, political, and theological complexities of the system of slavery and the racial ideologies that supported it are being addressed primarily through an ever-expansive and flexible return to the story of the Underground Railroad. This return to an all-too-familiar commemorative paradigm has been organized primarily through the National Park Service Network to Freedom program, supported in part by federal legislation passed in 1990 and 1998. In its brochure, the program claims to be "illustrative of a basic founding principle of this Nation, that all human beings embrace the right to self-determination and freedom from oppression." Places associated with the network include everything from "a site that might be a water or overland route" to "a plantation where an escape began." Those familiar with the representation of slavery at plantation museums can attest to the freedom that this network, taken as a whole, is most likely to celebrate. In short, visitors are encouraged to follow a carefully marked heritage trail while the social, economic, political, and theological traces of the past, along with the ideologies that supported racial oppression, continue to map the present in ways that are either safely removed from or meticulously contained in public memory. Guided by the markers that join highways to historical tourism areas, people can continue to hold their marriage ceremonies on former plantations, or stay in bed-and-breakfast inns modeled after slave cabins, or shop for gifts in renovated slave quarters. They can continue to imagine the North as either the refuge of freedom or a conduit to a possible freedom, or perhaps even believe that the nation's mythology as a land of justice and liberty was momentarily disrupted but ultimately untroubled by its reliance on the system of slavery and white supremacist ideology. Public memory is linked to the conditions of its financial support and the cultural imperatives of its presentation. More often than not, it is directed to promote the ideological mission of "official stories" about the past while obscuring the capitalist and white supremacist structures behind those ideological screens.[15]

To a great extent, as I have suggested, my purpose in this book is to offer a different kind of map by exploring the enduring value of the African American fathers' and mothers' guidebooks. Against the simple stories we sometimes tell about this body of literature is a world of complexity that has everything to do with the fragmented narratives, the sudden narrative shifts, the often unexplained juxtapositions, the generic complexity, and the frequently unstable or elusive perspective so common to nineteenth-century African American narratives, fiction, histories, and other texts. In her study of nineteenth-century Rhode Island, Joanne Pope Melish has outlined the significant resistance to the black-white racial binary then very much under development both regionally and nationally. "Racial designations," Melish observes,

were locally inflected and relational, indexed by local readings of
a host of different factors—cultural conventions, economic relationships, gender conventions, status relationships, national identities, citizenship status, religion, and perhaps others. Place and
social context could give similarly descended people variant racialized identities; very specific circumstances could produce different racial identities for closely related people and could change
either an official or a colloquial racial identity of the same person.
Well into the antebellum period, an increasingly rigid set of abstract racial categories defined by the state sat uneasily upon a
much more complex and contradictory set of racial characterizations in practice, reflecting not only local meanings of distinctions based on color, descent, and class among long-settled U.S.
populations but also attempts to coin racialized social identities
for a shifting matrix of new immigrants. ("Racial Vernacular" 18)

Those engaged in various regional studies will no doubt observe that
Melish's conclusions are not exclusive to Rhode Island, though the particular features of this racial complexity might be regionally distinct while
still influenced by various forms of interstate intercourse. "Such a set of
locally inflected, negotiated, complex, contradictory, and polymorphous
racial characterizations," Melish suggests, "may be called a 'racial vernacular'"—and different regions might speak in different racial vernaculars (18).

Nineteenth-century African American activists and writers understood
this and other racial vernaculars, a world of "locally inflected, negotiated,
complex, contradictory, and polymorphous" characterizations, social
roles, historical possibilities, narrative lines, and philosophical ideals.
To draw again from Hartman, identifying, negotiating, and articulating
the "community among ourselves" was always a complex affair—for it
was a community "defined not by the centrality of racial identity or the
selfsameness or transparency of blackness nor merely by the condition
of enslavement but by the connections forged in the context of disrupted
affiliations, socially amid the constant threat of separation, and shifting
sets of identification particular to site, location, and action" (59). These
attempted identifications, negotiations, and articulations are the primary
focus of nineteenth-century African American literature. This is a body
of literature that involves fundamentally the exploration of the relations,
connections, and tensions that Melish describes—a process circumscribed

by the binary and complicated by the more complex social landscape, as well as by habits, associations, and rituals that have either tended toward the mainstream African American traditions, fed directly into them, or departed from them. It involves as well a world of white writers who have directly or indirectly enforced, commented on, or been defined by the structures, assumptions, and networks of race.

As is the case of other literary traditions whose context is U.S. history—that is, literature usually viewed as having nothing to do with race—the history and interactions I address based on the concept of race have been central to the development of African American literary history. Indeed, African Americans have worked hard to identify the kinds of concerns I have outlined in this chapter, since doing so was often a matter of basic survival and a necessity for individual and collective self-determination. They brought those issues to the world of writing, where the contingencies involved in "the unbridled chaos at the heart of American democracy" could be viewed, considered, and reconfigured. Raymond Eve has noted that chaos theory can be seen to emphasize only an overwhelming and unpredictable complexity and so might not seem especially encouraging to those just beginning to understand it. "On the other hand," Eve points out, "we now may be able to at least *describe* many of the actions of complex systems that we see around us, those that hitherto remained mysterious. The signature of chaos is no longer written in invisible ink. We may not be able to predict the result of the next iteration of a set of equations that describes a chaotic system, or when a system will be in chaos and when not. However, we can at least now understand what a chaotic system is doing, and how it is doing it, when we see it" (278). There is great value in this—and throughout this book, I suggest that nineteenth-century African American writers were devoted to doing just that: describing the actions of the complex systems that they experienced.

I have in mind Hayles's distinction among the representations we might construct in the face of overwhelming complexity. Working from the proposition that "no unambiguous or necessary connection can be forged between reality and our representations," Hayles says that "within the range of representations available at a given time, we can ask, 'Is this representation *consistent* with the aspects of reality under interrogation?'" "If the answer is affirmative," she allows, "we still know only our representations, not reality itself. But if it is negative, we know that the representation does not mesh with reality in a way that is meaningful to us in that context" (*Chaos Bound* 223). African Americans in the ante-bellum United States (and long afterward) regularly observed that the literature, the national mythology and textbook histories, the rhetoric of Fourth of July celebrations, the discourse of churches, and a host of other public documents, proclamations, and stories were drastically inconsistent with the realities of nineteenth-century cultural life in the United States. In trying to account for the realities of race that cannot be reduced to simple crossings of a racial line or heroic performances in the otherwise stable theater of the other—that is, those narrative lines expected and celebrated by those who gathered in fascination to witness, as if first hand, the spectacular horrors of African American oppression—African American writers attempted to construct representations that were consistent with reality. In a nation of strategic (as Toni Morrison would have it, pathological) misrepresentations of reality,[16] African American writers faced the challenge of representing the chronicles, the assumptions, and the complex social forces that first made their stories necessary and then directed the available means for telling them.[17]

These representations have retained their enormous value over time, drawing us into the complex history of the dynamics of a chaotic system and enabling us to ask the right questions about more recent configurations and manifestations of that system. In making the case for chaos theory as a framework for sociological research, Eve, Horsfall, and Lee observe:

> The complex pattern of a strange attractor is produced by the repetitive iteration of very simple rules. Often the total system resulting from the operation of simple equations with feedback terms included begins to manifest *emergent properties* that could never have been predicted ahead of time by looking only at the original very simple rules for interaction among concepts. Could this be telling us, for example, that social structure is actually composed of emergent properties that very simple rules for individual interactions create in ways that we have but dimly understood? If so, it follows that changes in very simple rules about how we interact with one another socially, politically, or economically might result in a completely different social structure after a few million cycles of interaction. (xxx–xxxi)

The point here, in part, is that chaos theory has highlighted, as Frederick Turner puts it, "the primacy of history" (xvii), the necessary recognition "that time is irreducible, irreversible, and asymmetrical" (xix). But the point as well is that there is great value in identifying basic patterns of human interaction within a cultural system. The underlying hope in a great deal of nineteenth-century African American literature in an otherwise hopeless context is that simple recognitions, simple changes, shifts in the terms of human interactions "might result in a completely different social structure," if only after the brighter-day coming of "a few million cycles of interaction" (Eve, Horsfall, and Lee xxx).

In his essential study *African Fractals: Modern Computing and Indigenous Design*, Ron Eglash demonstrates the centrality of fractal knowledge systems in African cultures and offers a thoughtful approach to negotiating what he terms "the politics of African fractals" (192). Drawing on the work of Paul Gilroy, Eglash asserts that in representing "the ability for geometric expansion within bounded space," fractals offer a productive "analogy for oppositional political expansion in human bondage" (200). This expansion, I suggest, can begin with the challenge of literary representation, the means by which a representation consistent with reality itself shifts the terms by which the cultural landscape, including notions of both human bondage and freedom, can be understood. It is no surprise that the overwhelming majority of African American works published before the Civil War are characterized by fractal narrative methods. Perhaps, too, it is not surprising that this body of literature is so often viewed as rough, awkward, or otherwise uncrafted. In the face of an overwhelming and killing complexity, many African American writers struggled merely for an accurate representation—perhaps aware that the escape from slavery so often considered to be the end of their story was just the beginning of an infinite journey that would require a literature adequate to the task. In the chapters that follow, I examine the dynamic properties of that literature, consider the difficulty of confining those properties to a linear narrative of literary history, and suggest that when we recover the complexity that is vital to an understanding of nineteenth-century African American literary performances, we will remind ourselves of the equally complex but compelling concept of justice to which this literature was devoted.

## CHAPTER TWO

# Truth Stranger than Fiction

## African American Identity and (Auto)Biography

> As we learn to bear the intimacy of scrutiny and to flourish within it,
> as we learn to use the products of that scrutiny for power within our living,
> those fears which rule our lives and form our silences begin to lose
> their control over us.—AUDRE LORDE, "Poetry Is Not a Luxury"

In his 1880 memoir, *My Southern Home; or, The South and Its People*, William Wells Brown begins with a note about his autobiographical reflections. The book's "earlier incidents," he explains, "were written out from the author's recollections. The later sketches here given, are the results of recent visits to the South, where the incidents were jotted down at the time of their occurrence, or as they fell from the lips of the narrators, and in their own unadorned dialect" (113). Brown is being typically disingenuous, for what readers actually find in *My Southern Home*, albeit beyond their awareness, is a narrative partially made up of many other texts that Brown had published through the years. The book reprints, verbatim, passages, episodes, and narrative snippets from a wide range of Brown's publications, including his *Narrative of William W. Brown*, first published in 1847; both the 1853 *Clotel* and 1864 *Clotelle*; his 1858 play *The Escape*; his first historical study, *The Black Man*, appearing in 1863; and another historical work, *The Negro in the American Rebellion*, brought out in 1867.

Brown's complexly multitextual and multivocal performance in *My Southern Home* is largely a new iteration of his ongoing self-transformations comprising a series of autobiographical statements and strategies that appeared throughout his publishing career.[1] Included are not only Brown's own four American and five British editions of the *Narrative*, but also the accounts of his life that open *Clotel* and *The American Fugitive in Europe* (1855); William Farmer's "Memoir of William Wells Brown," which comes at the beginning of Brown's *Three Years in Europe* (1852); and Alonzo Moore's "Memoir of the Author" that opens *The Rising Son* (1874).[2] The various versions correspond generally, though sometimes their details are contradictory, and they often present inaccurate information—to the point where it is easy to wonder whose authority should be accepted in any given account. In addition to this biographical mix, a blending of genres weaves the author's life in and out of fiction, autobiography, biography, and history. For example, among the biographical sketches in *The Black Man* is a fictionalized account of Brown's own life, under the title "A Man without a Name," which later becomes chapter 36, "A Thrilling Incident of the War," of his history *The Negro in the American Rebellion*. As Russ Castronovo has argued, "These diverse autobiographical accounts do not so much constitute a complete life, inviolable in the authority of its own experiences, as they subtly reconstitute history, implying its mutable and selective aspects" (*Fathering* 167).

The chaotic turns on his autobiographical trail make Brown a particularly complex illustration of a characteristic pattern in nineteenth-century African American (auto)biographical publications—the subject of this chapter. Against the background of the understanding of race presented in Chapter 1, I will consider those narrative characteristics and contextual contingencies that make nineteenth-century African American (auto) biography *African American*. In other words, I wish to deviate from the usual approach to understanding the role of race in African American experience and identity in order to account for the ongoing and complex construction of identity, the highly contingent dynamics of social and individual experience in the nineteenth century. Instead of viewing these autobiographies, implicitly or explicitly, as narratives that proceed *from* race, from the identity of their authors or putative narrators, I suggest we view them as strategic representations *of* race—that is, attempts to represent the cultural process and dynamics of the ongoing but shifting (and shifty) construction of race, the means by which narrators tried to locate themselves and claim authority over their own autobiographies. How did the chaotic constructions of race shape individual lives? By what means can these constructions be identified, negotiated, and represented? And what are the implications of these constructions for readers of African American (auto)biographies? These questions are often at the heart of the autobiographical texts we study.

Nineteenth-century African American (auto)biographies are narrative performances that take place within a chaotic and incoherent culture.

They are performances devoted to representing an absent subject—not only the historically and culturally isolated narrator or the narrative subject, but also and more importantly the variable dynamics of racial construction, identification, and positioning that are rendered virtually invisible in a white supremacist culture. To return to the example that opened this chapter, we can say that Brown's *My Southern Home* is an important autobiographical work not in spite of but because of its representation of various texts from the author's publishing career. We can also say that this is an accomplished work not because it is a seamless reconfiguration of these various texts but because the seams show so clearly, the narrative perspective shifts so often, and the generic core of the book is so difficult to identify. *My Southern Home* is, in fact, the record of various autobiographical engagements and disengagements, various attempts to tell a story without allowing that story to be easily contained, and various negotiations with the delimited possibilities for African American self-presentation. I will return to *My Southern Home* and these concerns in Chapter 5. For now, drawing from Brown's example, as well as from the collective performances of and negotiations with the dynamics of African American subjectivity and experience in various texts, we can more comprehensively identify the core challenges of understanding African American (auto)biographical writing in the nineteenth century. Doing so might shift the terms of the primary question in *Chaotic Justice*, leading us to ask not what is *African American* about these autobiographies but rather what is *autobiographical* about them? That is, how should we interpret the dynamics of individual and collective self-representation during this period? The answers, I believe, are more complex than we have imagined, as are the texts that will guide us to satisfying and just readings.

## Reframing Autobiographical Equations

Too often, the textual terrain of nineteenth-century African American (auto)biographies is reduced to a manageable landscape, the kind that seems familiar even to those who have glanced at it from a distance—something that can be negotiated with a simple map. This is true particularly of those many (auto)biographies classified as slave narratives.[3] James Olney has argued that "the conventions for slave narratives were so early and so firmly established that one can imagine a sort of master outline . . . drawn from the great narratives and guiding the lesser ones." Such an outline would include the presentation of the book; testimonials or prefaces

TRUTH STRANGER THAN FICTION

written by white abolitionists, "or by a white amanuensis/editor/author actually responsible for the text"; and a number of narrative episodes on a variety of subjects—the struggle to become literate, "Christian" slave-holders who were more cruel than others, the nature of whippings, a "description of the amounts of food and clothing given to slaves, the work required of them, the pattern of a day, a week, a year" ("'I Was Born'" 152–53). This outline, Olney states, was largely the result of the focused concern that inspired the writing and publishing of slave narratives, and that provided an audience for them. Accordingly, Olney presents the situation of this field of writing as a rather simple equation: "Unlike auto-biography in general the narratives are all trained on one and the same objective reality, they have a coherent and defined audience, and have behind them and guiding them an organized group of 'sponsors,' and they are possessed of very specific motives, intentions, and uses understood by narrators, sponsors, and audiences alike: to reveal the truth of slavery and so to bring about its abolition. How, then, could the narratives be anything but very much like one another?" (154).[4]

But given the conditions under which they were writing, given the organized group of "sponsors" who often guided or edited the writing (or did the writing themselves), and given the cultural forces that shaped the audience for the narratives, we might well ask what "truth of slavery" could African American narrators in white America hope to present? This brings to mind Dwight McBride's important meditation on this question in *Impossible Witnesses: Truth, Abolitionism, and Slave Testimony*, in which he explores "the rhetorical markers that constitute the terrain of abolitionist discourse" and locates autobiographical performance on the "discursive terrain" of the transatlantic antislavery movement. McBride asks, "What does it mean for a slave to bear witness to, or to tell the 'truth' about, slavery?" (1, 16). His answer is that, since abolitionist discourse "produced the occasion for bearing witness," it regularly prepared audiences for "an experience that had already been theorized and prophesied." "In this way," he explains, "the slave serves as a kind of fulfillment of the prophecy of abolitionist discourse. . . . Before the slave ever speaks, we know the slave; we know what his or her experience is, and we know how to read that experience" (5). Or, as Frances Smith Foster puts it, "While white abolitionists were eager to privilege the authenticity of black writers' descriptions of slavery, it was only insofar as their descriptions confirmed what white readers had already accepted as true" (*Written by Herself* 82).[5] The exposure of the abuses under bondage had become a set of conventional and frequent performances, which is surely the operating assumption behind the tendency to treat one or a handful of slave narratives as representative of the many.[6]

The terrain of African American (auto)biographical publications is more complicated than is usually acknowledged. Olney's "master outline" actually applies to only a relative sprinkling of slave narratives, though we might see a version of some features in many of them. But the geographical diversity of the accounts, the ways in which local contexts shape the larger story (just as the larger story shapes local contexts), the multiplicity of authors and voices that sometimes commingle in a single text, and the publication of successive, overlapping, or contradictory versions of the same life story complicate any claims we might want to make about this kind of writing. In all of the situations and contexts in which they worked, African American writers, narrators, or textual subjects faced the challenge of representing a life defined by race, resisting that definition while also cultivating community, negotiating the cultural politics of readership as well as the occasions for publication, and redirecting the trajectory of—and the possibilities and settings for—African American identity. Indeed, because they were, of necessity, so directly, consistently, and profoundly engaged in the multifarious contradictions of American history and culture, African American autobiographers developed approaches to life writing capable of explaining a nation that often appears inexplicable. These explanations are not supplemental to their autobiographies; rather, they are maps to a history of experience that cannot be captured in a single, self-contained autobiographical portrait and certainly not in any "master outline" or simple generic overview.

Among the challenges posed by this body of writing broadly identified as (auto)biography is deciding, first, what narratives to read and, second, how to approach those narratives in terms of authorship, style, and implied reader. But since nineteenth-century African American autobiography is often reduced to the neatly conceptualized contours of the pre– and post–Civil War slave narrative, it is useful to begin by distinguishing the variety of African American (auto)biographical narratives. Although my schema may not be all-inclusive, I have identified at least eight categories of texts that can be included under that heading: (1) autobiographies published specifically in the service of particular organizations—like the first autobiographies of William Wells Brown and Frederick Douglass; (2) autobiographies published independently—for example, those by the Reverend G. W. Offley, William Grimes, and Eliza Potter before the Civil War, and virtually all of those published after the war; (3) multiple versions of autobiographical narratives—including those by William Wells Brown, Frederick Douglass, and Jerena Lee; (4) biographies by white authors on black subjects—among them, the narratives devoted to Sojourner Truth and Harriet Tubman (both of which appeared in more than one version); (5) autobiographies written by a white amanuensis—such as the narratives of Henry Box Brown (particularly the 1849 version) and Solomon Northup; (6) multiple versions of (auto)biographies written by a white amanuensis—for example, the various, and increasingly disturbing, versions of Josiah Henson's story; (7) hybrid narratives of fiction and autobiography, including that of Harriet Wilson and the novelization of other narratives; and (8) singular tales of discovered or local stories, such as Henry Trumbull's *Life and Adventures of Robert, the Hermit of Massachusetts* and Frances Whipple Greene's *Memoirs of Elleanor Eldridge*.

Of course, these categories cannot account for the dynamic narratives they attempt to organize, for we are still faced with pressing questions about how to *locate* these narratives. Is this the literature of the new southern studies, the old northeastern studies, or some manifestation of transatlantic or transnational studies? Do we account for them by their points of departure or by their points of arrival and publication sites? One thinks, for example, of William Andrews's collection of North Carolina narratives, Arna Bontemps's collection of Connecticut narratives, and Eugene McCarthy and Thomas Doughton's collection of narratives associated with Worcester, Massachusetts. Some narratives were written in England, such as William and Ellen Craft's *Running a Thousand Miles for Freedom* or the "First English Edition" of Henry Box Brown's story. Others are associated with historical sites (Elizabeth Keckley in the White House). Still others were published and promoted in social spaces generally (and sometimes strangely) not marked in current scholarship as significant sites of nineteenth-century African American history (Lucy Delaney's, published in St. Louis—an important site of African American history, but one only gradually earning the attention of scholars—or Louis Hughes's, published in Milwaukee). Moreover, in virtually all of these narratives, we need to account for significant movement involving different social spaces, shifting social and political contingencies, and often fundamentally different manifestations of "blackness" or "whiteness" as the narrative subject travels from place to place, including but beyond the movement central to most African American (auto)biographical narratives—for example, Eliza Potter's travels from Cincinnati to various places North and South, Nancy Prince's experiences abroad, or the itinerant missions of Jerena Lee, Zilpha Elaw, or Sojourner Truth.

Although it is tempting to say that identifying these narratives with specific geographical locations is unimportant, it *is* important to remember that geographical location was crucial to African American writers, and that the liberating potential of boundary crossing and movement was for many of them a mixed blessing at best, especially the authors of slave narratives, since some boundaries could not be recrossed safely—particularly those leading back to home, family, and community. Accordingly, how we discuss the relation between geographical sites and autobiographical performances has a great deal to do with the understanding we will draw from these narratives. In approaching any slave narrative, then, we face a deceptively simple question: What exactly are we reading and where?

What are we reading? Consider Harriet Wilson's *Our Nig; or, Sketches from the Life of a Free Black, in a Two-Story White House, North, Showing That Slavery's Shadows Fall Even There, by "Our Nig"* (1859), which arguably has become a different book, and obviously a more complicated one, over the course of the research by Henry Louis Gates Jr., Barbara White, Eric Gardner, Gabrielle Foreman, and Reginald Pitts.[7] Given what is now known about Wilson's life, we might well ask, Is this a novel or an autobiography? Do we even have terms to identify the genre of this book?[8] My point is not just to question whether *Our Nig* should be identified as a work of autobiography or a work of fiction. Rather, it is to recognize that the text itself blends the two genres. In other words, it is not merely a matter of deciding, through research, whether this book is an autobiography or a novel, but rather of noting the narrator's shifting focus and voice throughout the work. Chapters narrated in the third person have titles indicating that they present another episode in the life of the writer—the titles of chapters about Frado's experience refer to "my mother" or "my father," and the chapter about Frado's entrance into the Bellmont household is entitled "A New Home for Me" (5, 14, 24). The narrative relates the experiences of Frado, the author's representative in this story, but Wilson never allows us to view Frado as simply a character in a work of fiction. In other words, this book is about the need to turn to fictional representations in order to construct an autobiography.

Part of what makes Wilson's book so significant is that it concerns life not in the South but in New England—indeed, a town in New Hampshire known for its antislavery sentiments. As Wilson admonishes her readers to remember that slavery's shadows fell even north of Boston, so we should keep in mind that even beyond the racism in the North there were strong investments in the system of slavery in the South. As James Brewer Stewart has noted, many of Boston's most prominent white families added "new fortunes to old by linking their assets with those of 'king cotton.' By developing sophisticated textile factories outside Boston that processed vast amounts of raw cotton, these powerful entrepreneurs linked their city's banking, shipping, trading, and investment enterprises to the economy of the slave states." "By the 1840s," Stewart writes, "it had become common to equate Boston's 'lords of the loom' with the 'lords of the lash' who held sway in the Deep South" (107). Not incidental to this economic connection to the South was the developing selective memory by which the presence of slavery and of African Americans generally were removed from New England's vision of itself as a region.

Joanne Pope Melish is particularly instructive on this point. "New England whites," she observes, "employed an array of strategies to effect the removal" of people of color "and to efface people of color and their history in New England" (*Disowning Slavery* 2). Melish cites a host of measures used by New England whites to render African Americans, along with the history of slavery in New England, invisible:

> Some of these efforts were symbolic: representing people of color as ridiculous or dangerous "strangers" in anecdotes, cartoons, and broadsides; emphasizing slavery and "race" as "southern problems"; characterizing New England slavery as brief and mild, or even denying its having existed; inventing games and instructional problems in which the object was to make "the negroes" disappear; digging up the corpses of people of color. Other efforts aimed to eliminate the presence of living people of color: conducting official roundups and "warnings-out"; rioting in and vandalizing black neighborhoods. Finally, some efforts involved both symbolic and physical elements, such as the American Colonization Society's campaign to demonize free people of color and raise funds to ship them to Africa. (2)

This extensive "array of strategies" employed by white New Englanders indicates the complex cultural theater in which African Americans were forced to perform in writing their autobiographies. As Melish notes, many of these strategies involved the representation of black character and of the black presence in national history (which was, for many, *white* national history). Even those who escaped from slavery to tell their stories in the North found those stories already anticipated and contained.

It is important, then, to place *Our Nig* within the absurdities of nine-teenth-century American culture, for this was a nation that regularly proclaimed its commitment to liberty while every aspect of its life—political, economic, social, legal, even theological—was devoted to slavery. This was a nation that regularly celebrated a founding document proclaiming that all men were created equal even as it created the fictions of race to enforce unjust, enslaving, and even murderous social distinctions. This was a nation whose champion of liberty, New Hampshire's Daniel Webster, helped to craft a political compromise in 1850 that violated the rights of African Americans, both those who had escaped from bondage and those who were nominally free. This was a nation whose highest legal authorities declared in 1857 that black Americans had "no rights which the white man was bound to respect."[9] This was a nation whose most popular and influential form of entertainment was blackface minstrelsy and, in fact, a nation almost obsessed with defining and controlling the terms of black identity.[10] Constantly confronted by violations of celebrated national principles, by white supremacist legal practices, and by popular caricatures, even African Americans born and raised in the North understood all too well that northern whites had stories of their own to tell about black identity—at their occasional best, seemingly sympathetic stories that demonstrated white benevolence, but at their more frequent worst, overtly racist stories. All of white culture seemed to be creating fictions about what it meant to be black, and the interest of even the most trusted white Americans in the life stories of black Americans was almost always a mixed blessing. Scholars and teachers still struggle to make the point, for example, that many of Sojourner Truth's speeches were later misremembered and misrepresented, as white writers not only put words in her mouth but also presented Truth's speech patterns in stereotypical black southern dialect, even though Truth was raised in a Dutch-speaking area of New York.[11] Sarah Bradford, looking to help Harriet Tubman, wrote a biography that begins by having the young Tubman sitting close to "a group of merry little darkies," a biography that praises Tubman by distinguishing her and her family from other African Americans, asserting that "all should not be judged by the idle, miserable darkies who have swarmed about Washington and other cities since the War" (13, 69). Such well-intended but prejudiced misrepresentations were not unusual, and almost all African American public figures of the time demonstrated a keen understanding of what it meant to live in a white supremacist culture.[12] African American narrators were cautious about the prospect of revealing the details of their lives even to benevolent white readers who were simultaneously being influenced by a culture bent on trivializing, eliminating, and otherwise controlling the African American presence in the North. To tell your story is to give someone control over your life, unless they are willing to reveal just as much about themselves. As Wilson's northern-based *Our Nig* suggests, to tell the truth of African American life in the United States was to tell a story that might alienate those whites on whom they relied, at least in part, for their readership.

Wilson's intriguing mix of autobiographical assertions with the conventions of storytelling associated with sentimental fiction suggests the dilemma she faced in trying to tell her story. The truth of her life was bound intimately with questions about *how* to tell that truth, *how* to relate her experiences; and the question of *how* to tell her story was shaped in part by the audience for whom she was writing. How could she tell the story of her life, then, through straight autobiographical narration? How could she and her contemporaries go about telling a true story in a land devoted to falsehoods? How did they give a realistic account of their life, their character, and their nature in an absurd social environment? They needed to account for these fictions, these absurdities, as being the primary forces shaping their life. They needed to represent the fictions of the larger culture in order to get at the realities of their life.

It is noteworthy that Wilson begins her narrative by tracing Frado's identity to her white mother's experiences in order to establish Frado as the most deliberately determined product of northern U.S. culture. That is, in her telling of Mag Smith's story, Wilson portrays the conceptual structures of cultural identity, structures that will later confine Frado even more tightly than they did her mother. As Mag successively crosses over into what might be called the concentric borders of cultural infamy, accumulating increasingly inflexible and restrictive cultural labels along the way, the system of values that distinguishes between acceptable and notorious identity, between cultural insiders and outsiders, becomes clear. Initially, Mag is a woman with a "loving, trusting heart" who has the democratic simplicity to believe that she can "ascend" to the social level of her duplicitous seducer and "become an equal" (5). Inevitably, she acquires a reputation that follows her wherever she goes, leaving her with a "home . . . contaminated by the publicity of her fall" and "a feeling of degradation," yet still with the hope that "circumspect" behavior might yet enable her to "regain in a measure what she had lost" (6). Finding the boundaries of morality carefully guarded, she is forced to remain in her assigned sphere of infamy. Aggravated further by the immigrant labor that altered so significantly the status of women in the workplace during the Jacksonian era, Mag is soon left "hugging her wrongs, but making no effort to escape" (7). What follows is what the narrator calls "the climax of repulsion," Mag's interracial marriage to Jim—by which she "sunder[s] another bond which held her to her fellows" and "descend[s] another step down the ladder of infamy" (9). Her final step into "the darkness of perpetual infamy" is the result of having "lived an outcast for years": her extramarital relationship with a second black man after Jim dies.

Had Mag deliberately set out to transgress the implicit boundaries of the dominant culture's standards, she could not have done a better job. The point here is that her acts are not deliberate and that in witnessing the consequences of seduction (for which the seducer himself receives only the admiration of his fellows), we witness the process by which collective cultural identity is maintained at the expense of individual moral character. After all, Mag's repentance does not prove to be the key that will reopen the cultural doors; she has been identified—and clearly she must remain—a cultural outsider, an example of moral transgression. Those doors closed to her, Mag marries and thereby comes to embody yet another cultural transgression: unacceptable intercourse between black and white. The product of these successive acts of transgression is the daughter Mag cannot support: Frado, the "titled" character of the narrative. Thus defined before birth, Frado's identity as cultural product is finalized when she becomes "our nig."

This is the process that has allowed us to locate Wilson within a generalized African American community, to identify *Our Nig* as a significant publication in African American literary history. But this same process should lead us to a more complicated understanding of what it means to identify Wilson as an African American writer. Against assumptions of a unified community—the very "colored brethren" that she invokes in her book's preface—Wilson portrays a world that is incapable of producing stable, uniform grounds for an imagined or assumed community. Instead, prevailing prejudices create the *appearance* of commonality by setting blacks apart and grouping them together as ideologically marked sites for political action in the form of either repression or repression's cousin, charity. By such logic, all blacks are either physical or ideological fugitives in need of white control and protection, and all fugitives look alike. The resulting dangers for the artificially delineated black community become clear in Wilson's final chapter, "The Winding Up of the Matter." Again, the author enters into delicate cultural territory, for she begins by alluding to "*professed* fugitives from slavery, who recounted their personal experience in homely phrase, and awakened the indignation of non-slaveholders against brother Pro" (70, my emphasis). Such false professions were an issue in both the North and the South. In newspapers and books, antiabolitionists warned potential fugitives that self-proclaimed representatives of the Underground Railroad could not be trusted; similarly, northern abolitionists and members of antislavery societies cautioned against free blacks who pretended to be fugitives to procure money and clothing from Underground Railroad sympathizers.[13] Wilson presents her protagonist as a victim of this kind of impostor; more importantly, though, she identifies the cultural mechanism of this victimization: "Such a one appeared in the new home of Frado; and as people of color were rare there, was it strange she should attract her dark brother; that he should inquire her out; succeed in seeing her; feel a strange sensation in his heart towards her; that he should toy with her shining curls, feel proud to provoke her to smile and expose the ivory concealed by thin, ruby lips; that her sparkling eyes should fascinate; that he should propose; that they should marry?" (70). Here Wilson tells a familiar story of courtship, love, and marriage. Doing so in a single sentence, she joins the sentimental associations readers would bring to it with the cultural divisions that make this particular love story seem like a series of nearly inevitable steps, one foregone conclusion leading to the next.

This conflation of the sentimental destinies of love and the limited destinies of cultural identity undermines the romance of it all, revealing the potential danger of innocent, unworldly love: its ability to shape one's understanding, to create a naive belief in what eventually prove to be deceptive appearances. We have heard this story before, at the beginning of *Our Nig*: Frado's story echoes that of her mother Mag. But whereas Mag's love led her to the naive hope of transcending the divisions of class, Frado's *extends from* an equally naive belief in the inherent community of race.[14] It is this belief—the product of "her own oppression"—that enables her to view Samuel's silence about his assumed enslavement, when they are alone, as evidence that they are joined by a shared experience, and that it is "painful to disturb oftener than was needful" (70). "There was a silent sympathy," the narrator emphasizes, "which Frado felt attracted her, and she opened her heart to the presence of love—that arbitrary and inexorable tyrant" (70). In the end, of course, the tyrant shows his face, as Frado's husband "[leaves] her to her fate . . . with the disclosure that he had never seen the South, and that his illiterate harangues were humbugs for hungry abolitionists" (71). Frado is the victim not merely of an oppressive culture but also of her own prior experience as a victim. The oppressive culture she has come to know, and against which she has begun to develop strategic modes of defense, reveals yet another level of power—for it has invaded not only her life but also her consciousness. The sense of a community of silent sympathy among the oppressed becomes yet another dimension of the force of oppression, yet another layer of cultural identity as defined by others.

Unable to control the terms of her own cultural identity, and unable to trust others similarly defined, Wilson speaks both to and against those—black or white, male or female—willing to see her as a cultural type, a familiar product. That is, as has been noted by almost all critics of this narrative, Wilson signifies on her own culturally determined identity in her use of "Our Nig" as the title of both the book and its author. Gates, for example, argues cogently that *Our Nig* enacts "the transformation of the black-as-object into the black-as-subject" ("Introduction" lv), and clearly he is right. But as Wilson makes painfully clear, this particular "black-as-subject" still must face a culture eminently capable of retransforming her into "woman-as-object" and, into yet another concentric circle of identification, "worker-as-object." In other words, Frado begins not only as a product of racist formulations, but also as a product of ethical, gender, and economic formulations. As this book demonstrates from the first page onward, troping one's way into black subjecthood simply changes the color of the corner one has been backed into.

This is exactly why it is important to question the terms of black subjecthood by locating it in the *process* that Wilson endeavors to represent in her narrative, the blackness Gates identifies in his emphasis on the dynamic over the static, the *transformation* that leads from the "Our Nig" of the title to the "Our Nig" of authorship. In having Frado's story echo her mother's, Wilson refers to the cultural constructions of identity as an iterative process. To some extent, Frado's story is simply the story of ongoing cultural patterns, as she faces the same cultural forces (involving economic and social frameworks, as well as the prejudices shaped by those frameworks) that determined her mother's life. Frado is the latest iteration of the female experience represented by her mother, an experience that involves negotiating such restricted cultural and social mobility that a single mistake can send her into an entirely different framework for subjectivity (but one still predictable in its overall trajectory). In effect, we witness feedback in Frado's story as "a portion of model, machine, or system output returns to be used again as input" (Stroup 126–27). Frado is the "output" of the cultural system that shaped her mother's life, and her story is a study of what happens when that output returns to be used again as input. Frado is both product and variable in a new iteration of the cultural equation, and the result is a life that follows that of her mother but on a different scale.

Wilson's response to this process offers—rather than any hope of escape to a fundamentally new system—the hope that comes from deliberately manipulating the terms of the equation. In identifying "Our Nig" as the author of *Our Nig*, she initiates a new feedback process, one that simply represents the equation, a representation that enables her to observe that on this new scale—the story of her life—the damaging effects of this system are especially evident, for there are no heroes in *Our Nig*, no signs of a stable community either within or outside the domestic sphere, and the cruelty inspired by the cultural patterns at play are excessive by any measure. Through this act of representation, Wilson attempts to reposition herself—and as we see "the transformation of the black-as-object into the black-as-subject" we are also witnessing the transformation of the object of chaos into its savvy student. The cultural terms that define Frado's (and Wilson's) life will not go away just because she escapes the cruelties of the Bellmont household, for that household (as Wilson makes clear on her title page) is simply the manifestation, on a smaller scale, of larger cultural patterns and processes. What Wilson *can* do is negotiate her status as a variable in this cultural equation. *Our Nig* is, in effect, a great rock in the cultural stream, an attempt to at least redirect the cultural currents that most directly affect the course of Wilson's life.

It is not surprising that scholars today find it difficult to locate *Our Nig* within existing generic definitions. Because Wilson attempted to represent the world of her life as well as her life in the world, *Our Nig* cannot be comfortably classified as either a novel or an autobiography. Perhaps we should think of it as a novel about autobiography—or as autobiographical reflections on social fictions. In constantly drawing attention to her blending and *bending* of literary genres, Wilson indicates to her readers that the story she has to tell is both inside and outside the story they are reading. Her concerns extend beyond the particular family implicated by the title page, for she never allows readers to settle into a familiar genre and in that way to determine their relation to this story. In the end, she asks them for financial aid as payment for her labor in writing the book and for the instruction provided by that labor—the lessons to be learned from Wilson's experiences, lessons available only from her perspective but vital to the moral health of the nation. Wilson's story of Frado's struggles—including her conflict with a religion that has itself been corrupted by white supremacist ideology—leads finally to an appeal to her readers to continue the moral work begun by Frado's own difficult conversion. This book, which appears to call into question our sense of what constitutes literary writing, builds to a challenge of the reader's own moral literacy—a new literary equation, if you will. The matter of how we respond seems ever more urgent as we actually learn how to *read* this book, a process that includes learning how to read the world of the book—indeed, the world that made this book necessary.

## The Uncle Tom School of Christianity

Of course, this blending of fiction and (auto)biography could work against African Americans as well as for them. Unavoidably, the fictional or novelistic presence, both in African American lives and in the narratives devoted to those lives, was the product of both the racial and the literary politics of the time; even white writers who were determined to support black reformers regularly displayed the effects of those politics. In an attempt to praise minister and abolitionist Samuel Ringgold Ward in 1853, for instance, a British journalist compared Ward to Harriet Beecher Stowe's character Uncle Tom—a testimonial subsequently reprinted in the U.S. antislavery newspaper *The Liberator*. According to the journalist:

> The friends of the Slave in the New World could not have selected a more meet human Sequel to "Uncle Tom." The "Key" was even more effective than the lock; but the arrival of a man, six feet high, and we presume sixteen stone weight, gifted with a vigorous understanding, endowed with a rich original eloquence, to turn the "Key"—that was the finishing stroke. There is the book! There is the man! Is there a line in the former that is not rendered credible by the exhibition of the latter? Never was a conjunction happier than the publication of "Uncle Tom," and the advent of S. R. Ward. ("Rev. Samuel R. Ward in England")

Ward was only one of many African American public leaders of the time who were subjected to this problematic comparison to Stowe's Uncle Tom. Frederick Douglass received similar treatment in *The Uncle Tom's Cabin*

*Almanack or Abolitionist Memento*, published in London in 1853, an image of Douglass presenting a speech, with text below promising readers that they would soon, in another image, see him being whipped by his former master. In fact, virtually every black public figure at all involved in the antislavery movement could expect to be contextualized and transformed into a kind of antislavery spectacle by *Uncle Tom's Cabin*—at times, representing the evidence in support of Stowe's novel, but almost always being transformed into a living type made understandable by the book.[15]

*Uncle Tom's Cabin* was not only the very large and white elephant in the antislavery room; it also quickly became the centerpiece of a field of discourse and perspective addressing especially African American Christianity and individual moral identity. Many African Americans, along with others involved in the antislavery movement, developed a distinctive approach to Christian understanding, organization, and practice, setting the foundations for various black religious movements in the twentieth century (a chaotic tale in itself) and for certain strains of black theology. This is one of many areas where we can see "the possibilities of resistance conditioned by relations of power and the very purposeful and self-conscious effort to build community" (Hartman 59). Nevertheless, we can only note that this was a particularly challenging mode of resistance, given that practitioners of Christian discourse faced a battle against other practitioners of that same discourse, and given that many white allies were all too ready to blur the lines between one configuration of an antislavery Christian community and another. It was not for nothing that Douglass so sternly resisted membership in any established church, though he continued to define his cause through a Christian lens. Interestingly, as the antislavery movement developed, certain key texts, rhetorical tropes, and narrative lines began to map out the culture's discursive terrain, always representing particularly charged rituals of association (those rhetorical gestures, for example, for which an orator could expect immediate and hearty applause). Key among these maps was *Uncle Tom's Cabin*. But the unavoidable references and comparisons to the world of Stowe's novel compromised the ethical mission of the antislavery movement by complicating or even obstructing the promotion of African American experiences and understandings of Christian practice and faith. My point goes beyond the obvious ubiquity of Uncle Tom as an identifier of character and sociopolitical behavior, for also involved here was the very possibility of representing and even engaging Christian belief as an active principle of conscious experience.

Immediately following the publication of *Uncle Tom's Cabin*, there was considerable commentary on the force of Stowe's novel in representing African American individual and collective identity. One especially interesting example was William J. Wilson's remarkable series of fictional sketches entitled the "Afric-American Picture Gallery," which appeared serially in the *Anglo-African Magazine* in 1859. Wilson, writing under the pen name "Ethiop," draws his readers to a pair of pictures—the first identified as the interior of "a negro church" in a southern plantation setting (216). The second, Wilson informs us,

> entitled *After Preaching*, represents the congregation standing about outside the church in groups around the faithful leaders, who, being men carefully selected by the white piety of the sunny South, are of course, all of the Uncle Tom school. . . . In the back-ground may also be seen a few young, determined-looking faces, on which are expressed disbelief in, and detestation of, the whole affair. . . . These faces, in contrast with the others of the congregation, give a most striking effect to the picture. They are the unruly, the skeptical, the worthless of the flock—the wicked ones, who would rather run the risk than be bound up in the religious love so feelingly and so faithfully proclaimed to them—the religious love of the land. (217)

It is from this skeptical class, we are told, that "comes our Nat Turners," our Margaret Garners, and our Douglasses (217).

Earlier in this series, readers were prepared to discover that even this class is not entirely free of the influence of the Uncle Tom school, for Wilson feels compelled to work toward the essence of this alternate school of African American subjectivity by breaking through the layers of possibility enforced by the prevalence of Stowe's characterization. Another image, entitled simply "A New Picture," is that of a boy. "This boy," the narrator explains, "*Thomas Onward* (I call him *Tom* for shortness, [*sic*]) though he has seen all of life—yea more, is not an *Old Tom* by any means; nor an *Uncle Tom*, nor a *Saintly Tom*, nor even what is commonly deemed a good Tom; but a shrewd little rogue, a real live *Young Tom*, up to all considerable mischief and equal to all emergencies." Ethiop says of Tom that "one would scarcely conclude that this boy has come down to us through nearly three hundred years of hard trial." "And yet," the narrator continues, "it is true. Such is his history. He was almost whipped into childhood, whipped up to boyhood. He has been whipped up to manhood, whipped down to old age, whipped out of existence. He was toiled into life; he has been toiled through life; toiled out of life. He has been robbed of his toil, robbed of his body, robbed of all but his soul" (100). Although thus shaped, the boy, as revealed by the discerning eye of the portrait's artist and interpreted by Ethiop, retains something that has been left untouched. "The American Nation," Ethiop suggests, "if it can, may try its hardened hand yet a few centuries longer upon our live little Tom; but it will hardly mould [sic] him to their liking." The portrait of Tom stands as the promise of African America, in sharp contrast to "the hard, grave, iron, half savage and half barbarous faces of Washington and Jefferson, of Clay, Webster and Calhoun" (101). In short, Wilson portrays a boy who represents the crucial distinction presented in Thomas Hamilton's opening editorial for the *Anglo-African Magazine*, in which he argues that "the negro is something more than endurance; he is a force," a force that "can hardly be measured to-day" (2).

Unlike Wilson's Tom are the many others locked by Stowe's *Key*. The most striking example of an African American life virtually lost to Stowe's novel is that of Josiah Henson, who became closely associated with the ideal of Christian endurance represented by Uncle Tom. Following the publication of his original narrative, *The Life of Josiah Henson, Formerly a Slave, Now an Inhabitant of Canada*, in 1849 and of *Uncle Tom's Cabin* in 1852, Henson gained renown, somewhat improbably, as the "model" for the Uncle Tom in Stowe's novel. In some versions of his own narrative he is referred to as "Stowe's Uncle Tom." By the time the last account of Henson's story appeared, his life had become so identified with that of Uncle Tom that any hope of understanding the actual man had vanished in the fame of the fictional character. As Robin Winks has observed, "Henson was seldom left free to be himself, to assimilate if he wished to into the mainstream of Canadian life—even of black Canadian life—for he became the focus of abolitionist attention, a tool to be used in a propaganda campaign which was not above much juggling with the facts, however proper its ultimate goals may have been" (Introduction to *An Autobiography* vi). Henson's 1849 *Life* was written by Samuel A. Eliot, "a former Mayor of Boston who was well-known for his moderate anti-slavery views" (Winks xiii). It tells the story of a man who escaped from slavery and eventually settled in the Dawn settlement in Canada, where he worked to promote that developing African American community. There is no evidence that this version provided Stowe with her model for the character Uncle Tom, but after *Uncle Tom's Cabin* was published the association developed all the same, perhaps aided by Stowe's preface to the "substantially revised" narrative of Henson's life brought out in 1858 (Winks xxxi). After that time, Henson's narrative was in the hands of English clergyman-editor John Lobb. The third version of Henson's narrative, published in 1877, was entitled *"Uncle Tom's Story of His Life": An Autobiography of the Rev. Josiah Henson (Mrs. Harriet Beecher Stowe's "Uncle Tom"), from 1789 to 1876.* In 1881, Lobb published *An Autobiography of the Rev. Josiah Henson ("Uncle Tom") from 1789 to 1881*, a version that includes a chapter entitled "Mrs. Stowe's Characters," another entitled "'Uncle Tom' and the Editor's Visit to Her Majesty the Queen," a "Summary of 'Uncle Tom's' Public Services," and an appendix offering "A Sketch of Mrs. H. Beecher Stowe."

The effect of Stowe's influence on Henson's significance as a Christian was to emphasize, from their first association in the pages of his narrative to the last, his patient suffering and willing submission to the evils of this world in preparation for the rewards of the next. In her preface to the 1858 *Truth Stranger than Fiction: Father Henson's Story of His Own Life*, Stowe remarks that members of "the African race appear as yet to have been companions only of the sufferings of Christ," but she looks for the day "when the unwritten annals of slavery shall appear in the judgment, [and] many Simons who have gone meekly bearing their cross after Jesus to unknown graves, shall rise to thrones and crowns!" (iv). Years later, in the 1881 version of his life, when the annals of slavery remain to be written, Henson is still not allowed any real achievement in this world, and he is still suffering—this time with the help of editor John Lobb, the British press, and the queen of England. "Windsor welcomed a visitor yesterday," a reprinted news story proclaims, "around whose name and history clusters an exceptional interest. He has done nothing, in the ordinary meaning of the phrase, to win fame. He has produced no work of genius, performed no feat of statesmanship, discovered no new lands. He has not devastated countries with conquest, or colonised them with venturous enterprise. He has done nothing but suffer" (153). At the beginning of this late version of his life is an "Editorial Note" explaining how Henson could be Uncle Tom when, after all, Stowe kills off Tom in her novel—but we could well say that Stowe's Tom still lived and Henson was killed off along the way.

What we are left with is the white appropriation of black history as symbol. I am reminded of Toni Morrison's argument that, through "the representation and appropriation" of the Africanist narrative, white Americans have long worked to transform African American experience into a domesticated tale that is capable of serving multiple functions.

The white narrative of African American life "provides opportunities to contemplate limitation, suffering, rebellion, and to speculate on fate and destiny"; it is "used for discourse on ethics, social and universal codes of behavior, and assertions about and definitions of civilization and reason"; and it is "used in the construction of a history and a context for whites by positing history-lessness and context-lessness for blacks" (*Playing* 53). Josiah Henson, whose essential narrative (and the history it represents) does not change significantly in its overall narrative trajectory from 1849 to 1881, similarly becomes the representative of an African American Christianity that lacks both history and context. Not an ongoing effort in this world, the Uncle Tom school of Christianity exists only for the postponement of justice, the rewards of the hereafter.

These lives, surrounded by and wrapped up in a culture promoted by *Uncle Tom's Cabin*, illustrate a larger concern—the ways in which a dominant culture can both acknowledge and contain faith, and the ways in which conceptions of Christianity are sometimes removed from history even while invoking the force of historical events. In her commentary on Henson's narrative, historian Robin Winks at one point imagines her readers wondering what harm there might be in linking Josiah Henson and Uncle Tom. And she answers: "Precisely this: as Canadians came increasingly to assign Henson's role to Tom, as the myth of the North Star, the Underground Railroad, and the Fugitives' haven 'under the lion's paw' . . . grew in the post–Civil War years, [white] Canadians also came increasingly to congratulate themselves upon their lack of prejudice and to contrast themselves favorably with the immoral and once slave-ridden United States" (xxvii). The problem, Winks notes, is that the contrast does not hold up under the slightest scrutiny. Similarly, *Uncle Tom's Cabin* more generally demonstrates the ways in which the discourse of white Christianity can present itself as transcending race, appropriate the available means for expressing alternative understandings of both faith and religious duty, and capture lives and entire cultures (with their histories in tow) in a seductive tale about a past brought to moral closure. Too often the narration of the history of African American spirituality and collective religious endeavors, like the narration of African American history itself, is reduced to neat and predictable stories of progress that amount to little more than various versions of Uncle Tom meeting the queen of England.[16]

It is no wonder that so much of African American autobiographical writing involves not just expressions of religious belief but examinations of the terms by which religion can be understood and experienced. Just as Harriet Wilson reformulated the equation of her life, many African American writers used their narratives to assess the products of what they sometimes called "American Christianity"—that is, their own life experiences marked by institutionalized inequalities and injustice, or by condescending and restricted benevolence—in order to reformulate the equation by which the experience of Christianity might be located, and by which the moral terms of individual and collective experience might be understood.

I say this not to suggest that all African Americans were Christian or even religious, but rather to emphasize that Christianity was a dominant force in U.S. culture (shaping, among other things, the understanding of benevolent behavior that many white readers brought to black experience, as with Stowe) and a dominant presence in an overwhelming number of nineteenth-century African American autobiographies. Christianity obviously pervades the spiritual autobiographies of Jerena Lee, Zilpha Elaw, Julia Foote, and Virginia Broughton, just as it does the great majority of slave narratives. Of course, Christianity was by no means a singular or stable frame of reference. In an 1859 essay entitled "The Great Conflict Requires Great Faith," abolitionist minister J. W. C. Pennington complains that "influences are constantly bearing upon us strongly calculated to affect us unfavorably towards the institutions of religion. Those institutions, professedly for the benefit of all classes of the family of man, are perverted to the vile uses of oppression" (343). This was the religious framework with which many African American writers and preachers contended in their autobiographical accounts. Some of these narratives proceed from experiences in black denominations like the African Methodist Episcopal Church, itself formed in response to racism within the white church; others address more broadly the operations of religion in the United States.

Frederick Douglass, Henry Bibb, and Henry Box Brown—to offer three prominent examples—each turn to religion at the end of their narratives. Douglass distinguishes between "the Christianity of this land" and "the Christianity of Christ"; between the two, he asserts, is "the widest possible difference—so wide, that to receive the one as good, pure, and holy, is of necessity to reject the other as bad, corrupt, and wicked" (*Narrative* 97). Bibb similarly worries in his closing chapter that he "might possibly make a wrong impression on the minds of some northern freemen, who are unacquainted theoretically or practically with the customs and treatment of American slaveholders to their slaves" (198). He proceeds to advance a detailed defense of his critique of slavery, focusing on the slaveholders' professions of Christian belief, and finally asks: "Is this Christianity? Is it honest or right? Is it doing as we would be done by? Is it in accordance with the principles of humanity or justice?" (203–4). Answering his own question, Bibb states directly, "I believe slaveholding to be a sin against God and man under all circumstances," then signs off, "prayerfully and earnestly relying on the power of truth, and the aid of the divine providence" (204). At the end of his narrative, Henry Box Brown declares: "I have no apology whatever to make for what I have said, in regard to the pretended christianity under which I was trained, while a slave" (92). Like Bibb, Brown presents a brief justification of his criticism of "pretended christianity," then says: "I pray that God may give them light to see the error of their ways, and if they know that they are doing wrongly, that he may give them grace to renovate their hearts!" (92–93). Following this pronouncement with a list of slave laws, Brown shows just how much is being done wrongly and how much must be involved in the attempt "to renovate their hearts."

Each of these narratives not only rejects a false religion but also presents a *religious* resistance to slavery and racism as its primary concern. They place their readers in a world of dangerous deception; they transform a story about those who are physically enslaved to encompass all of those, black and white, participating in a culture that relies on dangerous and fundamental deceptions. Thus they present the reader's response to their narrative as the first step toward a possible "renovation" of the heart— either by providing support for the moral labor of the narrators or by working to aid the narrators in the larger struggle against not only slavery but also racial oppression in all of its forms. Charity is not required in these narratives; action is. Christian benevolence also is not the goal; rather it is for readers to examine and renovate the foundations of their religion as they work to renovate their heart. In their juxtaposition of passages of tacit restraint and open denunciation, in their presentation of tensions between what is publicly professed and what is privately practiced, and in their determination to confront and confound expectations by both revealing and concealing the stories of their lives, these narrators make of their lives parables that speak of the unrepresentable "truth of slavery," a truth that involves not only the subjects of these autobiographies but also their readers. In short, at the end of each of these narratives lies a significant moral choice, and the artistry of the writer can be found most fully in the way the text crafts that choice, leaving readers to reflect on their own life stories as they read about those lives that have been most conspicuously affected by the system of slavery, North and South.

The confrontation with proslavery and racist Christianity is perhaps nowhere more dramatic than in *Narrative of the Life of Henry Box Brown, Written by Himself*, Brown's second autobiographical account, published in England in 1851. Few stories of the escape from slavery were so directly and regularly associated with religion as was Brown's. Images of his "resurrection" from a box were published soon after his escape, as was the biblical source for the "Hymn of Thanksgiving" that he sang after emerging from his "portable prison" (Stearns, *Narrative* v).[17] Although Brown quickly became famous for his unique mode of escape—the box that gave him his middle name—his flight was presented from the beginning as a distinctly religious event, with Brown associated with Lazarus in the introduction to his 1849 narrative and with Moses in the introduction to his 1851 narrative. But it is the latter narrative that proves most telling, for it contains far more detail than the earlier account, most of it having to do with the experience of religion under slavery that finally compelled him to escape. In his preface, he writes that he has been "impelled by the voice of . . . conscience" to address the inadequate response to the unrecognized crisis of slavery—that is, to the fact that "four millions of human beings, possessing immortal souls, are, in chains, dragging out their existence in the southern states" (41).

Considering that he was so complexly located, boxed in, by the cultures of both bondage and American Christianity, it is important that Brown presents in his *Narrative* a vision of "the Christianity of America" that is coextensive with the social and geographical landscape defined by the system of slavery. A few years later, Samuel Ringgold Ward would state in his *Autobiography of a Fugitive Negro* that the word "*religion* . . . should be substituted for Christianity; for while a religion may be from man, and a religion from such an origin may be capable of *hating*, Christianity is always from God, and, like him, is love" (41). While in many ways the *Narrative of the Life of Henry Box Brown* is designed to make this distinction, so familiar in antislavery writing, Brown emphasizes the extent to which, as Ward puts it, "the oppression and the maltreatment of the hapless descendant of Africa is not merely an ugly excrescence upon American *religion*" but rather "a cardinal principle, a *sin qoa non*, a cherished defended keystone, a corner-stone, of American faith" (41–42). Brown's experience could hardly have led him to different conclusions, even as he claimed the authority of Christianity in appealing to audiences shaped by American religion.

What hope could Brown, or his readers, entertain of entering a church that rests on different foundations, is devoted to different principles, and is marked by a different cornerstone? This is the question to which, I suggest, Brown's 1851 *Narrative* is primarily directed—and, indeed, the result of the most extensive revisions from the 1849 text. In successive chapters of the 1851 *Narrative*, containing material largely absent from the 1849 publication, the reader is introduced to a contextualized account of Brown's religious conversion—that is, his conversion to a religion apart from slavery—that is linked to the plan for his escape from slavery. The relatively brief fifth chapter addresses "the state of churches in slave countries" (69), focusing on the hypocrisies of slaveholding religion but including an account of the white northern evangelist and opponent of slavery, Jacob Knapp, who once visited and preached in Richmond. The sixth chapter, the longest in the *Narrative*, takes the reader from Brown's decision to marry to the scene where he watches first his eldest child, then his wife carried away in chains to another owner, never to see them again. Brown had witnessed slave coffles before, but the sight of his child and his wife being taken from him "made it assume the appearance of unusual horror"—a hellish vision of "little children of many different families, which as they appeared rent the air with their shrieks and cries and vain endeavours to resist the separation which was thus forced upon them, and the cords with which they were thus bound" (80). The next and final chapter includes Brown's account of his escape. Throughout his *Narrative*, Brown moves from situation to consequence to strategy—that is, from a culture of corrupt Christianity to the tragedy and trauma that necessarily follows from that corruption, then to the faith for which his traumatic experiences prepared him. Brown's successful escape is the product of the entire process. And just as his escape cannot be understood apart from his faith, so his faith cannot be understood apart from the traumatic experiences that enabled him to discover an understanding of and an approach to belief that can be known only through a conscious encounter with and deliberate resistance to the perversion of religion.

The turning point for Brown comes not when he is inspired to enter a box but rather when he is inspired to resist the box he is in—involving not the rejection of religion but rather a determined act of moral responsibility. The *Narrative*'s final chapter begins with Brown's disavowal of religion and the specific occasion of his return to the church. "The suspicion of these slave-dealing Christians," he reports, "was the means of keeping me absent from all their churches from the time that my wife and children were torn from me, until Christmas day in the year 1848; and I would not have gone then but being a leading member of the choir, I yielded to the entreaties of my associates to assist at a concert of sacred music which was to be got up for the benefit of the church" (81).[18] During the performance, a fellow choir member, James C. A. Smith, suddenly closed his hymnbook and sat down. Brown explains that "Dr. Smith's feelings were overcome with a sense of doing wrongly in singing for the purpose of obtaining money to assist those who were buying and selling their fellow-men. He thought at that moment he felt reproved by Almighty God for lending his aid to the cause of slave-holding religion." After "several other pieces" Brown sang lines that had a similar effect on him: "Vital spark of heavenly flame, / Quit, O! quit the mortal frame." What gave the lines special meaning was "the sting of former sufferings," the loss of his wife and children, prompting Brown to follow Smith's example: "I too made up my mind that I would be no longer guilty of assisting those bloody dealers in the bodies and souls of men" (82). The experience led to Brown's resolution to escape and, eventually, his successful plan. The idea of a box came to him following a "prayer to Almighty God" (84).

It is appropriate that Brown would believe himself divinely inspired to escape by having himself boxed in, for the Christianity he came to trust is a realm of belief itself boxed in by a culture claiming its authority. Where can a true Christianity be located in a culture devoted to slavery? Brown seems to find the answer only in the manifest image of its own containment, the shipping crate he took with him for his antislavery appearances. Contained by a culture devoted to the commercial exchange and ownership of both personal and social bodies, both individuals and families, the only Christianity imaginable was the one that delivered Brown first to nominal freedom and then to a career on the antislavery lecture circuit. As with his newfound and reformed beliefs, then, Brown presents in his narrative a theology of liberation through containment. Like all slave narratives, this is not just the story of an escape from slavery, nor is it simply the story of a Christian soul being delivered from the "demons" of the slaveholding South. Rather, the *Narrative of the Life of Henry Box Brown* is a meditation, both knowable and representable only through experience, on the possibilities of faith in a world that has appropriated the discourse and authority of Christianity.

Brown's *Narrative* is, in fact, an argument against the possibilities of a

Christian community in the United States. Throughout this work, he describes a world of variable character, the instabilities of identity promoted by the church of slavery. "The whole feature of slavery," he notes, "is so utterly inconsistent with the principles of religion, reason, and humanity, that it is no wonder that the very mention of the word God grates upon the ear as if it typified the degeneracy of this hellish system" (25). In the world that Brown describes, promises are made and broken, religious conversions are compromised, and sacred relations between fellow Christians are at once acknowledged and rejected. Indeed, he is faced with the reality that the language with which he might express both his discovery of faith and his "resurrection" from the social death of slavery is the very language that carries the weight of the trauma of enslavement and white supremacist control. More than presenting a mere rhetorical impasse, antebellum religious discourse constitutes the traumatic arena in which Brown must necessarily work in his ongoing efforts to claim the authority not only of his voice but also of his conscience. The "voice of conscience" in the *Narrative* finds expression in a vision of religion that can be realized only through the experience of the perverse imperatives of the multiple tensions that define American Christianity. The Christianity in the *Narrative* is one of unresolvable trauma—that is, not a belief that resolves the perversion of religion but rather one that emerges from it. Accordingly, Brown's voice of conscience is directed both to traumatic remembrance and to the necessity of traumatic encounters with audiences prepared to celebrate his "resurrection" from slavery. In this way, he can help us find our way through autobiographical narratives that address, either in their presentation or their reception, the Uncle Tom school of Christianity.

Whereas Josiah Henson never managed to distance himself from that school, and in fact seemed increasingly to embrace it, another famous Uncle Tom offers a rather different story. Thomas Jones's life did not end but began its entrance into print through its association with Stowe's novel. His first narrative, *Experience and Personal Narrative of Uncle Tom Jones, Who Was for Forty Years a Slave*, published in 1849, included a frontispiece image of a black man with a stovepipe hat and pipe hovering above a small dwelling identified in bold type as a cabin. Following the first version of his narrative, however, Jones did what Henson could not or would not do—extricate himself from *Uncle Tom's Cabin* so as to present a more challenging representation of the dynamics of Christian faith in U.S. culture. To be sure, in many ways Jones might seem to be very well suited to the Uncle Tom school. In his account, for example, suffering is both emphasized and somewhat exoticized. He prefaces the text by stating his hope for "a more fervent conviction of the necessity and blessedness of toiling for the desolate members of the one great brother-hood who now suffer and die, ignorant and despairing, in the vast prison land of the South." The brief preface, which ends with the golden rule, is followed by an appeal "To the Friends of Suffering Humanity" (*Experience of Rev. . . . Jones* 207, 209). But Jones also tells a more complex story about both the past and his reconciliation with the past. It is a story of how "the grace of God . . . makes all one, regardless of color or condition" (262) and of how "all distinctions as between different races seemed to have disap-peared altogether, and everybody recognized a common bond of interest and endeavor" (254). Jones promotes this ideal in the context of struggle and loss; he never seems to lose sight of the immense efforts required to make such occasional scenes occur with greater regularity. He tells a story that ends with references to John Brown and the Civil War, and with his own successful attempts to secure his mother's and father's liberty. In Jones's narrative, Christianity is revealed and its rewards are realized—in the struggles of this world, in energetic labors for justice, and in a faith defined by, forged in, and inseparable from the experience of injustice.

Jones's narrative is instructive, particularly in his vision of a Chris-tian union beyond racial distinctions. My point, in fact, is that identi-fying the religious presence in African American autobiographies is not simply a matter of locating black bodies in church pews or, in the case of slave narratives specifically, of identifying examples of the Christian discourse so prominent in antislavery writing. As is powerfully evident in the narratives of African American women who began their evangeli-cal careers in patriarchal religious institutions, black as well as white, African Americans were hardly in agreement about Christian doctrine, institutional order, and religious practice. Indeed, those who attended the National Convention of Colored Citizens held in Buffalo in 1843 saw the need to speak directly to African American Christians. After denouncing "slaveholding and prejudice sustaining ministers and churches (falsely so called)" as "the greatest enemies to Christ and to civil and religious liberty in the world," the convention passed another resolution: "That the colored people in the free States who belong to pro-slavery sects that will not pray for the oppressed—nor preach the truth in regard to the sin of slavery and all other existing evils, nor publish anti-slavery meetings, nor act for the entire immediate abolition of slavery, are guilty of enslav-ing themselves and others, and their blood, and the blood of perishing millions will be upon their heads" (*Minutes of the National Convention* 15). Exploring the religious presence in black autobiographical writing cannot be a matter of referring to black Christianity any more than general references to black autobiography will consider the great diversity of the actual autobiographical accounts of widely varying life experiences published in the nineteenth century.

The lessons to be drawn from the narratives of Frederick Douglass, Josiah Henson, Sojourner Truth, Henry Bibb, Zilpha Elaw, Henry Box Brown, Harriet Tubman, Thomas Jones, and many others have to do not with the singularity of African American religious experiences but rather with the necessity of negotiating a religious culture dominated by "slaveholding and prejudice sustaining ministers and churches (falsely so called)." All Americans, of whatever race or religious beliefs, found their culture shaped by religious, political, economic, and social practices that could not be separated from the ongoing iterations of the various legal constructions of race. No expression of belief, no explication of the Bible, no doctrinal argument, and no church ritual could operate separately from the deeply intertwined strands of the American cultural order. For African Americans to locate themselves by way of an autobiographical narrative thus involved the effort to define or redefine their position within this social environment, including their position before both imagined and actual readers. The work of nineteenth-century African American autobiography is not simply the work of resisting racism; it is also the work of negotiating the frameworks and the operations of race that led from Mag Smith to Our Nig, from Josiah Henson to Uncle Tom, or from endurance to force.

## Unspeakable Stories and Crowded Affiliations

How does one represent a force? This is the question to which a great deal of scholarship on African American autobiographical writing has been at least implicitly devoted. We might frame the question differently by returning to William Andrews's authoritative study of African American autobiography, for in many ways the question has to do with the need "to tell a free story." As Andrews observes, the African American turn to the novel began in the complex world of autobiography, especially the slave narrative—the turn to a form that Andrews has called "the novelized autobiography" (*To Tell a Free Story* 265). Involved in this novelization of narrative are a number of significant characteristics of African American autobiographical writing as it developed over the years: "the supplementation of one narrative by a sequel, or one style by another; the intrusion of suspect voices into black autobiography, especially those that appeal to diversionary sentiments of any sort; the deliberate fictionalizing of texts in the 1850s and 1860s, notably through the use of reconstructed dialogue; [and] the problem of interpreting the dialectic of 'romantic-realistic elements' that all these kinds of supplements introduce into autobiography" (271). Increasingly, writers drew from these strategies and negotiated with these narrative presences in clear attempts to present an autobiographical narrative capable of getting at the broader realm of experiences, social practices, and cultural frameworks that define the terms by which an individual life can be known and directed. The most prominent examples of such strategic engagements with the novelized autobiography, and the ones Andrews focuses on, are Frederick Douglass's *My Bondage and My Freedom* (1855), Jacob Green's *Narrative of the Life of J. D. Green* (1864), and Harriet Jacobs's *Incidents in the Life of a Slave Girl, Written by Herself* (1861). These narratives have been rightly celebrated for their ability to challenge the implicit terms by which African American autobiography was imagined, composed, and received in the nineteenth century.

Beyond recognizing the strategies of novelizations, scholars have also perceived the extent to which nineteenth-century African American (auto)biography frequently functioned through creative indirection and crafted silences. We might well apply to most African American autobiographies what Andrews identifies as a distinctive feature of those published from 1760 to 1810: narrative "seams or cuts" that appear "when facts are revealed—made tellable—in a way subversive to the text," moments when "the presence of colorless white screens is deconstructed long enough for the absence to call attention to itself and demand a creative hearing for the silences in the text" (*To Tell a Free Story* 37). Gradually, scholars seem to be making the turn away from just defending the apparent roughness of nineteenth-century African American autobiographical writing to exploring their often strategic seams or crafted silences. In other cases, like Wilson's *Our Nig* and Brown's *My Southern Home* especially, the blending of voices and techniques, and the mix of conventions associated with both autobiographical writing and fiction (as well as other genres), guide readers into a world of noisy contentions, and the identity of the narrator (indeed, even the cultural self-positioning that the author achieves by way of the narrative) is revealed largely through a deafening mix of voices. As Frances Smith Foster observes in her groundbreaking study of antebellum slave narratives: "Writers had long discovered that elements of mimesis, romance, history, and myth could be combined in ways which far exceeded the advantages offered by any one structure. The slave narrators, likewise, created a form which was an amalgam of traditional and innovative techniques" (*Witnessing Slavery* 82). Recent scholarship on *Our Nig*, or on *Clotel* as a fictional narrative grafted onto an innovative autobiographical performance, in particular, indicates the growing interest in learning to read these narratives as amalgams.

But a great deal of work remains, for beyond the obvious questions about mixed genres, the blending of fact and fiction, or the influence of literary and popular culture (*Uncle Tom's Cabin*, blackface minstrelsy, and the like) on the narration and reception of African American life stories, reading nineteenth-century African American (auto)biographies is a constant reminder of how little we know about the past, about the voices that speak to us from the past, and about the myths, legends, and assumptions that surround the lives we try to approach through the narratives left behind.[19] The research on Harriet Wilson, Jeffrey Ruggles's recovery of the life of Henry Box Brown, Eric Gardner's archival research on Lucy Delaney and numerous other African Americans, Peter Hinks's biography of David Walker, Jean Fagan Yellin's biography of Harriet Jacobs, Nell Irvin Painter's biography of Sojourner Truth—these and similar scholarly efforts have done much to indicate the rich complexity of individual lives, interwoven communities, and cultural environments. Together they add up to the makings of a story waiting to be told, a history of African Americans in the nineteenth century not reducible to the clean outlines of a Black History Month presentation. But these studies have also emphasized the huge of amount of work that remains, for each advance in our understanding of Wilson, Brown, Walker, Jacobs, Truth, and many others only underscores how little we know about most other authors or subjects of African American (auto)biographies. We regularly encounter lives that are still known only through their narratives, with a biographical entry that concludes, "Very little is known . . . ." Occasionally, we may stumble over something—for example, a 1915 interview with Betheny Veney's husband Frank published in the Virginia newspaper the *Page News and Courier* in which we get an inkling of Veney's life in her later years.[20] But such glimpses only emphasize how much more there is to learn, while also reminding us that there is much that we do not know simply because we have not looked—that is, because certain authors and texts have not yet been considered sufficiently important to justify the research time and effort needed for a full biographical and contextual account.

As the biographical recovery work thus far on Wilson, Jacobs, and others indicates, when we do look we are likely to find a great deal to unravel and new cultural, political, and narrative lines to follow. Certainly, it is significant that in the space of four years, three biographies were published on Harriet Tubman alone: Jean M. Humez's *Harriet Tubman: The Life and the Life Stories* (2004); Kate Clifford Larson's *Bound for the Promised Land: Harriet Tubman, Portrait of an American Hero* (2004); and Milton C. Sernett's *Harriet Tubman: Myth, Memory, and History* (2007). The interest in Tubman is much deserved, but as Humez's and Sernett's titles especially show, the interest in Tubman has become so much a part of the story of her life that it is difficult to distinguish between what we know and what we think we know, or between why we care and why we *should* care. This also has been a unique challenge in the case of Sojourner Truth. Truth continues to serve as the distinctively, authentically black female presence in a number of scholarly and popular forums, and scholars and general audiences alike have been reluctant to sacrifice the terms of their appreciation of Truth's life and work in the face of new evidence. "Much of the writing about [Truth], in her time and ours," Carleton Mabee has noted, "has been bent more toward making her into a myth for inspiration rather than toward documenting the reality of her life; and Sojourner herself sometimes contributed to the myth-making" (74). The resulting myth, as Nell Irvin Painter has said, often is invoked to define the boundaries of scholarly investigation. "As useful in scholarly discourse as in popular culture," Painter observes, "this eloquent genius of Sojourner Truth appears sometimes at the beginning, but usually at the end of scholarly writing. She cuts off discussion with one sharp comment" (285). The needs of the argument, or of the scholar's position, or of broader social or political affiliations, provide the framework for reading Truth's *Narrative*, and, like the Bible, her *Narrative* becomes a sourcebook that serves many interpretive masters, the great majority of whom still want to return us to the endlessly adaptable foundational word: "Ar'n't I a woman?"[21]

As in the case of Tubman and Truth, often the legends we cherish or the misinformation we accept were built into the original portrayal of the lives of those who serve as subjects of (auto)biographical narratives—the biographies of these two prominent activists or in various "as told to" or "personal recollection" narratives. Consider, for example, *The Kidnapped and the Ransomed: The Narrative of Peter and Vina Still after Forty Years of Slavery*, written by Kate E. R. Pickard and published in 1856. While Pickard's voice and opinions are prominent throughout the narrative, there is reason to trust the authenticity of her account. As Nancy Grant notes in her introduction to the 1995 reprint of this narrative, Pickard "played a very active role both as a transcriber of the remembrances of Peter and Vina Still and also as an observer and commentator on events in their lives" (xii). In fact, Pickard had much to bring to the narrative, for, "unlike most editors, Pickard had known Peter as a slave and had lived in Tuscombia, where she worked as a teacher in the female academy that employed Peter for several years. She also knew Peter's owner and many of the whites who appear in the narrative" (xii).

Yet we can trust this narrative only so far—not even so far as Peter Still might have trusted it, for the account of Peter's life in this narrative is directly contradicted by Peter's brothers: William Still in *The Underground Rail Road* (1872) and James Still in *Early Recollections and Life of Dr. James Still* (1877). "According to the narrative," Grant observes, "Peter and his brother Levin were taken away from the peace and tranquility of their home on the Delaware River by a slave kidnapper who sold them in Kentucky. Levin died in slavery but Peter lived to retain the memory of his lost family. Persevering through hard work, faith, and good fortune, he was able to return 'home'" (vii). This is a powerful story, standing next to Solomon Northup's as an example of those accounts of slavery that not only end in "freedom" but also begin there. Unfortunately, this part of Pickard's story is not true. As Grant explains, her narrative fails to "reveal the fact that Peter, despite the well-publicized title, had not been kidnapped. He was abandoned by his mother when she escaped slavery in Maryland to join her husband who had bought his freedom several years earlier. Peter's mother, Sidney, decided to take her daughters with her and elected to leave behind her eight-year-old and six-year-old sons." Grant adds that "it is not clear whether Peter was aware of his slave status and chose to hide it or had been too young to understand his abandonment" (viii). Years later, William Still would document much of the larger and more difficult story of Peter's life, noting that when *The Kidnapped and the Ransomed* was first published, in the face of the Fugitive Slave Law, it would have been unsafe to reveal so much about those who escaped and left Peter and Levin behind. In many ways, *The Kidnapped and the Ransomed* tells both more and less than its "editor" and narrative source realized—the story of lives lived under the veil of fictions shaped by the force of law, the tenuous relations of families, the improbable opportunities to change one's location and condition, and almost unimaginable choices.

Even in less dramatic circumstances, behind every slave narrative were experiences nearly impossible to relate. As William Wells Brown put it in 1847, "Slavery has never been represented; Slavery never can be represented" (*Lecture* 4).[22] No purely individual or factual account seemed adequate to explain the multifarious horrors of bondage; any description could only emphasize the many unknown lives and unrecorded violations of humanity that the culture of slavery largely omitted from the historical record. In an 1809 speech, Henry Sipkins concluded his imagined narration of the slave trade with the comment, "But why attempt to portray, in their true colours, scenes of oppression, which language the most descriptive is inadequate to delineate: or why any longer expatiate on a subject of such complicated misery" (370). Constructing a similar narrative, Russell Parrott asked in an 1814 oration, "What language can tell the feelings of his soul? what pen portray the intenseness of his grief?" (385). Nathaniel Paul echoed this in an 1827 address, remarking, "Its more than detestable picture has been attempted to be portrayed by the learned, and the wise, but all have fallen short, and acknowledged their inadequacy to the task, and have been compelled to submit, by merely giving an imperfect shadow of its reality" (8). Hosea Easton comments throughout his *Treatise on the Intellectual Character, and Civil and Political Condition of the Colored People of the U[nited] States* (1837) that "no language capable of being employed by mortal tongue, is sufficiently descriptive to set forth in its true character the effect of that cursed thing, slavery" (23). At one point, he exclaims: "Language is lame in its most successful attempt, to describe [slavery's] enormity; and with all the excitement which this country has undergone, in consequence of the discussion of the subject, yet the story is not half told, neither can it be" (26). "I have no language to express what I see, and hear, and feel, on this subject," Easton declares, adding, "Were I capable of dipping my pen in the deepest dye of crime, and of understanding the science of the bottomless pit, I should then fail in presenting to the intelligence of mortals on earth, the true nature of American deception" (33). Such disclaimers regularly appear in *Narrative of the Life and Adventures of Henry Bibb, An American Slave* (1850). "Reader," Bibb asserts, "believe me when I say, that no tongue, nor pen ever has or can express the horrors of American Slavery" (15). Later he continues to insist: "No tongue nor pen can describe the dreadful apprehensions under which I labored for the space of ten or twelve hours" (75), "No tongue could express the deep anguish of my soul when I saw the silent tear drops streaming down the sable cheeks of an aged slave mother, at my departure" (89), and "No tongue, no pen can ever describe what my feelings were at that time" (130).

In the face of such experience, it is understandable that Lucius C. Matlack would begin his introduction to the Bibb's *Narrative* by emphasizing the wonder of "the most brilliant productions" emerging from the experience of slavery. His opening lines are particularly instructive about his sense of how slavery served as, in effect, potent fertilizer for literary productions. "From the most obnoxious substances," Matlack states, "we often see spring forth, beautiful and fragrant, flowers of every hue, to regale the eye, and perfume the air. Thus, frequently, are results originally which are wholly unlike the cause that gave them birth. An illustration of this truth is afforded by the history of American Slavery" (1). On the other hand, Henry David Thoreau could just as easily argue that manure is manure. "Slavery and servility," he writes, "have produced no sweet-scented flower annually, to charm the senses of men, for they have no real life: they are merely a decaying and a death, offensive to all healthy nostrils. We do not complain that they *live*, but that they do not get *buried*. Let the living bury them; even they are good for manure" (2056). Thoreau, certainly aware of slave narratives though not addressing them here, speaks to the very grounds of this literature; Matlack, on the other hand, finds life in those grounds—though in describing the literature, he mixes metaphors wildly, characterizing slave narratives as fragrant flowers, "gushing fountains of poetic thought," and "productions, whose logical levers will ultimately upheave and overthrow the system" (1). Perhaps when that work is complete, the metaphorical complexity of slave narrative artistry will be resolved. These many years later, we might say that the work of these narratives remains, and that the "end" of slavery has highlighted both the ideological framework necessary for slavery and the ongoing effects of slavery's centrality to American history—a shift in emphasis that changes the original terms for understanding the artistry of slave narratives, especially that artistry devoted to the repressed, the elided, or the unspeakable.

With that larger framework in mind, it is important to remember that what Hartman has termed "the more mundane and socially endurable forms of terror" (42) were not limited to the experience of slavery, and the unspeakable was a presence in African American self-representation concerning life in the North as well as in the South. In *The American Prejudice against Color* (1853), William G. Allen, who was never enslaved, observes:

"I can assure you that language has yet to be invented in which to write in its fullness what, when the children of certain parents shall look back fifty years hence, they will regard as the darkest deeds recorded in the history of their ancestors" (51). David Walker, in his *Appeal to the Coloured Citizens of the World* (1830), extends his vision of such dark deeds still further, applying the unspeakable to the tensions among African Americans themselves. Accounting first for "the productions of ignorance" among those who were enslaved, Walker then turns his eyes to those who were nominally free:

> And when my curious observer comes to take notice of those who are said to be free, (which assertion I deny) and who are making some frivolous pretentions [*sic*] to common sense, he will see that branch of ignorance among the slaves assuming a more cunning and deceitful course of procedure.—He may see some of my brethren in league with tyrants, selling their own brethren into *hell upon earth*, not dissimilar to the exhibitions in Africa, but in a more secret, servile and abject manner. Oh Heaven! I am full!!! I can hardly move my pen!!!! (24).

Here Walker reminds us that one could not safely refer to an African American community in commenting on those writers who worked to foster an imagined community or a working solidarity. Moreover, in the tensions among the historically determined brethren, he claims, there are worlds of identity and experience that resist representation with such force that one can only strain against the limits of typographical symbols.

In nineteenth-century African American (auto)biography, thus are we regularly confronted by the unspeakable, by the repressed, and sometimes by information only imperfectly or even inaccurately gathered or remembered by the narrative subject. These accounts are directed less to the facts of individual lives than to the conditions that have marked those lives in significant ways; the chaotic processes by which race is experienced as one of the central and unavoidable forces in human experience; the cultural, political, and economic means by which the system of slavery was maintained; the "alchemy," as Frances E. W. Harper put it, "by which this blood"—the blood of "a hundred thousand new-born babes . . . annually added to the victims of slavery," of "twenty thousand lives . . . annually sacrificed on the plantations of the South"—can be transformed into gold" ("Could We Trace" 101). In approaching this demanding but larger story—that is, in writing a story in which subject and context, in

effect, trade places as the principal concern—African American (auto)
biographers often could only gesture to the story waiting between the
lines for those who could read. The stories told by many autobiographical
narrators address the "truth" of history through strategic omissions, indicating the untold stories that resisted representation, stories beyond what
white audiences were prepared to hear or capable of understanding. In
an expansion of the narrative he first set out to write, the Reverend G. W.
Offley says that friends had asked him to tell the story of a slave woman
and her two children that he had mentioned in passing. "I omitted several
stories," Offley notes, "because I did not design it as an anti-slavery book,
but merely a short sketch of my youthful life, as I am aware that the slave
is a hopeless victim in this country" (22). Turning to the larger antislavery
story that he was expected to tell based on his life experiences, Offley
emphasizes that the larger narrative remains mostly untold, as if to suggest that the hopelessness he feels is a product not only of slavery but also
of the controlled narrative of antislavery culture. "This is not a fictitious
tale," Offley cautions, "but a true story. I could write a book of facts more
sad than this story, but let this suffice" (28).

Like Offley, all African American (auto)biographers recognized that
there were many stories that could be told about their lives, and many
stories to respond to in their own telling, making autobiography an attempt to account for and reframe the multiple relations (legal, economic,
and social) shaped by a white supremacist culture that were fundamental
to their experience. By means of strategic narrative omissions or other
gestures both on and outside the printed page, they frequently reacted
to these multiple contingencies by locating moral authority beyond the
sphere of white readers' expectations or understanding. But the challenges of representing their own lives, and of negotiating their broader
representative status, required greater strategy still. Escaping the governing authority over identity in the South, many who fled slavery found
themselves governed again by white antislavery assumptions about the
meaning of a fugitive identity. African Americans born or resettled in
the North found themselves defined in relation to a generalized black
identity in white racist communities, and in relation to an unrepresented
and unrepresentable black community in the South. Often, they found
themselves representing a freedom that made a mockery of the concept. They understood well the ways in which they were limited—even
bound—ideologically, culturally, politically, and geographically, an understanding more often than not inscribed in the narratives they produced.

The dilemma of African American (auto)biographical narrators was to engage in an intricate play of representation from which a particular configuration or concept of historical truth could emerge. The field of African American (auto)biography, in short, is characterized by tremendous instability, dramatic movement (both geographical and perspectival), and turbulence, and any attempt to characterize this genre as a field of study must somehow account for its dynamic character.

The challenges outlined here are not entirely unfamiliar to anyone involved in the study of life writing, but they are particularly pressing, given that what counts as African American cultural and literary history is still spotty at best, misrepresented even in many of the available primary documents and official records, and in many cases seemingly lost. In his study of nineteenth-century African American women's autobiographies, William Andrews concludes with brief comments on Anna Julia Cooper, though he notes that he is not wholly equipped to *place* her views. "Only through further study of Cooper's contemporaries in black women's autobiography," he states, "will we be able to understand fully whether she spoke for the many or the few among black women at the end of the nineteenth century" ("Changing Moral Discourse" 239). African American (auto)biographical texts of the nineteenth century speak with and against one another in complex ways, they borrow from and echo other writers both black and white, they are sometimes themselves authored by white writers, they sometimes include standard antislavery or other familiar tropes of cultural discourse, and they are almost always composed in a mix of direct and indirect address. They keep some secrets and expose others, and they require attention to a rich network of texts, people, and historical currents. While there is still much to uncover in the shadows of the archives, much of the history and many of the lives addressed in African American (auto)biographies can be known only through the kind of intertexual work that Andrews describes—a matter sometimes of reading the patterned silences and suggestive gestures of the available narratives and other documents. What is African American about these lives and about this body of literature can be discovered in the complex interplay of the accounts of various individual lives, in the digressions that indicate a story beyond the clean lines of the promised plot, and in the stylistic roughness that suggests truths that do not quite fit into the discursive conventions and possibilities of the time. An African American literary history that settles for less than this dynamic and fractal complexity loses its hold on the center it claims as an organizing principle.

## CHAPTER THREE

# The Shortest Point between Two Lines

*Writing African Americans into American Literary History*

> To engage in a serious discussion of race in America, we
> must begin not with the problems of black people but with the flaws
> of American society—flaws rooted in historic inequalities and longstanding
> cultural stereotypes. How we set up the terms for discussing racial issues shapes
> our perception and response to these issues. As long as black people are viewed
> as a "them," the burden falls on blacks to do all the "cultural" and "moral"
> work necessary for healthy race relations. The implication is that only
> certain Americans can define what it means to be American—and
> the rest must simply "fit in."—CORNEL WEST, *Race Matters*

Some years ago, Eric J. Sundquist observed that "it remains difficult for many readers to overcome their fundamental conception of 'American' literature as solely Anglo-European in inspiration and authorship, to which may then be added an appropriate number of valuable 'ethnic' or 'minority' texts, those that closely correspond to familiar critical or semantic paradigms" (7). Today, we can point to a number of scholars for whom this statement does not apply, scholars devoted to what Sundquist has termed "the challenge of revising the contours of literary tradition" (19). It would be more difficult, though, to identify scholarly studies that attempt to come to terms with what Sundquist identifies as "the necessity of living with the paradox that 'American' literature is both a single tradition of many parts *and* a series of winding, sometimes parallel traditions that have perforce been built in good part from their inherent conflicts" (18). As I hope I have indicated by outlining the challenges of reading African American autobiographies, this is both a useful and a deceptive overview of the work ahead. It is useful in its reliance on paradox and geometrical complexity (winding and *sometimes* parallel) to chart a narrative course. One thinks of Hartman's comment that she uses "the term 'performing blackness' as a way of illuminating the entanglements of dominant and subordinate enunciations of blackness and the difficulty of distinguishing between contending enactments of blackness based on form, authenticity, or even intention" (56). Behind Sundquist's winding and (only sometimes) intersecting traditions, in other words, are the complex entanglements of racial history. However, Sundquist's description is deceptive in its assumption that in using the word "traditions" he can be taken to mean roughly equivalent literary and scholarly realms of historical attention and understanding. In fact, *tradition* should be understood to refer not simply to the world of texts but also to the history of attention to those texts. A literary tradition involves both the publications of the past and the history of recovering, preserving, conceptualizing, and creating the past, and the various traditions that form the American literary tradition exist in vastly different states of order and familiarity.

Although it is almost a commonplace today that writers from formerly segregated literary traditions should be placed in conversation with one another, my purpose in this chapter is to show that doing so is in fact very difficult, even if we limit our attention to white and black writers, as I will do here. The problem with many visions of an inclusive literary history is that we have been there before; it is a world in which a delimited black presence facilitates a superficially interracial exchange. Black and white writers have often been studied in relation to one another, but the burden of cultural translation and relocation has been unevenly borne. In her introduction to a collection of essays on Harriet Jacobs, Rafia Zafar notes that many writers considered to be "new voices in literary studies" have actually been there the whole time, and that what should be new are the literary studies in which they appear.[1] "The inclusion of Jacobs and *Incidents* within a syllabus on 'Classic' American literature does not by itself indicate a rethinking of the list itself; merely to add Jacobs, without reimagining the context of that syllabus, exemplifies the Band-aid approach to literary studies" ("Over-Exposed" 2). In scholarship over the last twenty years or so, Jacobs and a few other writers have emerged as regular presences in American literary studies, and many syllabi and books have included attention to African American writers. But often the attention to race that is inevitably a primary point of such classroom units or book chapters has had little discernible effect on the overall syllabus or the book's other chapters. Gene Andrew Jarrett has commented that while "the scholarly conception of African American literature has undoubtedly benefitted from canonical revisionism, . . . the critics engaged in such work have also committed the mistake of conflating authorial identity with literary identity, in this case for the sake of racial politics" ("Addition by Subtraction" 318). Jarrett is especially concerned about the marginalization of African American writers who do not perform overt (or conventionally recognizable) forms of black realism and politics, and he importantly reminds us that such writers "were well aware that they were writing in a field of power relations (literary, critical, commercial, social) in which their Black identities imbued their creative activities with political meaning" (318). That field of power relations is still an inevitable presence in any attempt to bring "sometimes parallel traditions" together in an integrated analysis.[2]

In the absence of a radical reconsideration not only of literary history but also of the cultural work of literature in the face of the instabilities of cultural identity, placing various literary and cultural traditions together, or even placing different African American writers together under established historical paradigms at best is an extremely difficult and complex endeavor, and at worst amounts to a kind of ritualized reenactment of the protocols of U.S. racial history.[3] Often, this conversation involves a chapter in a book devoted to a thesis that could have been formulated with little or no attention to the complexities of African American literary or cultural history, which I take to be a problem, however much such concerns are accounted for in the relevant chapter. In 1853, at the Colored National Convention in Rochester, New York, the Committee on Social Relations and Polity noted the importance of "schools adapted" to the needs of the African American male (education for females was addressed in a separate report). The committee observed of the black male student that "neither schools nor educators for the whites, at present, are in full sympathy with him; and . . . he must either abandon his own state of things which he finds around him, and which he is pledged to change and better, or cease to receive culture from such sources, since their whole tendency is to change him, not his condition—to educate him out of his sympathies, not to quicken and warm his sympathies" (*Proceedings* 22–23). In bringing African American and white writers into conversation with one another, we similarly must be careful not to educate black writers out of their sympathies, nor to praise their achievements by merely bringing them into the fold of the literary and philosophical concerns and protocols defined by a historically white approach to the American literary tradition. In other words, we must be careful to avoid denying the realities of race and implicitly absorbing African American literature into the ranks of a literary tradition that still accounts for the multiple and often contending literary traditions of the United States largely through selective inclusion, strategic revision, or occasional examinations of the category of race. Such conversations, I suggest, need to be negotiated among different cultural spaces and different historical continuums, and such negotiations should return our attention to a concept of African American literature that includes but extends beyond the identity of its authors.

## Inverted Epistemologies and Interpretive Battles

Those who enter this field of concern by way of nineteenth-century African American literature quickly discover that there is no need to talk of *placing* African American and white writers in conversation with one another, for there actually were a great many interracial conversations, collaborations, and debates in the nineteenth century, many of them central to, often even constituting the occasion for, African American publications. Of course, some of the these conversations do not rise to the level of the *literary* as traditionally understood. As noted in my introduction, Dwight McBride recognized the need to emphasize, even in 2001, the importance of considering a range of publications, including "literary texts, political pamphlets, speeches, essays, newspaper articles, historical and scholarly treatises on both the institution and the morality of slavery, and, of course, slave narratives" (2). "This broad-ranging approach to understanding abolitionism," McBride observes, "rather than assuming a hierarchy among these forms, is concerned with the production of meaning that is possible when one considers the interplay of these forms taken together in the terrain that is abolitionist discourse" (2–3). That hierarchy, though, far beyond the field of antislavery studies, has a great deal to do with the ways in which texts by African American writers find their way into scholarship on the broader field of American literature and culture, as well as a great deal to do with how they are received, valued, and put to work upon their arrival in that scholarship. My point here and throughout this book is not that hierarchies are irrelevant when one considers African American texts—that is, not that we should be inattentive to differences in literary achievement. Rather, we are not in a position to determine such hierarchies—we are not in a position to identify aesthetic standards that emerge from literary history—unless and until we have surveyed the full range of publications and cultural conditions that influenced African

American texts and textual production. Placing African American writers in conversation with writers who already enjoy the status that results from a long, sometimes contentious, and decidedly biased history of thinking about aesthetics or other concepts of literary value is not sufficient. Nineteenth-century African American writing is not a series of texts applying for our recognition; it is an aesthetic and discursive field that operated within a complex environment, and what we need most are "conversations" that take us deeper into that environment.

The point is not about putting writers together or keeping them apart; to a great extent, the point involves simply asking questions about how and why certain authors end up in certain courses or scholarly arguments. What are the occasions for the conversations we arrange in scholarship, either by considering a group of writers together in an article or book chapter or by including chapters representative of different (though related) concerns, different (though intertwined) cultural traditions, and different (though overlapping) literary fields of production? What questions are we hoping to answer? What problems are we trying to address or resolve? What are the implicit or explicit frameworks, contexts, or understandings of history (or of the priorities of historical research) that we bring to these groupings? And how do we arrive at the pairings or groupings that we stage in our work? Sometimes, the answers to such questions are rather limited in scope, dealing with individuals rather than traditions. As many have noted in the past, Frederick Douglass is often included in scholarship as the sole representative of African American writers—and he finds himself in that position both as an accomplished and influential writer and public figure and, sometimes, as the writer with whom most readers are most familiar. One way to respond to Deborah E. McDowell's now famous observation that Douglass has been treated as "the part that stands for the whole" by scholars who have "privileged and mystified Douglass's narrative" is to include other writers and to work toward "a reconfigured genealogical model" that "would examine the historical and cultural function of the slave narrative, both in the moment of its emergence and in contemporary scholarly discourse" (McDowell, "In the First Place" 56, 38, 58). But while there has been a broadening of attention beyond Douglass's 1845 *Narrative*, attention to Douglass, Jacobs, and only a few others still dominates the field, to the point where it can seem innovative to focus on a lesser-known writer or a relatively obscure narrative without the trouble of attending to the concerns informing McDowell's call for a reconfigured genealogical model.

When we allow evidence to precede argument, and when we look for evidence within the cultural fields marked out by African American history, we discover rich occasions for considering the relations between white print culture and black, occasions that speak of the tangled genealogies, to borrow from Jacobs, central to American history. Indeed, without in any way undermining the significant fostering of African American reading communities, and the publication of newspapers, pamphlets, and other publications directed specifically to black readers, one might say that African American print culture was *born* in conversation with white print culture—dating back at least to the various petitions to Congress and to state legislative bodies filed toward the end of the eighteenth century.[4] In a document that Herbert Aptheker identifies as "the earliest extant negro petition to Congress," four black men protested a North Carolina law that called for the capture and reenslavement of those who had been freed. Asserting that laws forbidding the manumission of slaves were "a stretch of power, morally and politically, a Governmental defect," and that such laws were "a direct violation of the declared fundamental principles of the Constitution," the petitioners asked "for redress of our grievances" (40–44). As Aptheker points out, the congressional debate over whether to accept this petition suggests that this was not the first such case. Representative William Smith, of South Carolina, argued: "The practice of a former time, in a similar case, was that the petition was sealed up and sent back to the petitioners" (qtd. in Aptheker 40). Breaking that seal and getting a just hearing is the story behind a great deal of early African American writing.

Given the existence of the culture so ably represented by the congressional response to this petition, a culture that developed an increasingly articulated white supremacist ideology, and given the facts of institutional racism and institutional or de facto slavery, both before and after the Civil War, it is hardly surprising that the white presence in black texts was much more prominent than was the black presence in white texts throughout the nineteenth century. For black Americans the world of white texts—from the U.S. Constitution and the legal code to minstrel humor and *Uncle Tom's Cabin*, from George Bancroft's *History of the United States* to Thomas Dixon Jr.'s *The Clansman*—was a world one could not afford to ignore or misunderstand. The study and interpretation of white print culture was necessarily a central presence in nineteenth-century African American intellectual and cultural history.[5]

In his famous *Appeal*, arguably one of the founding texts of African

American literary history, David Walker enters into conversation with white American literature quite directly and deliberately to make a point about historical, cultural, and textual interpretation. Throughout the *Appeal*, Walker reads various documents, including the Bible, the Declaration of Independence, articles in the *Columbian Centinel*, a sermon in South Carolina, and writings by Thomas Jefferson and procolonizationists Henry Clay, and Elias B. Caldwell. At one point he says to his black readers, "I hope you will try to find out the meaning of this verse—its widest sense and all its bearings: whether you do or not, remember the whites do" (27). As if to document this interpretive battle, Walker later quotes from speeches by Clay and Caldwell at a meeting on colonization, which texts Walker draws from the *National Intelligencer* of December 24, 1816. Again, he presents quotations interspersed with commentary. Following Clay's reference to Christianity, Walker inserts in brackets, "Here I ask Mr. Clay, what kind of Christianity? Did he mean such as they have among the Americans—distinction, whip, blood and oppression?" (46). At one point, Walker presents a partial quotation, followed by the symbols "&c. * * * * * * *," noting for his readers, "You know what this means" (46). Here Walker teaches his readers a kind of historical literacy, by which statements may be reinterpreted and reapplied. Similarly, he reads Caldwell's speech, drawing attention to the possibilities for misreadings: "The last clause of this speech, which was written in a very artful manner, and which will be taken for the speech of a friend, without close examination and deep penetration, I shall now present" (52). We might well say that all of the *Appeal*, in fact, is designed to penetrate such texts and to provide readers with similar interpretive skills.[6]

The conspicuous intertextuality of Walker's work is central to its purposes, for the racial presence in the *Appeal* can be located not in its author or even in "the coloured citizens of the world" that Walker invokes in his title, but rather in the cultural politics of interpretation. Charles W. Mills captures the dominant background of nineteenth-century African American literary history when he observes that "the requirements of 'objective' cognition, factual and moral, in a racial polity" enforce a tacit "agreement to *misinterpret* the world," an agreement supported by "the assurance that this set of mistaken perceptions will be validated by white epistemic authority, whether religious or secular." Indeed, while the boundaries of African American life in the nineteenth century were defined by this "epistemology of ignorance," this "pattern of localized and global cognitive dysfunctions," a great number of "racial incidents" that regularly marked the lives of African Americans were also the result of the disruption of these dysfunctional patterns, moments when white Americans were forced to confront the limits of or fundamental threats to their conceptual order. Such disruptions produce, Mills observes, "the ironic outcome that whites will in general be unable to understand the world they themselves have made" (18). But as the *Dred Scott* decision made clear, while such disruptions were recognized as having something to do with race, the structures and processes thus disrupted were quickly returned to the "inverted epistemology" of their normal state—that is, an envisioned stability threatened by potentially disruptive forces, often with the blame for the event going to those who pointed out that the occasional eruptions spoke of the underlying state of affairs.

In literary studies, this dynamic is often played out to similar effect. "Nonwhites," Mills observes, "find that race is, paradoxically, both everywhere and nowhere, structuring their lives but not formally recognized in political/moral theory" (76). African American writers, accordingly, are often brought into classrooms and scholarship to contribute the presence of race to a larger set of concerns. Given that they faced the challenge of accounting for life in a white supremacist culture (as one might need to do even in relating a simple romance), their work becomes racially significant regardless of whether they represent the consciousness of race or whether they do not. It is hardly surprising, then, that literary history has often assigned nonwhite writers the task of delimiting the "everywhere" to the usual politics of *somewhere* (and therefore, for many white writers and critics, *nowhere*). Race is what we expect when approaching African American literature, and the absence of significant commentary on race itself becomes a significant statement.[7] Those expectations do not apply to white writers, helping to make it seem especially noteworthy when white writers comment on race—particularly if they comment on the whiteness that defines the worlds they purport to represent—and helping to make it irrelevant or unnoticed when they do not.

What is distinctive about the African American literary tradition is not that all African American writers have written about race but rather that they have all had to negotiate with these dynamics, that the history of those negotiations has been a presence in subsequent literary efforts, and that patterns have emerged visible to those who study that history and even more visible to those who live intimately with those ongoing literary, cultural, and social negotiations. While we can easily understand the force of the considerations that led George Schuyler to denounce what he called "The Negro-Art Hokum" or that led Douglass to advise southern African Americans against westward migration, no one would think it at all unusual if one were to note that any number of white writers have had little or nothing to say about race as a presence in art or life. Even if we were to accept Schuyler's view that "the Aframerican is subject to the same economic and social forces that mold the actions and thoughts of the white Americans" (1222), we could hardly say that the inverse is true—that white Americans historically have been subject to the same economic and social forces that have molded the actions and thoughts of African Americans. It is only to be expected that, when reading African American and white American literary works together, many critics will be tempted to go with Schuyler's emphasis in setting up the equation for determining commonality and inclusion. In truth, a great deal of nineteenth-century white American literature seems woefully inadequate when it comes to representing, let alone explaining, the world as seen through the lens of African American experience and art. African American writing has been shaped, in large part, by the challenges of representing that world, by the necessity of doing so, and by the fact that such representations would need to operate in a world governed, in literature as elsewhere, by the "agreement to *mis*interpret the world."

Frederick Douglass's career is especially instructive in this regard, for not only was Douglass's work directed to the networks of affiliation that defined his public identity, but even his approach to his work was shaped by the racial frameworks and the dispersed but affiliated priorities of a community conditioned by relations of power. When Douglass wrote about slavery, his readers knew that he was not speaking metaphorically, and that the complex historical and political realities of the U.S. system of slavery were his primary subject; when he wrote about race, *he* knew that his readers would associate him with African Americans, and beyond with Africans and the African diaspora generally. One would need to willfully misread Douglass to read him apart from the enslaved millions, and the millions of stories untold, or from the question of basic recognition and civil rights for nominally free African Americans, or from the question of a vision of citizenship inclusive of African Americans. Indeed, not just the views expressed in his writings but the occasions and form of his writing were affected by his cultural position. Douglass never had the luxury of approaching writing as something separate from his activist labors or from his position as a public representative of an oppressed community. A list of his major writings would certainly include his autobiographical narratives, "The Heroic Slave," and a few of his best-known speeches—but ultimately what defined Douglass as a writer was the need to address specific concerns as they arose; the need to represent a cause that was variously ignored, misrepresented, or rejected; and the need to continually engage in the shifting cultural politics of a white supremacist nation. Douglass's career and achievements as a writer, in other words, are best represented by his indefatigable labor in producing newspaper articles, his ability to meet virtually every public occasion with the right words, the necessity of his attendance and the inevitability of his representative role on such occasions, and the pervasive presence of racial science and racist laws that not only defined the occasion for his words but also connected him to communities unrepresented by any image of a generalized American.

This is not to say that Douglass can be understood only within an African American context, but to emphasize that he approached his work from an African American perspective that must be accounted for but that is easy to overlook, simplify, or otherwise misrepresent. If we are to account for the complexities of race, and if we are to avoid educating Douglass out of his sympathies, then it is important to think about what role he is asked to play or is able to play in any comparative analysis. When paired with a white writer, is Douglass asked to serve as a representative man, and is it even possible for him to serve in that role? It seems that the choice is to recognize the significance of Douglass's status as an *African American* writer, in which case his representative status is both unavoidable and problematic, or to deny the significance of his racial status, and the work conditioned by that status, so as to focus on other concerns. In either case, such a pairing would make it very difficult for Frederick Douglass to be an African American writer, for what is African American about both Douglass and his writing is the complex of contingencies that defined his life and conditioned his sense of purpose. To understand him as a representative African American writer of his time would require that we consider a wide range of other African American writers, as well as the largely unrecovered history of African American communities from which writers emerged and to which they responded. This would enable us to determine how and why we might compare Douglass's work with that of any number of white writers. But to the extent that such a comparative approach restricts or even defines that wider range of concerns, such work runs the risk of leaving us with a Douglass whose representative role (and its limits) cannot be adequately determined, and perhaps even a Douglass largely removed from the field of relations that matters most.

## Multiplied Texts and Invested Readers

When we consider that field of relations, and the literature that emerged from that field, we find ourselves in a literary landscape that cannot be encompassed by any single author or text. In an essay about twentieth-century African American women writers, Karla F. C. Holloway addresses the dynamics of what she identifies as "a 'multiplied' text." "Recursive structures," Holloway explains, "accomplish a blend between figurative processes that are reflective (like a mirror) and symbolic processes whose depth and resonance make them reflexive. This combination results in texts that are at once emblematic of the culture they describe as well as interpretive of this culture." Included in the works she examines are such dynamic features as "a certain 'posturing' of the textual language" that "places the narrative language at a formative threshold," "a translucent flux," and "a shifting, sometimes nebulous text." Viewed individually, these narrative and stylistic features might be said to represent any number of literary texts, but Holloway suggests that a historical study of such features highlights the gathering patterns of a recognizable tradition. Contemporary literature by African American women "displays the gathered effects of these literary structures to the extent that, when we can identify and recognize them, we are also able to specify their relationship to thematic and stylistic emphases of the traditions illustrated in these works" (388). The specificity of the content in these novels (their devotion to and ability to account for the experience of black girls and women), joined with the gravitational pull that centers black women's reading and writing practices, leads to a tradition that might share features with other traditions (for included in that gravitational pull are a wide range of literary conventions). But that tradition finds its purpose when writers address the specific challenges of accounting for the lives of those who are forced to negotiate intimately with the anything-but-straightforward forces that define the shifting significance of both race and gender.

My point is that nineteenth-century African American literature is collectively a multiplied text, and that placing authors in conversation is not the same thing as studying "the paradox that 'American' literature is both a single tradition of many parts *and* a series of winding, sometimes parallel traditions that have perforce been built in good part from their inherent conflicts" (Sundquist 18). To place *traditions* into conversation is to enter into the interpretive battles that have pervaded African American literary history, which involves following fractal patterns of reference and significance. In a special issue of *Legacy* on "racial identity, indeterminacy, and identification in the nineteenth century," Frances Smith Foster emphasizes that the racial past cannot be limited to questions of embodiment or even the political priorities of authorship:

> Elements of style and structure, genre and tone, tropes, metaphors, repetition, details, and allusions challenge those who would compare or interpret gestures, meanings, or intentions among, between, or within texts. For example, is the "Freedom" in *Freedom's Journal*, published between 1827 and 1829 by African Americans as an African American paper, the same "Freedom" as in the *Herald of Freedom*, a mid-nineteenth-century publication edited by and intended for Euro-Americans? Are "marble brows," "raven hair," or "dark-complected" racial signifiers in a story by Frances E. W. Harper published in 1859 in the *Anglo-African*, a periodical published by African Americans and for African Americans? How do we compare such descriptions with the same or similar ones in an 1896 issue of the *American Jewess*? When the Rev. John H. Acornley writes *The Colored Lady Evangelist, Being the Life, Labors and Experiences of Mrs. Harriet A. Baker* in 1892, is his use of "Mrs." the same as that of Jarena Lee in her 1849 memoir, *Religious Experience and Journal of Mrs. Jarena Lee*? ("Hurry Up, Please" 326)

To some extent, Foster's point here aligns with Stephen Henderson's concept of cultural saturation and of the literary mascon—that is, those words and rhetorical tropes that will have special meaning, and particular weight and pull, for certain readers over others, depending on different readers' various cultural experiences.[8] But Foster underscores the sheer complexity of multiple contexts, shifting intonations, and different forums of and for rhetorical and literary performances. "When . . . we explore ways of thinking comparatively about such a complicated and continually changing idea as racial politics," she warns, "we find ourselves in the midst of thorny possibilities and implications. We must not try only to identify the appropriate direction or articulation of our question, but we must also re-search, re-view, and re-discover data, and we must decide what and how to interpolate what we and others find. In other words, when we jump—or are pushed—into the briar patch, things get very sticky indeed" (327). Stickier still is the assumption that a comparative analysis of various authors and texts can take place outside of or above the briar patch.

Foster's reflections on the challenges of comparative readings across racial, ethnic, gender, or class lines highlights the challenges of reading almost any text produced by an African American in the nineteenth century, for the principal conversations between white and black histories, literary and otherwise, are those inscribed in African American texts. In prefaces and introductions, in the often commanding presence of an amanuensis, in reprinted letters and other documents, in reprinted poems and other literary allusions, in references to legal codes and theological positions, and in perspectives informed by everything from social class to political activism, white Europeans and Americans are a pressing and often defining presence in nineteenth-century African American print culture. Indeed, when reading a great deal of nineteenth-century African American literature (and considering its subsequent and delayed appearance in mainstream American literary scholarship), one might well be tempted to think of a point that Douglass made in his 1865 lecture at the inauguration of the Douglass Institute in Baltimore—namely, that "when prejudice cannot deny the black man's ability, it denies his race, and claims him as a white man. It affirms that if he is not exactly white, he ought to be. If not what he ought to be in this particular, he owes whatever intelligence he possesses to the white race by contract or association" ("Lecture" 179). Such contracts and associations are complexly embedded in a great number of nineteenth-century African American texts, and the necessity of (re)negotiating such contracts and associations constitutes one of the most significant features of the craft of this tradition. As Beth A. McCoy observes, "The American spatial imaginary . . . still understands white domination almost solely as a series of public, bodily, and, indeed, *textualized* confrontations between white and black. Yet careful attention to texts by and about African Americans challenges this understanding and reveals the hidden, indirect, and *paratextualized* forces impelling and complicating those confrontations" (156–57). "Even as African Americans diagnosed paratextual space as one way through which white supremacy could be channeled," McCoy argues, "they also saw that same space as offering possibilities for resistance" (159).

Attention to such dynamic encounters would enable us to identify the most compelling and relevant sites of conversations between white and black writers. But such readings would also argue against merely identifying the accessible black presence behind the textual dynamics. We would have to consider the text itself, the history with which the text is associated, and the history of the text's reception and application over time—the conversations that take place not only when readers compare different texts but also when they read what they take to be a singular text. Commenting on the interaction between text and reader, John Reilly has observed that "communication by a literary text occurs as a transaction with an audience that, so to speak, completes the text by assimilating its signs and patterns through the grid of shared linguistic skills and cultural fields; thus, literature by its very nature coexists with other instances of social life as part of the institution of language within broader social life" (90–91). The challenge, of course, is that African American writers have often had to contend with the *appearance* or *assumption* of "shared linguistic skills and cultural fields"—as was the case when black abolitionists used the discourse of Christianity to battle against slaveholding Christians in the South and white supremacist Christians nationally.[9] Reilly adds: "It follows, of course, that history, so far as its interpretation and communication are concerned, also originates in language and offers its descriptive and documentary texts to reception by an audience in the same way that literature does" (91). Looking back on American intellectual and cultural history, we can hardly be encouraged by the prospect of nineteenth-century white readers completing black texts "by assimilating its signs and patterns through the grid of shared linguistic skills and cultural fields."

Consider, for example, a major but surprisingly understudied text, the last edition of the *Narrative of Sojourner Truth* (1884)—like William Wells Brown's *Clotel*, a work that includes a great number of texts, and, like various other nineteenth-century African American texts, one that appeared in different manifestations over time. The *Narrative*, I suggest, is what John Bryant has termed a "fluid text"—that is, "any literary work that exists in more than one version" (1). Bryant's definition concerns the revision and adaptation of single literary works—the varying forms of works such as *Moby-Dick* or *Leaves of Grass*, or the numerous reappearances of texts, artifacts, and performances under the name of *Uncle Tom's Cabin*. "A fluid-text historicism," Bryant explains, "focuses on the interpenetration of private and public pasts in order to make the evidence of literary versions, revision, and adaptation accessible to readers for critical and cultural analysis." The "subject matter" of this approach to literary history "is not texts per se but *texts that can be shown to have changed*; and the analytical focus is on the construction and meaning of the forces of change"

(61). Bryant's approach would be useful in exploring nineteenth-century African American literary history, that tradition so singularly focused on "the construction and meaning of the forces of change," and it is certainly a useful guide to the fluidity in and of the *Narrative of Sojourner Truth*. The fluidity of this *Narrative* is a function of *many* texts—including Olive Gilbert's 1850 narrative, Frances Titus's subsequent editorial work and commentary, reprinted publications by Harriet Beecher Stowe and Frances Dana Gage, and letters, newspaper articles, and the like—that collect to form the turbulent current of the text through which we approach that cultural icon, Sojourner Truth, as if to uncover the African American presence beneath the surface of white representation and appropriation.[10] Indeed, we could say that what is most characteristically *African American* about this text produced by white writers is the fact that it exists within and perpetually replicates the multiple and unstable ambiguities of black and white American identity. In the context of this significantly fluid text that represents a life of almost constant movement and itinerant preaching, what is most African American (or not) about the *Narrative* is neither its authorship nor its subject but, rather, the act of reading.

The *Narrative*'s complex bricolage of (auto)biographical narratives, sketches, letters, reviews, and even autographs, none of it authored directly by Truth herself, makes it a challenging but usefully revealing presence in African American literary history. It is a challenge even to identify the many textual layers, for involved in the multiplicity of genres are multiple authors of multiple texts shaped by multiple contexts—including sketches of Truth written for various newspapers serving different geographical, social, and ideological communities (from abolitionist papers to *Frank Leslie's Illustrated Paper*). We encounter different editorial styles, enter into historical situations that called for a certain mode of discourse, and move uneasily from author to author, text to text, state to state, and from one historical situation to another. The texts speak, both overtly and implicitly, of the political and racial tensions of their time. They speak more intricately still when placed together. Truth's story, we might say, is not some imagined core story, both indicated and obscured by these competing texts and narrative frameworks; rather, it is a cluster of competing and often conflicting representations, the narrative of both a private and a public figure always contending with the aims, means, and results of her publicity.

But this fractured portrait is, in many ways, the point of the life it represents, a life shaped by the unstable but potent contingencies of race. Robert F. Reid-Pharr has written of the importance of exploring "the ideological calculus by which our understanding of the black body is wedded to our understanding of black literature and literacy," noting that "it is taken almost without question that Black American literature is that which demonstrates the impress of the black hand, the black body" (4). Throughout the *Narrative of Sojourner Truth*, this ideological calculus is both displayed and disrupted, and we are reminded again and again that the personification of the cultural construct of race is a distortion perpetuated in the service of a white supremacist culture. Readers encounter both the attempt to fashion an ideological order and its breakdown, because that order is exposed in the act of performing its own racial fictions. Race in the *Narrative* is not something embodied in Truth herself but something constructed economically, politically, legally, and theologically—imagined by a complex congregation of social actors. To redirect Reid-Pharr's comment, one might say that in this narrative African American literature is demonstrated by the impress of many hands that themselves demonstrate the force of multiple cultural contexts. What is black about Sojourner Truth is a function of her situation within these raced contingencies and of her ongoing negotiation of the ideological currents that defined the course of her life.

In its conspicuous juxtaposing of these multiple contingencies, the *Narrative of Sojourner Truth* functions as a fluid text, and its fluidities draw readers into the complex currents of U.S. racial history and culture. While the *Narrative* itself can be studied as a single text that has appeared in different versions, has been revised, and has been the subject of numerous adaptations, it is also a constellation of texts that together constitute a study of "the construction of meaning and the forces of change" (Bryant 61). All of the texts brought together in the *Narrative* are transformed by virtue of having been placed in relation to one another, and the *Narrative* as a whole is transformed by readers engaged, consciously or not, in "a fluid-text historicism." The *Narrative* draws readers into what Bryant calls "an ontology of process" (61), and it is in the negotiation of that process that the text discovers its status either as a work of African American literature (with the definitive characteristic of this tradition focused on practices of reading rather than of writing) or as a site for Hartman's concept of "performing blackness" (57). The *Narrative*, as Sojourner Truth's legend over time has emphasized, operates as a site in which white readers can reimagine or reconfirm their status as white while all readers are invited to celebrate an isolated and exoticized blackness. The *Narrative*, in short, is less about Truth than about the many writers we encounter in this text, and it is less about those writers than about the readers who determine the order of this fluid representation of a complex culture.

This is what makes the *Narrative* at least potentially a work of African American literature, for that which defines *African American* is a cultural order that denies the realities of American history. The product of that cultural order, the subject of that denial—the woman named Isabella—realized herself as a symbolic entity, renamed herself Sojourner Truth, and lived a life engaged in the complex contingencies of social identity. As I noted in the introduction, Toni Morrison has spoken of her desire to "develop a way of writing that was irrevocably black." In many ways, the *Narrative of Sojourner Truth* is an altogether too fitting example of a black text, though not of the kind that Morrison describes. The *Narrative* performs blackness, in Hartman's terms, in the complex ways that it is situated in culture, in its partial and mixed awareness and acknowledgment of its status as a particular kind of cultural product, and in its interpretive instability. The blackness of this text is activated when someone reads it—that is, reads the complicated blackness of American culture: variously defined, endlessly appropriated, potentially powerful, and easily *mis*read. Just as Sojourner Truth exposed the moral inconsistencies and uncertainties of those she encountered, so this text exposes its readers, revealing our notions of what literature is and should be—and, specifically, what counts as African American literature and what that definition demands of readers. As the portions of the *Narrative* written by Gilbert, Titus, Stowe, Gage, and others work to place Truth within the white national narrative of progress (a point to which I will return in Chapter 5), readers are faced with the challenge of negotiating contending histories, literary and otherwise. The *Narrative of Sojourner Truth* can provide readers with a thoroughly domesticated Truth or it can provide an entry into an understanding of African American literature that emphasizes the systemic dynamics of racial ideology—those contingencies of U.S. cultural life that make the designation "African American" historically, ideologically, and morally significant. Thus we can follow the *Narrative*'s fluidities to a revised understanding of literary history, or we can channel them to serve the needs of a tradition that cannot afford to acknowledge its own ideological course. If we are not facing some version of these choices, then we are not placing this text in conversation with other texts of its time, and by default, our choice about what to do with this text becomes all too clear.

Such choices emphasize the challenging presence of race in staged conversations between black and white writers—race as a systemic principle
and as a dynamic, chaotic social process. In talking about black and white
writers, in other words, or about black and white communities, I do not
wish to suggest that individuals should be understood by way of a simple
black/white racial binary, or that there were homogeneous black and
white communities to which any individual should be relegated. Rather,
I mean to recognize that in the United States individuals live and work in
a white supremacist culture, that their lives and writing are conditioned
by that culture, and that they necessarily negotiate differently with the
intricate dynamics of systemic racism. The application of this recognition is a challenging concern, as many have acknowledged. It would be
difficult, at best, to group nineteenth-century African Americans into a
stable ideological field, for their disagreements were many, their cultural,
regional, and economic positions diverse, and their political affiliations as
fragile as those of any constituent body. Moreover, one can find considerable alliances between white and black thought and discourse throughout
the nineteenth century. Indeed, nineteenth-century African American
writing can reveal a nationalistic idealization of the United States every
bit as sweeping as that found in the work of white writers, though often
with a significant difference.

Consider, for example, an interracial conversation between white historian George Bancroft, African American educator and social reformer
William Watkins, and Watkins's son, William J. Watkins. Bancroft once
referred to the United States as an "empire of mind,"[11] a phrase that the
elder Watkins used in an 1834 speech praising the "blessings of civilization and the Gospel" associated with European and American culture. But
Watkins singled out the "art of printing" as "the grand medium through
which every species of useful knowledge is poured in one incessant flood
upon the vast 'empire of mind' in this lower world" (161). For Watkins,
the glorious civilization waiting to rise from that flood, while distinctly
American, required some interpretation:

> Yes, sir, the wings of the press are wafting to all lands the glorious
> tidings, the ennobling, the heaven-born truths, that "God hath made
> of *one* blood all nations for to dwell on *all* the face of the earth"; that
> man, *immortal* man, who bears the image of his Maker—who ranks
> but a little lower than the angels, may not be treated, as a brute,
> with impunity; "that *all* men are created *equal*, and endowed by

their Creator with certain *inalienable* rights; that among these are life, *liberty* and the pursuit of happiness." (161, Watkins's emphasis).

Some years later, the younger Watkins, responding to Bancroft's 1854 oration "The Necessity, the Reality, and the Promise of the Progress of the Human Race," argued that "our theory is well enough; but our practice is as far removed from it as the east is from the west." Noting Bancroft's assertion that "our country is bound to allure the world to Liberty by the beauty of its example," Watkins wondered: "Where has Mr. Bancroft been living that with all his wisdom and erudition he has not found out that the great object of this Government, *as developed in its policy*, is the extension, the consolidation, and the perpetuity of a system of robbery, of plunder, and oppression, aptly characterized the vilest that ever saw the sun" (Ripley 4:257). Race, then, is not simply what we encounter when we initially identify an author's cultural affiliations or ancestry, nor is race (by any stretch of the imagination) limited to those beyond the pale of whiteness. Rather, race has to do with the social, occupational, physical, and literary spaces writers inhabited and the ways in which they found themselves worlds apart even when standing next to one another.

## White Banners and the Current of Public Opinion

The tensions in and around such spaces are especially evident in the pages of slave narratives written by a white amanuensis.[12] Consider again the two narratives of Henry Box Brown's experience: the one by white abolitionist Charles Stearns, *Narrative of Henry Box Brown, Who Escaped from Slavery Enclosed in a Box 3 Feet Long and 2 Wide: Written from a Statement of Facts Made by Himself, with Remarks upon the Remedy for Slavery* (1849), and the later *Narrative of the Life of Henry Box Brown, Written by Himself* (1851). Together, the two narratives are less about the facts of Brown's life than about the terms by which Brown might tell his story or otherwise work toward self-definition and independence. The two narratives do not merely reflect a racial order that placed Brown in slavery and then in the tenuous position of a fugitive slave in antislavery culture. Rather, Brown's story (and the story of the means by which he came to tell his story) operates within the cultural dynamics by which the concept of race was and is constantly reconstituted and maintained. Race is not simply what marks the difference between slaveholder and slave, or between Charles Stearns and Henry Box Brown; race is what takes place in their situated and highly mediated negotiations toward a narrative that must always fall short of

articulating Brown's understanding of his life. Moreover, the independence Brown sought was not just a matter of producing a narrative "written by himself," for the authorship of the later narrative is complicated.
Although Richard Newman suggests that preparing the 1851 version was
a matter of editing "Stearns' overblown rhetoric [in the 1849 version] out
of the narrative" (xii), Stearns's narration in fact remains a guiding presence in the 1851 *Narrative*. And although the 1851 text includes in its title
the familiar phrase "written by himself," Brown probably did not write it
himself.[13] The 1851 *Narrative*, then, extends beyond the edited palimpsest to a more complex narrative and cultural performance—indeed, a
multivocal performance involving a range of those invested in antislavery
discourse.[14]

Although many antislavery activists joined word and deed, rhetoric and
practice, at considerable personal sacrifice, still the limitations of white
benevolent rhetoric was a constant theme in black abolitionist writing. In
a call for the establishment of a national African American press in 1847,
for instance, a committee of black leaders argued that "the amount of the
hatred against us has been conventional antipathy; and of the favorable
feeling has been human sympathy. Our friends sorrow with us, because
they say we are unfortunate! We must batter down those antipathies,
we must command something manlier than sympathies" (*Proceedings of
the National Convention . . . , 1847* 19–20). Minister and activist Samuel
Ringgold Ward pressed the point in his 1855 autobiography:

> Those who have done us injury think it a virtue to express sympa-
> thy with us—a sort of arms'-length, cold-blooded sympathy; while
> neither of those would, on any account, consent to do towards us
> the commonest justice. What the Negro needs is, what belongs to
> him—what has been ruthlessly torn from him—and what is, by
> consent of a despotic democracy and a Christless religion, with-
> holden from him, guiltily, perseveringly. When he shall have that
> restored, he can acquire *pity* enough, and all the sympathy he needs,
> cheap wares as they are; but to ask for them instead of his rights was
> never my calling. (86–87)

In 1860 Frederick Douglass similarly complained: "The effect of all antislavery effort thus far is this: It has filled the whole North with a sentiment opposed to slavery. Sentimental Abolitionism is abundant. It may
well be met with in the pulpit, sometimes in the religious newspapers,
and more frequently still we meet it in the meetings of the Republican

party; yet among them all there is neither will nor purpose to abolish slavery" ("Abolition Movement" 522). While all of these writers valued both the public forum and the political potential facilitated by the developing organization of antislavery culture from the 1830s to the Civil War, they also recognized the strict limitations of this culture.

When Henry Box Brown entered the public stage in 1849, and as he worked with others to produce his 1851 autobiographical narrative, he faced both the dubious promise and the complex limitations of sentimental abolitionism. As Susan M. Ryan observes of "the competing rhetorics of benevolence that circulated among mid-nineteenth-century Americans . . . [,] not only did these conversations draw on and, in turn, shape the era's social crises, but they also overlapped with and helped to construct its ideologies of race and nation" (1). Recent scholarship has suggested that white sentimental possession, self-affirming benevolence, and voyeuristic engagements were central not just to the reception of slave narratives but also to the fundamental argument for their necessity.[15] In one of his most well-known speeches, presented in Rochester, New York, on July 5, 1852, Frederick Douglass asserted: "I submit, where all is plain there is nothing to be argued"—and then he emphasized his point: "Must I undertake to prove that the slave is a man?" "Would you have me argue that man is entitled to liberty?" "Must I argue that a system thus marked with blood, and stained with pollution, is *wrong*?" ("What, to the Slave" 256–57). The logic of the slave narrative, as it functioned in antislavery culture, was based on the premise that, yes, such arguments were necessary. To a significant extent, the theatrical imagination pervading antislavery culture virtually required the regular restaging of the spectacle of slavery in the relative safety of the North. Clergyman Henry Ward Beecher, for example, staged a female slave auction at his church, as did, in effect, black abolitionist William Wells Brown both on the lecture circuit and in the pages of his fictional narrative *Clotel; or, The President's Daughter* (1853).[16] Ultimately, such stagings served the needs of a larger cultural theater, one in which the drama of white Christian authority was the primary concern. While authors of slave narratives (most prominently, Douglass) worked not only to invite but also to avoid, undermine, or otherwise deflect the dynamics of imagined white empathy, the reader's imaginative engagement and ethical investment in slavery's scenes of horror were always a formidable presence in the relation between narrator and reader.[17]

Inevitably, then, the imperatives of white Christian antislavery culture framed the box in which Brown was contained in the first published account of his escape, the 1849 *Narrative* written by Charles Stearns. Stearns was, as Jeffrey Ruggles has observed, an "unusual man," "very individual" in both his beliefs and his "radical" commitment to social reform (59, 60). His Christianity "drew on the ecstatic meetings of the [revival] tents and was molded by his pacifism and abolitionism. He was probably influenced as well by the writings of his uncle George Ripley and the other Transcendentalists who emerged in the 1830s" (60). In his essay "Cure for the Evil of Slavery," which Stearns included in the 1849 text, he advocates "the immediate formation of *a new government at the North*" while condemning the corruption of Christianity in the United States (Stearns, *Narrative* 67). "Our God," Stearns declares, "is emphatically Slavery. To him we address our early matins, and in his ear are uttered our evening orisons. More devoutly do we render homage to our god, Slavery, than the most pious of us adore the God of heaven, which proves that we are a very religious people, worshipping, not crocodiles, leeks and onions, snakes, and images of wood and stone, but a god, whose service is infinitely more disgusting than that of any heathen idol, but one who *pays* us well, for our obeisance, as we imagine" (81–82). It is not surprising that, before his partnership with Brown, Stearns had been publicly critical of more moderate approaches to Christianity that were not sternly opposed to slavery, war, and alcohol; he had suggested that "there is so much bad" in the Bible that "in its present form, I doubt its utility to the world" (qtd. in Ruggles 61). Having established himself as a printer in Boston by 1847, and having published various antislavery and political tracts, Stearns was prepared to be of great service to Brown. The narrative that they produced together during the summer of 1849 appeared in September with "Brown & Stearns" listed as the publishers.[18]

As others have indicated, Stearns's religious and political views, along with his elaborate rhetoric, overwhelm the 1849 version of Brown's story. In the preface, Stearns presents Brown as one who experienced "a *portable prison*, shut out from the light of heaven, and nearly deprived of its balmy air" (Stearns, *Narrative* v). Readers might well feel that Stearns's extravagant prose has made the narrative itself a kind of portable prison of a resolute moral position that presses against the discourse available for its expression. Even in his most conventional moments, Stearns inflates antislavery rhetoric both conspicuously and insistently, as if by pure excess sentiment might overwhelm the implicit terms of its usual restraint. In the preface, readers are addressed directly and assigned a role: "O reader, as you peruse this heart-rending tale, let the tear of sympathy roll freely from your eyes, and let the deep fountains of human feeling, which God has implanted in the breast of every son and daughter of Adam, burst forth from their enclosure, until a stream shall flow therefrom on to the surrounding world, of so invigorating and purifying a nature, as to arouse from the 'death of the sin' of slavery, and cleanse from the pollutions thereof, all with whom you may be connected" (Stearns, *Narrative* v). Firmly convinced of the rightness of his position, Stearns draws from the imagined wells of what he believes to be a pure Christianity to flood the Christianity contaminated by slavery. All that is needed to initiate the process is a tear inspired by Brown's story. But the story itself stands in danger of being lost in the flood, and Brown himself has moved from one portable prison to another as he is drawn along the currents of Stearns's elaborate narrative performance.

I do not mean to imply that Brown did not enter into his partnership with Stearns as a free agent, or that Brown was dissatisfied with this arrangement, but rather to indicate the ways in which Brown was situated as he entered the public stage of antislavery activity, and to suggest that he would be challenged to direct his experience to something more than an overflowing response of white antislavery sympathy. For all of Stearns's resistance to conventional Christianity and politics, in the pages of the 1849 *Narrative* Brown becomes a rather familiar figure—or, rather, a familiar occasion for familiar forms of rhetorical and racial performance. Consider, for example, the opening statement of the narrative proper, given in the first person as if to represent Brown's own voice:

> I am not about to harrow the feelings of my readers by a terrific representation of the untold horrors of that fearful system of oppression, which for thirty-three long years entwined its snaky folds about my soul, as the serpent of South America coils itself around the form of its unfortunate victim. It is not my purpose to descend deeply into the dark and noisome caverns of the hell of slavery, and drag from their frightful abode those lost spirits who haunt the souls of the poor slaves, daily and nightly with their frightful presence, and with the fearful sound of their terrific instruments of torture; for other pens far abler than mine have effectually performed that portion of the labor of an exposer of the enormities of slavery. Slavery, like the shield discovered by the knights of olden time, has two diverse sides to it; the one, on which is fearfully written in letters of

blood, the character of the mass who carry on that dreadful system of unhallowed bondage; the other, touched with the pencil of a gentler delineation, and telling the looker on, a tale of comparative freedom, from the terrible deprivations so vividly portrayed on its opposite side. (Stearns, *Narrative* 11)

The elaborate rhetoric here leads to a promise to relate, "if possible, the beautiful side of the picture of slavery" (11–12)—that is, Brown's "comparative enjoyment" of a less severe form of slavery. But obviously this passage has less to do with slavery than with its representation, the fraught and heavily laden rhetorical performance that suggests everywhere Stearns's signifying expertise, traveling freely through time from the suggested Christian significance of Brown's age when he escaped to the two-sided shield of "the knights" of an "olden time" that Brown was unlikely to draw from in his own narrative of his life.

Stearns's insistent moral imagination, as he effectually performs Brown's role in this narrative, places Brown in the "noisome caverns" of Stearns's invention and transforms him into the knights' shield—an embodied story written in blood and an imminent story awaiting the skilled "pencil of a gentler delineation." Stearns's approach to Brown's life, as indicated by this initial framework, provides an unsettling illustration of what Hartman has identified as "the uses made of the black body [which] established continuities between minstrelsy and melodrama that surpassed their generic differences" (Stearns, *Narrative* 26). Stearns's is a particularly melodramatic version of blackface abolitionism—an extravagant performance of an imagined consciousness for which the enslaved subject serves primarily as the violated embodiment and interpolated voice. The excess of significance pressed through the white narrator's elaborate rhetoric both associates itself with and distances itself from the narrative's putatively speaking subject, delivering to the reader an account, beyond all else, of epic fascination. For Stearns, the antislavery cause involved an epic battle of sensibilities, an attempt to win hearts swayed by the seductions of a wayward culture. "If man is blinded to the appreciation of the good, by a mass of selfish sensibilities," Stearns asks in his opening remarks, "may he not be induced to surrender his will to the influence of truth, by *benevolent* feelings being caused to spring forth in his heart?" (vi). But this is a sympathy that requires elaborate staging, calling on associations of an imagined "olden time" that reconfigure the contingencies of Brown's experience in order to stage Stearns's epic moral battle: "That this may be the case with all whose eyes gaze upon the picture here drawn of misery, and of endurance, worthy of a Spartan, and such as a hero of olden times might be proud of, and transmit to posterity, along with the armorial emblazonry of his ancestors, is the ardent desire of all connected with the publication of this work" (vi). The more Stearns tries rhetorically to break an opening into the fabric of the social order so as to place the events of Brown's experience within sacred history, the more he seems drawn to the mythology of a secular analogue to that sacred realm, the legendary foundations of the developing Anglo-Saxon historical consciousness.[19]

But while it is relatively easy to isolate Stearns's presence in the 1849 narrative, the same cannot be said of the writer or writers of the "First English Edition," the *Narrative of the Life of Henry Box Brown, Written by Himself*. This version of Brown's narrative was published in Manchester in 1851, but Ruggles argues persuasively that "there is every reason to conclude that the main text . . . was actually produced in Massachusetts in the spring of 1850." But whether written in England or in the United States, "the writer of the 1851 *Narrative* remains unidentified" (132). To be sure, traces of Stearns's rhetoric remain—meaningful words, phrases, and sentences are retained and rearranged throughout the text, though usually displayed in less elaborate settings. Other voices are also present. Following a preface attributed to Brown, for instance, there is an introduction by the Reverend Thomas Gardiner Lee of Salford, England, which in addition to standard British antislavery rhetoric ("the roar of the British Lion" [Brown, *Narrative* 44]), includes testimonials from a number of individuals—among them, antislavery activists James Miller McKim and Samuel J. May, along with various individuals who had seen Brown's panorama. Quoted lines from poetry, presented in the original narrative, reappear in 1851, though sometimes augmented (such as the lines from Barnard Barton's "A Child's Dream" in chapter 1 [52]), as well as new verses—including the lines gathered from James Marrick's *The Psalms* and from Isaac Watts's "Hymn 99" that close chapter 2 (59). Elder Jacob Knapp, a white Baptist evangelist from New York State, not mentioned in 1849, makes an important appearance in 1851, along with the text (from Matthew 23:37) for a sermon he delivered in Richmond (70–71). There, too, is the less encouraging Reverend Robert Ryland, of Virginia, to whom "the coloured people had to pay . . . a salary of 700 dollars per annum, although they neither chose him nor had the least control over him" (71). Church hymns, absent in 1849, are quoted in 1851.

The 1851 version, in short, directs the reader to various people, texts, and events not mentioned in 1849 and in this way contextualizes Brown's life more complexly; it both documents and raises questions about the narrative agency at the center of these contextualizing presences. It is possible that a more restrained Stearns served as the primary writer for the 1851 version, for, as previously noted, the "First English Edition" borrows from the rhetoric of the original narrative—but here Brown finds himself in a somewhat less dramatic setting. Gone from Brown's introductory comments are the knights of old with their two-sided shields. Instead, Brown notes more simply: "The tale of my own sufferings is not one of great interest to those who delight to read of hair-breadth adventures, of tragic occurrences, and scenes of blood—my life, even in slavery, has been in many respects comparatively comfortable" (42).[20]

But Brown still speaks occasionally in Stearns's register, usually to comment on the incoherence of the social order as a context for understanding individual character. In the 1849 version, Stearns has Brown address "those inner pangs which rend the heart of fond affection," the effects of being separated from family that extend "far beyond, in terrible suffering, all outward cruelties of the foul system." Commenting on a separation "more dreadful to all of us than a large number of lashes, inflicted on us daily," the passage focuses on the cruelty of comparatively kind slaveholders: "Tell me not of kind masters under slavery's hateful rule! There is no such thing as a person of that description" (Stearns, *Narrative* 13). In his 1851 preface, Brown addresses the same concerns—the inherent evil of slavery, apart from its abuses, as well as the psychological, emotional, and spiritual suffering of enslaved people (thus emphasizing their humanity and relating their experiences to those of white readers). But the 1851 version, while still dramatic, is selective in echoing this passage: "The whip, the cowskin, the gallows, the stocks, the paddle, the prison, the perversion of the stomach—although bloody and barbarous in their nature—have no comparison with those internal pangs which are felt by the soul when the hand of the merciless tyrant plucks from one's bosom the object of one's ripened affections, and the darlings who in requiring parental care, confer the sweet sensations of parental bliss" (Brown, *Narrative* 42). Here, though surrounded by an array of devices of torture (a standard feature in antislavery writing), Brown turns his attention less to the violating actor than to the disrupted agency of those acted upon, and thus he underscores not just the pain of family separations but also the joys of parental responsibility. He refers to both emotional and spiritual pain, the pain of being kept from one's responsibilities—a point often lost in considerations of Brown's life and narratives.

As Brown asserts the importance of individual responsibility against all odds, so he emphasizes as well his distrust of reliance on any secular order to promote moral integrity. Both narratives, for example, end with a discussion of the legal system necessary for the maintenance of slavery, but with a significant difference. As I have mentioned, the 1849 version concludes with the essay "Cure for the Evil of Slavery," in which Stearns argues against the authority of the nation's "cannibal laws" and calls for "the immediate formation of *a new government at the North*" (Stearns, *Narrative* 71, 67). In the essay, Stearns speaks in his own voice, but in the narrative, he speaks for Brown, and so Stearns uses his role as Brown to introduce his own essay, thus indicating the dynamics that define his role-playing throughout the narrative. "I do not understand much about laws, to be sure," Stearns has Brown say, "as the law of my master is the one I have been subject to all my life, but some how, it looks a little singular to me, that wise people should be obliged to break their own laws, or else do a very wicked act" (65). Noting the need for one prepared to address the subject adequately, Stearns's Brown then presents Stearns: "I now wish to introduce to your hearing a friend of mine, who will tell you more about these things than I can, until I have had more time to examine this curious subject" (65–66). By 1851 Brown apparently had found time to examine the subject—but instead of a disquisition on the grounds for overthrowing the government, Brown merely reprints antislavery commentary on and examples from the laws of the South, and he enters the subject casually. "A few specimens of the laws of a slave-holding people," he states, "may not be out of place here" (Brown, *Narrative* 93). Brown's placement of this discussion at the end of the narrative emphasizes its seriousness, but his casual introduction of the subject also underscores his belief that a legal analysis is insufficient to address the situation of the enslaved. In part, Brown suggests, law simply does not consider the whole of human life—that is, "the various circumstances, which, independent of the law, in civilised and free countries, constitute the principle sources of happiness and misery." But a discussion of law is insufficient as well because unchecked power has rendered the law a very limited instrument of social organization and control. "In the slave-holding states of America," he states, "there is a strong current of public opinion which the law is altogether incompetent to control." The problem, Brown suggests, is that the law has been so warped by the needs of the system of slavery as to become an incoherent text. "In many cases there are ideas of criminality, which are not by statute law attached to the commission of certain acts, but which are frequently found to exist under the title of 'Lynch law' either augmenting the punishment which the law requires, or awarding punishment to what the law does not recognize as crime" (93).

In printing these laws, the Brown of the 1851 *Narrative* is not framing a call for secession or revolt but merely following a practice common in antislavery literature. Various slave narrators—most prominently, William Wells Brown—reprinted the laws of slavery in their narratives, as did antislavery newspapers and antislavery sourcebooks such as Lydia Maria Child's *An Appeal in Favor of That Class of Americans Called Africans* (1833), Theodore Dwight Weld's *American Slavery as It Is: Testimony of a Thousand Witnesses* (1839), and William Goodell's *The American Slave Code in Theory and Practice* (1853). The point was to expose the convoluted and monstrous legal system required for the maintenance of slavery.[21] But there was often another point as well, one that the Henry Box Brown of the 1851 *Narrative* underscores by arguing that the logical incoherence of these laws provides dangerous loopholes for human nature as shaped by the absolute power of the system of slavery. "It may be also worthy of remark," Brown notes amid these reprinted laws and legal commentaries, "that in all cases in which we have strong manifestation of public opinion, in opposition to the law, it is always exhibited in the direction of cruelty; indeed, that such should be the case, no person intimately acquainted with the nature of the human mind, need be in the least surprised" (Brown, *Narrative* 94). In other words, what was important about the incoherence of the legal code was what it revealed about the culture both defined and unleashed by that law.

It is interesting that while the Brown of the 1851 account seems to gain agency in the way the laws are introduced, the message is, on the surface, less radical than Stearns's 1849 argument for constituting a new government. This apparent shift away from a revolutionary position is echoed in other parts of the narrative—for Nat Turner, mentioned three times in the narrative of 1849, appears only once in that of 1851, and missing in the 1851 text are the references to Turner that speak of the military suppression of liberty and the possibility of armed resistance to slavery.[22] "How was Nat Turner's insurrection suppressed," Stearns has Brown ask in 1849, "But by a company of United States troops, furnished the governor of Virginia at his request, according to your Constitution?" (Stearns, *Narrative* 40). "Many people tell me," Brown says, as he prepares for Stearns's discussion of law, "that if the slaves should rise up, and do as they did in Nat Turner's time, endeavor to fight their way to freedom, that the Northern people are pledged to shoot them down, and keep them in subjection to their masters" (65). In 1851, Turner appears only when Brown explains a time in Richmond when "the whites seemed terrified beyond measure" and when "many slaves were whipped, hung, and cut down with the swords in the streets" (Brown, *Narrative* 63). The mention of Turner in Stearns's version—in the context of both a call for white political action and an implicit warning against black insurrectionist alternatives—indicates the transformation of the concept of revolutionary action as it passes from black theology to white antislavery activism. In Stearns's hands, one might say, Turner serves as a provocation for a more "civilized" reconstitution of the social order. But as Brown adjusted to the transition from a life in slavery to a life as a "free" black man in a white supremacist culture, he might well have had doubts about the efficacy of Stearns's desire for a new government under "a white banner, with the words, 'Emancipation to the Slaves,'" particularly given Stearns's opening acknowledgment that "the people of this country are not ready for a truly Christian government" (Stearns, *Narrative* 67). What hope, Brown might well have wondered, would African Americans find in a nation whose white banner marked their enslavement permanently as a defining cause?

## "O God, They Have Taken My Box": Brown and the Antislavery Pen

As if to answer that question, Brown assumes much greater editorial control over the second version of his narrative. In the final chapter, he draws from his public performances on the antislavery stage, which included a song about his escape set to the tune of Stephen Foster's "Old Uncle Ned," the chorus of which begins with the phrase "Den lay down de shubble and de hoe." These lines are retained in the chorus of Brown's song of escape, though without the dialect. More significantly, the song leads directly to the appendix, which opens with a short italicized statement that locates these lines in a different source: *"The allusion in my song to the shovel and the hoe, is founded on the following story, which forms the slave-holders' version of the creation of the human race"* (Brown, *Narrative* 91). The story that follows is, like the song before it, a representation of Brown's public appearances and, like the song, was undoubtedly part of his repertoire before the publication of the 1851 *Narrative*.[23] The story begins by slyly adopting the logic of the theories of polygenesis that were, by Brown's time, increasingly important in justifying white supremacy and race-based enslavement.[24] "The slave-holders," the story begins, "say that originally, there were four persons created (instead of only two) and, perhaps, it is owing to the Christian account of the origin of man, in which account two persons only are mentioned, that it is one of the doctrines of slave-holders that slaves have no souls: however these four persons were two whites and two blacks; and the blacks were made to wait upon the whites" (91). In this, of course, Brown distinguishes between Christianity proper and the "pretended Christianity" necessary for the system of slavery, and he extends the story to a discussion of the means by which the distinction is both veiled and maintained. Since the four people exist in "man's original state," the whites find no need for black servitude and are "plagued with the incessant attendance of the two colored persons, and they prayed that God would find them something else to do" (91). Responding to this prayer, God sends down two bags. The black man, "being the strongest and swiftest," takes the largest bag and the white man is left with the smaller one—but when they open the bags, the black man discovers "a shovel and a hoe" and the white man, "a pen, ink, and paper; to write the declaration of the intention of the Almighty" (92). Thus does the white couple maintain control over the black.

The authorship of the 1851 *Narrative* might still be in the hands of the white man who works with pen, ink, and paper, but here Brown manipulates the shovel and hoe of his public performances to shift the current of the narrative's declarations to his own experience of "the intention of the Almighty." In both versions of the narrative, Brown begins with an emphatic statement of the philosophical and moral violations by which he was made a slave upon birth "in the midst of a country whose most honored writings declare that all men have a right to liberty." Both accounts present a version of the statement that, at Brown's birth, there was not "any angel" who "stood by, at the hour of my birth, to hand my body over, by the authority of heaven, to be the property of a fellow-man" (Stearns 14; Brown, *Narrative* 51). Thus both versions emphasize that Brown was made a slave by a national usurpation of divine authority—in the struggle between man's governance and God's. Still, there are clear differences between the two presentations of this struggle. In the 1849 version, Stearns looks ahead to his call for the creation of a new government, and he has Brown say that he was made a slave "for the reason that nearly all the people of this country are united in legislating against heaven, and have contrived to vote down our heavenly father's rules, and to substitute for them, that cruel law which binds the chains of slavery upon one sixth part of the inhabitants of this land" (14). The 1851 version acknowledges a more formal correspondence between secular and sacred law, indicating that the former should operate in the framework of the latter but without the suggestion of an ideal state governed by "our heavenly father's rules." "I was a slave," the 1851 Brown states, "because my countrymen had made it lawful, in utter contempt of the declared will of heaven, for the strong to lay hold of the weak and to buy and to sell them as marketable goods" (51).

To be sure, both versions characterize slaveholding law as anti-Christian, but the 1851 version focuses more on wicked men than on a demonic system. I use these terms advisedly, for in the same paragraph Stearns has Brown describe his enslavement as a total possession in a satanic social and legal system: "Tyrants, remorseless, destitute of religion and principle, stood by the couch of my mother, as heaven placed a pure soul, in the infantile form, there lying in her arms—a new being, never having breathed earth's atmosphere before; and fearlessly, with no compunctions of remorse, stretched forth their bloody arms and pressed the life of God from me, baptizing my soul and body as their own property; goods and chattels in their hands!" (Stearns, *Narrative* 14–15). Although we cannot know the ways or extent to which Brown influenced the revisions for the 1851 *Narrative*, we can imagine him protesting that this statement gives entirely too much to the slaveholders. Indeed, here we can see a formalization, with attending ritual, for creating, as Christopher Castiglia has it, "the distinction between *two* interior states: affect, which characterizes white Americans as fully feeling subjects, and civic abstraction, which becomes the possession of black Americans" (34). There is nothing left of Brown but the cause to be fought by those who have avoided the satanic baptism that would make them citizens of the state of slavery.

In the 1851 version, then, we are not surprised to discover that Brown retains his soul: "Tyrants—remorseless, destitute of religion and every principle of humanity—stood by the couch of my mother and as I entered into the world, before I had done anything to forfeit my right to liberty, and while my soul was yet undefiled by the commission of actual sin, stretched forth their bloody arms and branded me with the mark of bondage, and by such means I became their property" (51). Brown is enslaved less by a system of evil than by men using pen, ink, and paper, and the great violation is not a forced baptism but rather a restriction of his rights without cause—for he had not yet "done anything to forfeit [his] right to liberty," and he had not yet committed any "actual sin." He loses his rights but not his soul, and thus he is armed by those who violate principles that should be held sacred. In short, both the enslavers and the enslaved retain their humanity in the 1851 account, and on those grounds the struggle is staged—a struggle in which Brown has a chance to pursue "a mission from God to the human family" (44).

For all of the righteous indignation of Stearns's rhetoric in the 1849 version, the 1851 *Narrative* is the one that highlights Brown's experience and perspective as a Christian struggling against what he calls the "pretended christianity" of the enslaving nation (92). In presenting his enslavement as a philosophical and theological violation—that is, by stating that he committed no sin and had done nothing to "forfeit" his "right to liberty"—Brown retains his agency by associating his moral agency not with an abstract freedom but against the experience and consciousness of enslavement that he could not escape even after his arrival in the North. At the end of his 1849 preface, Stearns presents Brown as a modern-day Lazarus, "clothed not in the habiliments of the grave, but in those of slavery, worse than the 'silent house of death'" (viii). Stearns is the pious stage manager of this performance, covering Brown in the "habiliments" so as to raise again not the body but the clothing—for the primary subject of the 1849 narrative is less Brown's story than Stearns's extended antislavery spectacle and sermon. In the 1851 *Narrative*, Brown's voice exists not apart from Stearns's performance but rather is complexly implicated in it. It is difficult to imagine by what means he might hope for a resurrection, still mediated by others, that saves the subject while still displaying the "habiliments" of slavery. That Brown's spectacular escape and his performative approach to his subsequent career have been the primary subjects of both his public and his scholarly reputation since that time only emphasizes the extent to which antislavery sympathy has insisted on baptizing him ever again in a vision of slavery that allows for a corresponding celebration of an idealized freedom.

The two narratives of Brown's experience tell a more complex and haunting story; they lead us from the performative box to a box of always vexed departures and always imminent arrivals, for lost in the accounts of Brown's escape is the family he left behind and the moral and parental responsibilities still in chains. In this way, Brown's famous box resembles a less famous one, that of Thomas H. Jones, as related in his own narrative of enslavement and vexed liberation. Like Brown, Jones saw his wife and family sold away from him. Unlike Brown, however, Jones took another wife while still enslaved, and the couple worked to secure their union by saving money toward his second wife's purchase. "So we made a box," Jones reports, "and, through a hole in the top, we put in every piece of money, from five cents up to a dollar, that we could save from our hard earnings" (*Experience of Rev. Thomas H. Jones* 232). But whereas the visibility of Brown's box was the means of his escape and subsequent fame, Jones needs to keep his hidden. The box becomes the center of Jones's attention, as he worries that patrollers will find it when they come to search the cabin, or that "some prowling enemy" will hear him dropping money into it (232). "How often have I started up in my sleep as the storm has beat aloud upon my humble home," he exclaims, "with the cry of unspeakable agony in my heart, 'Then, O God, they have taken my box, and my wife and babes are still slaves!'" (232–33). Eventually Jones saves most of the money he needs, and with additional help he is able to purchase his wife's freedom (though not that of a child born before the purchase was possible and still enslaved when Jones wrote the narrative). One might say that Brown's box, so spectacularly visible, was discovered even after he thought it safe, and one can only observe that Brown's wife and babes remained enslaved, largely invisible even to those who have celebrated his ingenious escape and equally ingenious career in the North and in England. His negotiations within the narrative to give voice to his own conscience can be seen as his effort to create another box destined for an uncertain and partial arrival, the story of a life not reducible to a single individual's fortunes. Brown's performance in his narrative, related to but separate from his performance on the antislavery stage, is an attempt not only to transport but also to preserve a self all but lost in the story of liberation contextualized by the discursive, narrative, and theoretical demands of a white supremacist culture.

WHETHER Henry Box Brown preserved his concept of self is an open question, though Stearns certainly preserved his. Brown went on to an active, sometimes controversial career in England and, after 1875, in the United States, eventually lecturing on electrobiology and giving performances that involved mesmerism and hypnotic trances. Marcus Wood presents Brown as "the most forward-looking of all abolitionist propagandists," noting that he "drew on commercial and creative resources which white abolitionist shied away from" (116, 107); Daphne A. Brooks similarly observes that Brown's "complex network of performance strategies posed a representational crisis to viewers who were seemingly tethered to narrow and troubling racial authenticity politics" (95). Audrey Fisch, on the other hand, comments on "Brown's success in commodifying his sufferings for display in front of English strangers, in combining celebration of spectacle with English nationalism, but also in catering to the racism of that nationalism" (*American Slaves* 81). The character of Stearns's subsequent career is easier to identify, for he continued his work under the white banner, most prominently in his postwar book, *The Black Man of the South, and the Rebels; or, The Characteristics of the Former, and the Recent Outrages of the Latter* (1872). Still confident of the moral superiority of the white North to the white South, and of his own superiority to both, Stearns says in his introduction that he will not follow the custom of offering "'rose-colored' views of those in whose behalf you plead" (xii). "With me," he declares, "it will be the very misery I shall depict, moral as well as physical, that I shall rely upon to re-awaken public interest in the victims of this depravity and woe" (xii). He still claims to be the channel of the voice of those he identifies as victims:

> "*Les Miserables*" shall plead for help, not by having exhibited the bright and shining traits in their characters, but rather, by having exposed to public view the shocking faults indigenous to their former condition, and in their very helplessness, uttering such a wail of anguish as shall touch all hearts imbued with the spirit of mercy. It is not the righteous I call upon you to save, O ye disciples of Jesus, but those morally "bruised and mangled" ones, whose "lost and ruined" condition, so excited the sympathy of him who "came to save" the sons and daughters of woe, who were "plunged" into this "gulf of dark despair." (xii)

With friends like these, African Americans came to understand the dubious benefits of the white-banner cause long after the Civil War. Of course, not all of the white abolitionists of old struck quite this tone after the Civil War—and even African American writers like William Wells Brown sounded at times like Stearns in their own postwar and post-Reconstruction commentaries (covered in Chapter 5). But Stearns emphasizes the force of the white framework with which African American writers had to contend and the challenges of locating a common literary tradition without deliberately interrogating the terms of that framework.

Stearns is, as I say, an exceptional example of the white presence in the black text, but in many ways he is representative. He is the presence Douglass responds to in *My Bondage and My Freedom*, that text which is, in William Andrews's persuasive reading, a declaration of independence not only from the paternal authority of William Lloyd Garrison and the Garrisonian mode of antislavery activism but also from the narrative conventions that determined the history that Douglass could draw from his life in 1845.[25] The white banner is what one encounters as well in the tensions between Harriet Jacobs and Harriet Beecher Stowe, as Jacobs looked for assistance in publishing the story of her experience, and it is the flag that Martin R. Delany conspicuously resists in his response to *Uncle Tom's Cabin*: *Blake; or, The Huts of America*. Echoes of Stearns emerge in Anna Julia Cooper's commentary on write writers who address the subject of race, those "preachers" who have "had a point to prove or a mission to accomplish" (185).[26] "The art of 'thinking one's self imaginatively into the experiences of others,'" Cooper observes, "is not given to all, and it is impossible to acquire it without a background and a substratum of sympathetic knowledge. Without this power our portraits are but death's heads or caricatures and no amount of cudgeling can put into them the movement and reality of life" (185–86). Echoes of Stearns's presence are even evident in the work of Frances E. W. Harper, who admired Stowe (as did Cooper), but who devoted her best-known novel, *Iola Leroy; or, Shadows Uplifted*, to the story of a woman who is finally encouraged to write "a book to inspire men and women with a deeper sense of justice and humanity" (262). When Iola doubts both her ability and the receptiveness of readers to a black woman's writings, Dr. Latimer responds: "Miss Leroy, out of the race must come its own thinkers and writers. Authors belonging to the white race have written good racial books, for which I am deeply grateful, but it seems to be almost impossible for a white man to put himself completely in our place. No man can feel the iron which enters another man's soul" (263). In short, nineteenth-century African American writers recognized very well and intimately the necessity of dialogues between white writers and black writers, and they were necessarily engaged in such conversations in virtually everything they wrote—but they also understood the terms of those discourses. We can hardly afford to initiate calls for interracial approaches to American literary history that do not begin by acknowledging that such approaches have been fundamental to certain literary traditions. Such exchanges abound, and nineteenth-century African American literature can help us considerably in learning when, where, and how to listen and join in the conversations that started, in fact, long ago.

CHAPTER FOUR

## Choreographing Chaos

*African American Literature in Time and Space*

Sometimes, in his room or on the sidewalk, the world seemed to him a
strange labyrinth even when the streets were straight and the walls were
square; a chaos which made him feel that something in him should be able
to understand it, divide it, focus it. —RICHARD WRIGHT, *Native Son*

Henry Box Brown's decision to conclude his 1851 *Narrative* by reprinting
laws regulating slavery was not unique. Such reprintings frequently appear in slave narratives, antislavery newspapers, and such books as William Goodell's *The American Slave Code in Theory and Practice* (1853) and
George M. Stroud's *Stroud's Slave Laws: A Sketch of the Laws Relating to
Slavery in the Several States of the United States of America* (1856). Law is a
regular feature and often a major plot device in a great number of nineteenth-century African American novels as well. William Wells Brown
begins *Clotel* by noting that marriages among the enslaved were unrecognized by both church and state—and the legal implications of that reality
informs the novel throughout. Frances E. W. Harper's *Iola Leroy* is about
a woman who believed herself to be white but learns that she is legally
black, a discovery that not only repositions her significantly before the
Civil War but also informs her decisions about her future after the war.
Harper's public career itself was inspired in part by one of the many eruptions of the expulsion movement in the South, the attempt to force free
African Americans to leave the state, often under threat of enslavement.[1]
J. McHenry Jones's *Hearts of Gold* (1896) explores the manipulation of law
after the Civil War in the service of the convict labor system—a system
that, as Douglas A. Blackmon documents, involved "practices almost
identical to those emerging in slavery in the 1850s" (57). One of the
novel's central characters, an African American doctor, is falsely accused

and convicted of a crime and sent to the coal mines; he is rescued only when a friend, an African American newspaper editor, finally succeeds in acquiring a pardon from the governor. In these and numerous other works, African Americans confront the consequential force of law—measures designed to restrict their fundamental rights, their geographical and social mobility, even their identity. Those of African heritage found themselves variously restricted, unrecognized, or unprotected by law, on the one hand, and regularly characterized as a threateningly lawless mass, on the other.[2]

Among the many historical and cultural factors that have combined to shape African American culture(s) and identities, we should remember that in the nineteenth century African Americans were also black by law. What this meant varied according to locale, situation, and historical moment, but the legal definitions and enforcement of racial identity and group affiliation were everywhere a primary determinant of possibilities and pathways. I do not mean simply the many and varying laws that defined what constituted nonwhite status, though of course they were important, but also the many laws and social customs that followed from such definitions. Without the force of that imposing legal structure and its corresponding social codes, one might be able to identify African American identity purely in terms of ancestral heritage, inherited folkways, traditions, or other cultural formations that developed among historically affiliated people through the years, connecting them back to generally identifiable roots in Africa, Europe, and elsewhere and recognizing the self-professed contours of a diverse group identity. But just as African religions were both transformed by and transformative of religious practices in the United States—precisely because diverse, established traditions encountered one another in a repressive setting, leading to hybrid practices over time[3]—so the identities of those of African heritage, carrying the combined possibilities of a broad range of cultural roots, were pressed into the pervasive structures and forced through the restrictive channels of U.S. racial law. Out of this turbulent process emerged ever-new iterations of patterns of cultural life, and these iterations are central to nineteenth-century African American literature.

In this chapter, with an eye toward the background of American legal history, we will address certain laws—juridical, social, and historical—that were pivotal in the representation of African American life: laws of time, laws of mobility, and laws of affiliation. Nineteenth-century African American literature is characterized fundamentally by the need to consider the legal realities of African American life and by various attempts to realize the possibilities of the instabilities in American legal and social practice. That is, the representation of nineteenth-century African American life required attention to the force of the various laws that both restricted and inspired not only approaches to resistance and community organization but also concepts of individual independence and agency. Indeed, speeches, essays, treatises, pamphlets, and newspaper publications are central to nineteenth-century African American literary history because it was through such forums that African American writers responded to misrepresentations, appealed legal injustices, promoted social reform, established the contours of a history marginalized by the dominant culture, and worked to foster concepts of collective identity and agency. These various concerns, and the social contexts in which they were conceptualized and acted upon, became fundamental to nineteenth-century African American aesthetics. In effect, this chapter explores the ways that nineteenth-century African American writers attempted to represent the dynamics of African American life in social time and space.[4]

Another way to put this is to say that I will examine African American writers as cultural choreographers, though what follows is not a study of the relative dynamics of black dance and print culture, as valuable as such a study would be. Instead, I am suggesting that African American writers' attempts to represent a chaotic social system required complex textual performances, and that those performances involve the representation of the dynamics of African American life—choreographies, in a sense, that *follow* performance rather than precede it, attempts to capture on the page the dynamics of African American subjectivity and experiences in American social life. I draw from the language of choreography, then, to follow the representations, in nineteenth-century African American literature, of social time and space. Particularly useful in this regard are the theories of Rudolf Laban, one of the pioneers of dance notation. In explaining my approach by way of Laban's work, I am deeply cognizant of the irony of invoking the theories of a man who promoted racist views in service to Nazi Germany. But appropriating those theories in the service of African American literature, which so often involves complicated interracial appropriations and maneuvers, seems very much to the point. Ultimately, the performances I consider are textual and include a choreography crafted by African American writers in a threatening theater of engagement long before Laban formulated his theories and brought them to the stage.

I am reaching so far beyond the context of African American culture to redirect Laban's useful observation that "space is a superabundance of simultaneous movements," and that "movement is one of man's languages and as such it must be consciously mastered. We must try to find its real structure and the choreological order within it through which movement becomes penetrable, meaningful and understandable" (3, viii). Following those structures of movement, Laban wrote of "trace-forms," the "living architecture" that is "created by movement," the structures "made up of pathways tracing shapes in space" (5). In studying the multiple perspectives and modes of experience involved in dance, Laban looked for a synthesis, asserting that "we are all emotional dreamers, and scheming mechanics, and biological innocents, simultaneously: sometimes we waver between these three mentalities, and sometimes we compress them in a synthesized act of perception and function" (7). Considered individually, the texts constructed by African Americans can productively be understood as compressed and synthesized acts of perception and function. Considered together, we can see "trace forms," recurring ideological patterns, social concerns, and discursive gestures that indicate the living architecture of what Toni Morrison terms "a culturally formed race" ("Unspeakable" 370).

Importantly, Laban's language of movement extended to a reconceptualization of the relations among performers, audiences, and the theaters of engagement. As Ann Hutchinson Guest has observed, "It is significant that until Laban's system (Vienna, 1928) all floor plans were written from the audience's point of view and not as experienced by the performers. It was as though the dancers were not to be involved, but only those watching them" (54). One can only observe that many African American works also have been approached primarily from the audience's point of view—with an emphasis in slave narratives, for example, on the spectacle of suffering under slavery and the sublimity of eventual liberation.[5] The challenge for a great many writers was to make the theater of the narrator's experience and subsequent performance—most prominently, the world of slavery, antislavery spectacle, and/or a white supremacist and patriarchal culture—itself the subject of the narrative. In the face of a culture that exoticized the racialized body, and that abstracted from those bodies concepts of humanity and theoretical freedom, African American writers reconstructed the stage upon which African Americanness might be understood and experienced by confronting, challenging, and otherwise attempting to reconfigure readers' understandings of the ways in which "motion and emotion, form and content, body and mind, are inseparably united" (Laban viii). At the end of this chapter, I focus on a particularly revealing cultural performance, that of William and Ellen Craft, and on William Craft's attempt to choreograph the dynamics of their performance in *Running a Thousand Miles for Freedom*. But first it is important to identify the laws that restricted and otherwise directed the possibilities for African American performance—both in various cultural theaters and on the printed page.

## Laws of Time

At the opening of his 1845 *Narrative*, Frederick Douglass says that he can only guess at his age. "I do not remember to have ever met a slave who could tell of his birthday," he writes. "They seldom come nearer to it than planting-time, harvest-time, cherry-time, spring-time, or fall-time" (15). Douglass begins, in other words, by observing that among the conditions defining the experience of the enslaved was the inability to locate oneself in historical time; locating oneself in that way, he says, was a sign of racial privilege. "The white children could tell their ages. I could not tell why I ought to be deprived of the same privilege" (15). The alignment of the enslaved with natural time rather than historical time is not surprising, for in most slave narratives we might well expect to encounter a broad range of manifestations of the racialized experience of time. What I mean by this is suggested by Bridget T. Heneghan's comment about Frederick Law Olmsted's reports on his travels in the South. Olmsted, Heneghan relates, had trouble following the directions from a local farmer, "which include fallen-in cabins, fences, unidentifiable schoolhouses and hidden log houses"; he has trouble as well when he "asks the distance to a certain house," and the slave he questions "can only estimate how long the journey will take." "His frustration," Heneghan observes, "comes from a difference in perspective: the farmer's directions draw from a knowledge of the history of the area and of the endpoints of each small path. The slave's concerns are for the traveling time that he might control, rather than the measured land that he cannot. Olmsted only becomes confused when directed through ruined cabins and unused fields: these are the hidden and ignored elements of a planter's formal landscape" (22). Those who enter the racialized terrain of nineteenth-century American history might find themselves similarly confused, for white and black Americans of a great many regions, slave and nominally free, lived in a cultural landscape divided by labor and time, and they necessarily negotiated their way through that landscape differently. Although they lived in the same historical period, they lived in different complexes of community, space, and time—and therefore, to a large extent, in different historical continuums.

Given the effects of such differentials, time was naturally a central preoccupation in African American life and thus a central presence in African American literature. Representing African American life required a challenging choreographic rendering of constant encounters with and pressures from overlapping experiences of time, as governed by the competing demands of labor, travel, family, and community, as well as by the cultural politics of historical understanding and historiographical authority. Recent scholarship has highlighted different conceptions of time among different regional and racial constituencies in the United States. In his groundbreaking study, *Mastered by the Clock: Time, Slavery, and Freedom in the American South*, Mark M. Smith has been especially instructive about the developing alliance of white northern and southern concepts of time, and of the relationship to both natural and mechanical time among the enslaved in the South. But while such scholarship is promising, it is clear that the experience of time both separated and connected various groups and social classes across regional lines in ways we have only begun to understand. As Thomas M. Allen argues, "The heterogeneity of time . . . provided opportunities for diverse agents with different interests to produce competing accounts of American national identity" (3)—and, I would add, for competing approaches to agency itself. In Heneghan's example, time for the enslaved in the South can be measured by the negotiation of labor and space, the ways in which the enslaved either claimed relative freedom from the demands of their condition or performed resistance through slowed or delayed labor.[6] For those who escaped bondage, the extended time of risky and usually nighttime travel was rewarded not by the luxury of time but by their relative authority over their time in the North, the ability to claim compensation for their time. In the North, time was also a function of the extra trouble required to get to and from places of work, commerce, and worship in a culture of segregated transportation and limited institutional access. And time was certainly a factor for those seeking an education beyond what the dominant culture was prepared to offer, especially for those who turned to writing as a vital part of their public lives.

Indeed, the reception of African American literature has in many ways been marked by the kinds of assumptions about the literary importance of an author's authority over time that British novelist Anthony Trollope offers in relation to American literature generally. "Literature," he asserts in *North America* (1862), "is the child of leisure and wealth. It is the produce of minds which by a happy combination of circumstances have been enabled to dispense with the ordinary cares of the world. It can hardly be expected to come from a young country, or from a new and still struggling people" (273). Trollope notes that significant literature had come from American authors all the same, though he limits his attention to white male writers. We can say the same of African American writers—but with greater emphasis on the achievement of producing this literature in the absence of leisure and wealth. John Quincy Adams—whose *Narrative* emphasizes the pressures and relative comforts of time from its subtitle (*When in Slavery, and Now as a Freeman*) to the refrain that punctuates his account ("But how is it now?")—concludes by telling his readers: "This book was written at night—every line of it after I had performed the duties of the day" (50). Many other narratives, novels, orations, pamphlets, and poems might well end with the same line. Free time was, for nineteenth-century African Americans, as rare and as restricted as the other freedoms they knew in the North.

Beyond the experience of time in travel and labor, African Americans encountered the racial laws of time in their experience of and relation to history. As I argued in *Liberation Historiography*, locating African Americans in history was a major preoccupation of nineteenth-century African American writers. African Americans found themselves variously misrepresented, omitted, or problematically inserted into white nationalist histories; accordingly, African American historical writing required recontextualized readings of biased historical archives, strategic manipulations of literary forms, and purposeful management of the available forums for public debate, collective self-definition, and literary representation. These matahistorical efforts were inscribed in virtually every form of literature, often punctuated by recurring tropes or references. Just as African American writers would return regularly to Thomas Jefferson trembling for the future of the country in *Notes on the State of Virginia*, or to Andrew Jackson hailing his black fellow citizens in proclamations in 1814, or to the outstretched arms of Ethiopia of Psalm 68:31, so African American writers relied on fragmented narratives, sudden narrative transitions, surprising but purposeful juxtapositions, and other narrative methods to represent an African American history (and an African American *approach* to history) that could be located only in the complex contingencies that defined black life in a white supremacist culture. By such means did African American writers attempt to choreograph their shifting positions on the crowded historical stage enclosed in the national theater.

The history in and of any literary tradition is anything but simple, as is emphasized by Wai-Chee Dimock's explorations of "deep time" in relation to American literature more broadly. "What we called 'American' literature," Dimock rightly observes, "is quite often a shorthand, a simplified name for a much more complex tangle of relations. Rather than being a discrete entity, it is better seen as a crisscrossing set of pathways, open-ended and ever multiplying, weaving in and out of other geographies, other languages and cultures. These are input channels, kinship networks, routes of transit, and forms of attachment—connective tissues binding America to the rest of the world" (3). To "capture this phenomenon," Dimock proses "a new term—'deep time,'" by which she means to highlight "a set of longitudinal frames, at once projective and recessional, with input going both ways, and binding continents and millennia into many loops of relations, a densely interactive fabric" (3–4).[7] Certainly, we can hardly think of African American history without recognizing such channels, networks, routes, and forms of attachment; what to make of such complex interconnections has been a pressing question within the various, sometimes overlapping, and sometimes competing realms of African American Studies, Africana Studies, and Black Studies—though this is not a topic that Dimock explores. Still, Dimock's concept of deep time accounts for a dynamic and unpredictable process that applies very well to African American literature, one of the many pathways she explores.

But following or even identifying that pathway might be difficult. We can, of course, look for an entrance into the African American "tangle of relations," or Hartman's "networks of affiliation," by attending to the historical markers that African Americans themselves identified, tracing cultural history so as to chart the deep time of literary history. Many of those markers are quite clear—constituting a commemorative calendar rather different from that of white Americans. As Marcus Wood has noted, "There was an unbroken history of African-American freedom festivals in the Northern free states, which focused upon dates which had special resonance for those of slave descent in the Americas," including "1 January, a date commemorating Toussaint l'Ouverture's declaration of the independent state of Hayti, and the outlawing of the American Atlantic slave trade; 5 July, because of the passage of 1799 and 1817 gradual abolition legislation; and 1 August, because it commemorated British Emancipation in the Caribbean colonies" (250). We might follow such commemorations to account for deep time, most evident in the form of the biblical, classical, African, and European histories that were so dramatically present in nineteenth-century African American orations, political pamphlets, and histories. But tracing that presence would soon lead us into what might more appropriately be termed chaotic time and space, for there is no neatly linear historical line connecting the reference with the referent, and no citation not complicated by both the inaccuracies of the historical record and the racial politics controlling or determining the archive. Contradictions, inaccuracies, flights of historical imagination, and even contending historical references abound in nineteenth-century African American literature. Moreover, as emphasized in previous chapters, this was not a literature that emerged from a stable entity that can be termed the African American population or community. African Americans were scattered and fragmented both geographically and ideologically, both in terms of the conditions under which they lived and in terms of the possibilities they entertained. As is underscored even by the anguished and sometimes contentious disagreements over group names—African, Colored, Anglo-African, and the like—this was a collective defined in part by a dominant culture and in part by their own variously organized efforts to understand themselves as a self-defining community.[8]

Complicating their efforts to construct a coherent historical narrative were the many manifestations, legal and social, of a white supremacist culture, both homegrown and imported, determined to obscure its own historical disruptions (including the obvious philosophical contradictions required for racial domination) by way of an essential stability—the rather different concept of deep time represented by nineteenth-century race science. Particularly interesting in this regard is James Cowles Prichard, author of (among many other works) *Researches into the Physical History of Man* (1813) and *The Natural History of Man: Comprising Inquiries into the Modifying Influence of Physical and Moral Agencies on the Different Tribes of the Human Family* (1843). Prichard resisted the approaches of those who argued for the existence of different species of humans—polygenesis, as viewed from a European-American religious perspective. Such arguments would become increasingly prominent in U.S. race science, especially in such works as John Campbell's *Negro-Mania: Being an Examination of the Falsely Assumed Equality of the Various Races of Man* (1851) and Josiah Clark Nott and George R. Gliddon's influential *Types of Mankind: or, Ethnological Researches, Based upon the Ancient Monuments, Paintings, Sculptures, and Crania of Races, and upon Their Natural, Geographical, Philological, and Biblical history* (1854). Prichard's work is itself deeply Eurocentric; he believed fundamentally that the European understanding of religion, beauty, and civilization was the global and human standard against which all other understandings should be measured. Still, there is some rationale for George W. Stocking Jr.'s 1973 assessment that "race was never a rigid category for Prichard," and that "the thrust of his whole work . . . was to defend the common humanity of blacks against those who sought to deny it on scientific grounds" (lvii).

Prichard offers an early manifestation of the concept of deep time. Like many philosophers and scientists of his day, Prichard was very much involved in gathering all of human history within the ideological borders of the nation. For his anthropological work, he drew, as Stocking notes, from a wide range of classical writers, eighteenth-century travel writers, "writings in the biological sciences," "the tradition of oriental studies associated with the name of Sir William Jones," and various other historical sources, including "most of the great chronological writers from Eusebius, through Sir Isaac Newton, right on down to Dr. William Hale's recently published attempt 'to remove the imperfection and discordance of preceding systems, and to obviate the cavils of sceptics, Jews, and infidels'" (xxxiv–xli). The prejudices of a white British writer of his time are obvious, but clearly Prichard accounted for a great deal of human history and cultural traditions in his research. Moreover, his research was often directed against the grain—particularly his central argument (which met with considerable criticism) "that all mankind constitute but one race or proceed from a single family" (iii). As Stocking observes, "not only did he insist on a considerable amount of individual variability, but he insisted on the variability of the groups which (with somewhat variable terminology) he called races, nations, and tribes" (lvii). Within this context, Prichard examines a world of difference, but in accounting for that variety, he looks for an understanding that, his obvious historical and cultural prejudices aside, might well work within the framework of deep time—including a sustained linguistic analysis similar to that in Dimock's work when she explores the African roots of African American literature.

There are two significant points to be made about Prichard's studies. The first is rather basic—that the underlying intent of nineteenth-century race science was to locate and stabilize the global and unstable dynamics of the developing concept of race. While Prichard admirably defended "the common humanity of blacks" and argued for variety within established racial categories, he still did much to establish such categories and to locate them in certain essential features. His study of race, like that of others, follows the processes of geographical and historical movement to ultimately provide a kind of global map for identifying different kinds of people. Race, however unstable or flexible a concept, was still viewed as embodiment, and one could follow even race mixture to identify the essential elements of one's identity—much like many look to do through DNA testing today. In effect, the argument behind race science was simple: No matter where you go, there you are.

My second point is that in the eighteenth and nineteenth centuries, the methodology associated with deep time existed not as a theoretical abstraction but rather as a cultural tradition or a set of cultural traditions that were influential in defining the very national and ideological boundaries that many scholars today are looking to address, and that those methodologies are especially evident in nineteenth-century race science and works of historical scholarship. What comes to mind is the historical mode that Washington Irving satirizes in *A History of New York, from the Beginning of the World to the End of the Dutch Dynasty, by Diedrich Knickerbocker* (1809). On the more serious side, one thinks of the historical scope of George Bancroft's *History of the United States*, in the ten volumes of which, published from 1834 to 1874, Bancroft struggles, as Henry Adams once noted, to reach his subject, finally concluding this history with the American Revolution, after reaching back at least as far as the "discovery" of the New World and the Protestant Revolution. Exploring nineteenth-century African American literature is thus a matter of exploring various and competing notions of deep time—from the commentary on African history in the American Colonization Society's monthly newspaper, *The African Repository and Colonial Journal*, to the extensive research included in *David Walker's Appeal*, some of it drawn from the society's newspaper.[9] The *time* of African American literature, in other words, or the *history* of African American literary history, continually leads back to a "complex tangle of relations." Indeed, we could say of African American literary history more broadly what Hortense J. Spillers has said of black women's writing, that it is "a matrix of literary *discontinuities* that partially articulate various periods of consciousness in the history of an African-American people" (251). These discontinuities themselves are the iterative links to a fractal narrative of the deep time in both African American literature and African American literary history, though the longing for a simpler narrative has always been seductive.

Her thoughtful but complex resistance to that longing is central to Hartman's reconsideration of the terms by which we might approach the history of slavery. Focusing primarily on the strands of African American history intertwined with the transatlantic slave trade, Hartman observes: "The discussion of memory in black cultural practice has been interpreted most often through continuist narratives of tradition grounded in the foundational status of Africa" (74), and such narratives are frequently replicated in grand narratives of African American history that focus on a linear notion of progress that enable some to dismiss the conditions of the present by contrasting them with those of the past. As for "the discontinuities of history and the complexity of culture practice," Hartman maintains that this particular approach to the past—the past of "the mystical and homogenizing Africanity of the discourse of 'survivals'"—"cannot be recovered, yet the history of the captive emerges precisely at this site of loss and rupture" (74). Entering at this site, we discover a fractured and fractal history both untranslatable and essential, leading to narratives less of historical recovery than of strategic iterations of an established historical pattern—the feedback mechanism fundamental to *Our Nig*, for example, or the eternal present tense of many African American narratives an idyllic Africa disrupted by the slave trade. What we discover, in short, are the ways in which experience both calls for and resists the priorities of historical narration and living memories that trouble any comforting hope of a community not informed by the history of race. As Hartman argues:

> In the workings of memory, there is an endless reiteration and
> enactment of this condition of loss and displacement. The past
> is untranslatable in the current frame of meaning because of the
> radical disassociations of historical process and the discontinuity
> introduced into the being of the captive as he is castigated into the
> abstract category of property. The Middle Passage, the great event
> of breach, engenders this discontinuity. Thus the reiterative invo-
> cation of the past articulated in practice returns to this point of
> rupture. In this instance, memory is not in the service of continuity
> but incessantly reiterates and enacts the contradictions and antago-
> nisms of enslavement, the ruptures of history, and the disassociated
> and dispersed networks of affiliation. It is by way of this reiteration
> or differential invocation of the past and by way of this memory of
> difference that everyday practices are redolent with the history of

captivity and enslavement. This working through of the past is a significant aspect of redress. (74)

Hartman's work is devoted precisely to this untranslatable history of "dislocation, rupture, shock, and forgetting" and the "fragmented existence" of memory. She enters this history, accordingly, through "considerations of memory that focus on rupture, breach, discontinuity, and crisis," and she finds "the subterranean history of death and discontinuity" through the performance of "repetition or iterability" (75). Exploring the fractal fault lines of history, finding communities formed by constant feedback and iteration, Hartman explores a history that requires a significantly fractured narrative approach. Thus does time enter African American literature not merely as a subject but as a fundamental condition, the terms by which a possible community might be narrated into consciousness.

As Hartman suggests, the contours of that community, while firm, resist definition and representation, for it is a community forged through tangled relations and understood through a troubled discursive subtext. Consider, for example, Alexander Crummell's "The English Language in Liberia" (1861), a speech that has for its background numerous Atlantic crossings—including Crummell's parentage, his birth in New York, his education in both the United States and England, and his emigration to Liberia. Challenging any formulaic conception of nineteenth-century African American politics, Crummell's speech is perhaps especially instructive about the difficult alliances, imagined and real, central to the transnational dynamics of African American literary and cultural history. Speaking in Liberia, Crummell explores the uneasy association of a colonizing language with the concept of liberty, just as he worked in the nation that was the product of the American Colonization Society to envision a grand destiny for Liberia and for Africa generally. Moreover, the speech is addressed to a cosmopolitan audience:

> We are here a motley group, composed, without doubt, of persons
> of almost every tribe in West Africa, from Goree to the Congo. Here
> are descendants of Jalofs, Fulahs, Mandingoes, Sussus, Timmanees,
> Veys, Congos, with a large intermixture every where of Anglo-Saxon,
> Dutch, Irish, French and Spanish blood—a slight mingling of the
> Malayan, and a dash, every now and then, of American Indian. And
> perhaps I would not exaggerate much, if I ended the enumeration
> of our heterogeneous elements in the words of St. Luke—"Jews
> and Proselytes, Cretes and Arabians." (288)

It is significant that Crummell finally gathers this "motley group" within biblical history, and that this cosmopolitan, trans-tribal, and transnational assembly represents intermixture while retaining the essential traces of a stubbornly tribal, national, and racial world.[10] This assembly is gathered in a nation founded on American slavery and racism and carries with it—indeed, embodies—the fractal course of history by which enslavement, colonization, and violent oppression become the foreground for a vision of liberty and an envisioned national power. Tracing that history might provide a useful complement to Dimock's study (which focuses on creolization and Black English), as Crummell celebrates the power of a colonizing language—for this motley group virtually speaks its troubled history. "And yet they all speak in a foreign tongue," Crummell points out, "in accents alien from the utterance of their fathers. Our very speech is indicative of sorrowful history; the language we use tells of subjection and of conquest. No people lose entirely their native tongue without the bitter trial of hopeless struggles, bloody strife, heart-breaking despair, agony and death! Even so we" (288). The most potent and promising reality in Crummell's vision of deep time is that the painful process of adopting a foreign tongue "is a common incident in history, pertaining to almost every nation on earth" (288).

Throughout his influential career, Crummell negotiated the difficult tensions between the discontinuities central to the scattered people he represented, in both Liberia and the United States, and the need for continuities by which those of African descent might know themselves and determine the terms of their historical agency. In fact, deep time for Crummell was something to be discovered not at the end but in the process of such negotiations, and one of his chief interests concerned the ways in which the racial politics that shaped African American life and thought disrupted that process. Liberia itself was itself a product of those politics, a historical intervention not only into African politics but also into African American "freedom." One might say that the work of the American Colonization Society was an attempt to relocate African Americans not only to another place but also to another time, another historical trajectory. The result was an ever-more complex relationship between African Americans and the understanding of deep time related to concepts of an ancestral home. In an 1894 letter to *The Southern Workman*, Crummell mentioned his failed attempt "to organize an 'African Society' for the preservation of traditions, folk-lore, ancestral remembrances, etc., which may have come down from ancestral sources" ("Letter" 81). The attempt had failed,

Crummell believed, because "the dinning of the 'colonization' cause into the ears of the colored people—the iteration of the idle dogma that Africa is the home of the black race in this land; has served to prejudice the race against the very name of Africa. And this is a double folly:—the folly of the colonizationists, and the folly of the black man; i.e. to forget family ties and his duty to his kin over the water" ("Letter" 81).

As Crummell suggests, the laws of time operating in the service of the system of slavery and of white supremacist racial control had reverberations far beyond the inconveniencing and dislocation of African Americans in social life. "America's manifold temporal cultures," Thomas M. Allen observes, "were like pieces of a puzzle that might be assembled into a variety of different pictures" (*Republic in Time* 3). The experience of time in African American life was similarly a puzzle, but the pictures that might be assembled from that puzzle were far from clear. From the manipulation of time that governed labor to the ancestral ties by which one might locate one's place in history, African Americans found themselves mastered by the clock and pinned into a delimited historical sphere. Nineteenth-century African American literature, accordingly, often functions as a meditation on time and often is devoted to attempts to discover or establish a historical framework by which the time *in* a person's life and the time *of* that life might be framed by an understanding of deep time, both retrospective and prospective, capable of offering a sense of order, the possibility of control, and the comforts of cognitive authority over envisioned process. Thus narrative time in African American literature is more often than not a complicated and even disjointed matter, but by such paths African American writers hoped to address the many dimensions of John Quincy Adams's simple question, "But how is it now?"

## Laws of Mobility

The racial politics of historical self-location were central to attempts by African Americans to locate (and relocate) themselves culturally and geographically as well. Here again, local and national laws constituted a cultural viaduct restricting the experience through which historical understanding and philosophical principles could be experienced, tested, and applied to the needs of individual and collective life. David F. Dorr begins his 1858 travel narrative *A Colored Man Round the World* with a commentary on slavery in the form of a dedication that amounts to a search for his mother obstructed by a world of controlled mobility: "Mother! wherever thou art, whether in Heaven or a lesser world; or whether around the freedom Base of a Bunker Hill, or only at the lowest savannah of American Slavery, thou art the same to me" (7). This search for his mother between heaven and earth, freedom and slavery, speaks volumes about the laws of mobility governing the life of the enslaved, as Dorr was no more free to follow his mother's path in life than he was to look for her in "the lowest savannah of American Slavery." But against this backdrop, Dorr presents a travel narrative in which he locates *himself* with great security and confidence, precisely because of the constant movement to which his book is devoted.[11] "The Author of this book," he begins his preface, "though a quadroon, is pleased to announce himself the 'Colored man around the world.' Not because he may look at a colored man's position as an honorable one at this age of the world, he is too smart for that, but because he has the satisfaction of looking with his own eyes and reason at the ruins of the ancestors of which he is the posterity. If the ruins of the Author's ancestors were not a living language of their scientific majesty, this book could receive no such appellation with pride" (11). Here Dorr is referring to "Luxor, Carnack, the Memnonian and the Pyramids," and his preface briefly defends the prevailing thesis among African Americans of the time that the Egyptians were black. While Dorr is aware, in his way, of the ways in which "speech is indicative of sorrowful history," he focuses on the "living language" of monumental and ancestral history to locate his sense of security and confidence.

This was a security that Dorr discovered through the negotiation of his restricted movement as a slave, for he was enslaved throughout his travels around the world. Born in New Orleans in the late 1820s, Dorr was owned by Cornelius Fellowes, a lawyer who promised Dorr his freedom following their three-year trip around Europe and the Near East. Upon their return, Dorr escaped from Louisiana when Fellowes failed to live up to his promise and settled in Cleveland, where he wrote and published *A Colored Man Round the World*. In one of the few commentaries on the book, Malini Johar Schueller rightly notes that the narrative's very existence highlights "fundamentally unequal rights of access: those available to a slave and those available to a citizen free to travel" (ix). "Travel," Schueller observes, "implies a certain freedom of mobility and access to sights and cultural spaces that then get reported in travel narratives. This does not mean that slaves did not travel but rather that their travel was circumscribed by the fact that they were part of an entourage" (ix). The question was not just the nature of one's travel but the status available to that person by way of traveling, for "slaves, like the servants of Victorian bourgeois travelers, scarcely ever achieved the status of 'travelers,' the power to comment and interpret being largely an 'Anglo' privilege. . . . Being a traveler meant assuming mobility and the complex network of race, class, and gender privileges accruing a genteel (Anglo) identity" (ix). Dorr was not alone in challenging such assumptions, but his narrative is a singular example of an attempt to claim the privileges of traveling while still within the restricted sphere of enslavement. It is an attempt that he presents as both a product and a gift of time, something that will enable readers to "gain time and knowledge in the stride of life" (189).

Dorr draws us to the laws of mobility that regulated antebellum African American life, laws that were reformulated in various ways after the Civil War and Reconstruction. I need not review here the fact that the mobility of the enslaved was flexible but highly policed, that mobility away from one's owners became a notorious national concern after the Fugitive Slave Act in the Compromise of 1850, or that mobility in company with one's owners became a central national concern in the Supreme Court's 1857 decision on Dred Scott. As Dorr reminds us, the white equation of national security with controlling the mobility of the enslaved did not break down at the nation's borders. Indeed, the challenge in approaching nineteenth-century African American literature is not to somehow "get beyond" the nation-state but rather to recognize the international web of economics, politics, law, and religion within which the nation-state operated. It was difficult, after all, if not impossible, for African Americans to ever leave the United States, whether or not they were physically located in the country. Like Dorr, Frederick Douglass, William Wells Brown, William and Ellen Craft, and many others were legally the property of U.S. slaveholders even as they traveled to Europe; for them, the experience of even nominal freedom was contingent upon what amounted to a bill of sale. But while mobility was hardly the same as freedom, it still offered some degree of liberty. In fact, great mobility was common in the case of many enslaved individuals who either escaped (temporarily or permanently),[12] hired themselves out in the cities, or traveled as personal servants to their owners. Manipulation of the limited mobility available to them was, moreover, a common form of slave resistance, a way of stretching out the time it took to go from one duty to the next. In the North, restriction of mobility most prominently took the form of segregated transportation—something that Douglass, Brown, and many others frequently comment on in their work, and something that William Still, Sojourner Truth, and many others actively fought through the press and the courts. Restricted mobility was, for virtually all African Americans, a fundamental fact of life.

It is hardly surprising that so much of African American history and literature involves the dynamics of movement, of painful departures and difficult arrivals, and the endless task of negotiating social spaces designed for a white supremacist culture. Pre–Civil War African American literature and history are especially marked by stories of strategic mobility—mobility as a form of resistance and self-determination. The overwhelming majority of slave narratives involve the dangerous journey from the South to the North, to the point that the journey to the North and to Canada became an established trope, an expected story. Some of the most celebrated slave narratives (among them, Henry Box Brown's and William Craft's) capitalize on their readers' expected fascination with impossible mobility; others (Frederick Douglass's, most prominently) make a point of refusing that story to the readers. No doubt Martin Delany's tale of much broader travels in his novel *Blake* was in part a response to such expectations—concluding the journey to Canada, as it does, not at the book's end but at its middle, with other necessary journeys to follow afterward. Spiritual autobiographies by African American women present travel as the necessary means by which a female preacher could assert her authority beyond the confines of the patriarchal church. It is hardly surprising, too, that so many of the emancipated population after the war first looked for the experience of freedom through a luxurious indulgence of both time and mobility, opportunities that were quickly suppressed after the failure of Reconstruction and the renewal of "slavery by another name" in the South.[13] Such repressive acts highlighted, in turn, another movement devoted to mobility, the emigration of African Americans to the west or to urban centers in the North.

Certainly, African American writers understood that there was a ready audience for stories of escape by subterfuge, with both state and national boundaries marking particular sites of narrative and even moral resolution. White British reformer Harriet Martineau spoke for many when she wrote in 1838 that "the finest harvest-field of romance perhaps in the world is the frontier between the United States and Canada." "The vowed student of human nature," Martineau suggested, "could not do better than take up his abode there, and hear what fugitives and their friends have to tell," for "there have been no exhibitions of the forces of human character in any political revolution or religious reformation more wonderful and more interesting than may almost daily be seen there" (*Retrospect* 253).

As Martineau's comments indicate, one did not need to be a reformer to feel the tug of this story; many students of human nature gathered at the shores of the slave narratives to explore the various frontiers that defined the boundaries of freedom in the United States. Nor has this situation changed much over the years. As David Blight has observed, "Despite all the changes in historical education related to the teaching of slavery that have occurred in recent decades, it is still likely that the average American encounters the subject first, and most often, through the *lore* of the Underground Railroad" ("Why the Underground Railroad?" 234). Frederick Douglass was one among many who understood the tug of this story, and he understood as well the ways in which the story, then as now, obscured or even undermined a more important historical understanding, one capable of promoting not just celebration of successful escapes but active resistance to the conditions that made such stories necessary in the first place. "I have never approved," writes Douglass, "of the very public manner in which some of our western friends have conducted what they call the *underground railroad*, but which, I think, by their open declarations, has been made most emphatically the *upperground railroad*" (*Narrative* 85).

One such story appears at the end of this chapter and the postwar situation is examined in Chapter 5, but here I wish to explore the ways in which the laws of mobility were negotiated as a major challenge of literary representation. Accordingly, I will consider the different transatlantic travel experiences represented in the accounts of two writers closely associated with the antislavery movement, William Wells Brown and Harriet Martineau. Brown wrote about his travels through Europe in *Three Years in Europe; or, Places I Have Seen and People I Have Met* (1852), generally considered the first travel narrative published by an African American. Martineau wrote of her travels in the United States in two important publications, *Society in America* (1837) and the two-volume *Retrospect of Western Travel* (1838). In these works Martineau and Brown present themselves essentially as cultural theorists who challenge the stability of white American and European assumptions about identity, civilization, and progress. They each embody a version of what I will call the "fugitive tourist," whose fugitive status (legal in Brown's case, cultural in Martineau's) becomes the necessary perspective for understanding the performative nature of individual and collective identity. They are fugitive tourists because they have stepped out of an assigned social position, a transgression that is liberating but that comes with a price. The fugitive tourist, exploring the theory and practice of society from shifting locations and shifting perspectives, remaps history and restages identity, leaving her or his readers with a world of possible performances but no stable script. Ultimately, Martineau and Brown present a choreographic rendering of a world in which instability and movement are the only consistent characteristics, in which the fugitive is the only reliable guide, and in which strategic negotiations of the laws of mobility become the means by which authority can be crafted in a narrative performance.

Of the two works, Brown's *Three Years in Europe* is the one most easily misread, for one can imagine Brown trying to imitate the cultural perspective of an established form of writing. William W. Stowe, for example, has studied the role of "travel and travel writing . . . in William Wells Brown's self-construction, . . . strengthening his claim to the cultural and political power of the cultivated gentleman of letters" (67). Stowe argues that the American edition of Brown's narrative is rather conventional, and that "its very conventionality supports its author's implicit claim that African Americans are the spiritual and intellectual equals of their white compatriots" (70). But while Brown is attentive in *Three Years* to the conventions of travel writing and aesthetic appreciation, he never allows the reader to forget that he is a fugitive slave and that this extended commentary on European culture is the backdrop for his ongoing self-construction as a black abolitionist.[14] Brown recognized well the challenges he faced in this attempted self-construction. It should be emphasized that when he added chapters to his travel narrative for the American edition, entitled *The American Fugitive in Europe*, he included a portrait of the role-shifting, African-born Joseph Jenkins. Brown encounters Jenkins time and again in England—each time Jenkins is playing a different professional role, including preaching and acting. Brown identifies Jenkins as "the greatest genius that I had met in Europe" (275). Interestingly, when Brown speculates about the identity of this man whom he encounters in so many situations, he presents a figurative portrait of his own position in the constellation of black male antislavery leadership—for Jenkins is "too black for Douglass, not black enough for Ward, not tall enough for Garnet, too calm for Delany, [and] figure, though fine, not genteel enough for Remond" (279). The more we know about each of these men, and about the tensions that characterize their relationships with one another, the more they seem to represent an ideological profile of Brown himself. Brown, in other words, was not merely equal to his white "compatriots"; he was a genius uniquely suited to his situation, a man who thought carefully about his own culturally scripted role as a black public figure.

Like Joseph Jenkins, Brown avoids being neatly positioned, in part by assuming the role of a cultured traveler constantly recontextualized as he moves from place to place. As Jenkins performed the various social roles available to a black male in England, assuming authority over each but contained by none, so Brown constantly repositions himself in relation to people, art, and history in his travels. In short, Brown approached the considerable challenge of self-definition by restaging the multiple contingencies of identity and the positional codes of American cultural understanding. Brown was an astute observer of antislavery culture, and often he looked with wry humor on the public sphere that provided him with a public role. In *Three Years in Europe*, significantly, he surveys the field of reform lecturers he knew, characterizing reformist culture as he describes each man. Of the white abolitionist Charles C. Burleigh he says, "If he did not speak so fast, he would equal Wendell Phillips; if he did not reason his subject out of existence, he would surpass him" (265). He praises a temperance reformer for his ability to cry on cue and explains that the reformer's habit of falling off the wagon is one of his strengths as a temperance advocate. What is particularly interesting, though, is Brown's description of the antislavery ally James N. Buffum. "Were we sent out," Brown says, "to find a man who should excel all others in collecting together new facts and anecdotes, and varnishing up old ones so that they would appear new, and bringing them into a meeting and emptying out, good or bad, the whole contents of his sack, to the delight and admiration of the audience, we would unhesitatingly select James N. Buffum as the man" (267). Brown did not question the ideals behind the reform movement, but he often demonstrated an insightful understanding of the culture of reform, including its reliance on an established discourse that shaped both what one could say and what one's audience could be expected to hear, its stock of various public performers who stood somewhere between devotion to their cause and devotion to themselves, and its implication in the ideology of race that supported the very platform upon which Brown stood. To a great extent, Brown's task was to reconstruct that platform without losing his footing, a task that he handles, in effect, by taking his show on the road, recontextualizing antislavery discourse in the shifting settings of cultured travel.

Harriet Martineau stood on a considerably different platform, but she similarly faced the challenge of constructing an identity on the public stage. Martineau's role as a reformer is well known, and she was rather consistently a controversial figure—in her antislavery views, in her promotion of women's rights, in her challenges to Christianity, and generally in her determination to redefine her assigned role as a woman. Indeed, *Society in America* was controversial largely because of her comments on white women, Northern American racism, and slavery. To be sure, Martineau was well received during her travels through the states by Southerners and Northerners alike, and in *Society in America* she expresses her belief that her views were in no way an obstacle to her attempt to understand all of the regions she visited. "My opinions of slavery were known," Martineau asserts, "through the press, before I went abroad: the hospitality which was freely extended to me was offered under a full knowledge of my detestation of the system. This was a great advantage, in as much as it divested me entirely of the character of a spy, and promoted the freest discussion wherever I went" (2:147).

But though Martineau was not exactly a spy, and though she did enjoy the luxury of candor during her travels, she found that free discussion sometimes came at a price. As a result of her comments at an 1835 meeting of the Boston Ladies Anti-Slavery Society—at which she declared her commitment to the cause of the abolitionists—she was largely ostracized by Boston society. As she related in "An Autobiographic Memoir" many years later, "she was subjected to insult and injury, and was even for some weeks in danger of her life while traveling where the tar-barrel, the cow-hide, and the pistol were the regimen prescribed for and applied to abolitionists, and threatened especially in her case" (*Daily News*, June 1876; qtd. in Pichanick 90). The experience did not soften Martineau's approach to *Society in America*, for as she stated in a letter to William Johnson Fox in 1837, "I have never hesitated a moment as to how to write this book, though there has been no end to the importunity with wh[ich] I have been instructed to make it *moderate & popular*" (Burchell 43). "It is many years," she continues, "since I became fully convinced that I could not live for any other purpose than ascertaining & avowing truth: & the witnessing & being implicated in the perils & struggles of the abolitionists in the present martyr age of America has, of course, strengthened my convictions" (Burchell 44). Martineau rightly associated herself with the work of the abolitionists and, if not quite a spy, was by this time a fugitive tourist—someone who traveled under the guise of other people's assumptions, someone who had taken from her travels something more than what her hosts wanted her to have, and someone whose presence in print was an indictment against the system of slavery.

In the stability of its shifting perspective, the travel narrative is an apt vehicle by which to explore the presence of ideological contradictions of a complex society. While sailing to the United States, Martineau sketched out her method for such explorations in *How to Observe Morals and Manners*; published in 1838, the book has been called "the first substantive treatise on sociological methodology" (Hill xi). In this work Martineau notes that "a good deal may be learned on board steamboats, and in such vehicles as the American stages" (62). Adopting this advice both literally and philosophically, Brown and Martineau both present travel narratives of which the only unifying principle is the stable perspective of the narrator. In using one travel experience to draw out the underlying principles of another, both writers construct what I am calling a "choreographic unity"—a unity of philosophical stability in cultural movement. This choreographic unity is the result of their efforts to expose and juxtapose the contending forces of an unstable culture, and to identify the principle that caused the instability.

In Martineau's *Society in America*, the spectator's gaze is constantly disrupted by the ideological contradictions that define the fugitive. At one point, the author asks: "What social virtues are possible in a society of which injustice is the primary characteristic? in a society which is divided into two classes, the servile and the imperious?" (1:313).[15] Later she answers this question implicitly with another: "What security for domestic purity and peace can there be," Martineau wonders, "where every man has had two connexions, one of which must be concealed; and two families, whose existence must not be known to each other; where the conjugal relation begins in treachery, and must be carried on with a heavy secret in the husband's breast, no words are needed to explain?" (2:327). The moral perspective behind these questions reoccurs time and again throughout *Society in America* and *Retrospect of Western Travel*, disrupting and transforming what would otherwise be a conventional scene. For example, the conventionally sublime portrait of Niagara Falls gives way to the ultimately sublime sight of the fugitive slave's leap for freedom from the United States to Canada (*Retrospect* 253). Boston society is disrupted by the narrative of the riotous abuse of abolitionist William Lloyd Garrison by a "monied mob" of respectable gentlemen (*Society* 1:175). A survey of the U.S. Congress reveals mainly the extent to which American principles have been supplanted by the geographical and ideological divisions of the system of slavery (*Retrospect*, 164–84). What is fugitive in Martineau's narrative is the stable ideological position of the narrator as revealed by the shifting cultural locales she visits. A single concern arises, and the changing objects of the spectator's gaze map out the ideological contours of the fugitive perspective.

But to say that both Harriet Martineau and William Wells Brown transgressed their assigned social boundaries is not to say that they found themselves in the same fugitive space. Brown understood all too well that the fugitive slave was literally the embodiment of the American contradiction between professed principle and practice. To achieve the status of "fugitive slave" was but to step into another assigned role. To be publicly a fugitive slave was to become the site of ideological conflict. Gestures toward the fugitive became political statements, and the qualities of the fugitive body and character were itemized as plainly as they would be at any slave auction. It became significant, for instance, to recognize Brown as a man, to treat him as an equal; every public sign of recognition was a reminder of his spectacular visibility. Brown was, in effect, a traveling spectacle, a kinetic cultural artifact, and in *Three Years in Europe* the black spectator's gaze becomes itself the object of the white spectator's gaze. One observes the fugitive slave as he observes the monuments and celebrities of European culture.

It is important, then, to recognize what is often missed in readings of *Three Years in Europe*—that the fugitive is not merely the figure in the narrative but also the guiding perspective *of* the narrative. In *Three Years*, Brown's self-construction involves continual recontextualization, so that the collective achievements of European civilization gradually frame an identity that is undefinable in American society. The assumptions behind Martineau's and Brown's understanding of cultural achievements as they relate to group identity are, in this respect and others, significantly different. In thinking about the effects of racial hierarchies in America, Martineau offers a view of African American identity that reveals much about the limits of her understanding of the position Brown occupied, for Martineau presents a rather stereotypical generalization of African American character to suggest the principles that define white American national character. She writes:

> The Americans possess an advantage in regard to the teaching of manners which they do not yet appreciate. They have before their eyes, in the manners of the coloured race, a perpetual caricature of their own follies; a mirror of conventionalism from which they can never escape. The negroes are the most imitative set of people living. While they are in a degraded condition, with little principle,

little knowledge, little independence, they copy the most successfully those things in their superiors which involve the least principle, knowledge, and independence; viz. their conventionalisms.
(3:99)

Brown, who knew something about this image of "the coloured race,"
presents a different kind of imitative performance, that of the cultured
traveler, and uses this context to suggest an identity not yet contained,
not yet definable—the identity most fully realized by Joseph Jenkins,
who succeeds by playing with and against his assigned roles. In writing
a narrative of European travel, Brown was similarly open to the charge
of imitativeness—as I have noted, the conventionalism of *Three Years in
Europe* and *The American Fugitive in Europe* has often been highlighted
by Brown's readers. But any reasonably careful reader will see that these
are narratives that both feature and study reactions to Brown and to William and Ellen Craft—reactions that are, arguably, the primary subject of
the narratives. In short, Brown makes himself the object of the cultivated
spectator's gaze only to make that gaze itself the object of his study as he
travels.

In the end, both Martineau and Brown leave us with an image of an unformed national character. The only stable identity is that of the fugitive
tourist—the one who can juxtapose the multiple contingencies of public
life to suggest an identity not quite revealed in any given situation. And
where does this lead? What is the eventual destination for each of these
tourists? For Martineau, the United States remained a realm of promise.
In *Society in America*, she exclaims: "I regard the American people as a
great embryo poet: now moody, now wild, but bringing out results of absolute good sense: restless and wayward in action, but with deep peace at
his heart: exulting that he has caught the true aspect of things past, and at
the depth of futurity which lies before him, wherein to create something
so magnificent as the world has scarcely begun to dream of" (1:39).

Many years later, Brown seems to respond to Martineau in his travel
narratives, for the organizing principle of both *Three Years in Europe* and
*The American Fugitive in Europe*, I would argue, is in fact the cultural
geography of national poetry. As he takes up the work and habitats of
European poets, Brown gradually transforms the fugitive tourist into
the figure of the poet. Perhaps it is significant, then, that Brown's most
pointed pronouncement on national poetry comes in his chapter on Harriet Martineau. As he states there:

No one can look back upon the lives of Dante, Shakspeare [*sic*], Milton, Goethe, Cowper, and many others that we might name, without being reminded of the sacrifices which they made for mankind, and which were not appreciated until long after their deaths. We need look no further than our own country to find men and women wielding the pen practically and powerfully for the right. It is acknowledged on all hands, in this country, that England has the greatest dead poets, and America the greatest living ones. (*American Fugitive* 187)

In short, Brown addresses the subsequent development of the embryo poet of which Martineau wrote; the European fugitive tourist's perspective finds embodiment years later in the American fugitive tourist in Europe. In his reflections on the moral challenge of poetry, Brown remarks: "The poet and the true Christian have alike a hidden life" (*American Fugitive* 187). By way of that hidden life, Brown, like Martineau, presents us with a story of travels through a landscape transformed by the fugitive tourist's visible but unseen presence.

The necessity, and liberating or political possibilities, of fugitive or strategic mobility was a fact of life for many African Americans, North and South, and such movement is often central to the narrative strategies of African American literature. Harriet Jacobs famously negotiated her escape in part by creating the illusion of mobility even as she faced her extensive confinement in a crawl space, arranging for letters to be sent from New York—in her narrative those and other letters play a pivotal role, as readers are asked and even taught to interpret the fraudulent letters she received from the South. Solomon Northup's narrative draws readers into the story of his kidnapping and enslavement, then brings that account to a head as Northup struggles to fashion the pen and ink (and stolen foolscap) he needs to get a letter to friends in the North. Thomas Jones, who had purchased his wife's freedom, reprints the letters she wrote him from New York, along with his warnings to write as if she does not like New York and plans to return to him, so as to throw off Jones's owner, whom Jones knew would intercept and read the letters. David Walker smuggled his *Appeal* to the South; copies of *Freedom's Journal* and other newspapers also reached the South. Box Brown, of course, had himself shipped to the North, following correspondence with antislavery agents in Philadelphia to ensure that someone would attend to that all-important crate upon its arrival. Moreover, the many activities gathered under the heading of "Underground Railroad" involved both fraudulent and actual accounts of movement, sometimes to create the illusion of significant networks, sometimes to veil actual movement, and sometimes (as in the case of Ellen Craft) to use the publication of an escape as a way of getting word to those who remained in the South that their loved ones had safely arrived.[16] Many African American writers understood very well the role of the printed page in the achievement of both virtual and actual mobility, the means by which the controls they faced might be destabilized and used for other purposes. Moreover, they understood the advantages of presenting familiar configurations of racial performances in settings that would expose the injustice or absurdity of the U.S. racial order. In numerous ways, then, nineteenth-century writers contended with, manipulated, and otherwise represented the laws of mobility central to African American life.

## Laws of Affiliation

William Wells Brown, like many other writers, seized upon the possibilities of movement to renegotiate the terms and possibilities of his public identity as an "American fugitive," and also to claim an identity and an authority different from the ones that white readers generally associated with people of African descent. Although Brown had published the *Narrative of William W. Brown, a Fugitive Slave, Written by Himself* in 1847 and *Clotel* in 1853, an 1855 review of *Three Years in Europe* appearing in the *Liberator*, a paper particularly supportive of Brown, carried the significant title "A Fugitive Slave Turned Author." The piece began by asserting (implicitly drawing a distinction between slave narratives and other antislavery publications and literature), "It is a new thing in this country for a slave to become an author" (5). No doubt, Brown understood the assumptions behind this gesture. In the same month, another article in the *Liberator* celebrated "the first attempt of a colored man to give a course of Lectures, embracing other topics than the anti-slavery subject," referring to a series of lectures that Brown presented in Philadelphia. In that forum, Brown covered such subjects as "the great men and women of the Old World," "The Humble Origin of Great Men," "Mahomet and Confucius," and his published lecture, "St. Domingo, Its Revolutions and Its Patriots" ("William Wells Brown at Philadelphia" 14). Through these and other lectures, and through the publication of self-consciously *literary* performances in fiction, drama, and travel narratives (as opposed to the expected autobiographical narratives and antislavery orations), Brown indeed tried to negotiate a shift from "fugitive slave" to "author." The response of most white readers emphasizes the extent to which Brown's attempts to define himself on his own terms were constantly trumped by a reading public that associated him with a narrow understanding of a black man's public role and cultural affiliations, including their assumptions about what constituted a literary performance.

The laws of affiliation in the nineteenth century were in some ways flexible but in many ways strict. Although many African Americans, north and south, crafted exceptional lives that gained them substantial wealth and a broad world of social relations, it was impossible to craft lives that operated in some imagined cultural zone in which race was of no consequence. It was also impossible to avoid entirely the legal insistence on whiteness as a defining characteristic for the rights and privileges of citizenship, as the *Dred Scott* decision made painfully clear. In her examination of Abby Guy's suit against William Daniel in 1855, in which Guy "complained that he held her and her children unfairly in slavery despite the fact that she was white," Ariela Gross underscores the importance of affiliation as a legal distinction. "Witnesses," Gross observes, "testified about Guy's appearance, her reception in society, her conduct, her self-presentation, and her inherited status," and the jury was left to decide Guy's racial status ("Litigating Whiteness" 111). Such trials, "at which the central issue became the determination of a person's racial identity," as Guy's case documents, "were a regular occurrence in Southern county courts in the nineteenth century" (111). Consequently, Gross argues, "law made the 'performance' of whiteness increasingly important to the determination of racial status," a performance that included "the performance of acts of citizenship" unavailable to those recognized in their communities as nonwhite. Among the means by which such performances were judged was "what nineteenth-century judges and lawyers commonly called 'reputation evidence,'" which referred to "testimony about a person's acceptance in the community, including the person's associations with blacks or whites and the racial status his neighbors assigned to him—what he 'passed for'" (147).[17]

"Reputation evidence" played a prominent role as well in both the crafting and the reception of nineteenth-century African American literature. As is abundantly clear to anyone who has read William Wells Brown's *Clotel* (1853) or Frank Webb's *The Garies and Their Friends* (1857), African American writers did not seek to represent simple racial binaries in their work—but they contended all the same with what I am calling "laws of affiliation," and in various ways. As Brown's example suggests, African American writers contended with white concepts of literary and cultural affiliations, which both complicated any writer's attempt to extend his or her range of subjects and placed pressure on writers to represent the possibilities of those of African descent generally. To illustrate, Frances Smith Foster points out that Frances Harper faced a heightened challenge not only to her own reputation but also to her inevitable role as a representative of her race when she turned from her successful career as a poet and lecturer to an author of novels. Harper first published novels serially in the *Christian Recorder*, a forum sponsored by the African Methodist Episcopal Church and therefore one directed primarily to African American readers. But when she published her fourth novel, *Iola Leroy*, in book form, she confronted in a different way the laws of affiliation that led her to devote so much energy to black communities. "Were she to fail to produce a novel that would refute the myths created by writers such as Thomas Nelson Page," Foster observes, "were she to fail to arouse sympathies equal to those stirred by writers such as Helen Hunt Jackson, Harper knew her failure would be cited as evidence not only of her own declining abilities [she wrote the novel at age sixty-seven], but also of the artistic inferiority of Afro-Americans in general" (Introduction to *Iola Leroy* xxxiv).[18] Similarly, Samuel Ringgold Ward comments in his *Autobiography* about his role as pastor of a church in which the "congregation were all white persons save my own family" (80). "If I should acquit myself creditably as a preacher," Ward recalls thinking, "the anti-slavery cause would thereby be encouraged. Should I fail in this, that sacred cause would be loaded with reproach" (81). In a somewhat different experience of the laws of affiliation, Charles W. Chesnutt, frustrated over the social boundaries in which he was forced to live, once complained in his journal about his life in the South: "I occupy here a position similar to that of the Mahomet's Coffin. I am neither fish[,] flesh, nor fowl—neither 'nigger,' poor white, nor 'buckrah.' Too 'stuck-up' for the colored folks, and, of course, not recognized by the whites" (*Journals* 157–58). He imagined that life would be better in the North; for although he knew his Mahomet's Coffin of selfhood would not "reach *terra firma*" in his relation to either the black or the white population, he still envisioned that it would be a relief to "be in sight of land on either side" (158). Such laws of affiliation did not necessarily determine one's subject, but as Brown's example again suggests, racial status was inevitably a factor in the reception, or even the terms of recognition, of one's work.

Regardless of the subjects of their work, African American writers had to contend with such laws—either to write a work that would draw them into the chaotic and contested terrain decided by juries ruling on racial identity or to produce a work capable of defining the authority of authorship on different terms. Certainly, such efforts were behind Brown's approach to *Clotel*, which opens with the third-person narration of his own life, involves the imagined experiences of the enslaved daughter of Thomas Jefferson, and begins the first chapter with commentary on the "fearful increase of half whites, most of whose fathers are slaveowners, and their mothers slaves" (81). Toward the end of the century especially, Harper would make the uncertain status of racial identity, and the moral choice required for addressing laws of affiliation, a central point of her novels. In *Minnie's Sacrifice* (1869), in fact, one of the novel's major characters, Louis, first believes himself to be white, and he takes a kind of backward Underground Railroad journey during the Civil War to join the Confederacy. When informed of his mixed parentage, he learns to read himself differently, as well as to trust those more skilled readers who had lived with that kind of self-knowledge all of their lives, and who had lived on an idea now in the process of being translated into action. And so he takes an Underground Railroad journey northward, aided by various black conductors risking time and blood to help him.

African American authors often spoke of the temptation to restrict the laws of affiliation to the clear divisions of a racial binary, but their experiences would not allow them to do so. To be sure, despite the many affiliations between white and black laborers and social reformers in the nineteenth century, many African Americans believed themselves to be united not only by their legal status or a shared cultural heritage but also by a deep-seated resentment of the white supremacist culture in which they found themselves. Samuel Ward addresses this resentment in his reflections on leading an all-white congregation:

> Being deprived of the right of voting upon terms of equality with
> whites—being denied the ordinary courtesies of decent society,
> to say nothing of what is claimed for every man, especially every
> freeborn American citizen—I very well know, from a deep and pain-
> ful experience, that the black people were goaded into a constant
> temptation to hate their white fellow-citizens. I know, too, how
> natural such hatred is in such circumstances: and all I know of the
> exhibition of vindictiveness and revenge by the whites against *their*

injurers—and the most perfect justice of the Negro regarding the white man according to daily treatment received from him—caused me to see this temptation to be all the stronger: and convinced me also, that the white had no personal claim to anything else than the most cordial hatred of the black. (84–85)

Ward had no trouble reconciling the justice of such feelings with what he believed to be the equal justice of Christian love, and his alliances with white people in the United States and especially in Great Britain were strong. But his understanding of the natural results of U.S. racial history guided his approach to such alliances, leading him to resolve that he would not appeal to white audiences for sympathy, and that he would not degrade himself "by arguing the equality of the Negro with the white," particularly given his belief that "to say the Negro is equal morally to the white man, is to say but very little" (86–88). Like Ward, African American writers generally mentioned the challenge of negotiating the impossible binaries of U.S. racial life, even as they worked to characterize a generalized African American life and character in distinction against a generalized white standard.

But as Chesnutt's lament indicates, the laws of affiliation governing black life in the nineteenth century were not always embraced in the name of an idealized black community. Many slave narratives include commentary on the absence of *any* community of trust, black or white—a central dynamic in Harriet Wilson's North as well. Henry Bibb tells the story of being betrayed by two black men, and of being offered his freedom in exchange for information about other runaway slaves, an offer he refuses. Frederick Douglass similarly relates how he was betrayed in one escape attempt; when he finally made his way to the North, his motto was clear: "Trust no man!" (*Narrative* 90). The unified black community of the North in Douglass's narrative, in fact, is defined not by a threat by whites but by a black man's threat to inform on a fugitive slave. "Straightaway," Douglass relates, "a meeting was called among the colored people," to which the betrayer was invited, only to find his life threatened by a unified force directed by the appointed president of the meeting (94–95). In such cases, the laws of slavery guided the laws of affiliation, even as these accounts make clear that such affiliations were negotiated in the face of a splintered community. While often presenting such accounts, African Americans also represented numerous other divisions within black communities—tension inspired by differences of color, former or current condition, occupation, religious affiliation, social class, or the numerous other distinctions by which people everywhere define themselves with and against one another. A frequent motif in African American writing involves the experience of riding in the Jim Crow car of a train and feeling disgust at the company one is forced to keep—a theme that is lifted to the status of a major plot device in J. McHenry Jones's *Hearts of Gold*. In that novel, Regenia Wilson, who had previously traveled south without incident, is forced by a conductor to suffer the indignity of riding in the smoking car of the train. Later, the budding romance of Wilson and Dr. Stone is disturbed when Stone fails to show up to accompany Wilson to the train. Subsequently, the doctor reveals to his beloved his reasons for staying away. "If you had not been accompanied on your return," he explains, "the second trip South would have been as barren of annoyance as the first. If I had escorted you to the station in any other capacity than servant, you would have left Grandville in a smoking car. Under those circumstances you would not have returned. For ten minutes' pleasure I would have sacrificed many happy hours" (205). The doctor's certain racial status and the woman's ambiguous racial status meet, in effect, in the racialized space of the train station, where by the laws of affiliation Regenia would face "the perils of a lone woman on a southern railway car" (206). His logic is instructive, for African Americans often had to ride in the Jim Crow car of the American train, that train in which the laws of time, mobility, and affiliation came together.

Laws of affiliation were especially evident when prominent African American leaders were placed on the national stage to comment on the progress of American history. Frederick Douglass is a case in point, for like many African Americans of the nineteenth century, he was a sharp student of the rituals of history that marked the racialized sites of his public appearances, but unlike many others, he had frequent occasion to participate in those rituals before interracial audiences. In most of his speeches, Douglass focused on two primary modes of historical commentary: one located hope for the future in a carefully historicized understanding of the present moment, and the other argued that hope was all but lost in the current of its context. In his 1876 "Oration in Memory of Abraham Lincoln" at the unveiling of the Freedmen's Monument to Lincoln, Douglass is quite pointed in his management of these competing contextual frameworks. Calling attention to the great progress represented by the ceremony, he exclaims: "In view, then, of the past, the present, and the future, with the very long and dark history of our bondage behind us, and with liberty, progress, and enlightenment before us, I again congratulate you upon this auspicious day and hour" ("Oration" 310). But Douglass recontextualizes the moment in his identification of Lincoln as "preeminently the white man's President, entirely devoted to the welfare of white men," emphasizing that "in his interests, in his associations, in his habits of thought, and in his prejudices, [Lincoln] was a white man." Identifying the white audience as "the children of Abraham Lincoln" and the black audience as "at best only his step-children, children by adoption, children by forces of circumstances and necessity" (312), Douglass places the event, the monument, and the history they represent within a fractured embodiment of U.S. history, an agent of progress that represents fundamentally the sweeping force of the undercurrents of U.S. cultural, political, and racial life.

Douglass knew, too, the limits of "circumstances and necessity," a point brought home again and again in his public appearances, and a point emphasized by even less dramatic engagements in the commemorative impulse. At the 1892 unveiling of the statue of John P. Hale in Concord, New Hampshire, Douglass contrasts past racist violence in that state with the present moment. Then he expands the contrast by comparing the strength and principles of a previous generation of abolitionists to the present weakness of the Republican Party in the face of white southern violence and denials of African American rights. Although he looks to a hopeful future, his clear argument is that progress involves remembrance, and that remembrance both defines and complicates the terms by which progress can be identified. The recorded speech includes calls from the audience for Douglass to address some of the concerns of the day. One person asks, "What about suffrage down South?" Douglass responds, calling on the Republican Party to acquire "a little more backbone" and to defend the rights of African Americans. "The soul of a nation is its honor," Douglass states near the end of his recorded remarks, "and you bound yourselves when you gave the negro his liberty, when you gave him the right to vote, you pledged yourselves that you would see to it that that right would be protected" (*Statue of John P. Hale* 122–23).

What is interesting about the record of this address is that it emphasizes the position in which Douglass often found himself at such events—that of the renowned black man with an antislavery or civil rights message. Douglass claims that he did not prepare a written speech for the occasion—his remarks were influenced by the event and by his exchanges with the audience. The audience clearly respects him, enjoys his presentation, engages with him in parsing the message, then asks him to speak to and for broader concerns of African Americans—the civil rights theme is all too easily compartmentalized and reduced to what the white audience could view as a black message; it is only one of an array of issues to be considered. When Douglass finishes, the master of ceremonies offers a transition to the next speaker, a clergyman: "Not only did Mr. Hale attach to himself all reasonable anti-slavery workers, but scholars and all men striving for the upbuilding of character in their fellows" (*Statue of John P. Hale* 124). In this statement, as in the transition itself, the chairman of the event refers back to the terms of Douglass's invitation (to discuss his mid-century antislavery work), defines the context even of that limited field of activities ("all *reasonable* anti-slavery workers"), and contextualizes that realm of concerns within a much larger or more generalized cultural field ("scholars and all men striving for the upbuilding of character in their fellows"). Douglass's effort to present the issue of "negro suffrage" as a national concern is thus reversed, as national concerns are presented as a broader field inclusive of the issue of African American civil rights (or, at least, "reasonable" antislavery work) but not defined by it.

As these experiences of Douglass and other nineteenth-century African American writers suggest, what I call the laws of affiliation, while having everything to do with the operations of systemic race in the United States, could encourage but are not reducible to what Eddie S. Glaude Jr. terms "bad racial reasoning"—that is, "reasoning that assumes a tendentious unity among African Americans simply because they are black, or that short-circuits imaginative responses to problems confronting *actual* black people" (*In a Shade* x). In fact, African Americans recognized many factors leading toward the instability of any concept of black unity, and they regularly considered the means by which such instability might be addressed. In an 1865 lecture, on the occasion of the inauguration of the Douglass Institute in Baltimore, Douglass commented instructively on the results of U.S. laws of affiliation: "Now, what are those elemental and original powers of civilization about which men speak and write so earnestly, and which white men claim for themselves and deny to the Negro? I answer that they are simply consciousness of wants and ability to gratify them. Here the whole machinery of civilization, whether moral, intellectual or physical, is set in motion" ("Lecture" 181). Those who promoted African American uplift understood very well that there were many reasons why African Americans might struggle even to achieve "consciousness of wants," but, in any event, such consciousness, once attained, would face a "machinery of civilization" geared toward obstructing or denying the "ability to gratify" such wants. Consider, in this light, another example drawn from segregated public transportation, a story that William Wells Brown relates in *The Negro in the American Rebellion* (1867) about the daughter of Philadelphia activist William Still:

> I was much amused at seeing his little daughter, a child of eight or nine years, and her cousin, entering the omnibus which passed the door, going towards their school. Colored persons were not allowed to ride in those conveyances; and one of the girls, being very fair, would pay the fare for both; while the dark complexioned one would keep her face veiled. Thus the two children daily passed unmolested from their homes to the school, and returned. I was informed that once while I was there the veil unfortunately was lifted, the dark face seen, and the child turned out of the coach. How foolish that one's ride on a stormy day should depend entirely on a black veil! (366)

In this tale of fair complexions and public fares, Brown makes a point about the tenuousness of racial identifications—but he also suggests that what is most *racial* about this episode is not the face behind the veil but the veil itself, a culture of delusional constructions and crafted illusions, but a culture in which race is no less potent in relying on what we might call, adapting Douglass's statement, the "machinery of racial civilization."

The challenge for African American writers was not simply to claim racial identity or to avoid it, but rather to negotiate the various laws governing African American life so as to claim authority over their texts and over their identities. For such public figures as Douglass, Brown, and Harper, involved in the work of social reform, deliberate statements about the terms of racial identification were unavoidable, and their careers demonstrate the range of strategies by which they attempted to represent possibilities beyond the usual racial associations, a subject to which I will return in Chapter 5. For other writers, though, substantially different strategies were available.

One of the most remarkable narrative performances in terms of racial laws of affiliation is Eliza Potter's *A Hairdresser's Experience in High Life* (1859), a text that refuses to reveal any solid clues about the racial identity of its author. Sharon Dean reports that no author is listed on the title page of the original edition. Instead, she found "just underneath the title itself, a fine nineteenth-century hand had neatly penciled (librarians always use pencil), 'by Eliza Potter (colored)" (xxxiii–xxxiv). Dean imagines, and with good reason, that "Eliza Potter would have greeted the librarian's 'clarification' with a mixture of humor and ridicule," and she asserts that "what emerges as truly subversive in this protofeminist autobiography is her translation of that racist parenthetical identity into a potent angle of vision" (xxxiv). Surely this is so, for Potter does not make her own racial status in any way a part of her narrative, somewhat to the frustration of critics looking to the text for an example of nineteenth-century African American women's writing. Indeed, the most prominent scholar of Potter and her text, Xiomara Santamarina, has suggested that many critics have seemed anxious to enter *A Hairdresser's Experience* only by way of the librarian's pencil, thus recasting this text that refuses to locate its author in terms of the racial laws of affiliation. Many critics approach this work as a text that itself passes, in effect, for white. Refuting such approaches, Santamarina argues convincingly that it is Potter's "emphasis on women's entrepreneurial labor" that "marks her text's particular contribution to the African American literary tradition, a contribution that consists, ironically, in her unapologetic refusal to depict herself as a victim of racial and sexual domination in the antebellum United States" (*Belabored Professions* 108).

Potter engages readers in a consideration—and, often, an exposé—of the standards, the dynamics, and sometimes the illusions of social class, and her narrative makes clear just how resistant she was to any laws—of time, mobility, or affiliation—that anyone might think should govern her behavior. She does not do this by transcending such laws, but rather by drawing us into a story in which a deliberate and principled manipulation of such laws enables Potter to claim her authority on her own terms—as someone who had to come to grips with the pressures of her gender (marriage and motherhood, especially) and the priorities of her entrepreneurial labor, as someone who understands social status as it relates to character above all. Like Brown in Europe or Dorr around the world, Potter negotiates her narrative authority through an emphasis on movement and unexpected affiliations, though her own mobility would have set even Brown's head spinning. "Being at liberty to choose my own course," she notes, "I determined to travel, and to gratify my long-cherished desire to see the world" (11). Directed toward "the setting sun," her desires hit the obstacle of marriage in Buffalo, but she was not stalled for long, as her life and work took her to Canada, France, and other places in addition to her new home in Cincinnati, where her book was published. Readers of *A*

*Hairdresser's Experience* encounter numerous people of all social classes, including many pointed episodes concerning African Americans and slavery. Throughout, however, Potter rejects all formulas as she places these various episodes in juxtaposition—speaking against the injustices of slavery and abolitionism alike while also noting the existence and practices of black slaveholders, interracial relationships, and the social interactions of upper-class black and white men and women in the South, among numerous other concerns. By avoiding the racial inscription later added by the penciling librarian, Potter draws readers into a world in which we can plainly see that the laws we might have applied in approaching her life—of history, mobility, and affiliation—cannot account for the operation of those same laws in the world she inhabits.

African Americans knew very well that the laws governing black life in the United States did not add up to a coherent social system governed by a principled philosophical framework. Potter herself is quite clear about this in her commentary on the enslaved men and women she meets during her travels, as well as in her observations of the white upper-class clientele she serves. In this way, Potter offers "a particular contribution to the African American literary tradition," one that exemplifies from the perspective afforded by entrepreneurial labor what many African American writers tried to achieve in other contexts. In what she terms the harum-scarum presentation of her narrative, Potter addresses the harum-scarum order of the world in which she found herself, when quite young, "a stranger among strangers," someone "self-exiled from home and friends" (12). African American writers generally looked for ways to contend with the incoherent laws that governed racial identity, both in the service of slavery and in the service of systemic white supremacy. What was racial about those attempts had little to do with the author's own racial status and everything to do with her manipulation of the dynamics of history, mobility, and affiliation. Like Potter, many African American writers—indeed, most—worked to claim an identity beyond the usual formulas for understanding black life in the United States. Often their narrative performances represent their attempts to negotiate similar performances in social life, performances that were often played out in life-and-death situations.

## Representing African American Time and Space

Nineteenth-century African American literary history is the story of the terms by which such performances were managed over time, the attempts by various authors to represent new possibilities for African American life while working within the constraints of an incoherent but insistently restrictive set of social laws. I have generally referenced such attempts as examples of cultural feedback or determined iterations of established cultural patterns. Perhaps another way to identify the ways in which African American writers responded to the incoherence of racial law and a constrained theater of social performance is to gather these chaotic processes under the heading of Henry Louis Gates Jr.'s concept of signifying—one that he presents as itself unruly. For Gates, who focuses on traditions of the Signifying Monkey in approaching this concept, "the Monkey . . . is not only a master of technique . . .; he *is* technique, or style, or the literariness of literary language; he is the great Signifier. In this sense, one does not signify something; rather, one signifies in *some way*" (*Signifying Monkey* 54). This formulation describes well the work of nineteenth-century African American writers—not only in the obvious examples of tricksterism to which the critical eye is so often drawn, but also in their "motivated repetition" of the patterns of life they experienced and observed, and of the technique they embodied and enacted in their lives (66).

The dynamics of such performances are especially evident in one of the best-known but still understudied narratives that emerged from the U.S. system of slavery in the nineteenth century, the story of William and Ellen Craft's escape from bondage. The Crafts escaped in 1848, traveling from Georgia to Philadelphia by train and steamer. Ellen, whose complexion was light, was disguised as a white gentleman, and William played the role of her slave. They traveled very publicly, stopped at a southern hotel, and dealt with a number of close calls along the way, as white authorities challenged the young slaveholder's plans to take "his" slave to the North. Their risky public performances made their escape a celebrated story almost immediately upon their arrival in the North. In his narrative, *Running a Thousand Miles for Freedom*, published in London in 1860, William Craft tells the unique story of their journey and subsequent escape from Boston to England following the enactment of the Fugitive Slave Law.

*Running a Thousand Miles for Freedom* has been valued as an intriguing study of the winding color line in the nineteenth-century United States, one that operates in the margins "between male and female, white and black, and master and slave" (Andrews, *To Tell a Free Story* 213).[19] The account of the Crafts' escape has been identified as both a fugitive text and an "anti-passing narrative."[20] Ellen Craft has been characterized as an example of the "racial grotesque" that exposes the absurdity of U.S. racial culture and as a protagonist in a nineteenth-century cross-dressing tale.[21] *Running* has been praised as "a riveting story" that successfully combines various antislavery strategies of argumentation and narration (Blackett 106), though one scholar believes that "artistically . . . [it] is weakened by frequent digressions" (Starling 209). The Crafts' drama is often cited as a central story in the national narrative of slavery and race even as its particular features are misremembered or misrepresented—making it, for example, the most famous tale of the Underground Railroad even though the Crafts managed the journey on their own. Upon reaching representatives of the Underground Railroad in Philadelphia, they became instant and very public celebrities.

As these studies indicate, *Running a Thousand Miles for Freedom* works as a revealing site of the cascading ideological forces that constitute (and continually reconstitute) race in the United States. Indeed, the color line runs through the marriage of William and Ellen Craft, and they negotiate that line in a journey, first actual and then narrative, that requires not a Euclidian delineation of social space but rather a map informed by fractal geometry. In portraying the course and the terms of their journey, first to the North and then to England, William relies on a narrative style that attends to the realities of that fractal line. That is, *Running* follows the pattern of the cultural terrain it represents. Craft's narration replicates the tension between a linear story and the nonlinear chaotic realms out of which his experience, his consciousness, and his book emerge. This central tension both defines and is stabilized by a dynamic domestic realm, as William and Ellen move not simply their bodies but their marriage from enslavement to nominal freedom. Addressing the couple's attempt to maintain the security of their marriage—that relationship that their friend and fellow abolitionist William Wells Brown called the "foundation of all civilization and culture" (*Clotel* 83)—Craft refigures the terms by which "freedom" might be understood in a nation in which the fractal color line, connecting the system of slavery with the imperatives of white supremacist ideology, branches out endlessly into "free" social space.

In *Running a Thousand Miles for Freedom*, Craft is very direct in indicating the ideological terms of the journey he describes. In the preface, he quotes from both the Bible and the Declaration of Independence. From the Bible, Craft has chosen a phrase from Acts 17:26: "God made of one blood all nations of men"; from the Declaration of Independence, he cites the contested opening lines about the "self-evident" truth that "all men are created equal" (1). Both of these quotations were standard in antislavery rhetoric, often repeated, and regularly presented as evidence that, even when judged by the nation's own professed ideals, the nation still came up short. Craft echoes what would have been heard from most abolitionists when he writes, "This shameful conduct gave me a thorough hatred, not for true Christianity, but for slaveholding piety" (8). He extends this standard critique by citing proslavery laws near the beginning of his narrative and proslavery ministers (who supported the Fugitive Slave Law of 1850) toward the end.

But *Running* is best understood less as protest literature than as an attempt to chart a course through the cultural terrain shaped by this ideological instability. As his preface indicates, the Crafts' run for freedom is a journey through an opening identified years earlier by the author of the Declaration of Independence, Thomas Jefferson. In *Notes on the State of Virginia*, Jefferson wonders:

> Can the liberties of a nation be thought secure when we have removed their only firm basis, a conviction in the minds of the people that these liberties are the gift of God? That they are not to be violated but with his wrath? Indeed I tremble for my country when I reflect that God is just: that his justice cannot sleep for ever: that considering numbers, nature and natural means only, a revolution of the wheel of fortune, an exchange of situation, is among possible events: that it may become probable by supernatural interference! (163)

By the time William Craft wrote *Running*, Jefferson's concerns were well known in abolitionist circles. Antislavery writers regularly glanced at this southern statesman trembling before a just God, and Jefferson's ominous lines were especially prominent in the work of African American writers.[22]

In drawing from this tradition, though, Craft does not simply present this escape as a journey from slavery to freedom, from injustice to justice, or from violated policy to regenerated ideals, for the situation over which Jefferson trembled had become overwhelmingly complex. It was intertwined with everything from emerging narratives of national history to the dynamics of individual identity and the available scripts for social interaction and collective self-definition. Craft highlights the chaotic realities of race throughout *Running*, a text that is far more an indictment of the contradictions and instabilities inherent in white supremacist thought and culture than of the system of slavery itself. Obviously, the Crafts' successful escape relied on Ellen's light complexion and on her ability to play the social role associated with that complexion. Ellen's performance takes her into the dynamic contingencies of social identity—contingencies, as her presence makes clear, directed by the social fictions and assumptions of race. But even beyond the social world exposed by Ellen's performance, Craft takes every opportunity to identify and comment on the instabilities of race. He tells of white people kidnapped and enslaved, of other light-complexioned slaves making their escape through the guise of whiteness, and of white people who variously befriended, supported, even courted the young white slaveholder on "his" journey north. The world of *Running* cannot be described in simple racial terms, for Craft's narrative maps a social landscape marked by predictable patterns of social engagement overlaying surprising disruptions of the assumed social order.

Representing that larger story takes Craft beyond the demands of linear narration and into a highly digressive style. Although he regularly promises to return to his story, he stops just as regularly to give accounts of others in the South—those he knew, those he had heard of while enslaved, and those he had heard of or read about after his escape. Some of the digressions provide a context for understanding that Ellen's white appearance was not entirely unique. Craft tells the story of Salomé Müller, a white woman who had been enslaved. Müller failed in her first attempt to regain her freedom in New Orleans in May 1844, but won her case in June 1845, when she appealed to Louisiana's supreme court. Craft also repeats a story, drawn from George Bourne's *Picture of Slavery in the United States of America* (1834), about a white boy of Ohio who was "tanned and stained in such a way that he could not be distinguished from a person of colour, and then sold as a slave in Virginia" (6). He pauses "to quote some passages from the fundamental laws of slavery in order to give some idea of the legal as well as the social tyranny from which we fled" (10). When he finally reaches his promised story of the Crafts' escape, William pauses almost immediately to reprint an indictment against a white woman who taught a black girl to read the Bible (22–23). He later presents an overview of laws restricting the mobility of "free negroes" in the South (24), and commentary on the *Dred Scott* Supreme Court case (26). In the very brief second part of his narrative, Craft pauses again—this time to give an overview of various clergy views on the Fugitive Slave Law, reprinted verbatim from tract 33 in Wilson Armistead's *Five Hundred Thousand Strokes for Freedom*, a collection of antislavery tracts published in London in 1853. Other digressions are more pointed commentaries on what Harriet Jacobs calls in *Incidents in the Life of a Slave Girl* the "tangled skeins" of "the genealogies of slavery" (88), as Craft explores a world of mixed relations and a social system devoted to maintaining the illusion, against all evidence, of a stable color line.

Such digressions, of course, are essential if the reader is to understand how the Crafts' escape was even possible. Indeed, the account of a light-complexioned black woman capable of passing through the white social landscape with her visibly black husband, *Running* is *necessarily* a narrative of digressions. African Americans in the antebellum United States (and long afterward) regularly observed that the literature, the national mythology and textbook histories, the rhetoric of Fourth of July celebrations, the discourse of churches, and a host of other public documents, proclamations, and stories were drastically inconsistent when it came to the realities of nineteenth-century U.S. cultural life. Craft's challenge was to represent the world created by such inconsistencies, to account for the stories, the assumptions, and the complex social forces that made his story necessary and then directed the available means for telling it. Most fundamentally, he had to account for the forces that constituted his identity as an enslaved black man and that reconstituted his identity as a free black man in England or as an author of a slave narrative. In effect, we are led to ask, How should we understand the *craft* of this narrative?

In a famous demonstration of the limitations of simple assumptions about geometric representation and measurement, Benoit B. Mandelbrot asks: "How long is the coast of Britain?" (25). Framing this question in terms of the story Craft tells, we might ask, "How far is a thousand miles?" As N. Katherine Hayles notes of Mandelbrot's question, the matter of asking the length of a coast "is more devious than it appears, because the answer is scale-dependent" (*Chaos Bound* 210). If measured with a large ruler, the coast will be much shorter than if measured by a very small one, especially one more sensitive to each twisting bend of the coast—in fact, "Britain's coastline *continues to grow without limit* as the ruler scale decreases" (210). Pointing out that standards of and motives behind measurement vary greatly and always reflect deeply invested choices, political and otherwise, Mandelbrot states: "In one manner or another, the concept of geographic length is not as inoffensive as it seems. It is not entirely 'objective.' The observer inevitably intervenes in its definition" (27). Mandelbrot thus looks for another way to consider the highly variable boundaries between land and water, attending not to differing measures of length but to predictable patterns across different scales of measurement, an identifiable regularity in the variations. Having observed that "coastlines' geometry is complicated," he points out that "there is also a great degree of order in their structure," for "in a rough approximation, the small and large details of coastlines are geometrically identical except for scale" (34).

In applying this concept to the Crafts' experience, I am not simply being metaphorical, for the real measure of their journey involves the relation between local and national configurations of racial practices. However precisely one might measure the miles between their point of departure and their point of arrival, the Crafts embarked with a deep realization of "the solemn fact that we had to take our lives, as it were, in our hands, and contest every inch of the thousand miles of slave territory over which we had to pass" (Craft 28). Taking lives over which they had no legal right into their own hands—"our lives, as it were"—the Crafts recognized that their journey involved complex social forces that shaped their identities while also providing for their disguises during the trip (including William's disguise as a slave, the role enforced on him from his birth). These same forces shaped the theater of each engagement along the way, from the cars on the train to the room in a hotel "which John C. Calhoun, and all the other great southern fire-eating statesmen, made their head-quarters while in Charleston" (34). Just as Mandelbrot says that "the concept of dimension should at the same time account for the coastlines' irregularity, their fragmentation, and the relationship between irregularity and fragmentation" (332), so the concept of social dimension in the Crafts' narrative should account for the irregularities of the social order, the bays and eddies they encounter along the way as they try to match their performances with the particular requirements of each situation. As they encounter black people who are white, white people who become black, porous and shifting boundaries between freedom and enslavement, and a world of relations that are both acknowledged and hidden, honored and violated, readers of the narrative enter into the fractal social geometry of the text and of the Crafts' world. To ask how far is a thousand miles, then, is simply to ask whether we can reasonably say that the Crafts' journey was equal to that of a white man making the same trip.

Through his digressive narration, Craft accounts for the fractal dimensions of the journey—measuring this journey, in effect, not in terms of miles but by the emerging regularity of a seemingly irregular journey. "Time in fractal geometry," Hayles has observed, "is not treated as the advancement of points along a number line" but instead "is conceptualized as small changes in the iterative formulae that are used to generate fractal shapes" (*Chaos Bound* 290). In representing the journey north, Craft draws readers into a world of complexly mixed relations and, we might say, mixed narrations. To measure this journey, we would need to account for a dynamic yet unstable complex of relations involving social time and space, cultural history and social theaters of performance.[23] Ellen's success, after all, depended on her performance of race, gender, and class, a performance that meant both anticipating and fulfilling the expectations of others. Told that it was against the rules "to take a slave out of Baltimore into Philadelphia" unless she could document her right to do so, Ellen, in her guise as William Johnson, draws the sympathy of the surrounding crowd "merely because they thought," William Craft reports, that "my master was a slaveholder and invalid gentleman, and therefore it was wrong to detain him" (46), at which point Ellen insists on her (rather, his) rights. Throughout the journey, "Mr. Johnson" is admonished that he should not treat his slave so well and that he should not risk taking a slave to Philadelphia. At times, Ellen/Mr. Johnson is given a pointed lesson on the proper treatment of slaves, as when one passenger on a steamer, as William relates, swears at his "poor dejected slave . . . merely to teach my master what he called the proper way to treat me" (33). In the second part of the narrative, readers encounter stories of racial prejudice and white assumptions about black identity that are, in many ways, extensions of the Crafts' experiences during their journey from the South. This is a journey, in short, that proceeds situation by situation, conversation by conversation, as the couple travels a racial—not just a geographic—landscape. Describing a white supremacist world in which language was strained to maintain its own philosophical groundings, in which social contexts were self-consciously created and maintained, and in which social identity was driven by increasingly elaborate cultural constructions, William Craft's narrative advances "through the evolution of underlying structures rather than through chronological time" (Hayles, *Chaos Bound* 294).

As previously noted, the basic terms of the tensions that drive this narrative are signaled by the tension between what Craft, following African American practice generally, identifies as the sacred and the secular realms of order, a tension between "true Christianity" and "slaveholding piety" (8). This is, after all, a narrative that begins with (slightly altered) lines from John Milton's *Paradise Lost*, associates the Crafts' journey with John Bunyan's *The Pilgrim's Progress*, and concludes with a warning of the consequences of a society "notoriously mean and cruel towards all coloured persons, whether they are bond or free" (69), a warning drawn from James Russell Lowell's "A Chippewa Legend":

Oh, tyrant, thou who sleepest
On a volcano, from whose pent-up wrath,
Already some red flashes bursting up,
Beware!" (Thelma M. Smith, *Uncollected Poems* 69)

The moral realm of this narrative, in other words, is complicated by a social world that both claims the authority and corrupts the discourse of "true Christianity." It therefore must be referenced through a highly inter-textual reading of the dominant culture's own commentary on its moral failings, commentary that must be resituated to expose the racial assumptions that define the culture's overriding imperatives. As Craft's use of his sources suggests, this referencing of the moral realm is not merely an exposure of hypocrisy—for there is, finally, relatively little difference between Lowell's warning against a demonized "tyrant" sleeping on a volcano and Jefferson's trembling reflection that God is just and that His justice cannot sleep forever, aside from the fact that the years between Jefferson's warning and Lowell's had worked to the advantage of the white northern conscience. Craft needed to not just refer to the recognition of injustice but to represent the workings of the social conscience, the means by which public displays of moral sentiment were necessary to white supremacist rule—"the work of affect," as Hartman has it, "in muting vio-lence and concealing injury" (168). Thus it is that Craft's presentation of this run for freedom is marked by narrative eruptions that represent the nature and terms of the Crafts' journey, the conditions that mark its path and measure its length—a journey negotiated by a couple who embody the social forces they resist and who seek to establish a new equilibrium in chaos, a domestic security within a differently configured system of relations.

Of course, the Crafts were not alone in this world, nor alone in their understanding of it, and *Running a Thousand Miles for Freedom* is not a singular example of an attempt to represent a cultural landscape shaped by the chaos of racial ideology. Variously guided and obstructed by vari-ous laws of time, mobility, and affiliation, African Americans found them-selves on a challenging and disjointed social terrain. Often what seems most rough about nineteenth-century African American texts are those moments when their authors are attempting to be most comprehensive and precise. By such means, African American writers worked toward a narrative authority that extended far beyond the usual concepts of authenticity based on the embodiment or the superficial performance of racial identity, for theirs was an authenticity forged through their encounters with a wealth of laws, juridical and social, governing their experience of time, mobility, and community, laws that would become particularly challenging in the new social order that followed the Civil War.

## CHAPTER FIVE

# The Story at the End of the Story

## African American Literature and the Civil War

Apparent failure may hold in its rough shell the germs of a success that will blossom in time, and bear fruit throughout eternity. —FRANCES ELLEN WATKINS HARPER, "The Great Problem to be Solved"

When describing the conclusion of the Civil War in his last autobiography, and the apparent success of the cause, the "great labor of [his] life" with which he had been identified and that had provided him with a clearly defined public role, Frederick Douglass writes of his "strange and, perhaps, perverse" reaction, a "great and exceeding joy . . . slightly tinged with a feeling of sadness": "I felt I had reached the end of the noblest and best part of my life; my school was broken up, my church disbanded, and the beloved congregation dispersed, never to come together again. The anti-slavery platform had performed its work, and my voice was no longer needed. 'Othello's occupation was gone'" (*Life and Times* 811). No doubt, there was a certain cultural inevitability in Douglass's identification with William Shakespeare's Othello. Douglass's marriage to a white woman, the story of which he presents briefly in the exhausted and defensive pages of the 1892 "Third Part" that supplemented the 1881 autobiography, could only have supported his self-assigned role as a U.S. Othello.[1] Discussing this "shocking offence" to "popular prejudice," Douglass deals briefly and bitterly with this time when "false friends of both colors were loading me with reproaches," and during which President Grover Cleveland stood firm "in the face of all vulgar criticism" by paying Douglass "all the social consideration due to the office of Recorder of Deeds for the District of Columbia" (961).[2] But although Othello remains a somewhat strange choice for his public role—certainly, Douglass does not want or mean to associate himself with the whole of Othello's character or with his tragic end—Shakespeare's tragedy still provides a sadly appropriate script for him to follow, speaking, as it does, of greatness that stands on tenuous cultural grounds. As Othello relies on war for his occupation, and the respect that he gains thereby, which would not otherwise be freely offered to a Moor in Shakespeare's Venetian world, so Douglass relied on the war against slavery for his own occupation, from which he gained respect and a public role. If he had been criticized and accused, he also was able to respond as Othello responds to the accusations against him early in the play: "My parts, my title, and my perfect soul / Shall manifest me rightly" (I.ii: 31–32). The confidence in these lines extends from the sure correspondence of public and private identity, the secure union of ability, social position, and character.[3]

The second time Douglass's role as Othello enters the narrative explicitly is in his account of his association with the Freedmen's Bank, an association that cost him much in reputation—bringing upon his head, by his estimation, "an amount of abuse and detraction greater than any encountered in any other part of my life" (*Life and Times* 842). Here his identification with Othello is a strange mix of defensiveness and intriguing metaphorical transformations. William Andrews has argued that in *My Bondage and My Freedom* Douglass appropriates the Prometheus metaphor to achieve a double identity by which he could alternately play devil and savior (*To Tell a Free Story* 231), and we might be justified in imagining an allusion to Prometheus in the same sentence from *Life and Times* in which Douglass quotes from *Othello*. Prometheus appears in the famous scene in Shakespeare's play where Othello prepares to take Desdemona's life and confronts the finality of his action:

> . . . but once put out thy light,
> Thou cunning'st pattern of excelling nature,
> I know not where is that Promethean heat
> That can thy light relume. (5.2.10–13)

Discussing his gradual realization that the Freedmen's Bank was a lost cause even before he was recruited to serve as president, Douglass states that although the institutional edifice of the bank remained, "the life, which was the money, was gone, and I found that I had been placed there with the hope that by 'some drugs, some charms, some conjuration, or some mighty magic,' I would bring it back" (*Life and Times* 842). The quoted lines, of course, come from Othello's statement to the Senators when accused by Brabantio of enchanting Desdemona (1.3.93–94). And just as Othello promises the Senators a "round unvarnished tale" of his courtship, so Douglass offers his readers "a fair and unvarnished narration of my connection with The Freedmen's Savings and Trust Company" (841). What makes his application of *Othello* here particularly strange is that he is defending himself against charges that his service was the death of the Freedmen's Bank, that he in fact failed to relume the light. Shakespeare's tragic story of a man who has been deceived to the point of killing his own wife seems an odd explanatory framework for Douglass's own tale of discovering that, upon accepting the presidency of the bank, "I was married to a corpse" (842).

As argued elsewhere in this book, Douglass, so often considered *the* representative African American of the nineteenth century, was representative as well in his inability to define for himself a stable framework for understanding his public role, the terms of his representative status, after the Civil War.[4] The war was, among other things, a conflict of various narratives— national, regional, religious, and racial. Its influence on American literature was profound, as various studies have demonstrated.[5] It was also a time when the meaning and centrality of race in the United States was variously exposed and veiled, and in the wake of hostilities the course of racial history was altered in significant ways. Following the Civil War, the racial presence in literature by white Americans became more pronounced, regional and national narratives were newly intertwined, and the forums for constructing and presenting national and literary history were becoming increasingly institutionalized. For African Americans, the Civil War was both the fulfillment of a collective narrative of liberation and justice and, following Reconstruction, a forceful reminder of the limitations of a linear, progressive narrative of history, albeit a reminder not evident to many at the time. African American autobiography changed dramatically after the war, both because it now operated outside of an antislavery context and because it now operated within a newly threatening and profoundly complex racial environment. And as conceptions of the possibilities for self-representation changed, so did African American approaches to literature generally.

But this was not simply a historical break that separates antebellum and postbellum writers, for as Douglass's example reminds us, some of the most important African American writers of the nineteenth century—Frederick Douglass, William Wells Brown, Frances Harper, and Martin Delany, among others—wrote and published both before and after the Civil War and Reconstruction, and these writers highlight the difficult transition into a newly chaotic narrative landscape. Anthologies typically struggle to represent this transition, usually placing these writers in the antebellum period, and literary histories generally follow the national narrative in defining the significant periods of African American literary production. These divisions serve the needs of periodization in anthologies, and they do emphasize the significant transition of the African American majority from slavery to nominal freedom, but they do not account for the challenges that African Americans faced in the final decades of the nineteenth century. As Leon Litwack has observed, "In what has been called the 'nadir' of African American history, a new generation of black Southerners shared with the survivors of enslavement a sharply proscribed and deteriorating position in a South bent on commanding black lives and black labor by any means necessary" (xiv). And just as the condition of the enslaved in the South had defined the collective identity of African Americans in the North—both by positive identification and by the laws and prejudices that were fundamental to a government and an economy dependent on the system of slavery—so the newly mobile, threatened, and elusive promise of the emancipated community and of subsequent generations influenced the active networks of affiliation by which African American writers understood the possibilities and responsibilities of their efforts.

This chapter looks at a few African American writers who attempted to represent the chaotic course of African American life and possibility after the Civil War. I suggest that their texts speak of a larger body of literature barely referenced by approaches that depend on race as a settled category of analysis and that view African American literature largely as a gathering of works produced by African Americans.[6]

## The Fluidity of Race

Of the many changes wrought by the Civil War—and by the economic, industrial, and political developments that followed—one of the most significant was that of race itself. As Matthew Frye Jacobson has demonstrated, from the 1840s to the 1920s U.S. culture was characterized by a "spectacular rate of industrialization," a corresponding "appetite for cheap labor" that encouraged migration, and a "growing nativist perception of these laborers as a political threat to the smooth functioning of the republic" (*Whiteness* 41). Responding to such changes and the shifting politics of American demographics, the nation moved "from the unquestioned hegemony of a unified race of 'white persons'" to "a contest over political 'fitness' among a now fragmented, hierarchically arranged series of distinct 'white races'" (42–43). These changes in conceptions of whiteness naturally presented challenges to black Americans in their efforts to define the terms of their collective identity. While many of the most prominent African American writers and political leaders had argued against the relevance and even the existence of race, they had recognized as well that those of African heritage were subject to prejudices, laws, social practices, and scientific theories that insisted on its existence and relevance. African Americans were defined by simplified conceptions of their complex relations with Africans, other African Americans, white Americans, and various immigrant groups—conceptions that often were played out in political articles and books, scientific treatises, literature, drama, popular songs, and the minstrel stage. As I have maintained throughout this book, race is a central presence in African American history and literature not because it exists as an embodied quality but rather because African Americans have faced the challenges of living in a white supremacist culture, in a nation that made the created category of race one of its foundational and central dynamics. Thus, it is virtually impossible to understand nineteenth-century African American literature without an understanding of racial history, and, as I have emphasized, it is all too possible to misunderstand that body of literature by approaching it with a simplistic concept of race.

We need not look far for reminders of these central concerns in nineteenth-century African American print culture—including the recognition of African Americans that they would need to assert authority over print culture itself if they were to have any hope of controlling or at least influencing the dynamics of racial definition. This was clear in the 1827 editorial that defined the mission of the first African American newspaper, *Freedom's Journal*:

> We wish to plead our own cause . . . [for] too long have others spoken for us. Too long has the public been deceived by misrepresentations, in things which concern us dearly, though in the estimation of some mere trifles; for though there are many in society who exercise towards us benevolent feelings; still (with sorrow we confess it) there are others who make it their business to enlarge upon the least trifle, which tends to the discredit of any person of color; and pronounce anathemas and denounce our whole body for the misconduct of this guilty one. ("To Our Patrons")

Similarly, the members of the Colored National Convention held in

Rochester, New York, in 1853 asked in their published proceedings: "What stone has been left unturned to degrade us? What hand has refused to fan the flame of prejudice against us? What American artist has not caricatured us? What wit has not laughed at us in our wretchedness? What songster has not made merry over our depressed spirits? What press has not ridiculed and contemned us? What pulpit has withheld from our devoted heads its angry lightning, or its sanctimonious hate?" (*Proceedings* 16–17). Toward the end of the century, Anna Julia Cooper would echo these same comments in her 1892 essay, "The Negro as Presented in American Literature." Noting the tendency of white writers to base their black characters on the writers' perceptions of whatever black people they happened to encounter, Cooper complains that "a few with really kind intentions and a sincere desire for information have approached the subject as a clumsy microscopist, not quite at home with his instrument, might study a new order of beetle or bug. Not having focused closely enough to obtain a clear-cut view, they begin by telling you that all colored people look exactly alike and end by noting down every chance contortion or idiosyncrasy as a race characteristic" (186–87).

This consistent concern with misrepresentations that defined the purpose of the overwhelming majority of nineteenth-century publications produced by African American writers operated within a national and international context defined by the instabilities and often dramatically shifting dynamics of racial identification and organization—what I have termed the "chaos of race." Indeed, Mark M. Smith has argued that, while many discussions of race worked from the default mode of visual markers, increasingly race was identified and experienced by a broader realm of sensory characteristics. These other racial markers, Smith observes, became increasingly prominent toward the end of the nineteenth century, a time when "many whites worried that blackness was in danger of becoming whiteness. The number of visually ambiguous 'black' people increased (the great age of 'passing' was 1880–1925), and sight became ever less reliable as an authenticator of racial identity" (*How Race Is Made* 7). Although sensory perceptions in interracial interactions had always played a role in antebellum racial politics, their importance increased during these years, to the point of constituting a significant reconfiguration of the dynamics of racial thought and experience:

> Ascertaining racial identity was even more important under segregation than under slavery because race had to be authenticated on

a daily basis between strangers in a modernizing, geographically fluid South. The basis of segregation, a system that argued for the utter, intrinsic, static, and meaningful difference between black and white, was a product of a late-nineteenth-century, largely Western questioning of vision, in which Western elites generally, southern segregationists included, found they could no longer rely solely on their modern eyes to verify all sorts of truths, racial ones included. Segregationists faced this visual tremor with aplomb. The problems with seeing gave further authority to nonvisual sensory stereotypes, such that smelling, tasting, feeling, and hearing race were now more important—and, whites liked to believe, more reliable—than ever. (7)

The effect was to centralize racial affiliation in the imagined racial consciousness or even subconsciousness, that complex of factors that theoretically made one comfortable or uncomfortable, attracted or repulsed, empathetic or distanced in social encounters—both those encounters that took place in a racial theater of sorts (that is, those segregated areas where one could be theoretically confident about those whom one might encounter) and those that took place in less certain interpretive contexts.

This "emotional, visceral, and febrile understanding of racial identity" (M. M. Smith, *How Race Is Made* 47) was often a glaring presence in late-century writing by white authors, constituting one of the many concerns African American authors needed to address in turn. When Thomas Dixon Jr. did all that he could to demonize African Americans in his pointedly white supremacist fiction at the turn of the century, prominent among his literary devices were appeals to the senses of smell and touch, appeals brought to a visceral head in the threat of interracial rape. In his own commentary on social divisions within the black community, Charles Chesnutt similarly appealed to the senses in his complaint against the Jim Crow cars on the train. And in his story of light-skinned African Americans, "The Wife of His Youth," Chesnutt contrasts social divisions based in part on visual distinctions with the tug of a felt allegiance to a historically constituted network of affiliations. One thinks as well of the exchange in Frances Harper's *Iola Leroy* between the white Dr. Latrobe and the African American Dr. Latimer, whom Latrobe believes to be white. Latrobe boasts, "The Negro . . . is perfectly comprehensible to me"; he can always identify a "nigger," no matter how white he or she may appear, for "there are tricks of blood which always betray them" (227–29). When Latimer points out Dr. Latrobe's error, Latrobe disappears from both the scene and the novel itself. The increasing prominence of dialect, too, in its appeal to the ear, helped to serve as a racial marker and a racial boundary, indicating a more primitive, essential consciousness that spoke of a fundamentally different world and mode of understanding. From Uncle Remus to the ongoing insistence that Sojourner Truth was somehow more authentic when speaking in a stereotypically black southern dialect, white representations of black identity on the page specialized in the transformation of visual difference into that world of intellectual and sensory cues by which such differences are represented on the page.[7] The experience of reading, we might say, always involves the illusions of visual experience presented by way of verbal appeals to a broader realm of sensory and psychological experience, and the representation of race in literature is a particularly insistent example of this. Robin Winks has characterized slave narratives as "the pious pornography of their day" ("General Introduction" vi). The same can be said of a great deal of the literature produced by white writers about black subjects, whether that literature is intended to be celebratory of folk wisdom or cautionary about threats to (white) civilization.

As Mark Smith argues, and as the ongoing appeal to white readers and audiences of late-century representations of race suggest, the very instabilities of racial thought led to a new and increasingly insistent stability, for those instabilities had produced an understanding of racial identity that was "immune to logic, impervious to thought, and, as such, a perfect foundation for segregation" (*How Race Is Made* 47). In the terms I have been using in this book, it might be said that we see in the history of race following the Civil War the self-organizing tendencies of a dynamic system as viewed through chaos theory. The white rage to explain the perceived necessity of black subordination was the subject of numerous books, both fiction and nonfiction, a tradition that has had considerable influence and ongoing appeal. From such overtly racist nineteenth-century volumes as J. H. Van Evrie's *White Supremacy and Negro Subordination; or, Negroes a Subordinate Race, and (So-called) Slavery Its Normal Condition* (1868) to Richard J. Herrnstein and Charles Murray's *The Bell Curve: Intelligence and Class Structure in American Life* (1994), from Joel Chandler Harris's *Uncle Remus* series (1881–1910) to Walt Disney's film *The Song of the South* (1946), and from Thomas Dixon's fiction to the silent film *Birth of a Nation* (1915) to Margaret Mitchell's immensely popular novel (1936) and film adaptation (1939) of *Gone with the Wind*, white culture has long provided

space for essentialized representations of black identity that fall into familiar patterns. "Segregationists," Smith observes,

> lived an illogical, emotionally powerful lie that relied on gut rather
> than brain to fix racial identity and order society. Their ability to
> make solid what was always slippery is annoyingly impressive. When
> it came to race, ordinarily thoughtful people contorted reason to fit
> a system of racial segregation riddled with so many exceptions and
> nuances that it should have imploded under its own nonsense. But
> that is not what happened. Sensory stereotypes—and the unthink-
> ing, visceral behavior they encouraged, even required—helped make
> the system seem entirely stable, reasonable, and appropriate to the
> people who sponsored it. This tension, along with the ability to rec-
> oncile the ostensibly contradictory, was present from the very begin-
> ning of formal segregation. (66)

In such a dynamic system, defining the course for African American uplift, individual and collective, involved much more than direct political
action or intraracial organization. Before the Civil War, African American
abolitionists well understood the ways in which slavery, racism, economics, and politics were intricately related, and the history of the black convention movements, fraternal societies, press, and educational initiatives
demonstrates both their awareness of the comprehensive efforts required
as well as the overwhelming complexity of the task. It is no wonder that
so many black abolitionists viewed the Civil War as the second American
Revolution. But the nation waiting at the other side of that revolution was
more complex still than the one that preceded it, and it was a nation in
which race played a new, if familiar, and even more threatening role than
it had before the war.

Jacobson, one of the best historians of race in the United States, has
offered the preeminent study of "the fluidity of race" in the late decades of
the nineteenth century, though he does so by noting that the subject can
be apprehended only in parts, by way of particular case studies (*Whiteness*
137). "If race is so mutable," Jacobson asks, "then how is its instability reg-
istered at a single historical moment or in a single group's history? How
is this instability manifest in social consciousness and in the political unconscious?" In answering these questions, he considers the constructions
of Jewishness in 1877, but his explanation of his methods applies more
broadly to the demands of locating any social group during this time. He
presents his analysis as an attempt "to illustrate the changeable character

of race" and "to trace the circuitry of race from the various historic encounters that generate this mode of ascribing 'difference' to the uneven
patterns of racial recognition which leave such encounters in their wake"
(138). Offering a "quick catalogue" of the events of 1877, Jacobson observes
that "this glacial process has left in play multiple, contradictory racial
understandings of who is who: competing 'phenotypical significations'
are etched upon the body (and the body politic) not only by the residual
power of prior events and renewing acts of their cultural representation,
but also by the untidiness of history itself" (141). In short, he finds the
same instabilities in the dynamics of race that Smith identifies, but Jacobson emphasizes that these instabilities are historical—indeed, competing
historical narratives that often combine in a single moment or even a
single individual's experience and consciousness. "Race," he argues, "is
a palimpsest, a tablet whose most recent inscriptions only imperfectly
cover those that had come before, and whose inscriptions can never be
regarded as final. Contradictory racial identities come to coexist at the
same moment in the same body in unstable combinations, as the specific
histories that generated them linger in various cultural forms or in the
social and political relationships that are their legacies" (142). "Culture,"
he adds later, "as a creature of history, destabilizes race by layering different conceptual schemes atop one another in response to shifting social
and political circumstances. The palimpsest of race maps the terrain of
ascription, perception, and subjectivity for a number of immigrant groups
whose 'American experience' has scarcely been recounted as a *racial* experience at all" (170).

African Americans, confronted with a newly threatening and more
emphatically national system of repression that included the competi-
tion with immigrant groups that so preoccupied such leaders as Booker T.
Washington, found themselves facing the challenge of entering and coun-
tering many histories, many narratives, in a complex racial palimpsest
that complicated even the terms by which their collective identity or
political unity could be defined. As has often been stated, the tenuous
alliance of the white North and South was a political union managed
by way of racial unity. "American reunion," David Blight observes, was
"achievable in the end only through new regimes of racial subjugation,
a fated and tragic struggle still only in its formative years. The sections
needed one another, almost as polar opposites that made the center hold
and kept both an industrial economy humming and a New South on
the course of revival. Some of the war's greatest results, the civil and

political liberties of African Americans, were slowly becoming sacrificial offerings on the altar of reunion" (*Race and Reunion* 139). The terms of this reunion would become the guiding terms of U.S. politics from that time to the present day, with any alleviation of the ongoing sacrificial offerings, any partial granting of African American rights, marked as progress, regardless of whether the historical effects of the original sacrifice were in any way addressed or compensated. At various stages of U.S. history, African Americans would find themselves in a new configuration of the palimpsest of race, approaching with a Du Boisian double consciousness what Alice Fahs has termed white America's "doubled consciousness of blacks" after the Civil War that "enabled whites to maintain older stereotypes while looking ahead to the possibility of new social realities for African Americans" (162). Progress for African Americans was itself folded into a historical narrative that looked back as insistently as it looked forward.

With so many stories to tell, so many overlapping and competing narratives, it is hardly surprising that the Civil War is still the most popular subject among publishers and readers alike. But while many of these publications address issues of race, relatively few have been examined for what they can tell us about the palimpsest of race in the late nineteenth century and beyond. To be sure, in *Black Reconstruction* (1935) W. E. B. Du Bois famously presented excerpts demonstrating the centrality of the racist assumptions informing many white historians' accounts of the failures of Reconstruction. Yet more difficult to counter was the "emotional, visceral, and febrile understanding of racial identity" behind such narratives that had already qualified Du Bois's faith in the efficacy of historical evidence and scholarly reason in a white supremacist culture.[8] Behind such official narratives were various influential, unofficial histories (the "imagined Civil War," as Fahs has it) in the form of "war poetry, sentimental war stories, sensational war novels, war humor, war juveniles, war songs, collections of war-related anecdotes, and war histories—literature that has often been designated, then dismissed, as popular" (1). "In both the North and the South," Fahs asserts, "popular war literature was vitally important in shaping a cultural politics of war. Not only did it mark the gender of men and women as well as boys and girls, but it also explored and articulated attitudes toward race and, ultimately, portrayed and helped to shape new modes of imagining individuals' relationships to the nation" (1–2). As Fahs suggests, scholarly devotion to delimited or exclusionary notions of aesthetics has helped to obscure the racial complexity of American literary history in this era as in others. But this was a literary history deeply involved in realigning various white networks of affiliation—and like race itself, and like the complex category of whiteness that stands at the forefront of U.S. racial history, the Civil War offered not one but many narratives, together constituting various historical palimpsests to complement and reinforce the ever-shifting, dynamic palimpsest of race. "This variegated literature," as Fahs puts it, "created not just one but a multitude of different imagined wars, complicating notions of what kind of national community was created through the auspices of print culture" (10).[9]

The effects of the racial landscape that supported these multiple wars, this national community organized by way of its own instabilities, were inscribed in turn in black expressive culture. Observing that "terror, organized and random, was a persistent part of politics in the postwar South," Blight rightly states that these conditions defined the needs of African American expressive culture, and that, accordingly, "black folklore, fiction, and reminiscence have reflected the legacy of violence that began during Reconstruction" (*Race and Reunion* 108).[10] Bernard Bell similarly notes the challenges faced by black American writers of the time, observing that "as twenty-first-century readers, we are inclined to forget the tenacity of the tradition of white supremacy with which postbellum and post-Reconstruction black novelists had to contend and the gravity of their dilemma" (*Contemporary* 98). Indeed, this was both an intimate and a practical dilemma for those interested in publishing their work, for "the black novelists of the period were compelled to have their works printed privately, or to make compromises to appeal to predominantly white readers" (97). In practice, this meant that African American writers, as Dickson Bruce has documented, were not directly representative of the broader communities with which they were associated, for in their occupations, and even in their religious denominational associations, they were often quite separated from the majority, a talented tenth living in a different world from that of most African Americans. Accordingly, the *African American* dimension of their writings—often, the overt purpose of their work—was a complex affair. It is hardly surprising—given the complex racial dynamics of the era, the competing historical and popular narratives for making sense of the era, and the racial politics involved in the production and distribution of literature—that, as Bruce says, "much of what post-Reconstruction literature reveals about black American thought and action lies in its unresolved contradictions, not in the answers it gave to the pressing problems of racial injustice" (*Black American Writing* xii). Unresolved contradictions, after all, had long been at the center of African American history, experience, and identity.

The question for African American writers in the late nineteenth century, then, was what to make of these unresolved contradictions, for previous methods for folding them into a reasonably secure or at least defined conceptual framework had been left behind with the abolitionist movement. Like Frederick Douglass, many African American writers found that Othello's occupation was gone, and that in its place was a white reading public anxious for work that would fall within the spectrum of possibilities defined by Joel Chandler Harris, Thomas Dixon, and Thomas Nelson Page, author of *Ole Virginia* (1887) and other sentimental tales about the Old South and the Lost Cause. As I have suggested, Douglass's own example is instructive. I agree with Gates that "anyone . . . who writes more than one autobiography must be acutely aware of the ironies implicit in the re-creation of successive fictive selves, subject to manipulation and revision in written discourse" (*Figures* 116), and the *Life and Times of Frederick Douglass* remains both revealing and understudied in this regard as in others. Among those ironies, as I have argued elsewhere, is Douglass's attempt to write into existence a historian who takes liberties with the facts and who is his own subject, a sociologist who is his own field, and an individual entity whose identity is not wholly his to define. It is in this role as autobiographer that Douglass looks to reconcile the conflict between his self-representation and his role as representative self.[11] The clear sphere of his antislavery labor provided a coherent framework for understanding and defining his public role, but beyond that coherent framework Douglass faced a world of multiple discourses that did not offer itself to a clear oppositional stance. Beyond the self he fashioned in his 1845 *Narrative*, and especially after the Civil War, Douglass faced the task of claiming authority over multiple discourses—legal, political, social, moral, scientific—affiliated only by the common assumption of racial domination. Ultimately, though, the self one encounters in 1855 and beyond increasingly is representative in its *inability* to provide a center that can hold against the conflicting pressures of the many discursive fields it contains.

It is, indeed, difficult to find a stable center by which African American history and identity can be located in the last few decades of the nineteenth century. It was a time of extensive mobility and new modes of white supremacist containment, a time when people found themselves or placed themselves in significant new locales, new contexts, and new theaters of performance, but also a time when many African Americans both North and South found themselves in new but familiar configurations of the possibilities for individual and collective expression and opportunity.[12] Many African Americans who were prominent leaders before the Civil War found themselves, like Douglass, facing the challenge of a new political landscape and undefined public roles. Martin Delany's varying course as a Civil War officer, an active supporter of the southern Democratic Party, a renewed emigrationist, and a commentator on racial science is a virtual study of the difficulties of surveying the new racial and political landscape without the help of the maps provided by abolitionism and black activism before the war. For others, it was a time of change characterized by continuity and more focused development. William Wells Brown and Frances Harper both took their writing to new forums and new levels—Brown as a historian and Harper as a novelist; both continued their activism by way of southern tours, with Brown extending the temperance work that had been important to him from the start of his career and Harper finding renewed purpose as a lecturer, teacher, and women's rights activist. Many African American women who had been active in the antislavery movement turned to teaching in the South—for many a significant return, as was the case for William and Ellen Craft, who moved back from England and purchased a plantation in their former home, Georgia, to establish a freedmen's cooperative. But the Crafts' experience is perhaps most representative in that they encountered racial violence and insidious financial stratagems that eventually cost them their property.

Through all of these changes, and in all of the new or reconfigured locales for establishing themselves anew, African Americans were reminded again and again that they lived in a culture characterized by "terror, organized and random." Perhaps the most pressingly continuous narrative connecting past to present was the reappearance of systemic slavery and racial oppression in new forms—this time without a clear center, legalized slavery, for rallying the cooperation of white allies. When the Supreme Court's ruling in *United States v. Stanley* helped to facilitate the proliferation of Jim Crow laws, Douglass declared: "It is the old spirit of slavery, and nothing else" (qtd. in Blight, *Beyond* 95). Douglass would repeat the point ten years later in his "Introduction to the Reason Why the Colored American Is Not in the World's Columbian Exposition," which invokes the standard commemorative rhetoric of progress and principle only to quickly and decidedly deny its application, noting that U.S. history remains guided by the "asserted spirit" of American slavery (470–71).

African American writing during and after the Civil War, in short, operated within an extremely complex and fluid racial, political, and economic culture. Although this period saw a publishing boom of sorts for African American letters, there is a reason why much of it has been largely ignored by literary scholars in favor of turn-of-the-century and, soon after, Harlem Renaissance literature. African Americans of this time published a great many histories—but histories have been only occasionally a presence in American literary scholarship, in sharp contrast to the days of David Levin, R. W. B. Lewis, and so many other scholars who emphasized that nineteenth-century readers recognized history as a form of literature. Those who do turn to these histories will find fragmented narratives and often uncertain frameworks as the historians of the time tried to negotiate the dual demands of the possibilities for progress and the energies of white supremacist suppression of those possibilities. It was an era that witnessed the publication of a great many autobiographical narratives, but readers today still prefer the seemingly clear politics of the antebellum slave narratives to the often contradictory and seemingly accomodationist stance of numerous postwar narratives. It was an era that saw considerable experiments in narrative development—as William Wells Brown adapted his 1853 Clotel to account for new contexts and new narrative and political possibilities, or as Frances Harper followed certain narrative lines from her serialized novels of the 1860s to the 1880s and reconfigured them in 1892 in Iola Leroy, a work that commented on political conversations, economic opportunities, and the importance of novels produced by African Americans. It was an era, too, that saw the publication of numerous poems and speeches that have yet to receive adequate scholarly attention. It was, one might say, an era that has posed numerous challenges to literary scholars, most of which remain unaddressed. Until such work is done, we will not be in a position to talk in any depth about this significant period of African American literary history. Until such work is done, too, those few texts considered at this time will remain at a considerable distance from the complex matrix that establishes the term "African American" as something more than a convenient and dismissible signifier for identifying an author. In what follows, I offer not that much-needed literary history but rather a few case studies that are intended to indicate directions and raise questions.[13]

207

## Uncontainable Stories: William Still
## and the Underground Railroad

In many ways, the last four decades of the nineteenth century constituted a golden age of African American historical writing, though most
of it remains virtually unknown even to many who study late-nineteenth-
century or turn-of-the-century African American literature. Certainly,
many readers know something about the historical and sociological work
of Booker T. Washington and W. E. B. Du Bois during this era, and the
political climate defined by the affiliation; the considerable differences
between these two public figures have often been used as a kind of shorthand for locating the ideological allegiances of other authors. William
Wells Brown's histories have received some attention, though perhaps
not as much as we would expect, given that Brown has won increasing
recognition as a literary artist and abolitionist leader. But far beyond the
work of such familiar figures, the field of historical writing during this period was both vital and productive. Important military histories included
George Washington Williams's *A History of the Negro Troops in the War of
the Rebellion, 1861–1865, Preceded by a Review of the Military Services of Negroes in Ancient and Modern Times* (1888), Joseph T. Wilson's *The Black
Phalanx: African American Soldiers in the War of Independence, the War of
1812 and the Civil War* (1887), and Edward A. Johnson's *History of Negro
Soldiers in the Spanish-American War, and Other Items of Interest* (1899).
Among the church and denominational histories were James M. Simms's
*The First Colored Baptist Church in North America* (1888), Wesley J. Gaines's
*African Methodism in the South; or, Twenty-Five Years of Freedom* (1890),
Daniel A. Payne's *History of the African Methodist Episcopal Church* (1891),
and Susan I. Shorter's *The Heroines of African Methodism* (1891). As Short-
er's title indicates, this was a time as well for that most central of African
American historical modes, the collective biography, notable examples
of which were William J. Simmons's *Men of Mark: Eminent, Progressive,
Rising* (1887) and Monroe Adolphus Majors's *Noted Negro Women: Their
Triumphs and Activities* (1893). Literary scholars usually are far behind
even those few professional historians who have explored these works,
though these decades constituted a prominent battleground fought on the
pages of histories.

The stories these histories tell are various and complex, often revealing
a troubled search for direction and the longing for resolution that had
been promised but denied by the Civil War.[14] As the titles of even the
few histories I have mentioned indicate, this was a time when historians

both celebrated and attempted to enter into the official record the significant *institutional* achievements of black men and women—such as the churches that now had a long history to claim or the many individuals and newspapers covered in I. Garland Penn's *The Afro-American Press, and Its Editors* (1891). Certainly, this was a time for celebrating the life achievements of various people of African origins, both to answer the charges of white racial science and to suggest, as did Martin Delany in *The Condition, Elevation, Emigration, and Destiny of the Colored People of the United States* (1852), that African Americans had the various skills, professional expertise, and leadership needed to function as an autonomous or politically unified community, a "nation within a nation," as Delany put it. Of course, in many cases these histories and collective biographies themselves undermine that same argument by demonstrating their own ideological assumptions. As Elizabeth Young has noted, "Black men's representations of the Civil War conformed to what Patricia Morton has analyzed as the primary project of black historiography in this period, that of 'restoring black men to a man's world'" (198). Examining a wide range of women's writings from and about the Civil War, Young contends:

> In a racist culture that denied not only civility but literary voice
> to African-Americans except under the most mediated of terms,
> issues of authentication and authorship constitute a particular
> battleground in black women's Civil War texts. In these and other
> issues, black women's texts are often openly at war with those of
> white women. For black women writers excluded from national
> discourse by virtue of both race and gender, "civil wars" involve
> battling not only the dominant national culture but also alternative
> iconographies—including those constructed by white women and
> African-American men—that would exclude them as well. (111)

A similar argument could be presented about a number of African American texts from this period when viewed in certain historical, cultural, literary, theological, or denominational contexts. There were wars both civil and uncivil, and alternative iconographies, everywhere—and the challenges of authentication, authorship, and community are often best found, in post–Civil War historical writing as in that which preceded the war, in the form of fragmented narratives and fractal narrative lines.

Consider, for instance, one of the most imposing histories published during this period and one often referenced as the beginning of African American historiography, George Williams's *History of the Negro Race in*

*America from 1619 to 1880: Negroes as Slaves, as Soldiers, and as Citizens; To-
gether with a Preliminary Consideration of the Unity of the Human Family, an
Historical Sketch of Africa, and an Account of the Negro Governments of Sierra
Leone and Liberia* (1883). This two-volume work explores everything from
the vagaries of race science to the challenge of recovering and even naming the history of various regions of Africa; however, most of it is devoted
to people of African descent in the United States. Williams's research for
this history was extensive, and he regularly involves the reader in that
research by providing commentary and reprinted documents. At the beginning of the first volume, he explains his rationale for this approach.
"Where I have used documents," he states, "it was with a desire to escape
the charge of superficiality. If, however, I may be charged with seeking to
escape the labor incident to thorough digestion, I answer, that, while men
with the reputation of Bancroft and Hildreth could pass unchallenged
when disregarding largely the use of documents and the citation of authorities, I would find myself challenged by a large number of critics"
(vii). In many ways, Williams offers readers a grand narrative of U.S. history, one that has become almost standard in accounts of American racial
history. Addressing the constitutional convention at the end of the Revolutionary War, Williams states: "It was then and there that the hydra of
slavery struck its fangs into the Constitution; and, once inoculated with
the poison of the monster, the government was only able to purify itself
in the flames of a great civil war" (1:vii). He asserts that he has been motivated "not as the blind panegyrist of my race, nor as the partisan apolo-
gist, but from a love for '*the truth of history*,'" and he presents the book in
the hope of an ideal world that would today be labeled color blindness,
wishing that "the day will hasten when there shall be no North, no South,
no Black, no White,—but all be American citizens, with equal duties and
equal rights" (1:x).

Yet Williams's *History* is representative of African American experience
less in the story it tells than in the historical perspective it embodies, in
its confrontation and negotiation with a world of experience that resists
not simply resolution but clear narrative lines. Indeed, as Williams gives
voice to what is at times a Bancroftian view of providential history (he
has been, in fact, called "The Negro Bancroft"), his subject is frequently
and ultimately overwhelmed by the documents that support it. Tracing
the origins of the great majority of African Americans to an inherently
inferior type, "the lowest strata of the African race" (1:109), Williams ret-
roactively endorses those who argued that slavery had a civilizing effect

on the enslaved, who having gained their freedom were again in danger of degradation. Williams, then, constructs a double narrative: the story of an ancient degradation and the story of a providential rise to a "higher," more "civilized" type of humanity. By these and other means, he effectively re-writes the untold stories of enslavement into an exclusionary narrative of citizenship. At the same time, his own involvement in that history, his failure to be as removed or as objective as he promises in the introductory pages, comes through in the various fissures of his narrative and in the commentaries he cannot help including. In the opening pages, Williams says that "I have avoided comment so far as it was consistent with a clear exposition of the truth" (1:x). Yet his comments are extensive, and they speak volumes about, as Mark Smith puts it, the "emotional, visceral, and febrile understanding of racial identity," which were as important to Williams as to white segregationists. At the beginning of his second volume, he comments on his position as a historian of slavery, noting: "I have tracked my bleeding countrymen through the widely scattered documents of American history; I have listened to their groans, their clanking chains, and melting prayers, until the woes of a race and the agonies of centuries seem to crowd upon my soul as a bitter reality." Approaching that scattered community through the evidence collected from scattered archives, Williams says that he brings more to this text than a hopeful ideal. "Many pages of this history," he states, "have been blistered with my tears; and, although having lived but a little more than a generation, my mind feels as if it were cycles old" (2:iii). Williams's *History* is, in effect, bursting at the seams, unable to contain the many narrative trajectories involved in the "history of the race."

Against this attempt to write a comprehensive and authoritative history, it is useful to consider a different narrative mode, that provided by William Still in *The Underground Rail Road: A Record of Facts, Authentic Narratives, Letters, &c., Narrating the Hardships, Hair-breadth Escapes and Death Struggles of the Slaves in Their Efforts for Freedom, as Related by Themselves and Others, or Witnessed by the Author; Together with Sketches of Some of the Largest Stockholders, and Most Liberal Aiders and Advisers, of the Road*, first published in 1872. Still was corresponding secretary and chairman of the Philadelphia Vigilance Committee, an activist in the struggle to desegregate public transportation in Philadelphia, and a founding member of the Social, Civil, and Statistical Association of the Colored People of Pennsylvania, formed in 1860. As its subtitle suggests, *Underground Rail Road* makes for an interesting narrative ride. Following the

"Author's Preface" and a collection of "Underground Rail Road Letters," most of the book is divided into separate narratives of escapes and arrivals, most including the names of the fugitives involved. Many of these entries are identified in rather businesslike headings—such as "Arrival from Maryland" or "Arrivals from Richmond"; some serve as a kind of headline to the escape—"Eight and a Half Months Secreted" or "Clarissa Davis, Arrived Dressed in Male Attire"; some address the determination or emotional state of the arrivals—"Liberty or Death, Jim Bow-legs, alias Bill Paul"; and a few convey a more satirical voice—"Ex-President Tyler's Household Loses an Aristocratic 'Article.'" The various entries are followed by an overview of the Philadelphia Vigilance Committee, including biographical sketches of its prominent members, ending with a rather extensive biography of Frances Ellen Watkins Harper, which constitutes the book's conclusion. This work is also a documentary history, providing newspaper accounts of escapes, numerous letters pertaining to the planning and execution of flights from slavery, and letters sent to Still after the fugitives had reached relative freedom.

*Underground Rail Road* is about significant travels, and the book itself traveled, for Still marketed it energetically, recruiting agents from across the country to help him sell it. As Stephen G. Hall writes: "At its height in 1874, Still's sales network included California, Indiana, Illinois, Iowa, Georgia, Massachusetts, Missouri, Nebraska, New York, North Carolina, South Carolina, Pennsylvania, Tennessee, and Texas. . . . Estimates indicate that Still had sold between five and ten thousand copies of his book by the late 1870s" (52–53). Hall's analysis of Still's sales techniques demonstrates that Still understood well why different readers, black and white, might be interested in his book. As Hall has documented, "The five major advertisements [usually illustrated] used for *Underground Rail Road* emphasized a variety of themes: intrigue, interracial cooperation, altered gender roles, and the impact of the peculiar institution on families" (47).[15] Some readers consulted the book for merely pragmatic reasons as they sought to locate and reunite families; others, for dramatic stories of "Hair-breadth Escapes." Some looked to the book to commemorate African American experiences under and beyond the system of slavery and to argue for the centrality of those experiences in the developing national story; still others, to find an alternate story of American history with which to displace the system of slavery by the more heroic tale of what has since been identified, in our own Orwellian historical moment, as the network of freedom.[16]

Obviously Still's work can serve a number of audiences representing different cultural and racial points of view. We could say that it documents Saidiya Hartman's concept of "performing blackness," a term that Hartman uses to convey "both the cross-purposes and the circulation of various modes of performance and performativity that concern the production of racial meaning and subjectivity, the nexus of race, subjection, and spectacle, the forms of racial and race(d) pleasure, enactments of white dominance and power, and the reiteration and/or rearticulation of the conditions of enslavement" (56). *Underground Rail Road* responds to and represents various modes of performance and performativity; various configurations of race, subjection, and spectacle; and various iterations of white dominance and power. In its decidedly loose coordination of the intertextual and intratextual interplay of narratives, documents, narrative modes, and cultural registers, Still's record of fugitive movement and activist organization against the slaveholding regime places in dynamic contention various possibilities for agency and purpose—including those of the various audiences with which Still hoped the book would find a home.

This is a book, in other words, that highlights both the motivations and the cultural contexts of its readers. There is little here to encourage a strictly sequential reading, and aside from scattered and loose indications of a chronological arrangement, the separate entries do not add up to anything resembling a sustained or developing narrative. While the entries all refer to escape attempts—some successful and some not, a few aided by representatives of the Underground Railroad but most not—the seeming similarity of hundreds of stories of escape is overbalanced or even disrupted by Still's emphasis on the individuality of the different attempts and especially by the individuality of the various fugitives recorded in the book. Moreover, Still reminds his readers that, despite its length and its voluminous records, the book can make no claim to being comprehensive, for, as he says in the preface, "In gathering narratives from unwritten sources—from memory simply—no amount of pains or labor could possibly succeed in making a trustworthy history." Further, although he has worked from "personal knowledge, and . . . the records of his own preserving," even *his* records "are quite too voluminous to be all used in this work" (1:xv). Indeed, Still cautions that the book cannot even claim to represent its primary subjects—the Underground Railroad and the history of enslavement—for "it scarcely needs be stated that, as a general rule, the passengers of the U.G.R.R. were physically and intellectually above the average order of slaves" (1:xii). Readers, then, are asked to be self-consciously involved in a book that points to its own inconclusiveness, its failure to be comprehensive—a book of fragments, often gesturing to the many stories that could be constructed from those fragments, woven together to tell a story whose suggested contours press against the available contexts for understanding its scope and significance.

Following the guidance of Still's historical record, we might say that mapping out "the history of the race" would be like initiating a Mandelbrot set, a world of fractals in which, to again borrow from Alice Fulton, "each part of a fractal form replicates the form of the entire structure. Increasing detail is revealed with increasing magnification, and each smaller part looks like the entire structure, turned around or tilted a bit" (55). In *Underground Rail Road*, Still provides just such a map, and in that way he documents a scattered but still coherent history. In resolutely allowing fragments to stand, gesturing toward stories untold, commenting on the inaccuracies and inadequacies of the historical record even as it works to construct that record, *Underground Rail Road* serves as a document not only of antislavery activity but also of the fluidity of African American history generally, a complex of various sites of dynamic interactions, a history defined by borders that are significant only because they can be crossed and, Still seems to argue throughout, a black community that can claim to be a community only by understanding itself as part of a larger dynamic process of arrivals and departures. In this way, Still's book is less a historical record than a call for a history capable of serving the ongoing needs of a community that cannot be defined by the usual protocols for identifying spacial, temporal, and political locale—a black America both inside and outside of history.

African American historical writing in the last decades of the nineteenth century operated in an uneasy balance between Williams's dreams of an authoritative and objective history and Still's fragmented and incomplete record of the past. The historical writings produced during this time remind us that one of the major concerns that has shaped African American literary culture from its beginnings has been the need to account for those whom James Weldon Johnson called "black and unknown bards" (79) and those whom Ralph Ellison famously locates outside of history. Writing African American history, then, includes the challenge of giving voice to the "historians without portfolio," as Geneviève Fabre and Robert O'Meally have termed them—those lives missing from the documents but clearly inscribed in the cultural landscape (8). No work better represents this challenge than Still's *Underground Rail Road*. A record of constant arrivals and departures, Still's account of the many who encountered the Underground Railroad agents upon their arrival in the North emphasizes the larger borders, and the dynamic cultural currents, that define black America. But Still's account also represents the challenge of channeling these chaotic currents into a stable documentary stream, one capable of developing into a narrative framework by which African American history might be known.

### Uncontainable Lives: Sojourner Truth as the Century's Twin

Many looked for such narrative streams in the seemingly clear waters offered by (auto)biographical accounts, but here as elsewhere the story was complex—for as Othello's occupation was gone, so too was the previous occasion (and the abolitionist cultural framework) for his story. As Andrews has demonstrated, "The abolition of involuntary servitude in 1865 forced the slave narrator in the postwar era to reevaluate the purpose of his or her prospective literary enterprise. Since ex-slaves no longer needed to denounce slavery to white America, the story of their past no longer carried the same social or moral import" ("Representation" 80). Andrews believes that the failures of Reconstruction provided renewed reason for autobiographical narratives, but that "the author of the new slave narrative . . . was no longer the rebel-fugitive whose ascent to freedom in the North had been celebrated in romantic fashion in the antebellum era" (80–81). Many of the postbellum narratives involve a return to a familiar life, a matter of shifting, expanding, or sometimes narrowing narratives established in earlier autobiographical accounts. Douglass returns to his former home in the South from the perspective of one of the most accomplished men of his generation. Josiah Henson finds himself in England, so fully associated now with Harriet Beecher Stowe's Uncle Tom that it is difficult to find any trace of his former self in his own narrative. William Wells Brown—well, his is a story that I will return to shortly. But those who find an unchanging account in pre–Civil War slave narratives would be especially challenged to do the same in the narratives published after the war; they would be challenged as well to imagine through these narratives a homogeneous black community. Elizabeth Young has observed of one of the most prominent of such narratives, Elizabeth Keckley's account of her experiences with President and Mrs. Lincoln in *Behind the Scenes*, that Keckley's "representation of black women . . . is sharply divided along class lines, and she offers no developed portraits of other black women, elite or nonelite. The version of 'redressment' offered in *Behind the Scenes* is idiosyncratic and uneven, and the text occupies an ambiguous relation to the very tradition—African-American women's Civil War writing—in which it would seem most welcome" (142). The same can be said of many other narratives published during this period, which might be one reason why they have received so little critical attention.

One significant narrative return after the Civil War is that of Sojourner Truth. In Chapter 3, I argued for the importance of understanding *The Narrative of Sojourner Truth* as a fluid text, a complexly intertextual record that both accounts for and represents (dynamically, as readers enter into the text's racial complex) Truth's multiply contingent subjectivity in a white supremacist and patriarchal culture. Inscribed in the *Narrative* is the complex process of its own development over the years, a process orchestrated primarily by Truth's two collaborators: Olive Gilbert and Frances Titus. Gilbert—whom Truth met at the Northampton Association for Education and Industry—served as author of the book's first edition, *Narrative of Sojourner Truth, a Northern Slave, Emancipated from Bodily Servitude by the State of New York, in 1828* (1850). When Harriet Beecher Stowe achieved great fame as the author of *Uncle Tom's Cabin*, Truth joined the many who sought and received Stowe's endorsement in the form of a preface. Stowe's brief statement, which assured readers that the narrative was "true & faithful" and that its subject possessed "a mind of no common energy & power" (qtd. in Painter 130), appeared in an 1853 edition of the *Narrative*. The *Narrative* was enlarged in 1875, with the help of Truth's Battle Creek neighbor Frances Titus, who added material from Truth's scrapbook, presented as the "Book of Life." Included in this new material are two of the most influential sources of Truth's legend: the "Ar'n't I a Woman?" speech for which Truth is most (mis)remembered, and Stowe's narrative sketch, "Sojourner Truth, the Libyan Sibyl," an account of Stowe's meeting with Truth published originally in the *Atlantic Monthly* in 1863. Following Truth's death in 1883, Titus produced the last edition of Truth's life story, the *Narrative of Sojourner Truth, a Bondswoman of Olden Time, Emancipated by the New York Legislature in the Early Part of the Present Century; with a History of Her Labors and Correspondence Drawn from Her "Book of Life"; also, a Memorial Chapter, Giving the Particulars of Her Last Sickness and Death* (1884).

In many ways, the final version of Truth's text (Gilbert and Titus, 1884) is a record of the interracial tensions central to the developing historical narrative of the Civil War and its aftermath. Throughout this *Narrative*, Truth stands at a point of history in which her essentialized embodiment of Christian providence can serve the needs of the post–Civil War white national narrative. Noting that the first part of this text is an abridged version of the 1850 account, Titus frames for her readers the emerging significance of Truth's story. Since 1850, Titus states, "momentous changes have taken place. Slavery has been swallowed up in a Red Sea of blood, and the slave has emerged from the conflict of races transformed from a chattel to a man" (4). What this might mean about our understanding of Sojourner Truth's role in the national story is suggested in Titus's subsequent prefatory comments at the beginning of "Part Second," in which Titus reprints an article "published in a Washington Sunday paper during the administration of President Lincoln." The article identifies Truth as "that old landmark of the past—the representative of the forever-gone age" (89), and its author uses this "land-mark" to measure the progress of the national narrative: "Truly, the spirit of progress is abroad in the land, and the leaven of love is working in the hearts of the people, pointing with unerring certainty to the not far distant future, when the ties of affection shall cement all nations, kindreds, and tongues into one common brotherhood" (90). The conflict of races behind and a common brotherhood ahead, Truth does seem to represent a "forever-gone age"—that is, a history hidden behind the revisionist national history that followed the Civil War.

Truth becomes, in fact, the representative of a largely deracialized story of progress, standing, Titus suggests, "by the closing century like a twin sister": "Born and reared by its side, what it knows she knows, what it has seen, she has seen" (169). The century's twin, Truth is transformed in the pages of the *Narrative* into a living archive, "her memory . . . a vast storehouse of knowledge, the shelves of which contain a history of the revolutions, progressions, and culmination of the great ideas which have been a part of her life purpose" (169). The woman celebrated for her oral delivery and her commanding presence, the woman presented as one who needed to rely on others to read and write for her, becomes a library for others to read. And as Truth comes to embody the century, so Titus's visions of the century come to contain and, ultimately, displace Truth. The towering figure of Sojourner Truth dissolves into a century so remarkable that it "towers above all preceding ones" and stands itself as the larger story of Sojourner Truth for which Truth herself is but a synecdoche, for "the century is a sibyl, too," and its achievements serve as "prophecies of the coming time" (170).

This, finally, is the narrative home in which Sojourner Truth is placed through the pages of the narrative written in her name. Her story subsumed by the white national story of progress, Truth journeys from the position of an outsider in the domestic sphere to that of a guest in the century's home. "Upon the foundation it [the century] has laid," Titus suggests, "a superstructure may arise more symmetrical than prophet has yet dared foretell. 'It builded better than it knew,' can truly be averred of it." Agency falls in the hands of a century guided by progress that enables readers to reenvision Truth's embodiment of prophetic power, for just as "numberless inventions and improvements are embraced within its circle," so Truth, the embodiment of a primitive African prophetic power, is herself contained by a new technology of prophecy, a world in which "mechanics, agriculture, commerce, science, and arts, the world of matter and the world of mind, have budded and blossomed, so to speak, as never before" (170). And with "the century's history . . . nearly written up," all that remains is for Sojourner's journey to find its natural course: "Her barque has been carried far out to sea, and now it nears the port. May she encounter no more storms upon her homeward course, but, wafted by soft, sweet winds through placid waters, peacefully enter the harbor of the 'King Eternal.' And when she glides from ship to shore, may she hear the welcome, 'Come unto me all ye that labor and are heavy laden, and *I* will give you rest" (170–71). The providential logic of the narrative Truth comes to serve in this account leads this sojourner to the end of her journey, safely housed in this world and safely home in the next.

What makes the *Narrative of Sojourner Truth* compelling in African American literary history is that Truth cannot be contained by Gilbert's and Titus's narrative frames. Sojourner Truth is, after all, a vocal presence throughout the narrative, however problematic the representation of her voice and however questionable the accuracy of any given quotation might be. And through that vocal presence, Truth introduces a different concept of the text's proper narrative home. Titus's preface to the *Narrative* concludes with a series of statements by Truth, offered in response to "a Chicago lady" who asked "for a thought to inspire and cheer her on her life journey" (7). In those responses, Truth distinguishes herself from the Christian communities she often encountered—in Titus's words, "the fashionable so-called *religious* world"—saying that this world "is empty as the barren fig-tree, possessing nothing but leaves." Truth finds her home elsewhere, asserting that "God is the great house that will hold all his children" and "we dwell in him as the fishes in the sea" (7). In these lines, Truth reminds her readers of the significance of her name and of the sojourning career that followed from her self-naming. In doing so, she speaks of a home barely referenced by the various writers of and in this text—Gilbert and Titus, and the legions of writers of the letters and articles reprinted in the *Narrative*—a home that works both with and against the narrative logic that both Gilbert and Titus construct, guiding readers finally to the dynamic confrontation of faith that was Truth's ongoing mission.

Truth's vision of the spiritual mission so central to all of her work is one of an encompassing domesticity, the house of God, within which her position as a representative embodiment—of religion and of nation—finds symbolic stability. That is, in the sphere of the "great house" of God, the relations among the symbolic embodiment (Truth herself), the grounds for the symbol (Truth's life and the world that both shapes and responds to that life), and the symbol's referents (an imagined model of moral duty in the secular world and of citizenship in the sacred) are defined and maintained. Like Titus, Truth associates her historical significance with that of the nation, but as resident in the house of God, Truth does not locate herself in the sort of regional logic by which, for example, the realm of slavery in the South was separated from the realm of national progress in the North. "Cosmopolitan in her nature," Titus reports, Truth "calls the world her home, and says she could never apply to a town for aid, but would sooner appeal to the whole United States, for the welfare of which she has labored and which is more her home than any single locality of town or State" (169). Truth's nation is not a regional habitat but a field of systemic relations, and the domestic realm she seeks is a realm in which sacred and secular are brought together in daily practice.

The force of Truth's vocal presence, in fact, most often has to do with the exposure of what should be the obvious contradiction between principle and practice, the obvious displacement of the godly home in the secular field. In the best-known example of Truth presenting herself as the embodiment of the nation, she looks not to transcendence over actual conditions but rather to an unstable nation in which the contradiction between principle and practice identifies an entrance to moral power. When she receives word that "her son had been sold South," Truth begins an extended and finally successful process to attain legal rights over her son. Looking back on her initial determination and conviction of her eventual success, she states: "I know'd I'd have him agin. I was sure God would help me to get him. Why, I felt so *tall within*—I felt as if the *power*

219

of a nation was with me!" (30). Similarly, in an account of her meeting with Abraham Lincoln (having moved from her experience of national power to an encounter with the representative of national power), Truth is shown "the Bible presented to [Lincoln] by the colored people of Baltimore" (120–21). Truth says of the Bible, "This is beautiful indeed; the colored people have given this to the head of the government, and that government once sanctioned laws that would not permit its people to learn enough to enable them to read this book. And for what? Let them answer who can" (121). The beauty Truth promotes is a beauty of a just exposure of injustice, a Bible that by its presence and by its symbolic status (as a gift from African Americans in Baltimore to the president of the United States) offers not only the guidance of the divine word but also a reminder of the need for such guidance, a gift given by those who had been denied the ability to read to the symbolic head of a people who had the ability but lacked moral literacy. In such acts, Truth resembles any number of antislavery activists, black and white, who worked to expose national contradictions in the hope of identifying both the need and the grounds for fundamental social reform.

Such passages emphasize the significance of Truth's self-definition as a preacher of the Word and not simply as a social activist, a self-definition that Gilbert and Titus both celebrate and contain. Under the heading of "Isabella's Religious Experience," for example, Gilbert turns "from the outward and temporal to the inward and spiritual life of our subject," telling a story of "truth and error strangely commingled" (40). Titus prefaces the *Narrative*'s second part by suggesting that at the time of the original (1850) publication, Truth had "but recently emerged from the gloomy night of slavery, ignorant and untaught in all that gives value to human existence" and so "was still suffering from the burden of acquired and transmitted habits incidental to her past condition of servitude" (89). Both Gilbert and Titus tell the story of Truth's rise from her original position (in childhood and then in the 1850s, respectively). Gilbert presents her comments as part of a narrative of Truth's early entrance into an understanding of Christianity, comparing Truth to "a landscape at early dawn" (40), a mix of sunshine and shadow—and, of course, the landscape becomes sunnier as the narrative progresses. Titus comments that Truth's "life forces and moral perceptions were so powerful and clear cut that she not only came out from this moral gutter herself, but largely assisted in elevating others of her race from a similar state of degradation" (89).

In such comments, contextualized by a narrative logic that leads finally to the imperatives of white nationalist history, Truth's religious beliefs are reformulated as part of the calculus of presence, the essence of a powerful but uncultured woman whose beliefs turn our attention to their essentialized source, an Africanist spirituality both primitive and prophetic. Truth becomes the subject of what Jon Cruz has termed "ethnosympathy." Here he is referring to the "humanitarian pursuit of the inner world of distinctively and collectively classifiable subjects" by which "black culture became aestheticized" and "a separation emerged between black political claims for a greater social and political inclusion within American civil society and a more acceptable spiritual (and eventually cultural) place for blacks in the hearts and minds of northerners who were championing the new mode of benevolent cultural reception" (3, 6). Truth has been and remains—in the pages of the *Narrative* and in American culture generally—the subject of ethnosympathy, for her insistence on the necessity of a strictly moral life, her moral critique of everything from property to women's fashions, would make her a challenging rather than a comforting figure had she not been successfully domesticated in the house of (white) American culture. Truth's status as a floating cultural symbol—applicable to a variety of cultural needs, a generalized symbol of justice variously applied—both overwhelms and overrules the more complex and demanding specificity of her life.[17]

It is therefore important to attend to the fluidity of the text that presents this ethnosympathetic rendition of Truth's life—that is, to note that the 1884 *Narrative* replicates the itineracy of Truth's ministry. In her travels, Truth simply followed her sense of a calling: "The Spirit calls me there, and I must go." Her travels were orchestrated by faith and chance: "Wherever night overtook her, there she sought for lodgings—free, if she might—if not, she paid; at a tavern, if she chanced to be at one—if not, at a private dwelling; with the rich, if they would receive her—if not, with the poor" (69). But the power of her ministry was not limited to her ability to preach, for each stop on her long sojourn was, in effect, a vital recontextualization of the local culture. Indeed, local cultures revealed themselves even in their reception of Sojourner Truth. On her travels, Truth "soon discovered that the largest houses were nearly always full; if not quite full, company was soon expected; and that it was much easier to find an unoccupied corner in a small house than in a large one; and if a person possessed but a miserable roof over his head, you might be sure of a welcome to part of it" (69). Locally secure cultural systems were forced open by Truth's presence, a presence that itself challenged the assumptions, the customs, and the values of local cultures in a ministry marked by confrontation and exposure. The 1884 *Narrative* is full of anecdotes of Truth's savvy exchanges with often-challenging audiences, exchanges for which she is most grandly remembered. A singular, insistent presence ("*I am that I am*," she once answered a policeman who demanded her name [214]) in a world of relativity ("the rich could always find religion in the rich," she once noted [69]). Truth became, in effect, the embodiment of an interpretive principle, the inhabitant of a great house against which all other houses might be measured.

This interpretive principle is the central dynamic of the 1884 *Narrative*, the story that Gilbert and Titus tell in their attempt to avoid or otherwise contain it. That is, reduced to an unformed essence—"truth and error strangely commingled," her blood like desert rivers, like "tropical fires" (40, 3)—Truth's religion, working both with and against its representation in the *Narrative*, becomes a fugitive theology. In calling attention to this containment of her spirituality, in other words, I am not suggesting a reading in which we piece together Truth's scattered statements to identify her religious views, views that can then be identified, categorized by denomination, and evaluated. Rather, I mean a reading of the narrative in which Truth's "outward and temporal" life and her "inward and spiritual life," to use Gilbert's distinction (40), are inseparable. Inhabitant of the domestic sphere of God, citizen of a nation that can be realized only when its ideological contradictions are placed in direct contention with one another so as to recognize the citizen precisely because her citizenship is not recognized, Truth embodies a nation unseen by Titus and Gilbert. As Samira Kawash has argued, "The framework of slavery in which the relation between property and the subject becomes socially meaningful demands that we recognize that this subject is always a historically and materially situated subject, emerging out of and in terms given by the social relations it appears to precede" (56). Truth's identification with the system of slavery and with the larger system of white supremacist ideology, an identification that both Gilbert and Titus enforce even in their sympathetic narratives, constitutes her as a particularly "socially meaningful" subject, the product of a world determined to both recognize and disclaim the cultural technology of individual identity, a world in which "the freedom of the politically recognized subject is a freedom conditioned and determined to be in some accordance with the being of such a subject" (56). Kawash offers these comments in an analysis of the status of the fugitive from slavery, but these comments can be applied as well

to those, like Truth, who were viewed as having acquired a legal separation (though never a divorce or liberation) from their identification with
slavery. And we might say of the itinerant preacher Sojourner Truth what
Kawash says of the fugitive slave: If the politically recognized subject "is
not simply given (by 'God' or by 'Nature') but is a socially achieved effect,
then the freedom of this subject cannot be the only possible freedom. And
insofar as the figure of the fugitive points to a space beyond or outside
this subject, it is in fugitivity that we may find the glimmerings of another
thought of freedom" (56). In the fugitive theology of Sojourner Truth,
we may find, in fact, a thought of freedom unrecognized by Truth's white
narrative collaborators.

Titus works to bring this fugitivity to the safe house of the American
narrative of progress. The "Book of Life" takes the reader, indeed, on a revealing cultural journey. Following the now-famous sketches by Gage and
Stowe, an account of Truth's meeting with Lincoln (and his autograph "for
Aunty Sojourner Truth" [Gilbert and Titus, 1884 121]), the "Book of Life"
presents an extensive section entitled "The Voice of the Press." The press
excerpts are arranged by locale: "From Fall River Papers," "From New
Jersey Papers," "From a Williamsburgh (L. I.) Paper," and so on. The press
accounts offer a complex portrait of Truth as a cultural presence—both
praised and condemned, recorded and misreported, a developing legend—with much of the information from earlier parts of the Narrative
(Stowe's sketch, for example, in addition to basic biographical information) variously repeated, reapplied, and decontextualized. Following the
press reports are personal testimonials to Truth's presence, public service,
and active faith—leading finally to a brief overview of her life ("Sojourner
Truth's Age," "Her Parentage," and "Extent of Her Labors" [212–13]), a last
series of "Anecdotes" (213), and a series of autographs. The brief overview,
categorized as it is, seems almost a prototypical scholarly treatment of
Truth, an attempt to identify fundamental facts about her—determining
her age, identifying her African and American Indian ancestry, and listing
the various states in which Truth lectured. The latter two entries are a
short paragraph apiece, and these bare "facts" battle with the more engaging series of "Anecdotes" that follow—a struggle for the terms by which
Truth might be known and remembered. We encounter Truth as cultural
legend, travel through the shadowy valley of her mixed public reception,
and arrive, finally, at the individual witnesses of her power, at which point
Truth's life can be safely summarized.

And yet there are tensions in this documentary journey, tensions emphasized in the text's closing autographs—the series of signatures by famous men and women. Carla Peterson, the preeminent reader of Truth's *Narrative*, has argued that these signatures represent a powerful act of self-definition, the formation of a community defined by Truth's pubic work. "At the moment of writing," Peterson tells us,

> the signer comes into existence only in relation to the signatee; thus, as they signed their autograph in her "Book of Life," Truth's friends and acquaintances received definition primarily in terms of their relationship to her. . . . The signature, while singular, is of necessity also iterable, reproducible, and thus detachable; it may, in fact, come to function as a quotation. Thus, in her "Book of Life" Truth compiled the signatures as a series of quotations, providing her own frame for them and, in a sense, creating her own written text. (*Doers* 39–40)

But it is important to note as well that although Truth reframes these signatures, gathering them into the community defined by her life's mission, Titus follows the signatures with a brief account of the signers and effectually reframes Truth's self-definition in turn—placing the figures within the sphere of white activism. We learn of Titus's respect for Lucretia Mott, the existence of a marble bust of another, and the public trials of others. And we are told that in the pages of *Uncle Tom's Cabin*, Stowe "opened the world's eyes to perceive . . . that Uncle Toms and Topsies were human beings after all" (Gilbert and Titus, 1884 220). Certainly, some identification of these signatures seems appropriate, and the signers are deserving of public memory and respect, but my point is that the form of the *Narrative* places these signatures back under the control of the narrative's primary author and the world that shapes her treatment of Truth's life.

Perhaps another way to state my concern here is to simply ask about the status of individual identity in the *Narrative*. As Peterson observes, "In its focus on Truth's individuality Gilbert's narrative (and Titus's as well) refuses to foreground Truth's search for community but focuses instead on those events that isolate her and mark her as extraordinary" (*Doers* 32). In its closing sections, the *Narrative* leads the reader from the mythic cultural stage (the white women's movement, Stowe's Libyan Sibyl, Lincoln's Auntie Sojourner) to the highly contingent cultural field represented by and in the press to, finally, a series of individuals testifying to Truth's power. The legend of Sojourner Truth relies primarily on the two ends of this journey—the mythic and the personal, the combination of which is aptly represented in the popular use of the phrase most associated with Truth, in which the individual and the generic are joined together: "ar'n't I a woman?" But the complexly contingent world represented by the press is largely contained in and by the pages of the *Narrative*—the world in which the realities of race are not reduced to a postabolitionist slogan, and in which the practice of religion overwhelms the pithy abstractions of its rhetoric. We see the extraordinary individuals represented by the closing autographs, but not their complex engagement in a white supremacist culture that made even the best of these figures, even Sojourner Truth, problematic at times. The disruptive logic of Truth's ministry—the exposure of the closed cultural systems she encountered in her travels—is brought under the narrative control of a different kind of closed system, a congress of extraordinary individuals fighting against the ordinarily blind, racist, or unjust persons of their day.

If we are to read this *Narrative* as an African American text, we need to resist the narrative logic that invites the reader, by way of a benevolent response or an easy affirmation of a generalized sense of social justice, to enter yet another signature at the end of this text. It is, finally, in the conspicuous struggle to define Truth, to bring her life to narrative closure by folding it into a larger, white national imaginary, that the *Narrative* represents not only Truth's fugitive theology but also the central terms of an African American poetics of self-documentation. Indeed, the determination to impose narrative order upon Truth's life is the saving grace of the *Narrative*, for in the contending forces of this text are the cultural dynamics that shaped Truth's thought of freedom. In his study of white national ideology, Russ Castronovo warns of "a political longing . . . to acquire a subjectivity freed from the necessity of grappling with factors that impinge on an 'essential' self," for "freedom is then truly free of all context." "Employed by persons with radically different positions in the social hierarchy such as slave and slaveholder," Castronovo argues, "this nationalized vocabulary traps experiences of freedom and unfreedom in a vague lexicon that expunges signs of systemic injustice, social trauma, private anguish, or any other remainders that refuse to fit a general definition" (*Necro* 50). As I have suggested, Gilbert and Titus seem determined to hold Truth to just this sort of vague lexicon—and their efforts are replicated by the many testimonials from the wide range of social actors whom we encounter in the pages of the *Narrative*. But the strained grandeur of that nationalized vocabulary calls attention to its own instability, for Truth never seems wholly contained or containable. The narrative houses in which she is placed seem like stations along the way rather than final destinations. The people we encounter struggle to name and claim her. Like the *Narrative*'s list of the states Truth visited, we have a world of information that fails to inform—for while we can be impressed by the extent of her travels, no single location seems quite the point, and all of the states, all of the homes, all of the people visited along the way are made roughly equivalent by a life that inherently tested the terms of the cultural order. Sojourner Truth is, in effect, a disruptive presence in her own narrative, a representative of the negotiated instabilities central to African American life and literature throughout the nineteenth century, instabilities that became more intricate still following the Civil War.

## Representing Chaos:
## William Wells Brown's Southern Home

The challenges of reading the *Narrative of Sojourner Truth* within a fluid and dynamic African American literary tradition come in part, I have suggested, because the narrative is authored by white writers, but one can find those same intertextual and interracial dynamics in what is perhaps the most strangely understudied text of this time, William Wells Brown's *My Southern Home: or, The South and Its People* (1880). In the opening paragraph of the first chapter of this memoir, Brown introduces his readers to a "mansion . . . surrounded with piazzas, covered with grape-vines, clematis, and passion flowers. . . . The Pride of China mixed its oriental-looking foliage with the majestic magnolia, and the air was redolent with the fragrance of buds peeping out of every nook, and nodding upon you with a most unexpected welcome" (119). Surrounded by this luxurious growth, Brown's story begins—a somewhat embellished return to the plantation where he had been enslaved in his youth. But in writing about this mansion toward the end of his career (in the last book he would publish, years after the Civil War and the legal end of slavery), Brown looks back at the mansion and finds both his former home and a qualified but lasting pride of place. "The tasteful hand of art," writes the man who spent most of his adult years in Massachusetts, "which shows itself in the grounds of European and New-England villas, was not seen there, but the lavish beauty and harmonious disorder of nature was permitted to take its own course, and exhibited a want of taste so commonly witnessed in the sunny South" (119). From this site Brown proceeds to tour both his life and the South in a book that itself has challenged the assumptions about taste among his readers, a work in which, we could say, "the lavish beauty and harmonious disorder of nature" is "permitted to take its own course." *My Southern Home* follows the harmonious disorder of nature to portray a culture in which instability is the only constant—combining, in effect, the dramatic documentary strategies central to Still's *Underground Rail Road* with the contingent and itinerant approach to self-representation that we see in Truth's *Narrative*.

Indeed, the remarkable, winding, and luxurious turns that character-ize *My Southern Home* make this Brown's most significant and challenging text. As Andrews has noted, "Historians of African American literature have praised *My Southern Home* as Brown's most finished book, a fitting capstone to the literary monument he built for himself during a writing career that spanned four of the most turbulent decades of American his-tory" (Introduction to *From Fugitive Slave* 5). Other readers have found it to be a problematic pastiche of a narrative, with shifting genres and perspectives, and sometimes shifty opinions and commentary. Brown presents this multigenre book as an autobiographical memoir that begins with an account of his life as a slave and concludes with reflections from his tour of the South during the post-Reconstruction era—including, as Brown notes in his preface, "incidents [that] were jotted down at the time of their occurrence, or as they fell from the lips of the narrators, and in their own unadorned dialect" (113).[18] Parts of the text are presented in dramatic form (for, in fact, they were drawn from Brown's plays), parts are presented as transcriptions of African American folk songs that Brown encountered in his travels, and parts are commentaries on the uncertain situation of African Americans recently emancipated from slavery and deep into what many historians take to be one of the most conflicted and threatening periods in African American history. Along the way, Brown manages to reprint material from virtually all of his publications, making *My Southern Home* less a capstone to a career than a lavish garden, with previously published texts "peeping out of every nook."

*My Southern Home* is about departures and returns, as Brown moves from present to past, city to city, telling of escapes from slavery, shifting demographics, and the promises and challenges, successes and failures, of the nation and of the African American community both before and after the Civil War. The early part of the book is based on Brown's life, though it is an account filtered through the autobiographical, dramatic, and even fictional versions of his experience that he had crafted for his other books. In describing escapes, as well as life under slavery, he largely presents himself as observer and commentator. In numerous ways, Brown provides readers with the narrative form and content of a great many publications after the Civil War that approached life on the antebellum plantation with a kind of idealized fascination—publications rife with dialect, song, and depictions of an earthy but crafty people largely at home in the difficult but romanticized world of slavery. But Brown's own position is never entirely clear—not only his former and present position in the world of slavery but also his position in relation to the settings, events, and opinions he presents throughout the book. He never tells of his own escape from bondage, for example, and only lightly refers to his youthful presence in the early scenes on the plantation in *My Southern Home* that stands in for and is based on the troubled "home" of his youth. Andrews has observed, "When compared to Brown's written *Narrative*, more than thirty years earlier, *My Southern Home* seems carefully designed to deindividualize the narrator, to distance his voice and his experience from that of Brown" (Introduction to *From Fugitive Slave* 9–10). As Andrews points out, we encounter in *My Southern Home* "a narrative mask, or persona, whose racial identity is often hard to determine," making it difficult to identify "a consistent and verifiable sociopolitical message" (11). On the one hand, we often have cause to "wonder if Brown in 1880 was trying to accommodate himself to a new generation of white readers in a post-Reconstruction era increasingly indifferent to the problems of slavery and racial justice over which the Civil War had been fought"; on the other hand, we meet in *My Southern Home* a narrator who is sometimes determined to "denounce the increasingly white supremacist governments of the post-Reconstruction South, attributing to them a 'cause of oppression scarcely second in hatefulness to that of chattel slavery' in the Old South" (10–11).

Such contesting perspectives and conclusions are very much the point here, for *My Southern Home* is less memoir than sociology. Harriet Martineau's *How to Observe Morals and Manners* (1838), which, as noted in Chapter 4, has been called "the first substantive treatise on sociological methodology" (Hill xi), had a profound influence on Brown.[19] Martineau was intimately associated with Garrisonian abolitionists and had been quite vocal in her commentary against slavery in her two books based on her travels in the United States: *Society in America* (1837) and *Retrospect of Western Travel* (1838).[20] In particular, *Society in America*, which originally Martineau had wanted to entitle "Theory and Practice of Society in America," is not only a commentary on the United States but also, more importantly, a consideration of the United States as a case study in sociological method. Martineau, who accounts for the challenges of generalizing from her limited experience in the United States, outlines a two-part method in presenting her findings. The first part is "to compare the existing state of society in America with the principles on which it is professedly founded; thus testing Institutions, Morals, and Manners by an indisputable, instead of an arbitrary standard, and securing to myself the same point of view with my readers of both nations" (viii). "The other method by which I propose to lessen my own responsibility," she continues, "is to enable my readers to judge for themselves, better than I can for them, what my testimony is worth. For this purpose, I offer a brief account of my travels, with dates in full; and a report of the principal means I enjoyed of obtaining a knowledge of the country" (ix). In this way, *Society in America* prepares for Martineau's general statement on sociological method a year later in *How to Observe Morals and Manners*, in which she proceeds from principle to focused observations, considering first the philosophical, moral, and mechanical "requisites for observation" and then "what to observe"—including "religion," "general moral notions," "domestic state," "idea of liberty," "progress," and "discourse" (vii–ix).

In *My Southern Home*, Brown similarly offers a brief account of his travels and provides readers with the means to judge for themselves the perspectives and opinions they encounter along the way. Like Martineau, too, Brown looks for opportunities to compare, as he had done throughout his public career, "the existing state of society in America with the principles on which it is professedly founded." In addition to the chapters based loosely on Brown's own experience of enslavement in and beyond St. Louis, Missouri, *My Southern Home* tours various locales, both urban and rural; it takes us to the Democratic State Convention of 1860; it has us enter a cabin for a reading of the Emancipation Proclamation; and it describes the churches built by African American congregations in the South after the Civil War. Moreover, it draws us into a complex social environment populated—either physically or historically—by whites, blacks, southerners, northerners, women, men, Jews, Arabs, Gypsies, Irishmen, Germans, and Frenchmen. Some of these groups and nationalities are mentioned in discussions of the challenges of oppression and collective self-determination; others illustrate the prevalence of prejudice. Often the stance and prejudices of our guiding narrator are themselves either unclear or all too clear but rather hard to reconcile with the tone and apparent purpose of the book. We are told, for instance, that "history shows that of all races, the African was best adapted to be the 'hewers of

wood, and drawers of water'" and that "the negro is better adapted to follow than to lead" (179). We encounter both assumptions and assertions of
white superiority, but also critiques of the effects of a white supremacist
culture, a culture that keeps African Americans from establishing their
equality. Thus Brown's southern tour, unlike Martineau's American tour,
offers no stable frame of reference, not even in the consistency of the narrator's commentary on history, culture, and collective character.

To be sure, *My Southern Home* is very much a book that measures actual social life against guiding or professed principles, one that builds to
a consideration of the best means of improving the condition of African
Americans, but it is also a book about a multiplicity of guiding principles,
competing "higher laws," and the challenges of applying and sustaining
principles in social practice. Part of what took Brown to the South for
this tour was his ongoing work for the temperance movement, a cause to
which he devoted himself from the beginning to the end of his career, and
one that took him just as far, in his travels and arguably in his writings, as
did his antislavery work.[21] This was a time of considerable tensions concerning the integration of the Good Templar lodges—similar to the tensions years earlier among the Freemasons that led to the establishment
of the Prince Hall lodge in Boston—with the white South determined
to establish and maintain segregated lodges and international groups
opening the doors for integrated lodges. According to David M. Fahey,
the Independent Order of Good Templars of the World "had sent its best
known black member, Dr. William Wells Brown, to organize blacks in
Virginia in 1877 and 1879–80" (16). "With the help of some True Reformers," Fahey states, Brown "formed a brief-lived Grand Lodge in Virginia
affiliated with [the] international organization"; he "returned to Virginia
in 1879 to reorganize the Grand Lodge" (232). Continuing these efforts,
Fahey says, in 1880 Brown "persuaded most of the [Grand Fountain of the
United Order of the True Reformers] in the state to dissolve the Grand
Fountain and establish Good Templar lodges" (16). This work within
the racially fractured temperance and fraternal organizations, work that
brought Brown to the travels he drew from for *My Southern Home*, could
only have reminded him that even shared principles and a guiding cause
were no guarantees of a stable social framework.

In many ways, then, *My Southern Home* is Brown's own attempt to both
identify and address the challenge of his onetime mentor Martineau:
"how to observe morals and manners." Brown, though, resituates and
recontextualizes this challenge, so it seems less the prelude to a method

than the frustrated plea that follows from observation and experience. His observations pose difficult questions about race, social relations, and political power. But rather than look for answers by surveying a complex cultural terrain and weighing the competing demands of different social groups, Brown echoes established social opinion and uses his survey—a tour of both time and social space—to examine the ways in which different historical situations promote different configurations of the exercise of power. In the opening line of the book's preface, Brown warns: "No attempt has been made to create heroes or heroines, or to appeal to the imagination of the heart" (113). This seems especially the case when the book turns to issues of race, for both white and black communities he observes seem to be subject to familiar patterns of power—as when he devotes a series of chapters to an exploration of the condition of free blacks before emancipation and the relationship of race and power during Reconstruction and beyond.

At the beginning of the book's fourteenth chapter, Brown addresses the suppression of some "fifty thousand free colored people in the slave States" in 1850. "In all the States these people were allowed but few privileges not given to the slaves," he says, "and in many their condition was thought to be even worse than that of the bondmen." Brown discusses the laws that restricted mobility and opportunity of free blacks, emphasizing the existence of laws "for the punishment of the free colored people" that did not apply to whites and the existence of "thirty-two offences more for blacks than had been enacted for the whites." He considers as well "public opinion, which is often stronger than law," which was "severe in the extreme." Brown then focuses on "a movement . . . made in several of the Southern States to put an exorbitant tax upon [blacks], and in lieu of which they were to be sold into life-long slavery" (216). Following general commentary on that movement, he quotes extensively from a southern dissenter, Judge Catron of Tennessee, though he shows how little such dissent was able to accomplish. That analysis leads to an even more extreme example of white supremacist control: "efforts . . . made to re-open the African slave trade" at the Democratic State Convention in Charleston, South Carolina, in 1860. Brown quotes from the convention's proceedings, concluding with one speaker's statement: "I believe that the African slave-trader is a true missionary, and a true Christian." Following this statement, Brown ends the chapter with one final comment: "Such was the feeling in a large part of the South, with regard to the enslavement of the negro" (220).

His pronouncement might seem to speak for itself, but in the next chapters Brown explores this "feeling in a large part of the South" from numerous angles. The fifteenth chapter addresses "the success of the slave-holders in controlling the affairs of the National Government" (221), this time leading to the opinion that such views created the tension between North and South that led to the Civil War. We then find ourselves, in the sixteenth chapter, in "a negro cabin in South Carolina" witnessing a reading of the Emancipation Proclamation—and this prepares us for the following chapter's discussion of "one question that appeared to overshadow all others" both during and following the Civil War: "Negro Equality" (224, 231). Brown's approach to this issue echoes that of Booker T. Washington ("Paddle your own canoe," is Brown's advice to African Americans), though with the difference that Brown's own racial position and allegiance remain ambiguous: "As if the liberating of a race, and securing to them personal, political, social and religious rights, made it incumbent upon us to take these people into our houses, and give them seats in our social circle, beyond what we would accord to other total strangers" (231). But if Brown begins with mild advice, offered from an immense social distance from southern blacks, the chapter quickly becomes more pointed in its commentary on the response of southern whites to the specter of social equality: "Through fear, intimidation, assassination, and all the horrors that barbarism can invent, every right of the negro in the Southern states is to-day at an end. Complete submission to the whites is the only way for the colored man to live in peace" (233). Brown concludes the chapter by suggesting that the "War of Races" had been ended only by the complete submission of blacks, and that the Ku Klux Klan and other white supremacist groups awaited any attempt by African Americans to change the situation.

Brown then turns from white southern feeling to African American experience, gradually both contextualizing his apparent sympathy with whites and his condemnation of white violence and suppression of even the most basic civil rights. His eighteenth chapter spotlights postemancipation Saturdays in the South, or "nigger day," when African Americans visited the city to spend their hard-earned pay. Focusing on this day of "gaudy-colored goods" in shop windows and the "gaudy articles of wearing apparel" favored by black women (234–35), this chapter is a blend of social description and folklore that would not be out of place in many magazines of the time that preferred the Uncle Remus school of exotic characterization.[22]

This extended consideration of the history and context of race relations in the South prepares Brown for one of his most direct statements of his assumed role during his travels. At the beginning of his nineteenth chapter, Brown states: "Spending part of the winter of 1880 in Tennessee, I began the study of the character of the people and their institutions" (243). Of course, we have been reading about just such a study for several chapters, including reprinted excerpts of primary documents and reportage from both secondary sources and direct experience. We have encountered political debates, legislative decisions, social politics, individual experience, shared social assumptions, and exoticized folkways. Now the author presents a mix of all those things. The chapter begins with a somewhat sympathetic account of white southerners, harkening back to Brown's commentary on social equality. Indeed, he goes out of his way to be objective—leading into the subject (rather strangely, by this point in the book) by saying, "I soon learned that there existed an intense hatred on the part of the whites, toward the colored population" (243). Arguably, this statement adds little to Brown's authority, making him seemingly the last person to realize what is obvious to everyone else, but he makes this assertion in large part to define his own role in these proceedings.

Brown here takes the part of a neutral observer by representing different perspectives—as shaped by different cultural experiences—on the source and significance of racial tensions. Throughout much of *My Southern Home*, his representation of African Americans in the South often seems to play to existing stereotypes—the very characterizations, indeed, being used at the time to justify white supremacist control. As noted earlier in this chapter, Andrews has suggested that, "given the uncompromising attack on slavery in the *Narrative*, one might wonder if Brown in 1880 was trying to accommodate himself to a new generation of white readers in a post-Reconstruction era increasingly indifferent to the problems of slavery and racial justice over which the Civil War had been fought" (10). This accommodation can be seen not only in Brown's criticism of African Americans but also in his explanation of white racism. "The older whites," he observes,

> brought up in the lap of luxury, educated to believe themselves superior to the race under them, self-willed, arrogant, determined, skilled in the uses of side-arms, wealthy—possessing the entire political control of the State—feeling themselves superior also to the citizens of the free States—this people was called upon to subjugate

themselves to an ignorant, superstitious, and poverty-stricken, race—a race without homes, or the means of obtaining them; to see the offices of State filled by men selected from this servile set made these whites feel themselves deeply degraded in the eyes of the world. (243)

This apparent sympathy for whites, however, is qualified—the statement addresses not only immense social inequality and white supremacist dominance but also the tools used to achieve and maintain that control (side arms, wealth, and political power). The hint of sympathy is amplified, though, when Brown turns to what he terms the "Comedy of Errors" resulting from the attempt by ignorant black men who were "congratulated as 'Statesmen'" by those northern whites and others seeking to take advantage of the temporarily "disfranchised" whites (244).

When Brown turns to a more heroic narrative of black achievement, this dark comedy still lingers, for the chapter does not end here. Brown is quite forceful in defending African Americans who stumbled on the public stage; he is forceful as well in praising their performance in the global theater of achievement. White resentment and black ignorance only emphasize the achievements of the race: "Nothing has been left undone to cripple their energies, darken their minds, debase their moral sense, and obliterate all traces of their relationship to the rest of mankind; and yet how wonderfully they have sustained the mighty load of oppression under which they have groaned for thousands of years" (245).[23] Thus does African American experience contrast with the response of whites who felt themselves, after only a few years, "deeply degraded in the eyes of the world." Brown's account, in other words, provides the reader with background not only on the law, professed ideals, and social tensions, but also on the dynamic history of racial interactions, mutual influences, and the intricate structures of social power that have shaped both individual and collective identity over time.

But this is not the whole point of Brown's commentary, for the chapter ends, perhaps strangely, with another darkly comic and exotic episode from black life, seemingly unrelated to everything else in the chapter—the story of how a father reconverted his daughter from Episcopalianism to Methodism (and, arguably, from recently acquired city manners and developing refinement back to country ways). But as the father whips his daughter into submission, we realize that Brown has prepared his readers to respond to such events at various levels, and to recognize in them a

culture of violence, a culture of difficult transitions, and a world of relations and histories that cannot easily be brought together. There are
no heroes here, as Brown has indicated; but there is a method of social
observation that attends to all sides and identifies the problems that call
for heroic efforts.

The competing contexts and racial struggles that Brown describes naturally complicate his claims to the South as his original and lasting home.
While he sharply critiques the white supremacist control that followed
the Civil War and Reconstruction, he also presents white southerners
as people caught up in the inevitable logic of a historical process driven
by shifting inequalities of power. And while he celebrates the achievements of southern blacks, he is also critical, even condescendingly so,
of the priorities and values of the emancipated population—a population that serves as the primary and sometimes the only black presence
in *My Southern Home*. The South of the book is a sort of perfect storm of
regional, racial, and class tensions, resulting in a destructive force that
is all too predictable: "This extravagance of black men, followed by the
heavy taxes, reminded the old Southerners of their defeat in the Rebellion; it brought up thoughts of revenge; Northern sympathy emboldened
them at the South, which resulted in the Ku-Klux organizations, and the
reign of terror that has cursed the South ever since." To be sure, Brown
asserts that this storm could have been anticipated and, if not avoided,
then at least diverted. "The restoring of the rebels to power," he states,
"and the surrendering the colored people to them, after using the latter
in the war, and at the ballot box, creating an enmity between the races, is
the most bare-faced ingratitude that history gives any account of" (245).
Once again Brown suggests that a region free from racial resentment and
hatred was, at one point, at least theoretically possible. This time, though,
the fault lies with the surrender and humiliation not of the defeated white
population but of the black—and the opportunity lost was historical in its
proportions. Indeed, the challenge of claiming a home in the South for
an expatriated black man is indicated even in the rhetorical conventions
that Brown follows here, whereby it is assumed that "southerners" and
"northerners" always refer to white people. And, as Brown reminds us,
those northerners and southerners could unite to enforce and extend the
white dominance of the land.

In books and magazines, in fiction and nonfiction, from legislative
halls to clergymen's pulpits, white Americans addressed the "problem"
of African Americans; more often than not they concluded that black

Americans should be restricted, controlled, or otherwise removed from the realm of social authority. As George M. Fredrickson has observed, late nineteenth-century "racial Darwinism" enabled some individuals to argue that the education of African Americans amounted to "the artificial preservation of the unfit," and that therefore the nation should not waste its time on such unscientific efforts (251). At the same time, racial Darwinism enabled other whites to reassure themselves that humanitarian efforts could be rather strictly defined, and that the nation was required to help blacks *only* through education. If blacks, thus aided, should fail, then the question of racial equality would be settled scientifically. In either case, education and various other cultural mechanisms for promoting rights, security, and opportunities were safely either held or withheld by the dominant culture, and both the premises and the results of these restrictive measures were used to define the "emancipated" community, either by implication or by design. Perhaps we should not be surprised, then, that Brown himself makes a great point of grappling with this problem, or that he does so in a way that emphasizes the social position both of commentators and of subjects.

Equally significant, perhaps, is that Brown largely avoids revealing his own social position. In fact, it is difficult to locate him even in the early chapters of *My Southern Home*, though we encounter various other people living in the home of his youth and even engaged in some of the incidents of his youth. But Brown seldom places himself in any scene, relying instead on his role as observer or peripheral participant—indeed, an observer of racially ambiguous status. Moreover, he rarely applies the words "I," "me," or "my" to himself through most of the early chapters—and when he does, he sounds less like an autobiographical narrator than a sophisticated observer, for all the world one of the many white social commentators or travel writers popular at the time. When a mistress looks for her slave, Brown enters the narrative merely to say, "I hastened out to look for the boy." And when the mistress worries that she will not have a clean cap to wear when greeting the guests who would soon arrive, Brown's comment seems intended to distinguish himself from the mistress's slaves: "I tried to comfort her by suggesting that the servants might get one ready in time" (123). During the mistress's visit with her company, Brown states simply: "I listened with great interest to the following conversation between Mrs. Gaines and her ministerial friend" (133). When he sees that "both Dr. and Mrs. Gaines were easily deceived by their servants," Brown does not seem to identify with those servants when he reports: "I often thought that Mrs. Gaines took peculiar pleasure in being misled by them" (154). And so it is through much of the early part of the narrative. Although readers might well be familiar with Brown's story, and although Brown draws liberally from his accounts of his early life published in his other books, the early chapters of *My Southern Home* are more a reflection of detached observation than of anything approaching autobiography or memoir. Brown only gradually reveals himself, as if his real purpose is to present the various social forces—people, geography, law, economics, and social custom—that shaped his identity day by day, year by year.

It might be said that in light of this approach to self-presentation, with Brown working behind the scenes in recounting his youth, instead of using this book to place himself in his former home, Brown uses the book to place his home in his life. The phrase "My Southern Home," in other words, refers not only or even primarily to a region but instead to the man we encounter on every page of the book that carries this title. This is to say nothing more than that Brown presents himself as a southerner, a man for whom "the South" is not simply a region but a world of experiences, as intimate as the blood that runs through his veins. This constitutes a rather significant transfusion for Brown, if we are to trust the racial logic of most white Americans of the time, but this is the point of his book. Brown's identity in *My Southern Home* is defined not by the history he relates but by his ability to relate that history—a history that goes beyond what can be recorded by personal observation or experience. That is, this is a history that encompasses the experiences, the histories, and the opinions of white and black, rich and poor—and it is a history that further represents these social groups by placing them in dynamic relation with one another. Who is Brown? He is the man behind the curtain, the participant-observer who is both a part of and apart from the events and people he describes. Brown does not just claim the South on his journey; he brings it with him.

When Brown emerges and asserts himself as a *black* man as well as a southerner, he recenters the race relations that have been so much a part of his story.[24] In much of his commentary on African American life before, during, and after the Civil War, he draws so often from standard frameworks for representing black life—minstrel humor, dialect folk recording, and the like—that we might assume he is directing his comments primarily to a white readership. But when Brown steps more deliberately into his text and presents himself as a black man, he also redefines his audience, addressing directly a black readership and assigning white readers to the periphery. "Emerging from the influence of oppression," he laments in a late chapter, "taught from early experience to have no confidence in the whites, we have little or none in our own race, or even in ourselves" (281–82). Brown turns the weight of the book to this cause, calling on his African American readers for "more self-reliance, more confidence in the ability of our own people; more manly independence, a higher standard of moral, social, and literary culture. Indeed, we need a union of effort to remove the dark shadow of ignorance that now covers the land. While the barriers of prejudice keep us morally and socially from educated white society, we must make a strong effort to raise ourselves from the common level where emancipation and the new order of things found us" (282). Suddenly Brown is not just a witness to but a participant in emancipation; finally his escape years ago is brought to closure as he rejoins the rest of the formerly enslaved community in a common cause. While certainly Brown presents himself here and elsewhere in *My Southern Home* as an assumed leader of the emancipated community, this is a dramatic if implicit reunion. If the South is something Brown brought with him in his travels, *My Southern Home* eventually finds the realization of that *something* in the cause of African Americans.

Brown's appeal to an imagined black community—the "we" that has emerged from the influence of oppression—might seem to require no explanation were it not for the dramatically contradictory statements and contending perspectives we encounter in *My Southern Home*. To be sure, it would be relatively simple to identify two primary positions to which this book seems devoted—a critique of white oppression and a defense of and praise for black achievement. It would be simple as well to account for the complexity of this book by noting that Brown modifies both of these positions—explaining the situation of the whites, and at times even sympathizing with them, and critiquing African Americans for everything from gaudy dress to irresponsibility. But, in fact, the world of *My Southern Home* is more complex than either of these positions, as is the imagined community held tenuously together, though only momentarily, by Brown's *we*. The community invoked throughout *My Southern Home* is the result of the complex and dynamic current of history. Brown's representation of that community would need to be just as dynamic.

Ultimately, *My Southern Home* works to locate Brown's southern home not in a region or even in the established divisions—primarily, race and class—of the communities of the South. Rather, Brown locates the South precisely in what he terms "inward culture, at the springs and sources of individual life and character" (288). Whereas Martineau adopted a method for observing and discerning the "manners and morals" of the social world, Brown presents a highly dynamic and unstable world that cannot be thus described—a world of contending opinions and interests, of violent and shifting struggles for power, a world lost in its own reliance on invested assumptions, caricatures, conventional wisdom, and stereotypes. Accordingly, he works in *My Southern Home* to invert Martineau's method in order to make the object of the observations the observing subject himself, William Wells Brown, whose method during his tours *becomes* the southern home he seeks. Brown's claim to the South as home, finally, is based on the fact that he is the product of this complex, dynamic push and pull of forces that constitutes the South—as a black man and a former slave, as a temperance man and an antislavery activist, as a fugitive southerner who has lived most of his life in the North, and as an internationally recognized writer and lecturer who is still subject to the same prejudices and restrictive laws that plague the recently emancipated communities of the South. *My Southern Home* represents this vision of the South in all of its complexity, in its unresolved conflicts, and in its play of opinions that neither begin nor end with shared premises.

Ultimately, Brown has no moral to offer for the interconnected but competing stories and ethical dilemmas described in *My Southern Home*. What he offers instead is a vision of history as palimpsest—both in his reuse of his own published material and in his examination of the many stories-upon-stories presented in the book. Castronovo, in a meditation on representations of a nation shaped by slavery and race, has commented insightfully on commemorative public history in the antebellum United States, arguing that "national narrative, once assumed as the site of cohesion, can be seen to fissure into sites of contestation, exclusion, and repression. 'Adding story to story' leads not to one larger story, but to dispersed histories that stand in uneasy relation to one another" (*Fathering* 6).[25] This is Brown's approach in *My Southern Home*. The region he encounters in his travels is, indeed, a region characterized by "dispersed histories that stand in uneasy relation to one another." The home he finds is not distinguished by a singular story but rather by a method, "adding story to story," by which this complex region can be known and understood.

In the penultimate chapter of *My Southern Home*, Brown discusses the importance of literature and expresses his belief that "never a shadow falls that does not leave a permanent impress of its image, a monument of its passing presence. Every character is modified by association. Words, the image of the ideas, are more impressive than shadows; actions, embodied thoughts, more enduring than aught material" (289). Brown's own life and character have been "modified by association," and the understanding he presents in *My Southern Home* is less the product of that life and character, the conclusions reached after a long and active life, than the process of its modification over time. We might say, in fact, that the home to which Brown returned did not fully exist until he wrote about his return, for the South he hoped to reclaim was a product of the many stories that had shaped his life, answered by the many stories he had written about his life and his world. Although it is, in many ways, an excellent guide to the South before, during, and after the Civil War, to find the South of Brown's book we need only follow the shifting perspectives, the competing histories, and the multilayered representations—"the lavish beauty and harmonious disorder"—of Brown's most seemingly detached but most intimate achievement, *My Southern Home*.

IN THE THREE TEXTS presented here as case studies of post–Civil War African American literature, the central features of this unique tradition are defined less by authorship than by the dynamics of common historical pressures and possibilities. In each case, the authors (both actual and, in Truth's case, conditional) represent the realities of African American life and history by underscoring the limitations of representation, even of basic documentation, and by locating the authorial or authorizing voice within a world of competing contingencies. Reading those contingencies requires that we attend to the whole of African American cultural and intellectual history, as well as the work of the many white writers and other public figures to which African Americans needed to respond, with whom they were sometimes associated, or against whose efforts they needed to devote themselves. That complex engagement with an almost overwhelmingly intertextual and interracial field of concerns was the principal fact of African American life during this period, a world in which race was both central and difficult to identify, and in which authorship was both essential and tightly contextualized. Nineteenth-century African American literary history is the history of such engagements, such concerns, and such contexts. It is also the history of the emergence of a complex poetics of both resistance and insistence, of representing the self claimed by the other, and of both inviting and accounting for readers who sometimes represented the possibilities of an imagined community and sometimes represented the improbability of that community's self-realization. This is a tradition that deserves to be studied on its own terms, one still very much in the process of being recovered. It is a tradition, to borrow again from Douglass, that is presently known largely by way of "glimpses," a subject "covered with mystery" and "enveloped in darkness." "Speaking of marks, traces, possibles, and probabilities," the writers of the nineteenth century come before their readers, still calling for a just response ("Heroic Slave" 474).

# Covenants and Communities

*The Demands of African American Literature*

"He's *so* worried about the history of the future."—Overheard during
a walk on campus, West Virginia University, April 28, 2008

In an essay published originally in 1996, Mae G. Henderson explores the
tensions between Black Studies (which emerged in the late 1960s and
early 1970s) and Black Cultural Studies (which appeared during the late
1980s and early 1990s). She begins by noting the similarities between
the two projects. Black Cultural Studies "continues the Black Studies
project in that it takes as its object of investigation the consequences of
uneven economic, social, and cultural development." Moreover, "like
Black Studies, cultural studies challenges received and conventional disciplinary paradigms in the construction of knowledge through its multi-
disciplinary and cross-cultural focus." Both schools, too, privilege "the
study of vernacular and mass culture." In short, "many, if not most, of
the central concerns of black cultural studies have been anticipated by
the Black Studies project and the challenge it brought to the academy
two decades ago" (95). So what is the problem? "The problem," Henderson explains, "is that the emergence of black cultural studies threatens to
re-marginalize a field of study that has become central during the Black
Studies movement. The voices and experiences of the objects of investigation—namely, African Americans—are subjected to interpretation by
scholars and theorists who draw on paradigms not grounded in African
American history and culture" (98).

As this statement suggests, Henderson is concerned about points of
intellectual departures and arrivals, about "intellectual space" and "institutional space" (98), and about the sites "of historical struggle and contestation" (100) that not only shape the theoretical and methodological

approaches to problems but also determine what might be identified as a problem worthy of study, sites where both the problem and the means toward a solution might be located. Working from the "community-based" discipline of Black Studies, itself "rooted in community culture," Henderson argues for an approach that looks "not only . . . to Birmingham, *England*, but to Birmingham, *Alabama*" for its definition of purpose and methodology (100). Henderson recognizes the value of transatlantic perspectives, but she is still concerned about the shift away from scholarly frameworks that emerged from the social struggles that produced the U.S. Black Studies movement. Accordingly, she cautions us to think carefully about the historical and cultural groundings of the frameworks and methodologies we bring to this work. "We need not only ask," she concludes, "'Where, by the way, is this train going?' We need also to ask 'where has this train been?'" (101).

The train, it seems, was transformed into a ship on the Black Atlantic destined for a cosmopolitan planetarity and was last seen sailing into the shadows of deep time. Within the academic realm, Black Studies, to be sure, still exists, but it has been rather forcefully marginalized and is generally treated as a suspect field carrying the perceived taint of the most prominent voices of Afrocentrism. Black Cultural Studies has developed considerably, though often in the very ways that so concerned Henderson in the mid-1990s. African American literary scholarship sometimes operates in various associations with these wider fields but has also become a reservoir of possibilities for scholars more broadly interested in American literary and cultural studies. Many of these developments are the result of the dismissal of race as a valid category of analysis, discussed in this book's first chapter—a dismissal often depending on the most vocal and simplistic examples of racialized logic associated with Afrocentrism, race politics, and popular culture. Addressing the "irrational rationalities, elisions, and performances" that emerge from "racial discourse," Paul Gilroy argues:

> In the resulting world of racial and ethnic common sense, it does not matter that all demands for the recognition of supposedly absolute difference presuppose extensive transcultural knowledge that would have been impossible to acquire if cultural divisions always constituted impermeable barriers to understanding. Appreciating the paradox of discrepant ontologies provides a chance to approach the problem of multiculture from a different angle and consider

instead why the alibis that derive from the cheapest invocations of incommensurable otherness command such wide respect. (*Postcolonial* 8)

Gilroy speaks for many who, in effect, argue that race has never had a stable existence, and that experience and identity in the world have always been transcultural and international. In the face of such arguments, what can seem like a hair-splitting distinction between Black Studies and Black Cultural Studies seems irrelevant, even parochial, or even a longing for simplistic assertions when sophisticated analytical tools are available.

Throughout this book, I have suggested that such distinctions are important. I have argued that simplistic assertions are those that assume race is simply an ideological construct reducible to generalizations easily dismissed in the face of "the paradox of discrepant ontologies." African American culture, I have contended, has been forged through its encounters with such discrepancies, and nineteenth-century African American literature is a valuable record of and commentary on that process. In many ways, in fact, I have followed the lead of Stephen Turner, whose work on cognitive science has led him to reject the ideal of inherently shared cultures and practices. Focusing on distinctly individual processes of adaptation to various inputs, Turner asserts that "the feedback mechanisms of experience that produce habituation are personal, or individual, but at the same time bound up with learning an idiom and experiencing the world" (12). I have maintained similarly that African American literature can be viewed productively as studies of those feedback mechanisms of experience—that is, of the controlling apparatus of a white supremacist culture that in many ways defined, restricted, or otherwise staged the production and reception of black self-representation. In nineteenth-century African American literature, we can often witness complex struggles with those shaping forces, assumptions, and expectations; and we can witness as well strategic efforts to expose, redirect, or otherwise resist the cultural mechanisms of racial definition and control. When we consider together a broad range of texts, I have suggested, we can see both the isolating and the productive tensions between the individual and the collective, and we can witness the development of an idiom for explaining and experiencing the world in different terms from those "the world" was prepared or willing to provide. We see, in short, the shift from imposed and isolating racial difference to patterns of "habituation," the discursive and narrative features of "the networks of affiliation enacted in performance" that are "conditioned by relations of power and the very purposeful and self-conscious effort to build community" (Hartman 59). We see, in effect, not simply narratives of African American lives but also African American narratives—the manifestations not of the simplistic concept of a shared culture that both Turner and Hartman denounce but rather of a complex of affiliations realized and gathered over time.

More than anything, then, I have tried to show in this book that those who read and comment on nineteenth-century African American literature need to look beyond selected texts and consider the broad range of African American expressive culture, the complex cultural history that shaped African American expressive opportunities and strategies, and the history of scholarly attempts to come to terms with this tradition. Of course, anyone familiar with that broad range might note that I do not fully practice what I preach in this book, for much of my argument is grounded in the work of writers with whom most readers are likely to be familiar. To some extent, I have relied for the background of this study on my consideration of African American historical writing in my last book, *Liberation Historiography*, in which I cover a wide range of writers and some of the most prominent cultural and publishing forums within which those writers worked. But even in *Liberation Historiography*, as in the present study, I say virtually nothing about poetry or oral culture, and one can hardly claim to represent this tradition with any justice without examining those central realms of expression.[1] While I hope that the value of my attention to such figures as Henry Box Brown, William Wells Brown, William and Ellen Craft, Frederick Douglass, Harriet Wilson, Sojourner Truth, and many others in *Chaotic Justice* is clear, I have tried to indicate a need for an understanding of the field that would not view a discussion of a wider range of examples from oral and print culture simply as a notable inclusion in scholarship, a mark of superior knowledge (as it generally is now). I have tried instead to show the need for a time when the failure to address a broad range of texts and other manifestations of expressive culture will be read as a notable omission, a serious flaw.

One might say, of course, that such attention to a broad range of concerns is only occasionally expected in scholarship on white American literary history; it is almost always considered a notable inclusion that offers an intriguing contextual setting for reevaluating our understanding of the great works of the tradition. We read a broad range of texts, but we generally keep them in the background. I am frankly unsympathetic to such approaches, rather uninterested in new arguments based on minor reconfigurations of the great authors and texts, and completely unconvinced that the usual logic of the canon is at all applicable to the special circumstances under which nineteenth-century African American literature was written, published, and circulated in a white supremacist culture. To understand the central features and dynamics of this literary tradition—one of the most conspicuous of which is that most frequently unexamined of critical concepts, race—we need to place text against text, story against story, and trope against trope, gradually reconstructing the contours of a dynamic field of expression designed to navigate the turbulent currents of mainstream American culture. What we often encounter instead is attention to a few familiar texts, revelations that are made with no awareness of similar insights presented years ago in African American literary scholarship, and working assumptions that race is both the defining feature of this literature and a category that can now be dismissed, aside from noting the political struggles necessary in a century that relied on this unfortunate cultural fiction. The assumptions about race in relation to African American literature become clear when we turn the page of the scholarly book we are reading and begin the chapter on a white woman writer, where gender but not race becomes the prominent concern, or on a white male writer, where headier or more metaphysical issues prevail.

This should not be the case, for there is a great deal of scholarship available to guide us through the concerns central to African American literature. Indeed, very little of what I have addressed in this book has involved the introduction of new concerns, and there is great value in reviewing regularly and integrating thoughtfully the critical history that has been so much a part of the development and recognition of what Houston A. Baker Jr. characterized in 1976 as "that body of written works crafted by authors consciously (even, at times, self-consciously) aware of the longstanding values and significant experiences of their culture" ("On the Criticism" 113). To be sure, many who write about or teach African American literature are aware of certain famous exchanges, such as the Joyce, Gates, and Baker exchanges in 1987, and certain pivotal publications—among them, Addison Gayle Jr.'s collection, *Black Expression* (1969); Michael S. Harper and Robert B. Stepto's *Chant of Saints: A Gathering of Afro-American Literature, Art, and Scholarship* (1979); the *Studies in Black American Literature* volumes (1980s) edited by Joe Weixlmann and Chester J. Fontenot; Marjorie Pryse and Hortense J. Spillers's edited collection *Conjuring: Black Women, Fiction, and Literary Tradition* (1985); the various collections edited by Henry Louis Gates Jr., including

*Black Literature and Literary Theory* (1984), *"Race," Writing, and Difference* (1985), and *Reading Black, Reading Feminist* (1990); the important collections published in 1989, including Cheryl Wall's *Changing Our Own Words*, Houston A. Baker Jr. and Patricia Redmond's *Afro-American Literary Study in the 1990s*, and Deborah E. McDowell and Arnold Rampersad's *Slavery and the Literary Imagination*; and prominent feminist collections, such as Gloria T. Hull, Patricia Bell Scott, and Barbara Smith's *All the Women Are White, All the Blacks Are Men, but Some of Us Are Brave: Black Women's Studies* (1982), and Beverly Guy-Sheftall's *Words of Fire* (1995). There are also good collections of African American criticism and theory that span a broad historical range, including Angelyn Mitchell's *Within the Circle* (1994), Hazel Arnett Ervin's *African-American Literary Criticism* (1999), and Winston Napier's *African American Literary Theory* (2000). These various collections (and this is only a partial list) portray a continuous, often contentious, and deeply thoughtful critical tradition that is often absent from scholarship that includes discussions of African American literature—either as direct sources or as a background presence. These collections richly demonstrate that the study of African American literature and literary history has always encompassed a broad range of concerns, from the literary to the historical, from the cultural to the philosophical, and from particular definitions of the imagined black community to various attempts to account for the geographical and ideological diversity of various understandings of African American communities and histories.

In some ways, then, my argument in this book is simple. It is that attention to African American authors and texts requires attention to a range of concerns—the same range that we would encounter in studies of white American writers—and that without that attention we can hardly be in a position to make sound claims and generalizations based on our study. If we were writing about an established white male author of the nineteenth century—Hawthorne, say, or Melville—we would certainly be expected to know something about the history most relevant to his life and work, as well as about the critical response to his work over the years. We would be expected to know his work beyond the text in question and to be familiar with the literary circles in which he is regularly placed. Without sufficient attention to the critical and historical tradition of these and other writers, we would be unable to publish our work. Even when there are lingering questions about authorship and biographical detail—as in the case of Shakespeare, for example—we are expected to have a precise sense of what is known and what remains unknown.

Yet for years, errors of established fact and of biographical and historical assumptions have been a commonplace in commentary on African American authors and texts. Why should this be? Why should we assume that it is unproblematic to focus on a certain author when we have not read a range of authors, to write about a handful of slave narratives without reading dozens, to account for "African American history" without becoming deeply involved in the historiographical challenges associated with that history, or to discuss an author as an African American writer without attending to the range of concerns and events that made such collective identifications continually unstable, politically necessary, and increasingly self-defined, significant, and problematic *within* the collective over time? If we are to place writers in conversation with one another, or if we are to construct newly integrated literary histories, it is important that we know where we have been (including all uncertainties we might have in this regard, with a strong recognition of the work that remains and of the gaps in the historical record) so we might know where we are and where we can go from there.

Central to my argument has been a reconsideration of race—not as a feature of African American identity but rather as a central dynamic in U.S. history. I contend, in effect, that there are two primary dimensions of the historical process of race: (1) the systemic manifestations and operations of racial ideology, and (2) the understanding, negotiation, and manipulation of various racial concepts in consciousness and experience, both individual and collective. To explore the systemic manifestations and operations of race, one would need to examine laws whose effects or limitations led to additional laws, institutions that inspired or enforced certain modes of public behavior, shifting discourses that followed from legal and institutional experience, and the ways in which the cultural scripts (and the human resistance to such scripts) shaped by legal, institutional, and social life led to shifts or revisions in various laws, institutions, and social practices. Involved in these processes but often viewed as if separate from them is the consciousness of race—that is, the simpler ways that we have of understanding and expressing our experiences within this chaotic process: the world of prejudices, the concepts of race as embodiment, the definition and manipulation of identity politics, and the like. These dimensions of racial history are reciprocal and dynamic, mutually modifying in constant interaction, and sometimes leading to attempts to bring the whole to a stable conceptual framework, such as multiculturalism or diversity, that might have not merely institutional and cultural force but also political and even commercial force, as people invest in such frameworks to address or at least to claim to address social problems and possibilities identified as racial. My argument is that we often attend to only a part of this process—usually, the most conscious level—and treat it as if it were the entire process.

African Americans have been prominent among those groups that have been forced to carry the burden of a more complex and comprehensive awareness of U.S. racial history. Some of the most prominent features of African American literature constitute, among other things, a record of the methods they have had to develop to manage a collective framework defined by something other than the priorities of white supremacist ideology. Out of these efforts has evolved a distinctive tradition, though it is a tradition challenged by those unwilling to face or determined to simplify what I have called the chaos of race. As Bernard Bell has observed:

> The complexity of racial and cultural identities includes . . . much more than class, religion, and geography. Contrary to the popularity in the academies of anti-essentialist arguments by postmodern critics, the authority, authenticity, and agency of the identities of most African Americans emanate most distinctively and innovatively from the particularity of our historical struggle against slavery and its legacy of antiblack racism in the United States. They also emanate from the shared cultural codes and language of our individual and collective political agency in reconciling our unique double-consciousness in the open-ended process of constructing our identities and reconstructing a new world order. ("Review" 477)

Although I have not called for an essentialist reading of African American identity, that is not Bell's argument, either. Rather, Bell accounts for a history that reveals regular patterns of both oppression and struggle, a struggle that is identifiable in its "particularity" and notable in that its proponents have developed "shared cultural codes" and a "language of our individual and collective political agency." In this book, I have argued that what is common in African American experience, as revealed by African American literary history, is not a homogeneous community but rather a community that has constructed such shared codes and languages (often, significantly, involving improvisational methods) out of their negotiations with the instabilities of the racial dynamics of cultural experience.

In fact, African American literature has been shaped, in part, by the determination of many writers to contribute to a black aesthetic without being bound by the simplistic notions of race that often have been the most predictable features of the dominant cultural field in which their work would be received and evaluated. They have worked within literary fields in which it was often safe to assume that white authors would have no consciousness of writing about or representing race until they reached a narrative moment involving a nonwhite person or a racially marked place or event, and within literary fields in which there was considerable reason to worry when white authors wrote consciously and deliberately about race. In both the unconsciously racialist and the consciously white supremacist texts, as Toni Morrison has pointed out, one usually discovers race as a pliable concept that serves as a kind of cultural warehouse for metaphors suited for metaphysical reflections capable of at once citing and transcending race. At the beginning of *Playing in the Dark*, Morrison reflects: "I do not have quite the same access to these traditionally useful constructs of blackness"—that is, those constructs common in writing by white authors. "Neither blackness nor 'people of color' stimulates in me notions of excessive, limitless love, anarchy, or routine dread. I cannot rely on these metaphorical shortcuts because I am a black writer struggling with and through a language that can powerfully evoke and enforce hidden signs of racial superiority, cultural hegemony, and dismissive 'othering' of people and language which are by no means marginal or already and completely known and knowable in my work" (x–xi). Morrison, in short, cannot afford the deceptive pleasures of a conveniently partial or delimited understanding of race, for she is far too intimate with the realities of racial history, and too complexly positioned by that history, to adopt what is itself a manifestation of the false consciousness central to racial history in a great number of white-authored texts. "The kind of work I have always wanted to do," she notes, "requires me to learn how to maneuver ways to free up the language from its sometimes sinister, frequently lazy, almost always predictable employment of racially informed and determined chains" (xi).

The work that Morrison is talking about is work badly needed in scholarship as well, though this is not work that can be accomplished by declaring race to be an inoperative concept. Indeed, Morrison addresses a world in which the illusion of racelessness prevails. "What," she asks, "does positing one's writerly self, in the wholly racialized society that is the United States, as unraced and all others as raced entail? What happens to the writerly imagination of a black author who is at some level *always* conscious of representing one's own race to, or in spite of, a race of readers that understands itself to be 'universal' or race-free?" (*Playing* xii). These have been the realities governing most of American literary history, and African American writers especially have produced a record of literary maneuvering capable not of getting us beyond race but rather of addressing the chaotic force of the racial world we are in. American literary scholarship has long been a profound example of Charles Mills's observation that "nonwhites . . . find that race is, paradoxically, both everywhere and nowhere, structuring their lives but not formally recognized in political/moral theory," and that "in a racially structured polity, the only people who can find it psychologically possible to deny the centrality of race are those who are racially privileged, for whom race is invisible precisely because the world is structured around them, whiteness as the ground against which the figures of other races—those who, unlike us, are raced—appear" (76). What is racially significant about African American literature is not that it was written by nonwhites, though this is what identifications of the role of race in this literary tradition sometimes amount to, particularly in the context of a study devoted primarily to white writers. What is significant about this literature in terms of race is its representational and analytical sophistication, its presentation of not simply the most conspicuous or crafted accounts of the conscious experience of race but also the best maps into the chaotic terrain of racial history and experience.

Nineteenth-century African American literature can guide us, I believe, to what a passing student has called (albeit dismissively) "the history of the future." As I indicated especially in Chapter 1, I think there is reason to feel more than a bit anxious about the future-oriented focus of much of the current commentary on race. I think that we have no chance of working our way into a stable and just future until we manage to work our way into the past, and I think our explorations of the past too often are guided by faulty maps. As noted in Chapter 1, I believe there might be some use for Redburn's guidebook, in Melville's instructive example—and more use still for those many guidebooks produced by those who had to chart indirect and savvy courses through the landscape of race. This was my primary concern in *Liberation Historiography*: to locate a few maps, which led me to explore not only African American history but also nineteenth-century African American approaches to historical method, approaches that I gathered under the heading of liberation historiography. Drawing from the methodologies of liberation theology, I argued that liberation historiography looks to the condition of oppression to determine the need and goals for historical research. It does not promise liberation from the complexly intertwined systems of power within which it functions, an escape to some imagined outside, some fundamentally new order, for there is no outside. Rather, liberation historiography envisions liberation as a manipulation of the instabilities of power in the service of empowering reinterpretations of the authoritative, and the authorizing, text of "history." In this book, I still turn to those texts that point to or emanate from the fissures of the white American ideological control over the past, those points where the conditions of oppression are most fully revealed. I am arguing for an approach to nineteenth-century African American literature that will promote more informed and productive readings of the maps that these texts provide.

I make no apologies for my belief that both historical and political agency are possible through literary scholarship. I have tried to indicate, though, the need to connect that scholarship with the communities most in need of sound historical maps. There are many today who could benefit greatly from studying the strategic conceptual negotiations of a threatening and "wholly racialized society," as Morrison put it, encountered in nineteenth-century African American literature, especially since this literature addresses so many aspects of the world in which we are still living, a world still significantly directed by nineteenth-century systemic forces.

Indeed, I think it might be useful to contrast the political energies of much of the current scholarship on American literary and cultural studies with a project—one hopes, a developing movement—initiated outside the academy, *The Covenant with Black America*. *The Covenant* is a book, a series of local conversations, and a number of community-based projects gathered together by a community of public leaders and activists under the leadership of Tavis Smiley. As Haki Madhubuti has observed, *The Covenant* "looks at the lives of Black folks in America and provides—in accessible language—analysis, solutions, and a call for self-reliance, self-sufficiency, and self-determination around the vital issues facing Black America" (Smiley 235). To my mind, *The Covenant* is a contemporary example of the historical approach I found among nineteenth-century African American writers—an attempt to define the terms *and the application* of historical scholarship by focusing on clear problems, manifest examples of an incoherent and unjust social system, and communities defined by an uneasy relation between local contingencies and national and global ideologies. In short, I found in this work, of both the nineteenth and the twenty-first centuries, important reminders of Maulana Karenga's admonition that the centerpiece of Black Studies is "a *relevant educa-tion*"—that is, an education devoted to solving "the pressing problems of the Black community" and to "the revolutionary struggle being waged to end racist oppression and change society and the world" (16–17).[2]

What especially interests me about *The Covenant with Black America* is that central to its work is a concept of Black America, but neither the book nor the ongoing work in this project depends on a simple or even a unified concept of a black American community, nor does that work ignore the fact that Black America exists and operates in the context of a global diasporic presence. Nevertheless, the Covenant locates itself by identifying clear problems in need of solutions—among them, problems concerning health care, education, the legal system, the environment, and the economy. Those problems define the parameters of the work ahead. Of course, those parameters, like the communities they help define, are themselves complex and constantly shifting. And as the project has pro-gressed, both in its organization and in its meetings with black communi-ties across the nation, it has reminded me very much of the attempts by nineteenth-century African American writers to assemble an imagined community, a community scattered geographically, ideologically, and ex-perientially, a community that could identify itself *as* a community only by discovering itself as a scattered people joined by a common historical condition and mission. In short, both the problems and the opportuni-ties outlined by the Covenant should be understood not simply as the social world confronted by African American communities but rather as the conditions, both positive and negative, that define African American identity, the world of contingencies that gives point and purpose to dis-cussions of blackness in communities, in culture, in history.

Such movements have often been fragile and short-lived, and the same might be true of the Covenant. But nineteenth-century African American literature could provide a powerful and stabilizing foundation for such efforts, stabilizing not because this literary tradition points to a world beyond the instabilities created by the chaos of race but rather because this tradition represents methods by which a common tradition can be forged through negotiated instabilities. It is worth repeating Gates's com-mentary on "the role of education in the reproduction of values," stated in my introduction. Addressing the arguments of the political right and the educational practices of a wholly racialized society, Gates observes: "The teaching of literature *is* the teaching of values; not inherently, no, but contingently, yes; it is—it has become—the teaching of an aesthetic and political order, in which no women or people of color were ever able to discover the reflection or representation of their images, or hear the resonances of their cultural voices" (*Loose Canons* 35). Gates argued for the importance of a literary canon capable of representing not only those lives but also the values implicit in the experience of those lives, the lessons learned along the way, the wisdom forged through intimate examinations of the terms of the world's always-delimited possibilities. Gates's point in publishing an anthology of African American literature was not just to allow us the luxury of having many readily available texts to choose from. The anthology represents a field of concerns and strategies, unlimited possibilities for representing and apprehending a world that resists representation and often frustrates understanding. Moreover, the anthology points to a broader field of writing still unrecovered or relatively unread, the field that the anthology is asked to represent but cannot contain. *Chaotic Justice* is a book about the need to continue that work, to read through and beyond imagined canons. And it is a book about the improbable faith of nineteenth-century African American writers and expressive artists we will discover when we do that reading. Theirs is a faith we still need today.

# NOTES

## Introduction

1  On Harper's use of significant names and historical references, see Ernest, *Resistance and Reformation*, chap. 6; and Foreman, "Reading Aright."

2  For a useful, informative consideration of commentary on "multipositionality" and African American identity, especially as the subject has been approached by historians, see Earl Lewis.

3  I am referring, of course, to the titles of influential books by Gilroy (*Against Race*) and Appiah (*The Ethics of Identity*).

4  One thinks here of John Reilly's awareness of the dangers of an uncritical approach to African American literary history even by those most devoted to the field. He says that one

> consequence of working with texts that display so openly their authors' sense of the burden of collective experience is the belief among critics of those texts that history—so evidently the property of others beyond literature—shows itself to be unconditionally objective. Since the presence of historical reference has made the design of inquiry seem so self-evident, Afro-American literary historians have tended not to ask questions about their own practice, even when it tends to contradict equally valued principles of practical criticism, such as the idea that literature cannot simply be equated with alternate realities; and the discipline has been the poorer for it. (89–90)

Although recent work has shown signs of attempting to address this problem, Reilly is quite right to note that the category of history itself needs to be interrogated in any effort to account for African American literary history.

5  For excellent examinations of the editing, publication, and distribution of African American literature in the twentieth century, see Hogue and John Young.

6  On *Clotel*, see the first chapter of Ernest, *Resistance and Reformation*; see also Reid-Pharr, 37–38. On *Our Nig*, see Buell, 301. On *Iola Leroy*, see Lauter, 28.

7  On the need for a broadly inclusive framework to account for the African American literary past—including unpublished work—and on the cultural politics that has obstructed the recovery of African American literature, see McHenry, "Toward a History of Access," 382–84, 398–99. See also Deck's "Response to Elizabeth McHenry." Based on the evidence he has gathered thus far, Gates believes Crafts's narrative to be the only known novel written by a female African American slave,

and possibly the first novel written by a black woman anywhere. However, many scholars believe that the evidence concerning Crafts's identity is insufficient to support any solid conclusions.

8 For a good overview of the development of American literary history, see Claudia Stokes.

9 In her consideration of the origins of African American fiction, Maryemma Graham observes that "one fundamental variant in all of this"—that is, "the interrelationship between the origin of black writing, especially black fiction, the issues of author-ship, and the problematic status of black writing and black writers in America"—"is whether one views literature as a product or process." She adds that "the concept of literature as a process is most useful for looking at the history of black literary pro-duction and the development of certain genres and identifiable traditions in black writing" ("Origins" 232). In explaining this, Graham notes the importance of under-standing "the history of Afro-American culture" in any attempt to understand "the history of Afro-American writing," a culture whose origins and terms are themselves matters of significant and ongoing debate (233; see also 235–37).

10 See Andrews, *To Tell a Free Story*, 270–91.

11 Obviously, I am drawing here from Kenneth Burke's injunction that "every docu-ment bequeathed us by history must be treated as *a strategy for encompassing a situ-ation.*" For Burke, a "strategy" is a "stylized symbolic act" that should be considered not "in isolation, but as the *answer* or *rejoinder* to assertions current in the situation in which it arose" (109, Burke's emphasis).

## Chapter One

1 The scholarship on the construction of race in the nineteenth century covers a wide range of disciplines. For legal background, see Franklin and McNeil; Gross (*What Blood Won't Tell* and *Double Character*); A. Leon Higginbotham Jr.; and Rogers M. Smith. For scientific background, see Stanton. For general cultural background on the United States as a "racial state," see Fredrickson; Gossett; Horsman; Jacobson (*Whiteness*); Roediger; Saxton; and Takaki. For general philosophical and theoretical frameworks that are especially relevant in this regard, see Goldberg (*Racial State* and *Racist Culture*); and Charles W. Mills.

2 Ron Eglash, in his consideration of the presence and significance of fractal knowl-edge systems in African cultures, provides the best overview of scholarship that draws from chaos theory and fractal geometry to explore the cultural effects of racial ideologies and racially oppressive systems. See especially his commentary on Paul Gilroy, Henry Louis Gates Jr., and others (179–202).

3 On economics, see Mandelbrot, 334–39; and Beinhocker. On "fractals in cross-cultural comparison," see Eglash, 39–57. On the "consequences" of chaos theory "for the humanities," see Hayles, *Chaos Bound*, 16–25. It is at least interesting and possibly revealing to note that much of the best work on race came out at the same time that many scholars, literary and beyond, were turning to chaos theory. No connections between the two were made then, but there are significant connec-tions to make and possibilities to be realized. Chaos theory in literary studies had a rather short life, but I have been struck by the developing importance of chaos and

complexity theory in the social sciences—as indicated, for example, by Raymond Eve, Sara Horsfall, and Mary Lee's *Chaos, Complexity, and Sociology* (1997); David Byrne's truly wonderful *Complexity Theory and the Social Sciences* (1998); and, more recently, Mark Mosko and Frederick Damon's *On the Order of Chaos: Social Anthropology and the Science of Chaos* (2005).

4  As variationist sociolinguist Kirk Hazen has observed (in an e-mail exchange), "The language system is so complex that we are still mucking with the foundations of our theories. When we consider subsocial systems like race, operating throughout the mind, then tie together how race is represented through language and how the social forces of racial identity constrain synchronic language variation and possibly diachronic variation, then we just hit points of bewildering complexity." For useful background on theological approaches to race in the nineteenth century, see Sylvester Johnson; Daly; and Irons.

5  For a useful and concise introduction to fractals, see Eglash, 8–19.

6  Even if we focus on race as embodiment, which I will argue is a superficial approach, we face a history of racism that goes beyond skin color or visual markers to include the full range of the senses. As Mark Smith has demonstrated in his cogent study of the racial past, nineteenth-century Americans, "particularly whites of all classes, racialized the senses in a deliberate effort to impose and maintain the artificial binary between 'black' and 'white.' . . . The senses were central to the creation of that clumsy world even as it was belied by everyday contingencies, compromises, and complications" (*How Race Is Made* 9). I discuss Smith's work at greater length in Chapter 5.

7  Useful studies of the legal history of race in the United States are noted above. For a useful overview of the shifting racial determinations of U.S. courts, see Okihiro.

8  It is no wonder, after all, that the Black Arts movement stressed the centrality of language in its attempts to define a black aesthetic. See especially Amiri Baraka (later Leroi Jones), "Expressive Language"; and Stephen E. Henderson, "Inside the Funk Shop" and "Saturation." Similarly important are the attempts of later scholars to define a black vernacular, of which the most direct and extended examples might be Baker, *Blues*; and Gundaker.

9  Appiah clearly understands the issues he addresses. He also understands the kinds of reactions he can anticipate to his approach. In his analysis, for example, he writes:

> There is a regular response to these ideas from those who speak for the identities that now demand recognition, identities toward which so many people have struggled in dealing with the obstacles created by sexism, racism, homophobia. "It's all very well for you. You academics live a privileged life; you have steady jobs; solid incomes; status from your place in maintaining cultural capital. Trifle with your own identities, if you like; but leave mine alone."
>
> To which I answer only: my job as an intellectual is to call it as I see it. I owe my fellow citizens respect, certainly, but not a feigned acquiescence. I have a duty to reflect on the probable consequences of what I say; and then, if I still think it worth saying, to accept responsibility for them. If I am wrong, I say,

you do not need to plead that I should tolerate error for the sake of human liberation; you need only correct me. But if I am right, so it seems to me, there is a work of the imagination that we need to begin. (*Color Conscious* 104–5)

One might wish to live in a world guided by the philosophy that Appiah imagines here. But behind his simple choice, I would argue, is a world of complexity that would complicate, in turn, the stance that Appiah assumes. The wrongness of one's opponents, of course, is not evidence of the rightness of one's approach, for both sides can be shortsighted about the numerous other historically informed perspectives that need to be part of the overall consideration of even possible philosophical approaches to the question of identity, let alone the realities of communities bound by the interplay of historical forces, misconceptions, and collective affiliations or allegiances.

10  I largely agree with Stuart Hall that "racism is always historically specific. Though it may draw on the cultural traces deposited by previous historical phases, it always takes on specific forms. It arises out of present—not past—conditions. Its effects are specific to the present organization of society, to the present unfolding of its dynamic political and cultural processes—not simply to its repressed past" (qtd. in Gilroy, "One Nation" 265). I do argue, however, that racism arises out of past as well as present conditions, and that it is impossible to isolate present *from* past conditions. On such concerns, Goldberg observes:

> It strikes me accordingly as altogether misleading to inquire into the determinants or causes of racism as such, for I want to insist that there is no generic racism, only historically specific racisms each with their own sociotemporally specific causes. There is no single (set of) transcendental determinant(s) that inevitably causes the occurrence of racism—be it nature, or drive, or mode of production, or class formation. There are only the minutiae that make up the fabric of daily life and specific interests and values, the cultures out of which racialized discourse and racist expressions arise. Racist expressions become normalized in and through the prevailing categories of modernity's epistemes and institutionalized in modernity's various modes of social articulation and power. (*Racist Culture* 90)

The process that Goldberg describes here is one of my primary concerns in this chapter.

11  Goldberg's critique of Gilroy should not be taken as a sign that Gilroy did not appreciate the importance of conceptualizing a theory of race that would enable us to account for its historical development and its various manifestations. Indeed, though he would later argue against the usefulness of race as a conceptual framework, Gilroy has always been both clear and sharp on the phenomena gathered under this heading. "Races are not," he asserted in an earlier essay,

> simple expressions of either biological or cultural sameness. They are imagined—socially and politically constructed—and the contingent processes from which they emerge may be tied to equally uneven patterns of class formation to which they, in turn, contribute. Thus ideas about race may articulate

political and economic relations in a particular society that go beyond the distinct experiences or interests of racial groups to symbolize wider identities and conflicts. Discussion of racial domination cannot therefore be falsely separated from wider considerations of social sovereignty such as the conflict between men and women, the antagonisms between capital and labor, or the manner in which modes of production develop and combine. Nor can the complexities of racial politics be reduced to the effect of these other relations. Dealing with these issues in their specificity and in their articulation with other relations and practices constitutes a profound and urgent theoretical and political challenge. It requires a theory of racisms that does not depend on an essentialist theory of races themselves. ("One Nation" 264)

More recently, Gilroy has similarly emphasized the importance of a historically informed, systemic understanding of race. In *Postcolonial Melancholia* (2005), he pauses to clarify his views: "This is probably a good opportunity to emphasize that by 'race' I do not mean physical variations or differences commonsensically coded in, on, or around the body. For me, 'race' refers primarily to an impersonal, discursive arrangement, the brutal result of the raciological ordering of the world, not its cause. Tracking the term directs attention toward the manifold structures of a racial nomos—a legal, governmental, and spatial order—that, as we have seen, is now reviving the geopolitical habits of the old imperial system in discomforting ways" (39).

12  For early African American literary responses to the vision of a fragmented community, see Ernest, *Liberation Historiography*, 39–93, 136–38. It is also, and just as significantly, the field of relations that has informed much of the fractal development of African American literary and cultural scholarship. Beyond obvious (and obviously problematic) examples such as the Black Arts movement, I am thinking, for instance, of the vision of community presented in literary scholarship by Gibson in "Individualism and Community in Black History and Fiction" and Christian in "The Highs and the Lows of Black Feminist Criticism," and in theology by Cone, *A Black Theology of Liberation*, 82–109. For an important admonition about the need to avoid visions of a homogeneous black community, see Santamarina, "Thinkable Alternatives."

13  For useful studies of "ethnic impersonators" and other reminders of the porous but insistent boundaries of racial identity, see Browder, 1–11; and Cassuto, 1–29.

14  In his examination of imperial violence in the early national period, Andy Doolen argues that

these practices occur when the state converts skin and blood into the legal justifications for slavery, when it polices racial hierarchies with a special class of penal laws, when it reinforces ideals of white racial purity through official rituals of execution and banishment, and finally when the state invents official narratives of insurrection and invasion as a strategy for reinforcing political authority. These racial fictions—taking the form of the official discourse of law, policy, proclamation, and public ritual—constitute the logic of U.S. imperialism in the late colonial and early national periods, transforming the terror of white supremacy into a rational and permanent presence. (xxi)

For historical background on the concerns raised by Doolen, see Theodore W. Allen's two-volume study, *The Invention of the White Race*; Saxton; and Horsman. For a related but different approach to these concerns, see Goddu.

15  For a more sympathetic overview of the National Park Service Network to Freedom program, see Miller.

16  See Gilroy, *Black Atlantic*, 221.

17  For a useful study of the white cultural appetite for spectacular presentations of racial others, see Frost.

## Chapter Two

1  On Brown's autobiographies and their changing emphases, facts, and claims, see Andrews (*To Tell a Free Story*); Yellin (*Intricate Knot*, 154–81); Gara (Introduction, ix–xvii); Castronovo (*Fathering*, 167–68); and Farrison, 133–63, 216–22.

2  Paul Jefferson reports that British journalist William Farmer is the author not only of the "Memoir of William Wells Brown" in *Three Years* but also of the "Narrative of the Life and Escape of William Wells Brown" that appears in *Clotel* and then again (with minor changes) as "Memoir of the Author" in *The American Fugitive in Europe* (Introduction 11). But Farrison, though acknowledging Farmer's authorship of the *Three Years* memoir, refers to the memoir in *American Fugitive* as "a reproduction of the first forty-six pages of the autobiographical sketch in *Clotel*" (252). On the narrative that opens *Clotel*, William L. Andrews follows Farrison in maintaining that "although written in the third person as though by a biographer, this installment of Brown's life, which included a good deal of information on his experiences in the North and in England, was more than likely his own creation" (Introduction to *From Fugitive Slave* 4). For an excellent discussion of the relation between the memoir—itself a collection of texts—and *Clotel*, see Stepto, *From Behind the Veil*, 26–31; for the ways in which Brown's more directly autobiographical texts shaped his other works, see Foster, *Witnessing Slavery*, 149.

   Farrison (82–83) reports that Alonzo Moore, a native of Aurora, New York, was the son of Brown's host for an 1844 visit in which Brown dealt effectively with an antagonistic crowd. Moore wrote his account of the event thirty years later.

3  For useful scholarship on slave narratives, see Andrews (*To Tell a Free Story*); Braxton; Davis and Gates; Fisch (*Cambridge Companion*); Fleischner; Foster (*Witnessing Slavery*); Gates (*Figures in Black*); Judy; McDowell and Rampersad; Valerie Smith; and Starling.

4  Olney is not just saying that all slave narratives look alike; rather, he is arguing that the narratives, by and large, were written under similar circumstances and within a restricted social forum, and that "all the mixed, heterogeneous, heterogeneric elements in slave narratives come to be so regular, so constant, so indispensable to the mode that they finally establish a set of conventions" ("'I Was Born'"152).

5  On the authenticity of slave narratives, particularly in terms of the racial dynamics of the narratives' reception, see also Browder, 13–46; Cassuto, 75–125; and Ernest, *Liberation Historiography*, 155–217.

6  On readers' expectations in slave narratives, including the reproducibility of images and tropes in antislavery culture, see Marcus Wood, 78–142.

7  I am referring to the process from Gates's original biographical research to Barbara White's biographical and regional research, to Eric Gardner's archival work, to Foreman and Pitts's research for the recent, and presently authoritative, Penguin edition of *Our Nig*.

8  For a useful discussion of such questions, see the following essays collected in Boggis, Raimon, and White: Gates, Foreword to *Harriet Wilson's New England*; Foreman, "Recovered Autobiographies"; Cassandra Jackson, "Beyond the Page"; and Ernest, "Losing Equilibrium." See also Ellis.

9  I am referring, of course, to the *Dred Scott* decision of 1857, in which Chief Justice Roger B. Taney, speaking for the majority, made this statement.

10  For background on minstrelsy, see Lott; Lhamon (*Jump Jim Crow* and *Raising Cain*); and Mahar.

11  For biographies that challenge our received image of Sojourner Truth, see Mabee; and Painter.

12  For the white presence in African American life stories, see Ernest, *Liberation Historiography*, 155–217.

13  The presence of false fugitives was simply a fact of antebellum life, as is suggested by the casualness of Frederick Douglass's claim, in discussing the character of the enslaved: "So uniformly are good manners enforced among slaves, that I can easily detect a 'bogus' fugitive by his manners" (*My Bondage* 70). On the complex deceptions and legends accompanying the pro- and antislavery movements generally and the Underground Railroad specifically, see Gara, *Liberty Line*.

14  On Mag's and Frado's similar situations and their different responses to them, see Claudia Tate, 37–38.

15  For excellent background and commentary on the ways in which various people were framed by *Uncle Tom's Cabin*, see Meer, 161–93.

16  On the centrality of spirituality in literary studies, primarily but beyond African American literary studies, see Victor Anderson; Bassard; Callahan; Cruz; Gerald L. Davis; Glaude (*Exodus!*); Haynes; Howard-Pittney; Juster and MacFarlane; Mizruchi; Moody; Moses (*Black Messiahs*); Pierce; and Theophus H. Smith.

17  The song sheet reprinted Psalm 40, from which Brown's hymn was drawn.

18  Brown is referring to the First African Baptist Church of Richmond. The Reverend Robert Ryland, a white minister and president of Richmond College, was pastor of Brown's church, which did not have a black pastor until James Henry Holmes, a longtime deacon of the church, replaced Ryland in 1866. The First African Baptist Church was formed in 1841, drawing its membership from the First Baptist Church of Richmond, in which blacks had long outnumbered whites. The First African had over two thousand members in 1843 and over three thousand in 1860. For background and commentary on the church, see Billingsley, 62–84.

19  For all of the many advances in the recovery of African American history during the time of legal slavery, as Orlando Patterson has noted, "we know next to nothing about the individual personalities of slaves, or of the way they felt about one another. The data are just not there" (11). One way to look at this is to think about constructing a study concerning the enslaved equivalent to Fox-Genovese and Genovese's *The Mind of the Master Class*. Certainly, a great deal of work has been

done in this regard, from Lawrence W. Levine's *Black Culture and Black Consciousness* to more local and specialized studies. But the challenge of recovering "the mind of the enslaved class" has always involved fundamental challenges to traditional historical methods, as well as a great deal of speculation based on scattered or partial evidence. For a useful introduction to slave narratives in this regard, see Gould. For an excellent study of the use of available evidence to recover slave life, see Franklin and Schweninger; and Vlach. For excellent approaches to the history of the enslaved that account for slave agency, see Berlin, *Generations* and *Many Thousands Gone*.

20 Robert H. Moore II, in turn, refers to the article in his column, "Heritage and Heraldry," in the July 2004 issue of the *Page News and Courier*. Moore writes that, according to Frank, after losing touch with Betheny after she moved north, they eventually communicated again. He had been in "correspondence with his former wife in Massachusetts, who has made many contributions to his comfort in his declining years." This in spite of the fact that, after he had not heard from her for three years, he had remarried (one of Frank's reported twenty-five marriages). On this, see Moore, "Clarifying a Few Details" and "Frank Veney."

21 Painter says that she met with a great deal of resistance to her findings about Truth, but also with examples of the persistent legend. "I was astonished when one presenter ended her paper by quoting Frances Dana Gage as Sojourner Truth. The historian spoke as though Carleton Mabee's 1993 biography and my 1994 'Representing Truth' had not been published" (284).

22 For the best analyses of the impossibility of representing the middle passage and the experience of enslavement, see Marcus Wood; and McBride.

## Chapter Three

1 Zafar credits "Genaro Padilla's remark about how mainstream scholars have discovered other new voices in literary studies": "These writers are not new, he said, they've been 'in the room' the entire time; they were not 'silent,' they just were 'not heard'" ("Over-Exposed" 2).

2 The best comparative or integrative approaches take on these concerns directly— by presenting either a thesis that deals with the challenge of a comparative analysis or an argument that addresses various perspectives on the central presence of race in American culture and literature. Even in such studies, though, the chapters often focus on the concerns of just one author or one racial or ethnic group within the racial (or, at times, racist) context central to that author or group, thus quietly avoiding the intricacies of racial culture and historical process. Such concerns, then, are only loosely applied to the contexts examined for other authors in other chapters. For especially successful approaches to interracial literary studies, see Castronovo (*Fathering the Nation*); Robert S. Levine (*Martin Delany, Frederick Douglass*); Nelson (*The Word in Black and White*); Sundquist; and Wald. See also Crane; Fabi; Jared Gardner; Sharon Harris; Heneghan; Herzog; Cassandra Jackson; Knadler; Kucich; Lemire; Levander; Charles D. Martin; Powell; Raimon; Barbara Ryan; Susan M. Ryan; Kimberly K. Smith; Stephanie A. Smith; Sollors; Sorisio; Vogel; Joyce W. Warren; Weierman; Wonham; Yellin (*Intricate Knot*); and Zafar (*We Wear the Mask*). Some of the most valuable interracial studies have centered on the complex

cultural relations forged through the antislavery movement. For such literary and cultural studies, see Bennett; DeLombard; Fanuzzi; Maurice S. Lee; Pierson; and Sanchez-Eppler.

Of course, some essay collections are designed specifically to bring a number of scholarly perspectives together in the same volume, standing as a call for attention to a broader realm of interdisciplinary concerns. For good examples of these literary, historical, and cultural studies, see Campbell, Guterl, and Lee; Shuffelton; and Siemerling and Schwenk.

Other collections focus directly on interracial relations and tensions by revisiting prominent authors (in the examples that follow, Twain, Douglass, and Melville) from perspectives informed by deep engagements in racial history. For the best illustrations of this method, see Leonard, Tenney, and Davis; and Levine and Otter.

More rare, but badly needed, are approaches to interracial conversations that explore the centrality of African American expressive culture within American culture generally, of which Sterling Stuckey's *Going through the Storm* is a notable example.

It is useful as well to differentiate interracial comparative studies from the work of those who approach literary history primarily or exclusively from the perspective afforded by African American literary and cultural studies. Throughout this book, I discuss some of the most prominent examples of studies in the field by Andrews, Baker, Foster, Gates, and others. These scholars demonstrate a sound understanding of the broader field of American literary and cultural studies, but their primary concerns are often substantially different from those who merely *include* a consideration of African American literature in analytical projects forged within the mainstream tradition.

Behind the best-known achievements in African American literary and cultural studies, too, is a history of attempts to address even very fundamental concerns so as to establish the foundation for further work. Starke, for example, examined "stock characters, archetypes, and individuals" in 1971, work not that far removed from Zackodnik's reconsideration of a standard literary figure in *The Mulatta and the Politics of Race*. Lawrence Levine did much to recover black folk thought in 1977, and Jarmon continues that work in *Wishbone: Reference and Interpretation in Black Folk Narrative* (2003).

The challenges of bringing these traditions together is not just a matter of including more texts by a wider range of authors representing various traditions. Indeed, each significant attempt to account for the shared interests of these traditions often reveals new manifestations of old problems of exclusion and misunderstanding. Such manifestations have certainly been a presence in scholarship touching on African American concerns, and African Americanists regularly have seen a need to address the assumptions of scholars only peripherally interested in African American life, culture, and history. Foreman's rereading of narratives featuring racial passing as "anti-passing narratives," for example, is an important response to the scholarship on racial passing. Foreman rightly notes that behind the scholarship on passing and on racial genealogies are critically unexamined histories of white supremacist and patriarchal assumptions. "Many contemporary scholars," she observes, "deploy 'white mulatto/a genealogies,' a term I use *not* to describe the lighter shades of a politically determined African-American racial classification but to highlight an overemphasis on patrilineal descent and an identification with and projection of white desire that continually revisits the paternal and the patriarchal, the phallic and juridical Law of the (white) Father" ("Who's Your Mama?" 506). Such correctives have been a regular presence in African American literary scholarship, but many interracial comparative studies that approach their subjects by way of frameworks defined within the mainstream tradition show no trace of the importance or influence of these correctives. In fact, to include multiple traditions in a single scholarly study is to risk multiplying such problems, since deep knowledge in all of the traditions is rare.

3  It could be said that I myself am reenacting the usual protocols of U.S. racial history by limiting my discussion to black and white writers. In doing so, I do not mean to discount or undervalue the many literary and cultural exchanges that we need to consider, perhaps especially the significant conversations between African American and Native American writers, the mixed racial ground between the two groups, or the commentary on the "three races" (red, black, and white) offered by Alexis de Tocqueville, George Bancroft, Henry Highland Garnet, and others. Rather, I focus on the black-white binary to address the fundamental racial framework, the white supremacist culture, with which African American writers had to contend. I offer this only as an initial entrance into this territory, one that emphasizes the need for additional work that is attentive to the dynamics of racial history as it relates to literary history.

   For useful studies of Native American and African American connections and tensions, see Brennan; Miles and Holland; Moos; Nelson (*The Word in Black and White*); and Shuffelton.

4  For commentary on the petitions, see Kaplan and Kaplan, chap. 1; Bradley, 101–3; and Nash, chap. 3.

5  For examples of black thought about white people, see Bay.

6  For a good analysis of the critical literacy I am referring to here—in this case, focused on Harriet Jacobs—see Cutter, "Dismantling." For a sustained discussion of the methods and priorities of nineteenth-century African American historical interpretation, see Ernest, *Liberation Historiography*.

7  For thoughtful considerations of these expectations, see Jarrett, *Deans and Truants*; and Zafar, *We Wear the Mask*.

8  For commentary on Henderson's approach, see Gates, "Preface to Blackness," 156–58; and Baker, "Generational Shifts," 206–9. Attention to such culturally grounded conventions have regularly led some to question the authority, or at least the informed sensitivity, that white readers can bring to African American literature. Most recently, this question was raised by McKay's essay in *PMLA*, "Naming the Problem . . . 'Who Shall Teach African American Literature?'"—even though McKay makes it clear that she is asking broader questions about preparation for the field, not simply about the cultural background and racial affiliations of those working in the field. See also Trudier Harris's "Miss-Trained"; Awkward's "Negotiations of Power"; Kenneth Warren's response, "From the Superscript"; and Awkward's response to Warren, "The Politics of Positionality." Awkward's reflections

on his own subject position in "Race, Gender, and the Politics of Reading" are valuable as well. The essays collected in Greg Tate's *Everything but the Burden* are also useful in this context.

9  For a useful consideration of the challenge of crafting "America's Anglo-African word," see Condit and Lucaites. See also Cutter (*Unruly Tongue*); Ericson; Hartnett; Holmes; Gavin Jones; and Robertson.

10  On the writing and publication of Truth's *Narrative*, see Douglass-Chin, 58–93; Glass, 17–36; Humez, "Reading"; Joseph; Lebedun; Mandziuk and Fitch; Peterson, "A Sign unto This Nation"; and Rohrbach. For the best biographies of Truth, see Mabee; and Painter.

11  George Bancroft to Evert Duyckinck, May 26, 1855, quoted in McWilliams, 7.

12  For a particularly thoughtful reconsideration of the role of the amanuensis and a critique of approaches that avoid such narratives or question their authority, see Worley.

13  Brown's agency is further complicated in 1851—a point I will focus on in this chapter—for as his biographer Jeffrey Ruggles notes, the familiar phrase "written by himself" in the title of this version of Brown's story is deceptive. "Although the 1851 *Narrative* is more directly Brown's expression than the 1849 *Narrative*," Ruggles asserts, "Brown did not put the words on paper" (129). Ruggles points out that "the new edition stays closer to the story, and it is clearer that Brown was the original source" (129); also, "the writer of the 1851 *Narrative* remains unidentified" (132). Newman, who wrote the introduction for the first U.S. publication of the 1851 *Narrative* in 2002, observes: "Unable to read or write and with little access to printers or publishers, Box Brown was not free from saying what other people wanted him to say. Only in England did he experience the freedom to express himself in his own way. The Manchester edition is obviously closer to Brown's own telling of his own story" (xii).

14  The textual range of Brown's story extends considerably further when we consider the fame of his story—and its retelling in other literary forums. For an excellent discussion of Box Brown's story in the context of "a rich field of intertextuality in which literary devices and rhetorical postures passed readily back and forth across racial and generic boundaries" (493), see Ostrowski.

15  Addressing in particular the ways in which "blackness . . . seemed to haunt earnest white activists," Susan Ryan notes that even the most committed white activists—Lydia Maria Child, for example—"shared a vision of white benevolence as a compulsion, one arising from and understood by means of a collective racial guilt" (2). For an excellent case study of the "masochistic erotic fantasy" available to white audiences through antislavery literature, see Noble, 126–46. On racism in the antislavery movement and white fascination over black life, see Ernest, *Liberation Historiography* 163–85. See also McBride on "the staging of abolitionism" (4) and "the overdeterminacy of the slave's testimony" (5).

16  On Beecher's use of mock slave auctions for fundraising purposes, see Filler, 235. William Wells Brown illustrates a slave auction in *A Lecture Delivered before the Female Anti-Slavery Society of Salem* (21); he presents a modified version of the same scene in *Clotel* (87–88). Elsewhere I have argued that in *The Escape* Brown satirizes

white northern antislavery sympathizers through the character of Mr. White, who loses his courage when he indulges in antislavery rhetoric during a visit to the South; see Ernest, "The Reconstruction of Whiteness," 1115.

17 For recent overviews of the theoretical purpose of slave narratives within antislavery culture and of the racial dynamics of their reception, see Bruce, *Origins*, 238–48; and Ernest, *Liberation Historiography*, 163–90, 202–17. On the development of a distinctively African American rhetorical approach to the definition of rights and of humanity, see Condit and Lucaites, 69–98.

18 Stearns was singular in many respects, but his strident views were not entirely unusual among white abolitionists. As Gienapp observes in his general overview of white antislavery activists:

> While they were often successful in their careers and were not a displaced social elite, they were nevertheless deeply alienated from American society. They deplored the lack of religion in American life, the rampant materialism, and the crassness and pragmatism of American politics. They were shocked by the failure of the campaign in the 1820s to stop the movement of the U.S. mails on the Sabbath. By the 1830s their vague discontent began to come into sharp focus, as they concluded that slavery was the fundamental cause of the nation's degradation. Abolitionism became the means to save the country. (32–33)

The most famous and influential white abolitionist, William Lloyd Garrison, exemplified this alienation. "Strongly influenced by John Humphrey Noyes's radical brand of Christian perfectionism," Gienapp explains, "Garrison endorsed a number of radical ideas, which constituted his 'broad program' of reform" (35–36).

19 Horsman's *Race and Manifest Destiny* provides the best background on the developing fascination with the Anglo-Saxon past and its connection to racial dominance in the nineteenth century.

20 Although Brown was most likely not the actual writer of the 1851 *Narrative*, scholars generally agree that he is the central narrative and *authorial* presence, shaping this new relation of the events of his life in detailed and intricate ways. Accordingly, I refer to the 1851 text as if Brown is the actual author, noting those moments or circumstances when it is important to remember that the writing of the 1851 *Narrative* was a complex authorial collaboration.

21 On this practice, see Bruce, *Origins*, 242.

22 For a thoughtful consideration of Brown's engagement with "a transnational political activism and discourse of diaspora resistance through a range of activities that can be considered an insurgent and insurrectionary Maroon corps," see Spencer.

23 Ruggles notes that "the earliest-located newspaper report" of presenting the story and the song together (as part of his performance with his panorama) was in 1852, following publication of the 1851 *Narrative*. However, Ruggles argues that the *Narrative* probably was written in 1850, "before the premiere of *Mirror of Slavery*." "If this dating of the text is correct," he reasons, "then Brown was presumably telling the story of 'the shovel and the hoe' to set up his song at appearances even before he began exhibiting the panorama" (208–9, n. 32). For my purposes, the important point is that in the 1851 *Narrative*, where the song is used to set up the story, both

the song and the story represent Brown's performative presence in and beyond the narrative.

24 For background on theories of polygenesis and the proslavery argument, see Fredrickson, 71–96; and Gossett, 44–67.

25 See Andrews, *To Tell a Free Story*, 217.

26 On Jacobs's editorial help, see Bruce Mills, "Lydia Maria Child"; Deck, "Whose Book Is This?"; and Yellin, *Harriet Jacobs*. See also the essays collected in Garfield and Zafar.

## Chapter Four

1 On the expulsion movement, see Berlin, *Slaves without Masters*, 360–64, 371–75.

2 The portrayal of African Americans, both enslaved and free, as actually or potentially lawless obviously ignores the ways in which the law failed to account for both the realities of African American life and the possibility of justice. The systemic lawlessness of the racial state, one might say, positioned African Americans in predictable ways. Nevertheless, such portrayals have had great persuasive force throughout U.S. history. As Blackmon observes, "Most scholars of American history have accepted that the repressive legal measures and violence of the post–Civil War era were the result, at least in part, of the lawless behavior of freed slaves. Charitable, if patronizing, iterations of this picture attributed the supposed criminal inclinations of freedmen to the psychic injuries of their generations of bondage, or simply to the difficulty of any emancipated people in adjusting to the dynamics of a life in freedom" (69). For a study that focuses on the role of lawlessness and the "black villains" in American life, see Van Deburg.

3 Studies of the roots and transformations of African American Christianity are many. For a useful sampling, see Altschul; Chireau; Frey and Wood; Paul E. Johnson; Henry H. Mitchell; Pinn; Raboteau (*Canaan Land*); and Theophus H. Smith.

4 In this context, it is useful to consider the ongoing relevance of Addison Gayle Jr.'s "Cultural Strangulation: Black Literature and the White Aesthetic." Focusing primarily on the literature and reception of twentieth-century black writers, Gayle's accounting of the effects of "historical conditioning and cultural deprivation" applies especially to nineteenth-century African American literature (96).

5 I am thinking especially of the narratives of Louisa Picquet (see H. Mattison in *Collected Black Women's Narratives*) and of Lewis and Milton Clarke, though the preface to the *Narrative of the Life of Henry Box Brown* also emphasizes this point.

6 Although there have been many studies of slave resistance, particularly useful to the concerns addressed in this chapter are those that consider slave communities' manipulations of or negotiations with the structuring of space and time. Especially valuable in this regard are Vlach; and McKittrick.

7 Actually, "deep time" is not a new term, for it has been used to discuss geologic time for quite a while now.

8 On the challenges of collective self-identification in the nineteenth century, see Stuckey (*Slave Culture* 193–244); and (Rael, 82–117). On the importance of constructing communities in nineteenth-century African American literature, see Bassard; Ernest (*Liberation Historiography*); and Glass.

9 On Walker's sources, see Robert S. Levine, "Circulating the Nation"; and Hinks's edition of Walker's *Appeal, To Awaken My Afflicted Brethren.*

10 Attention to the history of such motley groupings has sometimes led scholars to uncritical assumptions about race generally and African American identity specifically. Consider, for example, George Hutchinson's commentary on "black transnationalism" in a discussion of Nella Larsen. It is worth a long quotation to follow the operative assumptions here:

> We tend to think of races as extended families. The subordination of familial relationships to racial identity in American history has shaped the psychology of Americans of all races—but especially, I suspect, blacks and whites—so profoundly that it undergirds most theorizations of race and cultural identity in Americanist scholarship to this day, including, notably, theories of diaspora. Black transnationalism, as it is usually presented, opposes or transcends the confines of the national state with racial identities, and these racial identities have an irreducible genealogical component that is also presumptively familial and cultural. Without the genealogical component, the "political" identity and cultural affiliation cease to exist; with it, certain bonds of cultural affiliation and political identification are expected and others discounted. Such notions of black transnationalism may not be antidotes to American racial ideology and cultural colonialism so much as extensions of it. (55–56)

I have addressed, in Chapter 1, the dangers of assuming that race can be reduced to an intellectual problem that develops into a psychological problem that is the *real* problem we face in political and even academic life today. Here, I will just note the reliance of this analysis on its opening phrase—"We tend to think"—and say that Hutchinson follows many others in confusing misconceptions about race with the actual history of race. Political identity and cultural affiliation do not rely on an intellectual tendency, for they are supported, enforced, and complicated by virtually every institutional and ideological area of American culture. I should note as well that "we" tend to think much the same about white genealogies—perhaps especially when addressing Great Britain—though in that regard we recognize a more complex and conflicted political identity and cultural affiliation. Finally, such complaints against black thought "as it is usually presented" show little evidence of a sustained study of such presentations.

There have been a number of valuable transatlantic approaches to African American and interracial literary and cultural studies, as well as studies of white American perceptions of the racial world beyond the nation's borders. See, for example, Berman; Carr; Coles; Eudell; Fisch (*American Slaves in Victorian England*); Harvey; the essays collected in McKittrick and Woods; Magubane; Nwankwo; Rosenthal; and Skinner. Such studies draw us to African American history as a set of interactive sites of global cultural exchange, and nineteenth-century African American literature is often devoted to exploring the terms of such sites. Brickhouse, for example, explores the "opposition of official national history and an unofficial transamerican historical account" of Douglass's "The Heroic Slave," the "politically fraught conversation with a Cuban literary history" in Delany's *Blake*, the "unwritten, unofficial history exceeding the cultural and linguistic boundaries of national histories" found in Mary Prince, *The History of Mary Prince: A West Indian Slave*, and the confrontation of "the competing racial and literary ideologies emerging from an imperialist US presence in the larger Americas" in Seacole, *Wonderful Adventures of Mrs. Seacole in Many Lands* (126–30). We could add to this list considerably by including the work of William Wells Brown, James Theodore Holly, George Vashon, Pauline Hopkins, "and many others." We could also look at the extensive and often deeply problematic commentary on Africa in various speeches, or at the significant ties to European Romantic writers in an overwhelming number of texts, or at the sly appropriations and revisions of British antislavery writing that were central to black abolitionist writing. To complicate the picture further, we could examine Daniel Coker's journals concerning his emigration to Liberia or even Alexander Crummell's proclamation, "*Once more I remark, that the English language is the enshrinement of those great charters of liberty which are essential elements of free governments, and the main guarantees of personal liberty*" ("English Language" 291, Crummell's emphasis)— a statement in some ways not far removed from white nationalist historian George Bancroft's exclamation in the fourth volume of his *History of the United States*, "Go forth, then, language of Milton and Hampden, language of my country, take possession of the North American continent!" (4:456), about which, see Levin, 82.

    For one of the best studies of creolization and "vernacular practice in African America," see Gundaker. On motley groupings, consider Earl Lewis's survey of approaches to African American identity by historians. Lewis examines the relative neglect of the scholarship on African American history and addresses the need to consider the "history of overlapping diasporas" (765). Also useful in this regard is Lhamon's genealogical study of the gestures and cultures associated with blackface minstrelsy, *Raising Cain*.

11  For a useful consideration of Dorr's narrative, see William W. Stowe, 61–73.

12  The great majority of escapes were not from the South to the North or from slavery to freedom. The best study of the motives, methods, duration, and destinations of escapes is Franklin and Schweninger.

13  On the suppression of black mobility after the Civil War, see Cohen.

14  Brown's *Three Years in Europe* appeared in 1852; his freedom was purchased in 1854, the same year that he published (with an 1855 imprint) the U.S. version of his travel narrative, *The American Fugitive in Europe: Sketches of Places and People Abroad*. For commentary on Brown's travel writing, see Justin D. Edwards, 89–103; Lucasi; Stadler, 73–104; and William Stowe, 61–73. For useful background on mobility under slavery by way of steamboat culture, see Buchanan. For an excellent study of the somewhat different dynamics of American women's travel narratives, see Steadman. On black writers abroad, see Coles.

15  Brown reprints this sentence, with only a slight verbal change, in *Clotel*—arguably, the guiding question of that text. There is evidence as well that in *Clotel* Brown draws from several stories and commentaries in Martineau's work, including those of New Orleans quadroons and of Henry and Althesa Morton.

16  For the best studies of the Underground Railroad, see Blight, *Passages*; and Gara, *Liberty Line*.

17  The best study of law and race is Gross's *What Blood Won't Tell*. For a useful study of slavery and the legal system, including the significant challenges to slaveholding ideology posed by "evidence that slaves behaved as morally reasoning, self-governing agents" (73), see Gross, *Double Character*. For slave law and American literature, see Crane; DeLombard; and Macdonald. For legal commentary in African American literature, see Suggs.

18  For background on the southern women writers' roles in these literary battles, see Moss. For general background on sectional struggles in literature, see Faust; and Lively.

19  On the central question of ex-slave narrators, see Barrett, 315. For other commentaries on the Crafts and on *Running*, in addition to those of Cassuto, Foreman, McCaskill, and Weinauer mentioned below, see Andrews, *To Tell a Free Story*, 183–84, 213–14; Garber, 282–85; Kawash, 64–65; Reid-Pharr, 58–59; and Sollors, 260–61. Blackett (87–137) is the most comprehensive biographical source on the Crafts; for Blackett's commentary on *Running*, see 105–7.

20  See McCaskill, "'Yours Very Truly'"; and Foreman, "Who's Your Mama?"

21  For analyses that indicate the explanatory potential of chaos theory in relation to *Running*, see Cassuto on "the objectifier's unsound category system" (17); and Weinauer on the "endlessly mirroring relation" of "truth and illusion" (37).

22  On Jefferson's presence in early African American writing, see Ernest, *Liberation Historiography*, 87–88.

23  On genealogies of performance and the centrality of performance in African American social and political life, see Brooks; Lhamon (*Raising Cain*); and Roach 1–31.

## Chapter Five

1  By this act, in fact, Douglass steps into at least one reading of Shakespeare's play. As Robert Levine reports: "John Quincy Adams concluded, even as he was waging his heroic fight against the power of the slave South in the House of Representatives in 1836, that the moral of *Othello* was 'that the intermarriage of black and white blood is a violation of the law of nature. *That* is the lesson to be learned from the play'" (*Martin Delany, Frederick Douglass* 39). On Douglass's marriage, see Moses, *Creative Conflict*, 74–77. For useful background on "the Othello myth" in American culture more broadly, see Daileader.

2  Douglass's self-assigned role as a U.S. Othello might well have been in his thoughts as he discussed the power of unsubstantiated rumor, a "method of political warfare," he notes, that "has not escaped the vigilant eye of the Afro-American press or of the aspirant and office-seeker, who, when he has found a public man supposed to be in the way of his ambition, has resorted to this device" (*Life and Times* 955–56).

3  For additional commentary on Douglass's association with Othello, and his conflicted attempts to identify himself in the public sphere, see chap. 5 of Ernest, *Resistance and Reformation*, from which I am drawing here.

4  On "Minstrelsy, Race, and the Boundaries of American Political Culture" during this era, see Neely, 97–127.

5  The scholarship on literature related to the Civil War is extensive. For studies that represent a broad period of research, see Aaron; Diffley; Fahs; Faust; Sarah E. Gardner; James; Samuels; Sizer; Sweet; Edmund Wilson; and Elizabeth Young. For a useful sampling of southern fiction related to the Civil War, see Baro; for an outstanding sampling of historical interpretations of the conflict, see Pressly.

6  Little scholarship is devoted exclusively to African American literature produced during this time. Important studies that focus on or otherwise account for this period include Carby; duCille; Elder; Foster (*Written by Herself*); Moses (*Golden Age*); Peterson (*"Doers of the Word"*); and Claudia Tate. For other studies, which generally explore black writers in the context of American literary history more broadly, see Birnbaum; Eiselein; Boeckmann; Handley; Gavin Jones; Nabers; Claudia Stokes; Kenneth W. Warren (*Black and White Strangers*); and Wonham.

7  On the cultural politics of the use of dialect in literature at the end of the nineteenth century, see Gavin Jones.

8  Although Reconstruction has not fed the publishing industry nearly as much as the Civil War, a number of sound postwar studies have appeared; recent ones indicate that the complexities of this period, especially including but beyond race, will receive increasing attention. For a survey of scholarship on this subject, covering a broad span of years, see Chunchang; Laura F. Edwards; Foner; Franklin (*Reconstruction*); Holt; Hyman; Litwack: Michele Mitchell; O'Donovan; Rabinowitz; Richardson; Stanley; Upchurch; Valelly; and Forrest G. Wood.

9  For cogent commentary on the print and visual cultures that proliferated during and after the Civil War, see Nudelman; Samuels; and Sweet.

10  For background on the culture of racial violence, including its representation in literature, see Clymer; Cohen; Gillman; Gunning; Trudier Harris (*Exorcising Blackness*); Silver; and Wyatt-Brown.

11  James McCune Smith, for one, is quite explicit about Douglass's representative role (132). On Douglass as representative man, see Zafar (*We Wear the Mask*, 89–116); Olney ("The Founding Fathers" and "'I Was Born,'" 153–54); and Waldo E. Martin Jr. For an excellent analysis of the cultural politics of Douglass's representative status, see McDowell, "In the First Place."

12  For a fine study of the performative strategies of various African American public figures, see Brooks.

13  The best literary histories of this period are Bell (*Afro-American Novel*, 56–75, and *Contemporary*, 94–97); Bruce (*Black American Writing*); Blyden Jackson; and McCaskill and Gebhard.

14  William Andrews is characteristically instructive here: "The pragmatic reassessment of slavery and the rise of Afro-American realism illustrate a process of revisionism at work in black narrative of the late nineteenth century that exempted virtually nothing in the past from being remade anew. Whatever black reality *was* historically, whatever one generation of black narrators said it was, their successors refused to be bound by it. First pragmatic slave narrators, then the Tuskegee realists, and then novelists like Chesnutt and Johnson insisted on their right to reappropriate

the signifying potential of black reality and, through what we might call deconstructive acts, prepare the discursive ground once again for a new assay of the basis on which a usable truth could be constructed" ("Representation of Slavery" 89).

15 In addition to Hall's work, see Jeffrey, 61–91, for the best study of Still's book and marketing strategies to date. See also Gara, "William Still."

16 The National Park Service Network to Freedom program is supported in part by federal legislation passed in 1990 and 1998. In its brochure, it claims to be "illustrative of a basic founding principle of this Nation, that all human beings embrace the right to self-determination and freedom from oppression." The network's venues include everything from "a site that might be a water or overland route" to "a plantation where an escape began." Those familiar with the representation of slavery at plantation museums can attest to the freedom that this network, taken as a whole, is most likely to commemorate.

17 On the ideological appropriations and historical mismemory involved in invocations of Truth in white feminist thought, see Palmer, 152–53; McDowell, "Transferences," 98–99; and Zackodnik, 57–62.

18 As Andrews has observed, Brown sometimes represented dialect strategically, allowing the slaves in *My Southern Home* to "profanely redefine the very language of authority as the whites employ it" (Introduction to *From Fugitive Slave*, 12).

19 For Martineau's influence on Brown, see Ernest, "Fugitive Performances," 159–60.

20 "In 1838," Valerie Pichanick notes, Martineau "was made an honorary member of the Massachusetts Anti-Slavery Society, and in 1840 she was elected as a delegate from Massachusetts to the London Anti-Slavery Convention" (92). Martineau's articles were regularly reprinted in the United States. For background on her involvement in antislavery efforts, see Stange; and Taylor.

21 On Brown's activities during this period of temperance activity, see Farrison, 430–36; on Brown's interest in and presentation of temperance concerns, see Robert S. Levine, "Whiskey."

22 There is a good reason why Brown echoes the popular press in this episode, for he draws this material verbatim from "'Nigger Day' in a Country Town," an article that appeared in the *New York Times* on November 30, 1874, credited to "Our Own Correspondent."

23 Brown borrowed this statement from Wilson Armistead's *A Tribute for the Negro: Being a Vindication of the Moral, Intellectual, and Religious Capabilities of the Coloured Portion of Mankind; with Particular Reference to the African Race* (1848), x.

24 As Andrews observes, "The more the narrator of *My Southern Home* warms to his role as critic and advisor of southern blacks, the more openly he identifies with them" (Introduction to *From Fugitive Slave*, 15). "The narrator's impersonation of white in the first part of his text," Andrews argues, "looks more like an act of appropriation and empowerment through, than an act of betrayal of, color. Reading the narrator's behavior in this way makes his adoption of a black persona in the second half of *My Southern Home* a confirmation, rather than a contradiction, of the authority that the concluding lines of the text seek to summarize for all blacks" (16).

25 Castronovo notes that he draws the phrase "adding story to story" from Abraham Lincoln's 1838 "Address before the Young Men's Lyceum."

## Conclusion

1 Very little work has been done thus far on nineteenth-century African American poetry. For book-length treatments, see Keith D. Leonard; and Sherman. On folk culture, see Lawrence W. Levine.

2 Since relevance can be a suspect concept among teachers who have struggled to inspire their students to appreciate the importance of literary study, it is useful to consider Karenga's commentary on relevance in *Introduction to Black Studies*:

> One of the most important concepts in the general Student Movement and especially in the Black Student Movement which waged the struggle for Black Studies was the concept of a *relevant education*, a concept which had both academic and social dimensions. A relevant education for Black Studies Advocates was an education which was . . . meaningful, useful and reflective of the realities of society and the world. For Black Studies and Black Power advocates the central realities were: 1) the need to solve the pressing problems of the Black community, society and the world and; 2) the revolutionary struggle being waged to end racist oppression and change society and the world. To be relevant, education had to address these issues and contribute to these interrelated projects. Thus, Nathan Hare, one of the guiding theorists and founders of the Movement, argued for an African American education, which would contribute to solving "the problems of the race" by producing "persons capable of solving problems of a contagious American society." Moreover, he concluded, "a Black education which is not revolutionary in the current day is both irrelevant and useless." (16–17)

In this discussion, Karenga lists and explains seven "grounds of relevance":

(1) "The first ground of relevance of Black Studies is that it is a definitive *contribution to humanity's understanding [of] itself*";

(2) "A second ground of relevance of Black studies is found in its *contribution to U.S. society's understanding of itself*";

(3) "Thirdly, and as a logical consequence of the first two contentions, Black Studies has established its relevance as a *contribution to the university's realization of its claim and challenge to teach the whole truth*, or something as close to it as humanly possible";

(4) "Fourthly, Black Studies has demonstrated its relevance as *a contribution to the rescue and reconstruction of Black history and humanity*";

(5) "A fifth ground of relevance of Black Studies is that it is a a *critical contribution to a new social science* which will not only benefit Blacks, but also the U.S. and the world";

(6) "A sixth ground of relevance of Black Studies is *its contribution to the development of a socially conscious Black intelligentsia and professional stratum*";

(7) "A seventh and final ground of relevance of Black Studies is that it is a *vital contribution to the critique, resistance and reversal of the progressive Europeanization of human consciousness and culture* which is one of the major problems of our times." (21–25)

Obviously, here Karenga is concerned with defining and defending Black Studies as a discipline, but I appreciate the way he does so, and I think we can see how this translates into relevance in the classroom and beyond. Karenga says that "Black Studies advocates expressed two sets of basic concerns, i.e. academic and social ones. . . . On the academic level, they were concerned first with the intellectual inadequacy and injurious nature of traditional white studies." On the other hand, "The social concerns of Black Studies centered around the questions of exclusion, treatment on campus, academic conversions and production of a conscious, committed and capable intelligentsia and on what all this meant for the Black community" (17–18).

# BIBLIOGRAPHY

Aaron, Daniel. *The Unwritten War: American Writers and the Civil War*. Madison: University of Wisconsin Press, 1987.

Abdul-Jabbar, Kareem. *Black Profiles in Courage: A Legacy of African American Achievement*. New York: Avon/Eos, 1997.

Adams, John Quincy. *Narrative of the Life of John Quincy Adams: When in Slavery, and Now as a Freeman*. Harrisburg, Pa., 1872.

Adams, Nehemiah. *A South-Side View of Slavery; or, Three Months at the South, in 1854*. 1854. New York: Negro Universities Press, 1969.

Allen, Theodore W. *The Invention of the White Race: The Origin of Racial Oppression in Anglo-America*. Vol. 2. New York: Verso, 1997.

———. *The Invention of the White Race: Racial Oppression and Social Control*. Vol. 1. New York: Verso, 1993.

Allen, Thomas M. *A Republic in Time: Temporality and Social Imagination in Nineteenth-Century America*. Chapel Hill: University of North Carolina Press, 2008.

Allen, William G. *The American Prejudice against Color: An Authentic Narrative, Showing How Easily the Nation Got into an Uproar*. 1853. New York: Arno Press and the New York Times, 1969.

Altschul, Father Paisius, ed. *An Unbroken Circle: Linking Ancient African Christianity to the African-American Experience*. St. Louis, Mo.: Brotherhood of St. Moses the Black, 1997.

Anderson, Victor. *Beyond Ontological Blackness: An Essay on African American Religious and Cultural Criticism*. New York: Continuum, 1995.

Andrews, William L. "The Changing Moral Discourse of Nineteenth-Century African American Women's Autobiography: Harriet Jacobs and Elizabeth Keckley." In *De/Colonizing the Subject: The Politics of Gender in Women's Autobiography*, edited by Sidonie Smith and Julia Watson, 225–41. Minneapolis: University of Minnesota Press, 1992.

———. Introduction to *From Fugitive Slave to Free Man: The Autobiographies of William Wells Brown*, edited by William L. Andrews, 1–12. Columbia: University of Missouri Press, 2003.

———. Introduction to *Two Biographies by African American Women*. Schomburg Library of Nineteenth-Century Black Women Writers, xxxiii–xliii. New York: Oxford University Press, 1991.

———. "Mark Twain, William Wells Brown, and the Problem of Authority in New South Writing." In *Southern Literature and Literary Theory*, edited by Jefferson Humphries, 1–21. Athens: University of Georgia Press, 1990.

———. "The Representation of Slavery and the Rise of Afro-American Literary Realism, 1865–1920." In *African American Autobiography: A Collection of Critical Essays*, edited by William L. Andrews, 77–89. Englewood Cliffs, N.J.: Prentice-Hall, 1993.

———. *To Tell a Free Story: The First Century of Afro-American Autobiography, 1760–1865.* Urbana: University of Illinois Press, 1986.

———, ed. *African American Autobiography: A Collection of Critical Essays.* Englewood Cliffs, N.J.: Prentice-Hall, 1993.

———, ed. *North Carolina Slave Narratives: The Lives of Moses Roper, Lunsford Lane, Moses Grandy, and Thomas H. Jones.* Chapel Hill: University of North Carolina Press, 2003.

Andrews, William L., Frances Smith Foster, and Trudier Harris, eds. *The Oxford Companion to African American Literature.* New York: Oxford University Press, 1997.

Appiah, Kwame Anthony. *The Ethics of Identity.* Princeton: Princeton University Press, 2005.

Appiah, K. Anthony, and Amy Gutmann. *Color Conscious: The Political Morality of Race.* Princeton: Princeton University Press, 1996.

Aptheker, Herbert, ed. *A Documentary History of the Negro People in the United States: Volume I, From the Colonial Times through the Civil War.* 1979. Reprint, New York: Carol Publishing Group, 1990.

Armistead, Wilson. *Five Hundred Thousand Strokes for Freedom: A Series of Anti-Slavery Tracts: Of Which Half a Million Are Now First Issued by the Friends of the Negro.* London, 1853.

———. *A Tribute for the Negro: Being a Vindication of the Moral, Intellectual, and Religious Capabilities of the Coloured Portion of Mankind; with Particular Reference to the African Race.* London, 1848.

Awkward, Michael. "Negotiations of Power: White Critics, Black Texts, and the Self-Referential Impulse." *American Literary History* 2 (Winter 1990): 581–606.

———. The Politics of Positionality: A Reply to Kenneth Warren. *American Literary History* 4 (Spring 1992): 104–9.

———. "Race, Gender, and the Politics of Reading." *Black American Literature Forum* 22 (1988): 5–27.

Baker, Houston A., Jr. *Blues, Ideology, and Afro-American Literature: A Vernacular Theory.* Chicago: University of Chicago Press, 1984.

———. "Generational Shifts and the Recent Criticism of Afro-American Literature." In *African American Literary Theory: A Reader*, edited by Winston Napier, 179–217. New York: New York University Press, 2000.

———. "In Dubious Battle." *New Literary History* (1987): 363–69.

———. "On the Criticism of Black American Literature: One View of the Black Aesthetic." In *African American Literary Theory: A Reader*, edited by Winston Napier, 113–31. New York: New York University Press, 2000.

Baker, Houston A., Jr., and Patricia Redmond, eds. *Afro-American Literary Study in the 1990s.* Chicago: University of Chicago Press, 1989.

Bancroft, George. *History of the United States from the Discovery of the American Continent.* 10 vols. Boston: Little, Brown, 1872–74.

Baraka, Amiri (LeRoi Jones). "Expressive Language." In *African American Literary Theory:*

*A Reader*, edited by Winston Napier, 62–65. New York: New York University Press, 2000.

———. "Restaging Langston Hughes' *Scottsboro Limited*: An Interview with Amiri Baraka." *Black Scholar* (July–August 1979): 62–69.

Baro, Gene. *After Appomattox: The Image of the South in Its Fiction, 1865–1900*. New York: Corinth Books, 1963.

Barrett, Lindon. "Hand-Writing: Legibility and the White Body in *Running a Thousand Miles for Freedom*." *American Literature* 69, no. 2 (June 1997): 315–36.

Bassard, Katherine Clay. *Spiritual Interrogations: Culture, Gender, and Community in Early African American Women's Writing*. Princeton: Princeton University Press, 1999.

Bay, Mia. *The White Image in the Black Mind: African-American Ideas about White People, 1830–1925*. New York: Oxford University Press, 2000.

Beinhocker, Eric D. *The Origin of Wealth: The Radical Remaking of Economics and What It Means for Business and Society*. Boston: Harvard Business School Press, 2007.

Bell, Bernard W. *The Afro-American Novel and Its Tradition*. Amherst: University of Massachusetts Press, 1987.

———. *The Contemporary African American Novel: Its Folk Roots and Modern Literary Branches*. Amherst: University of Massachusetts Press, 2004.

———. Review of *Erasure*, by Percival L. Everett. *African American Review* 37, nos. 2/3 (Autumn 2003): 474–77.

Bell, Jeffery A. *Philosophy at the Edge of Chaos: Gilles Deleuze and the Philosophy of Difference*. Toronto: University of Toronto Press, 2006.

Bender, Thomas. *Community and Social Change in America*. Baltimore: Johns Hopkins University Press, 1982.

Bennett, Michael. *Democratic Discourses: The Radical Abolition Movement and Antebellum American Literature*. New Brunswick, N.J.: Rutgers University Press, 2005.

Bercovitch, Sacvan. Afterword to *Ideology and Classic American Literature*, edited by Sacvan Bercovitch and Myra Jehlen. Cambridge: Cambridge University Press, 1986.

———. *The Puritan Origins of the American Self*. New Haven: Yale University Press, 1975.

Berlin, Ira. *Generations of Captivity: A History of African-American Slaves*. Cambridge, Mass.: Belknap, 2003.

———. *Many Thousands Gone: The First Two Centuries of Slavery in North America*. Cambridge, Mass.: Belknap, 1998.

———. *Slaves without Masters: The Free Negro in the Antebellum South*. New York: New Press, 1974.

Berman, Carolyn Vellenga. *Creole Crossings: Domestic Fiction and the Reform of Colonial Slavery*. Ithaca, N.Y.: Cornell University Press, 2006.

Bibb, Henry. *Narrative of the Life and Adventures of Henry Bibb, an American Slave*. 1850. Madison: University of Wisconsin Press, 2001.

Billingsley, Andrew. *Mighty Like a River: The Black Church and Social Reform*. New York: Oxford University Press, 1999.

Birnbaum, Michele. *Race, Work, and Desire in American Literature, 1860–1930*. Cambridge: Cambridge University Press, 2003.

Blackett, R. J. M. *Beating against the Barriers: The Lives of Six Nineteenth-Century Afro-Americans*. Ithaca, N.Y.: Cornell University Press, 1986.

Blackmon, Douglas A. *Slavery by Another Name: The Re-enslavement of Black People in America from the Civil War to World War II*. New York: Doubleday, 2008.

Blight, David W. *Beyond the Battlefield: Race, Memory, and the American Civil War*. Amherst: University of Massachusetts Press, 2002.

———. *Race and Reunion: The Civil War in American Memory*. Cambridge, Mass.: Belknap, 2001.

———. "Why the Underground Railroad, and Why Now? A Long View." In *Passages to Freedom: The Underground Railroad in History and Memory*, edited by David W. Blight, 233–47. Washington, D.C.: Smithsonian Books, 2004.

———, ed. *Passages to Freedom: The Underground Railroad in History and Memory*. Washington, D.C.: Smithsonian Books, 2004.

Boeckmann, Cathy. *A Question of Character: Scientific Racism and the Genres of American Fiction, 1892–1912*. Tuscaloosa: University of Alabama Press, 2000.

Boggis, JerriAnne, Eve Allegra Raimon, and Barbara A. White, eds. *Harriet Wilson's New England: Race, Writing, and Region*. Hanover, N.H.: University Press of New England, 2007.

Bontemps, Arna, ed. *Five Black Lives: The Autobiographies of Venture Smith, James Mars, William Grimes, the Rev. G. W. Offley, James L. Smith*. Middletown, Conn.: Wesleyan University Press, 1971.

Boswell, James. *Life of Johnson*. London: Oxford University Press, 1953.

Bradford, Sarah. *Harriet Tubman: The Moses of Her People*. 2nd ed. 1886. New York: Citadel Press, 1991.

Bradley, Patricia. *Slavery, Propaganda, and the American Revolution*. Jackson: University Press of Mississippi, 1998.

Braxton, Joanne M. *Black Women Writing Autobiography: A Tradition within a Tradition*. Philadelphia: Temple University Press, 1989.

Brennan, Jonathan, ed. *When Brer Rabbit Meets Coyote: African-Native American Literature*. Urbana: University of Illinois Press, 2003.

Brickhouse, Anna. *Transamerican Literary Relations and the Nineteenth-Century Public Sphere*. Cambridge: Cambridge University Press, 2004.

Briggs, John. *Fractals: The Patterns of Chaos*. New York: Touchstone, 1992.

Brooks, Daphne A. *Bodies in Dissent: Spectacular Performances of Race and Freedom, 1850–1910*. Durham: Duke University Press, 2006.

Browder, Laura. *Slippery Characters: Ethnic Impersonators and American Identities*. Chapel Hill: University of North Carolina Press, 2000.

Brown, Henry Box. *Narrative of the Life of Henry Box Brown, Written by Himself*. 1851. Edited by John Ernest. Chapel Hill: University of North Carolina Press, 2008.

Brown, Michael K., Martin Carnoy, Elliott Currie, Troy Duster, David B. Oppenheimer, Marjorie M. Shultz, and David Wellman. *Whitewashing Race: The Myth of a Color-Blind Society*. Berkeley: University of California Press, 2003.

Brown, William Wells. *The American Fugitive in Europe: Sketches of Places and People Abroad*. 1855. Freeport: Books for Libraries Press, 1970.

——. *The Black Man: His Antecedents, His Genius, and His Achievements.* 1863. 4th ed. 1865. Salem, N.H.: Ayer, 1992.

——. *Clotel; or, The President's Daughter: A Narrative of Slave Life in the United States.* 1853. A Bedford Cultural Edition. Edited by Robert S. Levine. Boston: Bedford/St. Martin's, 2000.

——. *The Escape; or, A Leap for Freedom.* 1858. Knoxville: University of Tennessee Press, 2001.

——. *A Lecture Delivered before the Female Anti-Slavery Society of Salem, at Lyceum Hall, Nov. 14, 1847.* Boston: Massachusetts Anti-Slavery Society, 1847.

——. *My Southern Home; or, The South and Its People.* 1880. In *From Fugitive Slave to Free Man: The Autobiographies of William Wells Brown,* edited by William L. Andrews, 110–296. Columbia: University of Missouri Press, 2003.

——. *Narrative of William W. Brown, a Fugitive Slave, Written by Himself.* Boston, 1847.

——. *The Negro in the American Rebellion: His Heroism and His Fidelity.* 1867. New York: Kraus Reprint, 1969.

——. *The Rising Son; or, The Antecedents and Advancement of the Colored Race.* 1874. New York: Negro Universities Press, 1970.

——. *Three Years in Europe; or, Places I Have Seen and People I Have Met.* London: Charles Gilpin, 1852.

Bruce, Dickson D., Jr. *Black American Writing from the Nadir: The Evolution of a Literary Tradition, 1877–1915.* Baton Rouge: Louisiana State University Press, 1989.

——. *The Origins of African American Literature, 1680–1865.* Charlottesville: University Press of Virginia, 2001.

Bryant, John. *The Fluid Text: A Theory of Revision and Editing for Book and Screen.* Ann Arbor: University of Michigan Press, 2002.

Buchanan, Thomas C. *Black Life on the Mississippi: Slaves, Free Blacks, and the Western Steamboat World.* Chapel Hill: University of North Carolina Press, 2004.

Buell, Lawrence. *New England Literary Culture: From Revolution through Renaissance.* Cambridge: Cambridge University Press, 1986.

Burchell, R. A., ed. *Harriet Martineau and America: Selected Letters from the Reinhard S. Speck Collection.* Berkeley, Calif.: Friends of the Bancroft Library, 1995.

Burke, Kenneth. *The Philosophy of Literary Form.* 3rd ed. Berkeley: University of California Press, 1973.

Byrne, David. *Complexity Theory and the Social Sciences.* London: Routledge, 1998.

Callahan, Allen Dwight. *The Talking Book: African Americans and the Bible.* New Haven: Yale University Press, 2006.

Campbell, James T., Matthew Pratt Guterl, and Robert G. Lee, eds. *Race, Nation, and Empire in American History.* Chapel Hill: University of North Carolina Press, 2007.

Campbell, Jane. *Mythic Black Fiction: The Transformation of History.* Knoxville: University of Tennessee Press, 1986.

Campbell, John. *Negro-Mania: Being an Examination of the Falsely Assumed Equality of the Various Races of Man.* Philadelphia, 1851.

Carby, Hazel V. *Reconstructing Womanhood: The Emergence of the Afro-American Novelist.* New York: Oxford University Press, 1987.

Carr, Robert. *Black Nationalism in the New World: Reading the African-American and West Indian Experience*. Durham: Duke University Press, 2002.

Cassuto, Leonard. *The Inhuman Race: The Racial Grotesque in American Literature and Culture*. New York: Columbia University Press, 1997.

Castiglia, Christopher. "Abolition's Racial Interiors and the Making of White Civic Depth." *American Literary History* 14, no. 1 (Spring 2002): 32–59.

Castronovo, Russ. *Fathering the Nation: American Genealogies of Slavery and Freedom*. Berkeley: University of California Press, 1995.

———. *Necro Citizenship: Death, Eroticism, and the Public Sphere in the Nineteenth-Century United States*. Durham: Duke University Press, 2001.

Chesnutt, Charles W. *The Journals of Charles W. Chesnutt (1874–82)*. Edited by Richard Brodhead. Durham: Duke University Press, 1993.

———. "The Wife of His Youth." In *Charles W. Chesnutt: Selected Writings*, edited by SallyAnn Ferguson, 199–209. Boston: Houghton Mifflin, 2001.

Child, Lydia Maria. *An Appeal in Favor of That Class of Americans Called Africans*. 1833. Amherst: University of Massachusetts Press, 1996.

———. "The Quadroons." *Fact and Fiction: A Collection of Stories*. New York, Boston, 1846.

Chireau, Yvonne P. *Black Magic: Religion and the African American Conjuring Tradition*. Berkeley: University of California Press, 2003.

Christian, Barbara. "The Highs and the Lows of Black Feminist Criticism." In *Reading Black, Reading Feminist: A Critical Anthology*, edited by Henry Louis Gates Jr., 44–51. New York: Meridian, 1990.

———. "The Race for Theory." In *Within the Circle: An Anthology of African American Literary Criticism from the Harlem Renaissance to the Present*, edited by Angelyn Mitchell, 348–59. Durham: Duke University Press, 1994.

Chunchang, Gao. *African Americans in the Reconstruction Era*. New York: Garland, 2000.

Clarke, Lewis, and Milton Clarke. *Narratives of the Sufferings of Lewis and Milton Clarke, Sons of a Soldier of the Revolution, during a Captivity of More than Twenty Years among the Slaveholders of Kentucky, One of the So Called Christian States of North America: Dictated by Themselves*. Boston, 1846.

Clymer, Jeffory A. *America's Culture of Terrorism: Violence, Capitalism, and the Written Word*. Chapel Hill: University of North Carolina Press, 2003.

Coates, W. Paul. "Drusilla Dunjee Houston: An Introductory Note about the Author and Her Work." In *Wonderful Ethiopians of the Ancient Cushite Empire*, by Drusilla Dunjee Houston, i–v. Baltimore: Black Classic Press, 1985.

Cohen, William. *At Freedom's Edge: Black Mobility and the Southern White Quest for Racial Control, 1861–1915*. Baton Rouge: Louisiana State University Press, 1991.

Coles, Robert. *Black Writers Abroad: A Study of Black American Writers in Europe and Africa*. New York: Garland, 1999.

Collins, Julia C. [d. 1865]. *The Curse of Caste; or, The Slave Bride: A Rediscovered African American Novel*. Edited by William L. Andrews and Mitch Kachun. Oxford: Oxford University Press, 2006.

Condit, Celeste Michelle, and John Louis Lucaites. *Crafting Equality: America's Anglo-African Word*. Chicago: University of Chicago Press, 1993.

Cone, James H. *A Black Theology of Liberation*. 2nd ed. Maryknoll, N.Y.: Orbis, 1990.

Conner, Kimberly Rae. *Conversions and Visions in the Writings of African-American Women.* Knoxville: University of Tennessee Press, 1994.

Cooper, Anna Julia. *A Voice from the South by a Black Woman of the South.* 1892. Schomburg Library of Nineteenth-Century Black Women Writers. New York: Oxford University Press, 1988.

Craft, William. *Running a Thousand Miles for Freedom: The Escape of William and Ellen Craft from Slavery.* 1860. Athens: University of Georgia Press, 1999.

Crafts, Hannah. *The Bondwoman's Narrative.* Edited by Henry Louis Gates Jr. New York: Warner Books, 2002.

Crane, Gregg D. *Race, Citizenship, and Law in American Literature.* Cambridge: Cambridge University Press, 2002.

Crummell, Alexander. "The English Language in Liberia." 1861. In *Pamphlets of Protest: An Anthology of Early African-American Protest Literature, 1790–1860,* edited by Richard Newman, Patrick Rael, and Philip Lapsansky, 282–303. New York: Routledge, 2001.

———. "Letter on Ethnology." 1894. In *Destiny and Race: Selected Writings, 1840–1898,* by Alexander Crummell, edited by Wilson Jeremiah Moses, 81. Amherst: University of Massachusetts Press, 1992.

Cruz, Jon. *Culture on the Margins: The Black Spiritual and the Rise of American Cultural Interpretation.* Princeton: Princeton University Press, 1999.

Cutter, Martha J. "Dismantling 'The Master's House': Critical Literacy in Harriet Jacobs' *Incidents in the Life of a Slave Girl.*" *Callaloo* 19, no. 1 (Winter 1996): 209–25.

———. *Unruly Tongue: Identity and Voice in American Women's Writing, 1850–1930.* Jackson: University Press of Mississippi, 1999.

Daileader, Celia R. *Racism, Misogyny, and the Othello Myth; Inter-racial Couples from Shakespeare to Spike Lee.* Cambridge: Cambridge University Press, 2005.

Dain, Bruce. *A Hideous Monster of the Mind: American Race Theory in the Early Republic.* Cambridge: Harvard University Press, 2002.

Daly, John Patrick. *When Slavery Was Called Freedom: Evangelicalism, Proslavery, and the Causes of the Civil War.* Lexington: University Press of Kentucky, 2002.

Davis, Arthur. Introduction to *Clotel; or, The President's Daughter: A Narrative of Slave Life in the United States,* by William Wells Brown, vii–xvi. New York: Collier Books, 1970.

Davis, Charles T., and Henry Louis Gates Jr., eds. *The Slave's Narrative.* Oxford: Oxford University Press, 1985.

Davis, Gerald L. *I Got the Word in Me and I Can Sing It, You Know: A Study of the Performed African-American Sermon.* Philadelphia: University of Pennsylvania Press, 1985.

Dean, Sharon G. Introduction to *A Hairdresser's Experience of High Life,* by Eliza Potter, xxxiii–lix. New York: Oxford University Press, 1991.

Deck, Alice A. "A Response to Elizabeth McHenry." *American Literary History* 19, no. 2 (Summer 2007): 402–5.

———. "Whose Book Is This?: Authorial versus Editorial Control of Harriet Brent Jacobs' *Incidents in the Life of a Slave Girl, Written by Herself.*" *Women's Studies International Forum* 10, no. 1 (1987): 33–40.

Delaney, Lucy A. *From the Darkness Cometh the Light; or, Struggles for Freedom.* In *Six Women's Slave Narratives,* edited by William L. Andrews. Schomburg Library of Nineteenth-Century Black Women Writers. New York: Oxford University Press, 1988.

Delany, Martin R. [d. 1885]. *Blake; or, The Huts of America: A Tale of the Mississippi Valley, the Southern United States, and Cuba.* 1859–62. Boston: Beacon Press, 1970. [Published originally in serial form.]

———. *The Condition, Elevation, Emigration, and Destiny of the Colored People of the United States.* 1852. New York: Arno Press and the New York Times, 1968.

DeLombard, Jeannine Marie. *Slavery on Trial: Law, Abolitionism, and Print Culture.* Chapel Hill: University of North Carolina Press, 2007.

Diffley, Kathleen. *Where My Heart Is Turning Ever: Civil War Stories and Constitutional Reform, 1861–1876.* Athens: University of Georgia Press, 1992.

Dimock, Wai-Chee. *Through Other Continents: American Literature across Deep Time.* Princeton: Princeton University Press, 2006.

Doolen, Andy. *Fugitive Empire: Locating Early American Imperialism.* Minneapolis: University of Minnesota Press, 2005.

Dorr, David F. *A Colored Man Round the World.* 1858. Edited by Malini Johar Schueller. Ann Arbor: University of Michigan Press, 1999.

Douglass, Frederick. "The Abolition Movement Re-Organized." In *The Life and Writings of Frederick Douglass, Volume 2,* edited by Philip S. Foner, 520–25. New York: International Publishers, 1950.

———. *The Heroic Slave.* 1853. In *The Life and Writings of Frederick Douglass, Volume 5 (Supplementary Volume), 1844–1860,* edited by Philip S. Foner, 473–505. New York: International Publishers, 1975.

———. "Introduction to the Reason Why the Colored American Is Not in the World's Columbian Exposition." 1892. In *The Life and Writings of Frederick Douglass, Volume 4: Reconstruction and After,* edited by Philip S. Foner, 469–77. New York: International Publishers, 1955.

———. "Lecture at Inauguration of Douglass Institute, Baltimore, October, 1865." In *The Life and Writings of Frederick Douglass, Volume 4: Reconstruction and After,* edited by Philip S. Foner, 174–82. New York: International Publishers, 1955.

———. *Life and Times of Frederick Douglass.* 1881, 1892. In *Frederick Douglass: Autobiographies,* edited by Henry Louis Gates Jr. New York: Library of America.

———. *My Bondage and My Freedom.* 1855. In *Frederick Douglass: Autobiographies,* edited by Henry Louis Gates Jr. New York: Library of America, 1994.

———. *Narrative of the Life of Frederick Douglass, an American Slave.* 1845. In *Frederick Douglass: Autobiographies,* edited by Henry Louis Gates Jr. New York: Library of America, 1994.

———. "Oration in Memory of Abraham Lincoln, Delivered at the Unveiling of the Freedmen's Monument in Memory of Abraham Lincoln, in Lincoln Park, Washington, D.C., April 14, 1876." In *The Life and Writings of Frederick Douglass, Volume 4: Reconstruction and After,* edited by Philip S. Foner, 309–19. New York: International Publishers, 1955.

———. "Self-Elevation—Rev. S. R. Ward." 1855. In *The Life and Writings of Frederick Douglass, Volume 2,* edited by Philip S. Foner, 359–62. New York: International Publishers, 1955.

———. "What, to the Slave, Is the Fourth of July?" In *Lift Every Voice: African American*

*Oratory, 1787–1900*, edited by Philip S. Foner and Robert James Branham, 246–68. Tuscaloosa: University of Alabama Press, 1998.

Douglass-Chin, Richard J. *Preacher Woman Sings the Blues: The Autobiographies of Nineteenth-Century African American Evangelists.* Columbia: University of Missouri Press, 2001.

Du Bois, W. E. B. *Black Reconstruction in America: An Essay toward a History of the Past Which Black Folk Played in the Attempt to Reconstruct Democracy in America, 1860–1880.* 1935. Reprint, Cleveland: Meridian Books, 1998.

———. *The Souls of Black Folk.* 1903. In *Writings*, by W. E. B. Du Bois, 357–547. New York: Library of America, 1986.

duCille, Ann. *The Coupling Convention: Sex, Text, and Tradition in Black Women's Fiction.* New York: Oxford University Press, 1993.

Easton, Hosea. *A Treatise on the Intellectual Character, and Civil and Political Condition of the Colored People of the U[nited] States; and the Prejudice Exercised towards Them: With a Sermon on the Duty of the Church to Them.* Reprint, New York: Arno Press and the New York Times, 1969.

Edwards, Justin D. *Exotic Journeys: Exploring the Erotics of U.S. Travel Literature, 1840–1930.* Hanover, N.H.: University Press of New England, 2001.

Edwards, Laura F. *Gendered Strife and Confusion: The Political Culture of Reconstruction.* Urbana: University of Illinois Press, 1997.

Eglash, Ron. *African Fractals: Modern Computing and Indigenous Design.* New Brunswick, N.J.: Rutgers University Press, 1999.

Eiselein, Gregory. *Literature and Humanitarian Reform in the Civil War Era.* Bloomington: Indiana University Press, 1996.

Elaw, Zilpha. *Memoirs of the Life, Religious Experience, Ministerial Travels and Labours of Mrs. Zilpha Elaw, an American Female of Colour; Together with Some Account of the Great Religious Revivals in America.* 1846. In *Sisters of the Spirit: Three Black Women's Autobiographies of the Nineteenth Century*, edited by William L. Andrews, 49–160. Bloomington: Indiana University Press, 1986.

Elder, Arlene A. *The "Hindered Hand": Cultural Implications of Early African-American Fiction.* Westport, Conn.: Greenwood Press, 1978.

Ellis, R. J. *Harriet Wilson's Our Nig: A Cultural Biography of a "Two-Story" African American Novel.* Amsterdam: Rodopi, 2003.

Ericson, David F. *The Debate over Slavery: Antislavery and Proslavery Liberalism in Antebellum America.* New York: New York University Press, 2000.

Ernest, John. "Economies of Identity: Harriet E. Wilson's *Our Nig.*" *PMLA* 109 (1994): 424–38.

———. "The Family of Man: Traumatic Theology in the *Narrative of the Life of Henry Box Brown, Written by Himself.*" *African American Review* 41, no. 1 (Spring 2007): 19–31.

———. "The Floating Icon and the Fluid Text: Rereading the *Narrative of Sojourner Truth.*" *American Literature* 78, no. 3 (September 2006): 459–86.

———. "Fugitive Performances: William Wells Brown's *Three Years in Europe* and Harriet Martineau's *Society in America.*" In *Literature on the Move: Comparing Diasporic Ethnicities in Europe and the Americas*, edited by Dominique Marçais, Mark Niemeyer,

Bernard Vincent, and Cathy Waegner, 159–68. Heidelberg: Universitätsverlag C. Winter, 2002.

———. *Liberation Historiography: African American Writers and the Challenge of History, 1794–1861.* Chapel Hill: University of North Carolina Press, 2004.

———. "Losing Equilibrium: Harriet E. Wilson, Frado, and Me." In *Harriet Wilson's New England: Race, Writing, and Region,* edited by JerriAnne Boggis, Eve Allegra Raimon, and Barbara A. White, 203–11. Hanover, N.H.: University Press of New England, 2007.

———. "Outside the Box: Henry Box Brown and the Politics of Antislavery Agency." *Arizona Quarterly* 63, no. 4 (Winter 2007): 1–24.

———. "The Reconstruction of Whiteness: William Wells Brown's *The Escape; or, A Leap for Freedom.*" *PMLA* 113 (1998): 1108–21.

———. "Representing Chaos: William Craft's *Running a Thousand Miles for Freedom.*" *PMLA* 121 (2006): 469–83.

———. *Resistance and Reformation in Nineteenth-Century African-American Literature: Brown, Wilson, Jacobs, Delany, Douglass, and Harper.* Jackson: University Press of Mississippi, 1995.

———. "William Wells Brown Maps the South in *My Southern Home; or, The South and Its People.*" *Southern Quarterly* 45, no. 3 (Spring 2008): 88–107.

Ervin, Hazel Arnett, ed. *African-American Literary Criticism, 1773 to 2000.* New York: Twayne, 1999.

Eudell, Demetrius L. *The Political Languages of Emancipation in the British Caribbean and the U.S. South.* Chapel Hill: University of North Carolina Press, 2002.

Eve, Raymond A. "Afterword: So Where Are We Now? A Final Word." In *Chaos, Complexity, and Sociology: Myths, Models, and Theories,* edited by Raymond A. Eve, Sara Horsfall, and Mary E. Lee, 269–80. Thousand Oaks, Calif.: Sage, 1997.

Eve, Raymond A., Sara Horsfall, and Mary E. Lee. Preface to *Chaos, Complexity, and Sociology: Myths, Models, and Theories,* edited by Raymond A. Eve, Sara Horsfall, and Mary E. Lee, xxviii–xxxii. Thousand Oaks, Calif.: Sage, 1997.

Fabi, M. Giulia. *Passing and the Rise of the African American Novel.* Urbana: University of Illinois Press, 2001.

Fabre, Geneviève, and Robert O'Meally, eds. *History and Memory in African-American Culture.* New York: Oxford University Press, 1994.

Fahey, David M. *The Black Lodge in White America: "True Reformer" Browne and His Economic Strategy.* Dayton, Ohio: Wright State University Press, 1994.

Fahs, Alice. *The Imagined Civil War: Popular Literature of the North and South, 1861–1865.* Chapel Hill: University of North Carolina Press, 2001.

Fanuzzi, Robert. *Abolition's Public Sphere.* Minneapolis: University of Minnesota Press, 2003.

Farrison, William Edward. *William Wells Brown: Author and Reformer.* Chicago: University of Chicago Press, 1969.

Faust, Drew Gilpin. *Southern Stories: Slaveholders in Peace and War.* Columbia: University of Missouri Press, 1992.

Filler, Louis. *Crusade against Slavery: Friends, Foes, and Reforms, 1820–1860.* Algonac, Mich.: Reference Publications, 1986.

Fisch, Audrey. *American Slaves in Victorian England: Abolitionist Politics in Popular Literature and Culture*. Cambridge: Cambridge University Press, 2000.

———, ed. *The Cambridge Companion to the African American Slave Narrative*. Cambridge: Cambridge University Press, 2007.

Fisher, William W., III. "Ideology and Imagery in the Law of Slavery." In *Slavery and the Law*, edited by Paul Finkelman, 43–85. Lanham, Md.: Rowman and Littlefield, 2002.

Fleischner, Jennifer. *Mastering Slavery: Memory, Family, and Identity in Women's Slave Narratives*. New York: New York University Press, 1996.

Foner, Eric. *Reconstruction: America's Unfinished Revolution, 1863–1877*. New York: Harper and Row, 1988.

Foreman, P. Gabrielle. "Reading Aright: White Slavery, Black Referents, and the Strategy of Histotextuality in *Iola Leroy*." *Yale Journal of Criticism* 10, no. 2 (Fall 1997): 327–54.

———. "Recovered Autobiographies and the Marketplace: *Our Nig*'s Generic Genealogies and Harriet Wilson's Entrepreneurial Enterprise." In *Harriet Wilson's New England: Race, Writing, and Region*, edited by Boggis, JerriAnne, Eve Allegra Raimon, and Barbara A. White, 123–38. Hanover, N.H.: University Press of New England, 2007.

———. "Who's Your Mama? 'White' Mulatta Genealogies, Early Photography, and Anti-Passing Narratives of Slavery and Freedom." *American Literary History* 14, no. 2 (Fall 2002): 505–39.

Foreman, P. Gabrielle, and Reginald H. Pitts. Introduction to *Our Nig; or, Sketches from the Life of a Free Black*, by Harriet E. Wilson, edited by P. Gabrielle Foreman and Reginald H. Pitts, xxiii–l. New York: Penguin, 2005.

Foster, Frances Smith. "'Hurry Up, Please. It's Time,' Said the White Rabbit as S/he Followed Bre'r Rabbit into the Briar Patch." *Legacy: A Journal of American Women Writers* 22, no. 2 (2007): 322–30.

———. Introduction to *Iola Leroy; or, Shadows Uplifted*, by Frances E. W. Harper, xxvii–xxxix. Schomburg Library of Nineteenth-Century Black Women Writers. New York: Oxford University Press, 1988.

———. *Witnessing Slavery: The Development of Ante-bellum Slave Narratives*. 1979. 2nd ed. Madison: University of Wisconsin Press, 1994.

———. *Written by Herself: Literary Production by African American Women, 1746–1892*. Bloomington: Indiana University Press, 1993.

Fox-Genovese, Elizabeth, and Eugene D. Genovese. *The Mind of the Master Class: History and Faith in the Southern Slaveholders' Worldview*. Cambridge: Cambridge University Press, 2005.

Franklin, John Hope. *Reconstruction after the Civil War*. 2nd ed. Chicago: University of Chicago Press, 1994.

Franklin, John Hope, and Genna Rae McNeil, eds. *African Americans and the Living Constitution*. Washington, D.C.: Smithsonian Institution Press, 1995.

Franklin, John Hope, and Loren Schweninger. *Runaway Slaves: Rebels on the Plantation*. New York: Oxford University Press, 1999.

Fredrickson, George M. *The Black Image in the White Mind: The Debate on Afro-American Character and Destiny, 1817–1914*. New York: Harper, 1971.

Frey, Sylvia R., and Betty Wood. *Come Shouting to Zion: African American Protestantism in the American South and British Caribbean to 1830.* Chapel Hill: University of North Carolina Press, 1998.

Frost, Linda. *Never One Nation: Freaks, Savages, and Whiteness in U.S. Popular Culture, 1850–1877.* Minneapolis: University of Minnesota Press, 2005.

"A Fugitive Slave Turned Author." *Liberator,* January 12, 1855, 5.

Fulton, Alice. *Feeling as a Foreign Language: The Good Strangeness of Poetry.* St. Paul, Minn.: Graywolf Press, 1999.

Gaines, Rt. Rev. Wesley J. *African Methodism in the South; or, Twenty-Five Years of Freedom.* 1890. Chicago: Afro-Am Press, 1969.

Gara, Larry. Introduction to *Narrative of William W. Brown, a Fugitive Slave, Written by Himself.* In *Four Fugitive Slave Narratives,* edited by Robin W. Winks et al., ix–xvii. Reading, Mass.: Addison-Wesley, 1969.

———. *The Liberty Line: The Legend of the Underground Railroad.* Lexington: University of Kentucky Press, 1961.

———. "William Still and the Underground Railroad." In *Blacks in the Abolitionist Movement,* edited by John H. Bracey Jr., August Meier, and Elliott Rudwick, 44–52. Belmont, Calif.: Wadsworth Publishing Co., 1971.

Garber, Marjorie. *Vested Interests: Cross-Dressing and Cultural Anxiety.* New York: Routledge, 1992.

Gardner, Eric. "'Face to Face': Localizing Lucy Delaney's *From the Darkness Cometh the Light.*" *Legacy: A Journal of American Women Writers* 24, no. 1 (2007): 50–71.

———. "'This Attempt of Their Sister': Harriet Wilson's *Our Nig* from Printer to Readers." *New England Quarterly* 66, no. 2 (1993): 226–46.

———. "Two Texts on Children and Christian Education by Maria W. Stewart." *PMLA* 123, no. 1 (January 2008): 156–65.

———. "'You Have No Business to Whip Me': The Freedom Suits of Polly Wash and Lucy Ann Delaney." *African American Review* 41, no. 1 (Spring 2007): 33–50.

Gardner, Jared. *Master Plots: Race and the Founding of an American Literature, 1787–1845.* Baltimore: Johns Hopkins University Press, 1998.

Gardner, Sarah E. *Blood and Irony: Southern White Women's Narratives of the Civil War, 1861–1937.* Chapel Hill: University of North Carolina Press, 2004.

Garfield, Deborah M., and Rafia Zafar, eds. *Harriet Jacobs and* Incidents in the Life of a Slave Girl: *New Critical Essays.* Cambridge: Cambridge University Press, 1996.

Gates, Henry Louis, Jr. *Figures in Black: Words, Signs, and the "Racial" Self.* New York: Oxford University Press, 1987.

———. Foreword to *Harriet Wilson's New England: Race, Writing, and Region,* edited by JerriAnne Boggis, Eve Allegra Raimon, and Barbara A. White. Hanover, N.H.: University Press of New England, 2007.

———. Foreword to *The Works of William Wells Brown: Using His "Strong, Manly Voice,"* edited by Paula Garrett and Hollis Robbins, ix–xiv. Oxford: Oxford University Press, 2006.

———. Introduction to *Our Nig; or, Sketches from the Life of a Free Black,* by Harriet E. Wilson, xi–lv. New York: Vintage, 1983.

———. *Loose Canons: Notes on the Culture Wars.* New York: Oxford University Press, 1992.

———. "Preface to Blackness: Text and Pretext." In *African American Literary Theory:*

*A Reader*, edited by Winston Napier, 147–64. New York: New York University Press, 2000.

———. *The Signifying Monkey: A Theory of African-American Literary Criticism*. New York: Oxford University Press, 1988.

———. "'What's Love Got to Do with It?': Critical Theory, Integrity, and the Black Idiom." *New Literary History* (1987): 345–62.

———, ed. *Black Literature and Literary Theory*. New York: Routledge, 1984.

———, ed. *"Race," Writing, and Difference*. Chicago: University of Chicago Press, 1985.

———, ed. *Reading Black, Reading Feminist: A Critical Anthology*. New York: Meridian, 1990.

Gates, Henry Louis, Jr., and Evelyn Brooks Higginbotham, eds. *African American National Biography*. Oxford: Oxford University Press, 2008.

Gates, Henry Louis, Jr., and Nellie Y. McKay, eds. *The Norton Anthology of African American Literature*. 2nd ed. New York: W. W. Norton, 2004.

Gates, Henry Louis, Jr., and Hollis Robbins, eds. In *Search of Hannah Crafts: Critical Essays on* The Bondwoman's Narrative. New York: Basic Books, 2004.

Gayle, Addison, Jr. "Cultural Strangulation: Black Literature and the White Aesthetic." In *African American Literary Theory: A Reader*, edited by Winston Napier, 92–96. New York: New York University Press, 2000.

———, ed. *Black Expression: Essays by and about Black Americans in the Creative Arts*. New York: Weybright and Talley, 1969.

Geertz, Clifford. *The Interpretation of Cultures: Selected Essays*. New York: Basic Books, 1973.

Gibson, Donald B. "Individualism and Community in Black History and Fiction." *Black American Literature Forum* 11, no. 4 (Winter 1977): 123–29.

Gienapp, William E. "Abolitionism and the Nature of Antebellum Reform." In *Courage and Conscience: Black and White Abolitionists in Boston*, edited by Donald M. Jacobs, 21–46. Bloomington: Indiana University Press, 1993.

Gilbert, Olive. *Narrative of Sojourner Truth, a Northern Slave, Emancipated from Bodily Servitude by the State of New York, in 1828*. Boston, 1850. New York, 1853.

Gilbert, Olive, and Frances Titus. *Narrative of Sojourner Truth, a Bondswoman of Olden Time, Emancipated by the New York Legislature in the Early Part of the Present Century, with a History of Her Labors and Correspondence Drawn from Her "Book of Life"; also, a Memorial Chapter*. 1884. Edited by Nell Irvin Painter. New York: Penguin, 1998.

———. *Narrative of Sojourner Truth, a Northern Slave, Emancipated from Bodily Servitude by the State of New York, in 1828*. 1875.

Gillman, Susan. *Blood Talk: American Race Melodrama and the Culture of the Occult*. Chicago: University of Chicago Press, 2003.

Gilroy, Paul. *Against Race: Imagining Political Culture beyond the Color Line*. Cambridge: Belknap Press of Harvard University Press, 2000.

———. *The Black Atlantic: Modernity and Double Consciousness*. Cambridge: Harvard University Press, 1993.

———. "One Nation under a Groove: The Cultural Politics of 'Race' and Racism in Britain." In *Anatomy of Racism*, edited by David Theo Goldberg, 263–82. Minneapolis: University of Minnesota Press, 1990.

———. *Postcolonial Melancholia*. New York: Columbia University Press, 2005.

———. *Small Acts: Thoughts on the Politics of Black Cultures*. London: Serpent's Tail, 1993.

Glass, Kathy L. *Courting Communities: Black Female Nationalism and "Syncre-Nationalism" in the Nineteenth-Century North*. New York: Routledge, 2006.

Glaude, Eddie S., Jr. *Exodus! Religion, Race, and Nation in Early Nineteenth-Century Black America*. Chicago: University of Chicago Press, 2000.

———. *In a Shade of Blue: Pragmatism and the Politics of Black America*. Chicago: University of Chicago Press, 2007.

Gleick, James. *Chaos: Making a New Science*. New York: Penguin, 1987.

Goddu, Teresa. *Gothic America: Narrative, History, and Nation*. New York: Columbia University Press, 1997.

Goldberg, David Theo. *The Racial State*. Malden, Mass.: Blackwell, 2002.

———. *Racist Culture: Philosophy and the Politics of Meaning*. Cambridge, Mass.: Blackwell, 1993.

Goodell, William. *The American Slave Code in Theory and Practice: Its Distinctive Features Shown by Its Statutes, Judicial Decisions, and Illustrative Facts*. 1853. New York: New American Library, 1969.

Gossett, Thomas F. *Race: The History of an Idea in America*. 1963. Reprint, New York: Schocken, 1965.

Gould, Philip. "The Rise, Development, and Circulation of the Slave Narrative." In *The Cambridge Companion to the African American Slave Narrative*, edited by Audrey Fisch, 11–27. Cambridge: Cambridge University Press, 2007.

Graham, Maryemma. "The Origins of Afro-American Fiction." In *Proceedings of the American Antiquarian Society* 100, no. 1, 231–49. Worcester, Mass.: American Antiquarian Society, 1990.

———, ed. *The Cambridge Companion to the African American Novel*. Cambridge: Cambridge University Press, 2004.

Grammer, Elizabeth Elkin. *Some Wild Visions: Autobiographies by Female Itinerant Evangelists in 19th-Century America*. Oxford: Oxford University Press, 2003.

Grant, Nancy. Introduction to *The Kidnapped and the Ransomed: The Narrative of Peter and Vina Still after Forty Years of Slavery*, by Kate E. R. Pickard, vii–xv. Bison Books Edition. Lincoln: University of Nebraska Press, 1995.

Green, Jacob D. *Narrative of the Life of J. D. Green: A Runaway Slave, from Kentucky, Containing an Account of His Three Escapes, in 1839, 1846, and 1848*. Huddersfield, [England]: Henry Fielding, 1864.

Greenblatt, Stephen. "Culture." In *Critical Terms for Literary Study*, edited by Frank Lentricchia and Thomas McLaughlin, 225–32. 2nd ed. Chicago: University of Chicago Press, 1995.

Greene, Frances Whipple. *Memoirs of Elleanor Eldridge*. 2nd ed. 1843. Salem, N.H.: Ayer, 1971.

Grégoire, Henri. *On the Cultural Achievements of Negroes*. 1808. Translated by Thomas Cassirer and Jean-François Brière. Amherst: University of Massachusetts Press, 1996.

Grimes, William. *Life of William Grimes, the Runaway Slave*. 1855. Edited by William L. Andrews and Regina E. Mason. Oxford: Oxford University Press, 2008.

Gross, Ariela J. *Double Character: Slavery and Mastery in the Antebellum Southern Courtroom*. Athens: University of Georgia Press, 2000.

———. "Litigating Whiteness: Trials of Racial Determination in the Nineteenth-Century South." *Yale Law Journal* 108, no. 1 (October 1998): 109–88.

———. *What Blood Won't Tell: A History of Race on Trial in America*. Cambridge: Harvard University Press, 2008.

Guest, Ann Hutchinson. *Dance Notation: The Process of Recording Movement on Paper*. New York: Dance Horizons, 1984.

Gundaker, Grey. *Signs of Diaspora, Diaspora of Signs: Literacies, Creolization, and Vernacular Practice in African America*. New York: Oxford University Press, 1998.

Gunning, Sandra. *Race, Rape, and Lynching: The Red Record of American Literature, 1890–1912*. New York: Oxford University Press, 1996.

Guy-Sheftall, Beverly, ed. *Words of Fire: An Anthology of African-American Feminist Thought*. New York: New Press, 1995.

Hall, Stephen G. "To Render the Private Public: William Still and the Selling of *The Underground Rail Road*." *Pennsylvania Magazine of History and Biography* 127, no. 1 (January 2003): 35–56.

Handley, George B. *Postslavery Literatures in the Americas: Family Portraits in Black and White*. Charlottesville: University Press of Virginia, 2000.

Harper, Frances E. W. "Could We Trace the Record of Every Human Heart." 1857. In *A Brighter Coming Day: A Frances Ellen Watkins Harper Reader*, edited by Frances Smith Foster, 100–102. New York: Feminist Press at The City University of New York, 1990.

———. *Iola Leroy; or, Shadows Uplifted*. 1892. Schomburg Library of Nineteenth-Century Black Women Writers. New York: Oxford University Press, 1988.

———. *"Minnie's Sacrifice," "Sowing and Reaping," "Trial and Triumph": Three Rediscovered Novels by Frances E. W. Harper*. 1869. Edited by Frances Smith Foster. Boston: Beacon, 1994.

———. "We Are All Bound Up Together." 1866. In *A Brighter Coming Day: A Frances Ellen Watkins Harper Reader*, edited by Frances Smith Foster, 217–19. New York: Feminist Press at The City University of New York, 1990.

Harper, Michael S., and Robert B. Stepto, eds. *Chant of Saints: A Gathering of Afro-American Literature, Art, and Scholarship*. Urbana: University of Illinois Press, 1979.

Harris, Sharon M. *Executing Race: Early American Women's Narratives of Race, Society, and the Law*. Columbus: Ohio State University Press, 2005.

Harris, Trudier. *Exorcising Blackness: Historical and Literary Lynching and Burning Rituals*. Bloomington: Indiana University Press, 1984.

———. "Miss-Trained or Untrained? Jackleg Critics and African American Literature (Or, Some of My Adventures in Academia)." In *African American Literary Criticism, 1773 to 2000*, edited by Hazel Arnett Ervin, 461–70. New York: Twayne, 1999.

Hart, Albert Bushnell. Introduction to *The Underground Railroad from Slavery to Freedom*, by Wilbur H. Siebert. New York: Macmillan, 1899.

Hartman, Saidiya V. *Scenes of Subjection: Terror, Slavery, and Self-Making in Nineteenth-Century America*. New York: Oxford University Press, 1997.

Hartnett, Stephen John. *Democratic Dissent and the Cultural Fictions of Antebellum America*. Urbana: University of Illinois Press, 2002.

Harvey, Bruce A. *American Geographics: U.S. National Narratives and the Representation of the Non-European World, 1830–1865*. Stanford: Stanford University Press, 2001.

Hayles, N. Katherine. *Chaos Bound: Orderly Disorder in Contemporary Literature and Science*. Ithaca, N.Y.: Cornell University Press, 1990.

———. "Introduction: Complex Dynamics in Literature and Science." In *Chaos and Order: Complex Dynamics in Literature and Science*, edited by N. Katherine Hayles, 1–33. Chicago: University of Chicago Press, 1991.

Haynes, Carolyn A. *Divine Destiny: Gender and Race in Nineteenth-Century Protestantism*. Jackson: University Press of Mississippi, 1998.

Heermance, J. Noel. *William Wells Brown and Clotelle: A Portrait of the Artist in the First Negro Novel*. Hamden, Conn.: Archon Books, 1969.

Henderson, Mae G. "'Where, by the Way, Is This Train Going?': A Case for Black (Cultural) Studies." In *Postcolonial Theory and the United States: Race, Ethnicity, and Literature*, edited by Amritjit Singh and Peter Schmidt, 95–102. Jackson: University Press of Mississippi, 2000.

Henderson, Stephen E. "Inside the Funk Shop: A Word on Black Words." In *African American Literary Theory: A Reader*, edited by Winston Napier, 97–101. New York: New York University Press, 2000.

———. "Saturation: Progress Report on a Theory of Black Poetry." In *African American Literary Theory: A Reader*, edited by Winston Napier, 102–12. New York: New York University Press, 2000.

Heneghan, Bridget T. *Whitewashing America: Material Culture and Race in the Antebellum Imagination*. Jackson: University Press of Mississippi, 2003.

Henson, Josiah. *An Autobiography of the Rev. Josiah Henson ("Uncle Tom") from 1789 to 1881, with a Preface by Mrs. Harriet Beecher Stowe and Introductory Notes by George Sturge, S. Morley, Esq., M.P., Wendell Phillips, and John G. Whittier*. Edited by John Lobb. London, Ont., 1881.

———. *The Life of Josiah Henson, Formerly a Slave, Now an Inhabitant of Canada: As Narrated by Himself*. Boston, 1849.

———. *Truth Stranger than Fiction: Father Henson's Story of His Own Life, with an Introduction by Mrs. H. B. Stowe*. 1858. Williamstown, Mass.: Corner House, 1973.

———. *"Uncle Tom's Story of His Life": An Autobiography of the Rev. Josiah Henson (Mrs. Harriet Beecher Stowe's "Uncle Tom"), from 1789–1876*. London, 1877.

Hero, Rodney E. *Racial Diversity and Social Capital: Equality and Community in America*. Cambridge: Cambridge University Press, 2007.

Herzog, Kristin. *Women, Ethnics, and Exotics: Images of Power in Mid-Nineteenth-Century American Fiction*. Knoxville: University of Tennessee Press, 1983.

Higginbotham, A. Leon, Jr. *In the Matter of Color: Race and the American Legal Process: The Colonial Period*. Oxford: Oxford University Press, 1978.

———. *Shades of Freedom: Racial Politics and Presumptions of the American Legal Process*. New York: Oxford University Press, 1996.

Hill, Michael R. "Introduction to the Transaction Edition." In *How to Observe Morals and Manners*, xv–lx. 1838. New Brunswick, N.J.: Transaction Publishers, 1989.

Hinks, Peter P. *To Awaken My Afflicted Brethren: David Walker and the Problem of Antebellum Slave Resistance*. University Park: Pennsylvania State University Press, 1997.

Hogue, W. Lawrence. *Discourse and the Other: The Production of the Afro-American Text.* Durham: Duke University Press, 1986.

Holloway, Karla F. C. "Revision and (Re)membrance: A Theory of Literary Structures in Literature by African American Women Writers." In *African American Literary Theory: A Reader,* edited by Winston Napier, 387–98. New York: New York University Press, 2000.

Holmes, David G. *Revisiting Racialized Voice: African American Ethos in Language and Literature.* Carbondale: Southern Illinois University Press, 2004.

Holt, Thomas. *Black over White: Negro Political Leadership in South Carolina during Reconstruction.* Urbana: University of Illinois Press, 1977.

Horsman, Reginald. *Race and Manifest Destiny: The Origins of American Racial Anglo-Saxonism.* Cambridge: Harvard University Press, 1981.

Houston, Drusilla Dunjee. *Wonderful Ethiopians of the Ancient Cushite Empire, Book I: Nations of the Cushite Empire: Marvelous Facts from Authentic Records.* 1926. Reprint, Baltimore: Black Classic Press, 1985.

Howard-Pittney, David. *The Afro-American Jeremiad: Appeals for Justice in America.* Philadelphia: Temple University Press, 1990.

Hughes, Langston. "The Negro Artist and the Racial Mountain." In *The Norton Anthology of African American Literature,* edited by Henry Louis Gates Jr. and Nellie Y. McKay, 1311–14, 2nd ed. New York: W. W. Norton, 2004.

Hughes, Louis. *Thirty Years a Slave: From Bondage to Freedom: The Institution of Slavery as Seen on the Plantation and in the Home of the Planter: Autobiography of Louis Hughes.* 1897. Montgomery, Ala.: NewSouth Books, 2002.

Hull, Gloria T., Patricia Bell Scott, and Barbara Smith. *All the Women Are White, All the Blacks Are Men, but Some of Us Are Brave: Black Women's Studies.* New York: Feminist Press, 1982.

Humez, Jean M. *Harriet Tubman: The Life and the Life Stories.* Madison: University of Wisconsin Press, 2004.

———. "Reading *The Narrative of Sojourner Truth* as a Collaborative Text." *Frontiers: A Journal of Women's Studies* 16, no. 1 (1996): 29–52.

Hutchinson, George. "An End to the Family Romance: Nella Larsen, Black Transnationalism, and American Racial Ideology." In *Race, Nation, and Empire in American History,* edited by James T. Campbell, Matthew Pratt Guterl, and Robert G. Lee, 55–72. Chapel Hill: University of North Carolina Press, 2007.

Hyman, Harold, ed. *New Frontiers of the American Reconstruction.* Urbana: University of Illinois Press, 1966.

Irons, Charles F. *The Origins of Proslavery Christianity: White and Black Evangelicals in Colonial and Antebellum Virginia.* Chapel Hill: University of North Carolina Press, 2008.

Jackson, Blyden. *A History of Afro-American Literature, Volume 1: The Long Beginning, 1746–1895.* Baton Rouge: Louisiana State University Press, 1989.

Jackson, Cassandra. *Barriers between Us: Interracial Sex in Nineteenth-Century American Literature.* Bloomington: Indiana University Press, 2004.

———. "Beyond the Page: Rape and the Failure of Genre." In Me." In *Harriet Wilson's New England: Race, Writing, and Region,* edited by JerriAnne Boggis, Eve Allegra Raimon, and Barbara A. White, 155–65. Hanover, N.H.: University Press of New England, 2007.

Jacobs, Harriet A. *Incidents in the Life of a Slave Girl, Written by Herself.* 1861. Edited by Jean Fagan Yellin. Cambridge: Harvard University Press, 2000.

Jacobson, Matthew Frye. *Barbarian Virtues: The United States Encounters Foreign Peoples at Home and Abroad, 1876–1917.* New York: Hill and Wang, 2000.

———. *Whiteness of a Different Color: European Immigrants and the Alchemy of Race.* Cambridge: Harvard University Press, 1998.

James, Jennifer C. *A Freedom Bought with Blood: African American War Literature from the Civil War to World War II.* Chapel Hill: University of North Carolina, 2007.

Jarmon, Laura C. *Wishbone: Reference and Interpretation in Black Folk Narrative.* Knoxville: University of Tennessee Press, 2003.

Jarrett, Gene Andrew. "Addition by Subtraction: Toward a Literary History of Racial Representation." *Legacy: A Journal of American Women Writers* 22, no. 2 (2007): 315–21.

———. *Deans and Truants: Race and Realism in African American Literature.* Philadelphia: University of Pennsylvania Press, 2007.

Jefferson, Paul. Introduction to *The Travels of William Wells Brown, including "Narrative of William Wells Brown, a Fugitive Slave" and "The American Fugitive in Europe: Sketches of Places and People Abroad,"* edited by Paul Jefferson, 1–20. New York: Markus Wiener, 1991.

Jefferson, Thomas. *Notes on the State of Virginia.* 1787. Chapel Hill: University of North Carolina Press, 1982.

Jeffrey, Julie Roy. *Abolitionists Remember: Antislavery Autobiographies and the Unfinished Work of Emancipation.* Chapel Hill: University of North Carolina Press, 2008.

Johnson, Edward A. *History of Negro Soldiers in the Spanish-American War, and Other Items of Interest.* Raleigh, 1899.

Johnson, James Weldon. "O Black and Unknown Bards." In *Trouble the Water: 250 Years of African-American Poetry,* edited by Jerry W. Ward Jr., 79. New York: Mentor, 1997.

Johnson, Paul E., ed. *African-American Christianity: Essays in History.* Berkeley: University of California Press, 1994.

Johnson, Sylvester A. *The Myth of Ham in Nineteenth-Century American Christianity: Race, Heathens, and the People of God.* New York: Palgrave Macmillan, 2004.

Jones, Gavin. *Strange Talk: The Politics of Dialect Literature in Gilded Age America.* Berkeley: University of California Press, 1999.

Jones, J. McHenry. *Hearts of Gold.* 1896. College Park, Md.: McGrath, 1969.

Jones, Martha S. *All Bound Up Together: The Woman Question in African American Public Culture, 1830–1900.* Chapel Hill: University of North Carolina Press, 2007.

Jones, Thomas H. *Experience and Personal Narrative of Uncle Tom Jones, Who Was for Forty Years a Slave.* 1849. Worcester, Mass.: Henry Howland.

———. *The Experience of Rev. Thomas H. Jones, Who Was a Slave for Forty-Three Years: Written by a Friend, as Related to Him by Brother Jones.* 1885. In *North Carolina Slave Narratives: The Lives of Moses Roper, Lunsford Lane, Moses Grandy, and Thomas H. Jones,* edited by William L. Andrews et al., 203–78. Chapel Hill: University of North Carolina Press, 2003.

Joseph, Gloria I. "Sojourner Truth: Archetypal Black Feminist." In *Wild Women in the*

*Whirlwind: Afra-American Culture and the Contemporary Literary Renaissance*, edited by Joanne M. Braxton and Andree Nicola McLaughlin, 35–47. New Brunswick, N.J.: Rutgers University Press, 1990.

Joyce, Joyce Ann "The Black Canon: Reconstructing Black American Literary Criticism." *New Literary History* 18 (1987): 335–44.

———. "Black Woman Scholar, Critic, and Teacher: The Inextricable Relationship between Race, Sex, and Class." *New Literary History* 22 (1991): 543–65.

———. *Warriors, Conjurers and Priests: Defining African-centered Literary Criticism.* Chicago: Third World Press, 1994.

———. "'Who the Cap Fit': Unconsciousness and Unconscionableness in the Criticism of Houston A. Baker Jr. and Henry Louis Gates Jr." *New Literary History* 18 (1987): 371–84.

Judy, Ronald A. T. *(Dis)Forming the American Canon: African-Arabic Slave Narratives and the Vernacular.* Minneapolis: University of Minnesota Press, 1993.

Juster, Susan, and Lisa MacFarlane, eds. *A Mighty Baptism: Race, Gender, and the Creation of American Protestantism.* Ithaca, N.Y.: Cornell University Press, 1996.

Kaplan, Harold. *Democratic Humanism and American Literature.* University of Chicago Press, 1972.

Kaplan, Sidney, and Emma Nogrady Kaplan. *The Black Presence in the Era of the American Revolution.* Rev. ed. Amherst: University of Massachusetts Press, 1989.

Karenga, Maulana. *Introduction to Black Studies.* 3rd ed. Los Angeles: University of Sankore Press, 2002.

Kauffman, Stuart. *At Home in the Universe: The Search for Laws of Self-Organization and Complexity.* New York: Oxford University Press, 1995.

Kawash, Samira. *Dislocating the Color Line: Identity, Hybridity, and Singularity in African American Literature.* Stanford: Stanford University Press, 1997.

Keckley, Elizabeth. *Behind the Scenes; or, Thirty Years a Slave, and Four Years in the White House.* 1868. Edited by Frances Smith Foster. Urbana: University of Illinois Press, 2001.

King, Martin Luther, Jr. "I Have a Dream." In *The Norton Anthology of African American Literature*, edited by Henry Louis Gates Jr. and Nellie Y. McKay, 107–9. 2nd ed. New York: W. W. Norton, 2004.

Knadler, Stephen P. *The Fugitive Race: Minority Writers Resisting Whiteness.* Jackson: University Press of Mississippi, 2002.

Kolko, Beth E., Lisa Nakamura, and Gilbert B. Rodman, eds. *Race in Cyberspace.* New York: Routledge, 2000.

Krysan, Maria, and Amanda E. Lewis, eds. *The Changing Terrain of Race and Ethnicity.* New York: Russell Sage Foundation, 2004.

Kucich, John J. *Ghostly Communion: Cross-Cultural Spiritualism in Nineteenth-Century American Literature.* Hanover, N.H.: Dartmouth College Press, 2004.

Laban, Rudolf. *Choreutics.* Annotated and edited by Lisa Ullmann. London: MacDonald and Evans, 1966.

Larson, Kate Clifford. *Bound for the Promised Land: Harriet Tubman, Portrait of an American Hero.* New York: Ballantine, 2004.

Lauter, Paul. "Is Frances Ellen Watkins Harper Good Enough to Teach?" *Legacy* 5, no. 1 (1988): 27–32.

Lebedun, Jean. "Harriet Beecher Stowe's Interest in Sojourner Truth, Black Feminist." *American Literature* 46, no. 3 (November 1974): 359–63.

Lee, Jarena. *The Life and Religious Experience of Jarena Lee, a Coloured Lady, Giving an Account of Her Call to Preach the Gospel: Revised and Corrected from the Original Manuscript, Written by Herself*. 1836. In *Sisters of the Spirit: Three Black Women's Autobiographies of the Nineteenth Century*, edited by William L. Andrews, 25–52. Bloomington: Indiana University Press, 1986.

Lee, Maurice S. *Slavery, Philosophy, and American Literature, 1830–1860*. Cambridge: Cambridge University Press, 2005.

Lemire, Elise. *"Miscegenation": Making Race in America*. Philadelphia: University of Pennsylvania Press, 2002.

Leonard, James S., Thomas A. Tenney, and Thadious M. Davis, eds. *Satire or Evasion? Black Perspectives on Huckleberry Finn*. Durham: Duke University Press, 1992.

Leonard, Keith D. *Fettered Genius: The African American Bardic Poet from Slavery to Civil Rights*. Charlottesville: University of Virginia Press, 2006.

Levander, Caroline F. *Cradle of Liberty: Race, the Child, and National Belonging from Thomas Jefferson to W. E. B. Du Bois*. Durham: Duke University Press, 2006.

Levin, David. *History as Romantic Art: Bancroft, Prescott, Motley, and Parkman*. Stanford: Stanford University Press, 1959.

Levine, Lawrence W. *Black Culture and Black Consciousness: Afro-American Folk Thought from Slavery to Freedom*. New York: Oxford University Press, 1977.

Levine, Robert S. "Circulating the Nation: David Walker, the Missouri Compromise, and the Rise of the Black Press." In *The Black Press: New Literary and Historical Essays*, edited by Todd Vogel, 17–36. New Brunswick, N.J.: Rutgers University Press, 2001.

———. *Martin Delany, Frederick Douglass, and the Politics of Representative Identity*. Chapel Hill: University of North Carolina Press, 1997.

———. "'Whiskey, Blacking, and All': Temperance and Race in William Wells Brown's *Clotel*." In *The Serpent in the Cup: Temperance in American Literature*, edited by David S. Reynolds and Debra J. Rosenthal, 93–114. Amherst: University of Massachusetts Press, 1997.

———, ed. *Martin R. Delany: A Documentary Reader*. Chapel Hill: University of North Carolina Press, 2003.

Levine, Robert S., and Samuel Otter, eds. *Frederick Douglass and Herman Melville: Essays in Relation*. Chapel Hill: University of North Carolina Press, 2008.

Lewis, Earl. "To Turn as on a Pivot: Writing African Americans into a History of Overlapping Diasporas." *American Historical Review* 100, no. 3 (June 1995): 765–87.

Lewis, R. W. B. *The American Adam: Innocence, Tragedy, and Tradition in the Nineteenth Century*. Chicago: University of Chicago Press, 1955.

———. *Light and Truth, from Ancient and Sacred History*. Augusta, Maine, 1843.

Lhamon, W. T., Jr. *Raising Cain: Blackface Performance from Jim Crow to Hip Hop*. Cambridge: Harvard University Press, 1998.

———, ed. *Jump Jim Crow: Lost Plays, Lyrics, and Street Prose of the First Atlantic Popular Culture*. Cambridge: Harvard University Press, 2003.

Litwack, Leon F. *Been in the Storm So Long: The Aftermath of Slavery*. New York: Knopf, 1979.

Lively, Robert A. *Fiction Fights the Civil War: An Unfinished Chapter in the Literary History of the American People*. Westport, Conn.: Greenwood Press, 1957.

Loewen, James W. *Sundown Towns: A Hidden Dimension of American Racism*. New York: Touchstone, 2005.

Loggins, Vernon. *The Negro Author: His Development in America*. New York: Columbia University Press, 1931.

Lott, Eric. *Love and Theft: Blackface Minstrelsy and the American Working Class*. New York: Oxford University Press, 1993.

Lucasi, Stephen. "William Wells Brown's *Narrative* and Traveling Subjectivity." *African American Review* 41, no. 3 (Fall 2007): 521–39.

Mabee, Carleton, with Susan Mabee Newhouse. *Sojourner Truth: Slave, Prophet, Legend*. New York: New York University Press, 1993.

Macdonald, Christine. "Judging Jurisdictions: Geography and Race in Slave Law and Literature of the 1830s." *American Literature* 71, no. 4 (1999): 625–56.

Magubane, Bernard Makhosezwe. *The Ties That Bind: African-American Consciousness of Africa*. Trenton, N.J.: Africa World Press, 1987.

Mahar, William J. *Behind the Burnt Cork Mask: Early Blackface Minstrelsy and Antebellum American Popular Culture*. Urbana: University of Illinois Press, 1999.

Majors, Monroe Adolphus. *Noted Negro Women: Their Triumphs and Activities*. 1893. Salem, N.H.: Ayer, 1986.

Mandelbrot, Benoit B. *The Fractal Geometry of Nature*. San Francisco: W. H. Freeman, 1982.

Mandziuk, Roseann M., and Suzanne Pullon Fitch. "The Rhetorical Construction of Sojourner Truth." *Southern Communication Journal* 66, no. 2 (Winter 2001): 120–38.

Martin, Charles D. *The White African American Body: A Cultural and Literary Exploration*. New Brunswick, N.J.: Rutgers University Press, 2002.

Martin, Waldo E., Jr. *The Mind of Frederick Douglass*. Chapel Hill: University of North Carolina Press, 1984.

Martineau, Harriet. *How to Observe Morals and Manners*. 1838. New Brunswick, N.J.: Transaction Publishers, 1989.

———. *Retrospect of Western Travel*. 1838. New York: Johnson Reprint, 1968.

———. *Society in America*. 3 vols. London: Saunders and Otley, 1837.

Matlack, Lucius C. Introduction to *Narrative of the Life and Adventures of Henry Bibb, an American Slave*, 1–10. 1850. Madison: University of Wisconsin Press, 2001.

Mattison, H. *Louisa Picquet, the Octoroon; or, Inside Views of Southern Domestic Life*. 1861. In *Collected Black Women's Narratives*. New York: Oxford University Press, 1988.

McBride, Dwight A. *Impossible Witnesses: Truth, Abolitionism, and Slave Testimony*. New York: New York University Press, 2001.

McCarthy, B. Eugene, and Thomas L. Doughton, eds. *From Bondage to Belonging: The Worcester Slave Narratives*. Amherst: University of Massachusetts Press, 2007.

McCaskill, Barbara. "'Trust No Man!' But What about a Woman? Ellen Craft and a Geneological Model for Teaching Douglass's *Narrative*." In *Approaches to Teaching Narrative of the Life of Frederick Douglass*, edited by James C. Hall, 95–101. New York: Modern Language Association of America, 1999.

———. "'Yours Very Truly': Ellen Craft—the Fugitive as Text and Artifact." *African American Review* 29, no. 4 (1994): 509–29.

McCaskill, Barbara, and Caroline Gebhard, eds. *Post-Bellum, Pre-Harlem: African American Literature and Culture, 1877–1919*. New York: New York University Press, 2006.

McCoy, Beth A. "Race and the (Para)Textual Condition." *PMLA* 121, no. 1 (January 2006): 156–69.

McDowell, Deborah E. "In the First Place: Making Frederick Douglass and the Afro-American Narrative Tradition." In *African American Autobiography: A Collection of Critical Essays*, edited by William L. Andrews, 36–58. Englewood Cliffs, N.J.: Prentice-Hall, 1993.

———. "Transferences—Black Feminist Discourse: The 'Practice' of 'Theory.'" In *Feminism Beside Itself*, edited by Diane Elam and Robyn Weigman, 93–118. New York: Routledge, 1995.

McDowell, Deborah E., and Arnold Rampersad, eds. *Slavery and the Literary Imagination: Selected Papers from the English Institute, 1987*. Baltimore: Johns Hopkins University Press, 1989.

McHenry, Elizabeth. *Forgotten Readers: Recovering the Lost History of African American Literary Societies*. Durham: Duke University Press, 2002.

———. "Toward a History of Access: The Case of Mary Church Terrell." *American Literary History* 19, no. 2 (Summer 2007): 381–401.

McKay, Nellie Y. "Naming the Problem That Led to the Question 'Who Shall Teach African American Literature?'; or, Are We Ready to Disband the Wheatley Court?" In *White Scholars/African American Texts*, edited by Lisa A. Long, 17–26. New Brunswick, N.J.: Rutgers University Press, 2005.

McKittrick, Katherine. *Demonic Grounds: Black Women and the Cartographies of Struggle*. Minneapolis: University of Minnesota Press, 2006.

McKittrick, Katherine, and Clyde Woods, eds. *Black Geographies and the Politics of Place*. Cambridge, Mass.: South End Press, 2007.

McWilliams, John P., Jr. *Hawthorne, Melville, and the American Character: A Looking-Glass Business*. Cambridge: Cambridge University Press, 1985.

Meer, Sarah. *Uncle Tom Mania: Slavery, Minstrelsy and Transatlantic Culture in the 1850s*. Athens: University of Georgia Press, 2005.

Melish, Joanne Pope. *Disowning Slavery: Gradual Emancipation and "Race" in New England, 1780–1860*. Ithaca, N.Y.: Cornell University Press, 1998.

———. "The Racial Vernacular: Contesting the Black/White Binary in Nineteenth-Century Rhode Island." In *Race, Nation, and Empire in American History*, edited by James T. Campbell, Matthew Pratt Guterl, and Robert G. Lee, 17–39. Chapel Hill: University of North Carolina Press, 2007.

Melville, Herman. *The Confidence-Man: His Masquerade*. 1857. Evanston: Northwestern University Press and Newberry Library, 1984.

———. *Moby-Dick; or, The Whale*. 1851. Evanston: Northwestern University Press and Newberry Library, 1988.

———. *Redburn: His First Voyage: Being the Sailor-Boy Confessions and Reminiscences of the*

*Son-of-a-Gentleman, in the Merchant Service.* 1849. Evanston: Northwestern University Press and Newberry Library, 1969.

Michaels, Walter Benn. *The Trouble with Diversity: How We Learned to Love Identity and Ignore Inequality.* New York: Metropolitan Books, 2006.

Miles, Tiya, and Sharon P. Holland, eds. *Crossing Waters, Crossing Worlds: The African Diaspora in Indian Country.* Durham: Duke University Press, 2006.

Miller, Diane. "The Places and Communities of the Underground Railroad: The National Park Service Network to Freedom." In *Passages to Freedom: The Underground Railroad in History and Memory,* edited by David W. Blight, 279–89. Washington, D.C.: Smithsonian Books, 2004.

Mills, Bruce. "Lydia Maria Child and the Endings to Harriet Jacobs's *Incidents in the Life of a Slave Girl.*" *American Literature* 64 (1992): 255–72.

Mills, Charles W. *The Racial Contract.* Ithaca, N.Y.: Cornell University Press, 1997.

*Minutes of the National Convention of Colored Citizens: Held at Buffalo, on the 15th, 16th, 17th, 18th and 19th of August, 1843: For the Purpose of Considering Their Moral and Political Condition as American Citizens.* In *Minutes of the Proceedings of the National Negro Conventions, 1830–1864,* edited by Howard Holman Bell. Arno Press and the New York Times, 1969.

Mitchell, Angelyn, ed. *Within the Circle: An Anthology of African American Literary Criticism from the Harlem Renaissance to the Present.* Durham: Duke University Press, 1994.

Mitchell, Henry H. *Black Church Beginnings: The Long-Hidden Realities of the First Years.* Grand Rapids, Mich.: William B. Eerdmans, 2004.

Mitchell, Michele. *Righteous Propagation: African Americans and the Politics of Racial Destiny after Reconstruction.* Chapel Hill: University of North Carolina Press, 2004.

Mizruchi, Susan L. *The Power of Historical Knowledge: Narrating the Past in Hawthorne, James, and Dreiser.* Princeton: Princeton University Press, 1988.

Moody, Joycelyn. *Sentimental Confessions: Spiritual Narratives of Nineteenth-Century African American Women.* Athens: University of Georgia Press, 2001.

Moore, Robert H., II. "Clarifying a Few Details in the Narrative of Bethany Veney." *Page News and Courier,* August 24, 2000, <http://www.geocities.com/Heartland/Hills/1850/PageHH/handh08-24-00.html> (May 27, 2008).

———. "Frank Veney: The Other Half of the Bethany Veney Story." *Page News and Courier,* July 2004, <http://www.geocities.com/cenantuaheight/FrankVeney.html> (May 27, 2008).

Moos, Dan. *Outside America: Race, Ethnicity, and the Role of the American West in National Belonging.* Hanover, N.H.: Dartmouth College Press, 2005.

Morava, Jack. "From Lévi-Strauss to Chaos and Complexity." In *On the Order of Chaos: Social Anthropology and the Science of Chaos,* edited by Mark S. Mosko and Frederick H. Damon, 47–63. New York: Berghahn Books, 2005.

Morgan, Marcyliena. *Language, Discourse and Power in African American Culture.* Cambridge: Cambridge University Press, 2002.

Morrison, Toni. *Playing in the Dark: Whiteness and the Literary Imagination.* Cambridge: Harvard University Press, 1992.

———. "Unspeakable Things Unspoken: The Afro-American Presence in American Literature." In *Within the Circle: An Anthology of African American Literary Criticism from the Harlem Renaissance to the Present*, edited by Angelyn Mitchell, 368–98. Durham: Duke University Press, 1994.

Moses, Wilson Jeremiah. *Black Messiahs and Uncle Toms: Social and Literary Manipulations of a Religious Myth*. Rev. ed. University Park: Pennsylvania State University Press, 1993.

———. *Creative Conflict in African American Thought: Frederick Douglass, Alexander Crummell, Booker T. Washington, W. E. B. Du Bois, and Marcus Garvey*. Cambridge: Cambridge University Press, 2004.

———. *The Golden Age of Black Nationalism, 1850–1925*. New York: Oxford University Press, 1978.

Mosko, Mark S. "Introduction: A (Re)Turn to Chaos: Chaos Theory, the Sciences, and Social Anthropological Theory." In *On the Order of Chaos: Social Anthropology and the Science of Chaos*, edited by Mark S. Mosko and Frederick H. Damon, 1–46. New York: Berghahn Books, 2005.

Moss, Elizabeth. *Domestic Novelists in the Old South: Defenders of Southern Culture*. Baton Rouge: Louisiana State University Press, 1992.

Murji, Karim, and John Solomos, eds. *Racialization: Studies in Theory and Practice*. Oxford: Oxford University Press, 2005.

Nabers, Deak. *Victory of Law: The Fourteenth Amendment, the Civil War, and American Literature, 1852–1867*. Baltimore: Johns Hopkins University Press, 2006.

Nakamura, Lisa. *Cybertypes: Race, Ethnicity, and Identity on the Internet*. New York: Routledge, 2002.

Napier, Winston, ed. *African American Literary Theory: A Reader*. New York: New York University Press, 2000.

Nash, Gary B. *Race and Revolution*. Madison, Wis.: Madison House, 1990.

Neely, Mark E., Jr. *The Boundaries of American Political Culture in the Civil War Era*. Chapel Hill: University of North Carolina Press, 2005.

Nell, William C. *The Colored Patriots of the American Revolution, with Sketches of Several Distinguished Colored Persons: To Which Is Added a Brief Survey of the Condition and Prospects of Colored Americans*. 1855. Salem, N.H.: Ayer, 1986.

Nelson, Dana D. *National Manhood: Capitalist Citizenship and the Imagined Fraternity of White Men*. Durham: Duke University Press, 1998.

———. *The Word in Black and White: Reading "Race" in American Literature, 1638–1867*. New York: Oxford University Press, 1993.

Newman, Richard. Introduction to *Narrative of the Life of Henry Box Brown, Written by Himself*, xi–xxxii. New York: Oxford University Press, 2002.

Newman, Richard, Patrick Rael, and Philip Lapsansky, eds. *Pamphlets of Protest: An Anthology of Early African-American Protest Literature, 1790–1860*. New York: Routledge, 2001.

Noble, Marianne. *The Masochistic Pleasures of Sentimental Literature*. Princeton: Princeton University Press, 2000.

Northup, Solomon. *Twelve Years a Slave: Narrative of Solomon Northup, a Citizen of New York, Kidnapped in Washington City in 1841, and Rescued in 1853, from a Cotton Plantation near the Red River, in Louisiana.* 1853. Baton Rouge: Louisiana State University Press, 1968.

Nott, Josiah Clark and George R. Gliddon. *Types of Mankind; or, Ethnological Researches, Based upon the Ancient Monuments, Paintings, Sculptures, and Crania of Races, and upon Their Natural, Geographical, Philological, and Biblical History.* 1854.

Nudelman, Franny. *John Brown's Body: Slavery, Violence, and the Culture of War.* Chapel Hill: University of North Carolina Press, 2004.

Nwankwo, Ifeoma Kiddoe. *Black Cosmopolitanism: Racial Consciousness and Transnational Identity in the Nineteenth-Century Americas.* Philadelphia: University of Pennsylvania Press, 2005.

O'Donovan, Susan Eva. *Becoming Free in the Cotton South.* Cambridge: Harvard University Press, 2007.

Offley, Rev. G. W. *A Narrative of the Life and Labors of the Rev. G. W. Offley: A Colored Man, and Local Preacher.* Hartford, Conn., 1860.

Okihiro, Gary Y. "Race and Ethnicity." In *The Oxford Companion to United States History,* edited by Paul S. Boyer et al., 642–44. Oxford: Oxford University Press, 2001.

Olney, James. "The Founding Fathers—Frederick Douglass and Booker T. Washington." In *Slavery and the Literary Imagination: Selected Papers from the English Institute, 1987,* edited by Deborah E. McDowell and Arnold Rampersad, 1–24. Baltimore: Johns Hopkins University Press, 1989.

———. "'I Was Born': Slave Narratives, Their Status as Autobiography and as Literature." In *The Slave's Narrative,* edited by Charles T. Davis and Henry Louis Gates Jr., 148–75. Oxford: Oxford University Press, 1985.

Ostrowski, Carl. "Slavery, Labor Reform, and Intertextuality in Antebellum Print Culture: The Slave Narrative and the City-Mysteries Novel." *African American Review* 40, no. 3 (Fall 2006): 493–506.

Painter, Nell Irvin. *Sojourner Truth: A Life, a Symbol.* New York: W. W. Norton, 1996.

Palmer, Phyllis Marynick. "White Women/Black Women: The Dualism of Female Identity and Experience in the United States." *Feminist Studies* 9, no. 1 (Fall 1983): 151–70.

Parrott, Russell. *An Oration of the Abolition of the Slave Trade . . . Delivered on the First of January, 1814, at the African Church of St. Thomas.* 1814. In *Early Negro Writing, 1760–1837,* by Dorothy Porter, 383–90. Baltimore: Black Classic Press, 1994.

Patterson, Orlando. *Slavery and Social Death: A Comparative Study.* Cambridge: Harvard University Press, 1982.

Paul, Nathaniel. *An Address, Delivered on the Celebration of the Abolition of Slavery, in the State of New York, July 5, 1827.* 1827. New York: Arno Press and the New York Times, 1969.

Payne, Daniel A. *History of the African Methodist Episcopal Church.* Nashville, 1891.

Peabody, Ephraim. "Narratives of Fugitive Slaves." In *The Slave's Narrative,* edited by Charles T. Davis and Henry Louis Gates Jr., 19–28. Oxford: Oxford University Press, 1985.

Penn, I. Garland. *The Afro-American Press, and Its Editors.* 1891. Salem, N.H.: Ayer, 1988.

Pennington, J. W. C. "The Great Conflict Requires Great Faith." In *The Anglo-African*

*Magazine, Volume 1—1859*, edited by William Loren Katz, 343–45. New York: Arno Press and the New York Times, 1968.

Peterson, Carla L. *"Doers of the Word": African-American Women Speakers and Writers in the North, 1830–1880.* New York: Oxford University Press, 1995.

———. "A Sign unto This Nation": Sojourner Truth, History, Orature, and Modernity." In *Black Women's Intellectual Traditions: Speaking Their Minds*, edited by Kristin Waters and Carol B. Conaway, 129–70. Burlington: University of Vermont Press, 2007.

Pichanick, Valerie Kossew. *Harriet Martineau: The Woman and Her Work, 1802–76.* Ann Arbor: University of Michigan Press, 1980.

Pickard, Kate E. R. *The Kidnapped and the Ransomed: The Narrative of Peter and Vina Still after Forty Years of Slavery.* 1856. Lincoln: University of Nebraska Press, 1995.

Pierce, Yolanda. *Hell without Fires: Slavery, Christianity, and the Antebellum Spiritual Narrative.* Gainesville: University Press of Florida, 2005.

Pierson, Michael D. *Free Hearts, Free Homes: Gender and American Antislavery Politics.* Chapel Hill: University of North Carolina Press, 2003.

Pinn, Anthony B. *Varieties of African American Religious Experience.* Minneapolis: Fortress, 1998.

Poirier, Richard. *A World Elsewhere: The Place of Style in American Literature.* New York: Oxford University Press, 1966.

Potter, Eliza. *A Hairdresser's Experience of High Life.* 1859. New York: Oxford University Press, 1991.

Powell, Timothy B. *Ruthless Democracy: A Multicultural Interpretation of the American Renaissance.* Princeton: Princeton University Press, 2000.

Pressly, Thomas J. *Americans Interpret Their Civil War.* New York: Free Press, 1966.

Price, H. H., and Gerald E. Talbot. *Maine's Visible Black History: The First Chronicle of Its People.* Gardiner, Maine: Tilbury House, 2006.

Prichard, James Cowles. *The Natural History of Man: Comprising Inquiries into the Modifying Influence of Physical and Moral Agencies on the Different Tribes of the Human Family.* 1843. 3rd ed. London: Hippolyte Bailliere, 1848.

———. *Researches into the Physical History of Man.* 1813. Chicago: University of Chicago Press, 1973.

Prince, Mary. *The History of Mary Prince, a West Indian Slave, Related by Herself.* 1831. In *Six Women's Slave Narratives*, edited by William L. Andrews. Schomburg Library of Nineteenth-Century Black Women Writers. New York: Oxford University Press, 1988.

Prince, Nancy. *A Narrative of the Life and Travels of Mrs. Nancy Prince, Written by Herself.* 2nd ed. 1853. In *Collected Black Women's Narratives.* New York: Oxford University Press, 1988.

*Proceedings of the Colored National Convention, Held in Rochester, July 6th, 7th and 8th, 1853.* In *Minutes and Proceedings of the National Negro Conventions, 1830–1864*, edited by Howard Holman Bell. New York: Arno Press and the New York Times, 1969.

*Proceedings of the National Convention of Colored People, and Their Friends, Held in Troy, N.Y., on the 6th, 7th, 8th and 9th October, 1847.* In *Minutes and Proceedings of the National Negro Conventions, 1830–1864*, edited by Howard Holman Bell. New York: Arno Press and the New York Times, 1969.

Pryse, Marjorie, and Hortense J. Spillers, eds. *Conjuring: Black Women, Fiction, and Literary Tradition.* Bloomington: Indiana University Press, 1985.

Rabinowitz, Howard N. *Race Relations in the Urban South, 1865–1890.* New York: Oxford University Press, 1978.

Raboteau, Albert J. *Canaan Land: A Religious History of African Americans.* New York: Oxford University Press, 2001.

———. *Slave Religion: The "Invisible Institution" in the Antebellum South.* Oxford: Oxford University Press, 1978.

Rael, Patrick. *Black Identity and Black Protest in the Antebellum North.* Chapel Hill: University of North Carolina Press, 2002.

Raimon, Eve Allegra. *The "Tragic Mulatta" Revisited: Race and Nationalism in Nineteenth-Century Antislavery Fiction.* New Brunswick, N.J.: Rutgers University Press, 2004.

Read, Rev. Hollis. *The Negro Problem Solved; or, Africa as She Was, as She Is, and as She Shall Be: Her Curse and Her Cure.* New York: Negro Universities Press, 1864.

Reed, Ishmael. *Flight to Canada.* New York: Atheneum, 1989.

Reid-Pharr, Robert F. *Conjugal Union: The Body, the House, and the Black American.* New York: Oxford University Press, 1999.

Reilly, John M. "History-Making Literature." In *Studies in Black American Literature, Volume II: Belief vs. Theory in Black American Literary Criticism,* edited by Joe Weixlmann and Chester J. Fontenot, 85–120. Greenwood, Fla.: Penkevill, 1986.

"Rev. Samuel R. Ward in England." *Liberator,* September 16, 1853, 1.

Richardson, Heather Cox. *The Death of Reconstruction: Race, Labor, and Politics in the Post–Civil War North, 1865–1901.* Cambridge: Harvard University Press, 2001.

Ripley, C. Peter, et al., eds. *The Black Abolitionist Papers.* 5 vols. Chapel Hill: University Press of North Carolina, 1985–92.

Roach, Joseph. *Cities of the Dead: Circum-Atlantic Performance.* New York: Columbia University Press, 1996.

Robertson, Andrew W. *The Language of Democracy: Political Rhetoric in the United States and Britain, 1790–1900.* 1995. Reprint, Charlottesville: University of Virginia Press, 2005.

Roediger, David R. *The Wages of Whiteness: Race and the Making of the American Working Class.* London: Verso, 1991.

Rohrbach, Augusta. "Profits of Protest: The Market Strategies of Sojourner Truth and Louisa May Alcott." In *Prophets of Protest: Reconsidering the History of American Abolitionism,* edited by Timothy Patrick McCarthy and John Stauffer, 235–55. New York: New Press, 2006.

Rosenthal, Debra J. *Race Mixture in Nineteenth-Century U.S. and Spanish American Fictions: Gender, Culture, and Nation Building.* Chapel Hill: University of North Carolina Press, 2004.

Ruggles, Jeffrey. *The Unboxing of Henry Brown.* Richmond: The Library of Virginia, 2003.

Ryan, Barbara. *Love, Wages, Slavery: The Literature of Servitude in the United States.* Urbana: University of Illinois Press, 2006.

Ryan, Susan M. *The Grammar of Good Intentions: Race and the Antebellum Culture of Benevolence.* Ithaca, N.Y.: Cornell University Press, 2003.

Sammons, Mark J., and Valerie Cunningham. *Black Portsmouth: Three Centuries of African American Heritage.* Durham, N.H.: University of New Hampshire Press, 2004.

Samuels, Shirley. *Facing America: Iconography and the Civil War.* Oxford: Oxford University Press, 2004.

Sanchez-Eppler, Karen. *Touching Liberty: Abolition, Feminism, and the Politics of the Body.* Berkeley: University of California Press, 1993.

Santamarina, Xiomara. *Belabored Professions: Narratives of African American Working Womanhood.* Chapel Hill: University of North Carolina Press, 2005.

———. "Thinkable Alternatives in African American Studies." *American Quarterly* 58, no. 1 (March 2006): 245–53.

Saxton, Alexander. *The Rise and Fall of the White Republic: Class Politics and Mass Culture in Nineteenth-Century America.* London: Verso, 1990.

Schueller, Malini Johar. Introduction to *A Colored Man Round the World*, by David F. Dorr, ix–xliii. Ann Arbor: University of Michigan Press, 1999.

Schuyler, George Samuel. "The Negro-Art Hokum." In *The Norton Anthology of African American Literature*, edited by Henry Louis Gates Jr. and Nellie Y. McKay, 1221–23. 2nd ed. New York: W. W. Norton, 2004.

Seacole, Mary. *Wonderful Adventures of Mrs. Seacole in Many Lands.* 1857. New York: Oxford University Press, 1988.

Sernett, Milton C. *Harriet Tubman: Myth, Memory, and History.* Durham: Duke University Press, 2007.

Shapiro, Thomas M. *The Hidden Cost of Being African American: How Wealth Perpetuates Inequality.* Oxford: Oxford University Press, 2004.

Sherman, Joan R. *Invisible Poets: Afro-Americans of the Nineteenth Century.* 2nd ed. Urbana: University of Illinois Press, 1989.

Shorter, Susan I. *The Heroines of African Methodism.* Jacksonville, Fla., 1891.

Shuffelton, Frank. *A Mixed Race: Ethnicity in Early America.* New York: Oxford University Press, 1993.

Siemerling, Winfried, and Katrin Schwenk, eds. *Cultural Difference and the Literary Text: Pluralism and the Limits of Authenticity in North American Literatures.* Iowa City: University of Iowa Press, 1996.

Silver, Andrew. *Minstrelsy and Murder: The Crisis of Southern Humor, 1835–1925.* Baton Rouge: Louisiana State University Press, 2006.

Simmons, William J. *Men of Mark: Eminent, Progressive, Rising.* 1887. Chicago: Johnson Publishing, 1970.

Simms, Rev. James M. *The First Colored Baptist Church in North America: Constituted at Savannah, Georgia, January 20, A.D. 1788: With Biographical Sketches of the Pastors.* 1888. New York: Negro Universities Press, 1969.

Sinnette, Elinor Des Verney, W. Paul Coates, and Thomas G. Battle, eds. *Black Bibliophiles and Collectors: Preservers of Black History.* Washington, D.C.: Howard University Press, 1990.

Sipkins, Henry. *An Oration on the Abolition of the Slave Trade: Delivered in the African Church, in the City of New York, January 2, 1809.* In *Early Negro Writing, 1760–1837*, by Dorothy Porter, 365–73. Baltimore: Black Classic Press, 1994.

Sizer, Lyde Cullen. *The Political Work of Northern Women Writers and the Civil War, 1850–1872*. Chapel Hill: University of North Carolina Press, 2000.

Skinner, Elliott P. *African Americans and U.S. Policy Toward Africa, 1850–1924*. Washington, D.C.: Howard University Press, 1992.

Smiley, Tavis, ed. *The Covenant in Action*. Carlsbad, Calif.: Smiley Books, 2006.

———, ed. *The Covenant with Black America*. Chicago: Third World Press, 2006.

Smith, James McCune. Introduction to *My Bondage and My Freedom*, by Frederick Douglass. In *Frederick Douglass: Autobiographies*, edited by Henry Louis Gates Jr., 125–37. New York: Library of America, 1994.

Smith, Kimberly K. *The Dominion of Voice: Riot, Reason, and Romance in Antebellum Politics*. Lawrence: University Press of Kansas, 1999.

Smith, Mark M. *How Race Is Made: Slavery, Segregation, and the Senses*. Chapel Hill: University of North Carolina Press, 2006.

———. *Mastered by the Clock: Time, Slavery, and Freedom in the American South*. Chapel Hill: University of North Carolina Press, 1997.

Smith, R. D. "Social Structures and Chaos Theory." *Sociological Research Online* 3, no. 1, <http://www.socresonline.org.uk/3/1/11.html> (May 27, 2008).

Smith, Rogers M. *Civic Ideals: Conflicting Visions of Citizenship in U.S. History*. New Haven: Yale University Press, 1997.

Smith, Stephanie A. *Conceived by Liberty: Maternal Figures and 19th-Century American Literature*. Ithaca, N.Y.: Cornell University Press, 1994.

Smith, Thelma M., ed. *Uncollected Poems of James Russell Lowell*. 1950. Reprint, Westport, Conn.: Greenwood Press, 1976.

Smith, Theophus H. *Conjuring Culture: Biblical Formations of Black America*. New York: Oxford University Press, 1994.

Smith, Valerie. *Self-Discovery and Authority in Afro-American Narrative*. Cambridge: Harvard University Press, 1991.

Sollors, Werner. *Neither Black nor White, yet Both: Thematic Explorations of Interracial Literature*. Cambridge: Harvard University Press, 1997.

Sorisio, Carolyn. *Fleshing Out America: Race, Gender, and the Politics of the Body in American Literature, 1833–1879*. Athens: University of Georgia Press, 2002.

Spady, James G. "Drusilla D. Houston: A Umum Commentary, a Search and Personal Notes." In *Wonderful Ethiopians of the Ancient Cushite Empire*, by Drusilla Dunjee Houston, v–viii. Baltimore: Black Classic Press, 1985.

Spencer, Suzette A. "Henry Box Brown, an International Fugitive: Slavery, Resistance, and Imperialism." In *Black Geographies and the Politics of Place*, edited by Katherine McKittrick and Clyde Woods, 115–36. Cambridge, Mass.: South End Press, 2007.

Spillers, Hortense J. "Afterword: Cross-Currents, Discontinuities: Black Women's Fiction." In *Conjuring: Black Women, Fiction, and Literary Tradition*, edited by Marjorie Pryse and Hortense J. Spillers, 249–61. Bloomington: Indiana University Press, 1985.

Stadler, Gustavus. *Troubling Minds: The Cultural Politics of Genius in the United States, 1840–1890*. Minneapolis: University of Minnesota Press, 2006.

Stalnaker, Robert C. *Context and Content: Essays on Intentionality in Speech and Thought*. Oxford: Oxford University Press, 1999.

Stange, Douglas Charles. *British Unitarians against American Slavery, 1833–65.* London: Associated University Presses, 1984.

Stanley, Amy Dru. *From Bondage to Contract: Wage Labor, Marriage, and the Market in the Age of Slave Emancipation.* Cambridge: Cambridge University Press, 1998.

Stanton, William. *The Leopard's Spots: Scientific Attitudes toward Race in America, 1815–59.* Midway Reprint. Chicago: University of Chicago Press, 1960.

Starke, Catherine Juanita. *Black Portraiture in American Fiction: Stock Characters, Archetypes, and Individuals.* New York: Basic Books, 1971.

Starling, Marion Wilson. *The Slave Narrative: Its Place in American History.* 2nd ed. Washington, D.C.: Howard University Press, 1988.

*The Statue of John P. Hale, Erected in Front of the Capitol and Presented to the State of New Hampshire by William E. Chandler of Concord: An Account of the Unveiling Ceremonies on August 3, 1892, with a Report of the Addresses Delivered by the Donor and His Excellency Governor Hiram A. Tuttle, Councillor George A. Ramsdell, Chairman, and Messrs. Daniel Hall, Galusha A. Grow, George S. Boutwell, Frederick Douglass, Augustus Woodbury, Amos Hadley, and Alonzo H. Quint.* Concord, N.H.: Republican Press Association, 1892.

Steadman, Jennifer Bernhardt. *Traveling Economies: American Women's Travel Writing.* Columbus: Ohio State University Press, 2007.

Stearns, Charles. *The Black Man of the South, and the Rebels; or, The Characteristics of the Former, and the Recent Outrages of the Latter.* 1872. New York: Kraus Reprint, 1969.

———. *Narrative of Henry Box Brown, Who Escaped from Slavery Enclosed in a Box 3 Feet Long and 2 Wide: Written from a Statement of Facts Made by Himself, with Remarks upon the Remedy for Slavery.* Boston: Brown and Stearns, 1849.

Stepan, Nancy Leys. "Race and Gender: The Role of Analogy in Science." In *Anatomy of Racism,* edited by David Theo Goldberg, 38–57. Minneapolis: University of Minnesota Press, 1990.

Stepto, Robert B. "Distrust of the Reader in Afro-American Narratives." In *Reconstructing American Literary History,* edited by Sacvan Bercovitch, 300–322. Cambridge: Harvard University Press, 1986.

———. *From Behind the Veil: A Study of Afro-American Narrative.* 2nd ed. Urbana: University of Illinois Press, 1991.

Stewart, James Brewer. "Boston, Abolition, and the Atlantic World, 1820–1861." In *Courage and Conscience: Black and White Abolitionists in Boston,* edited by Donald M. Jacobs, 101–25. Bloomington: Indiana University Press, 1993.

Still, James. *Early Recollections and Life of Dr. James Still.* [Philadelphia]: Printed for the author by J. B. Lippincott and Co., 1877.

Still, William. *The Underground Rail Road: A Record of Facts, Authentic Narratives, Letters, &c., Narrating the Hardships, Hair-breadth Escapes and Death Struggles of the Slaves in Their Efforts for Freedom, as Related by Themselves and Others, or Witnessed by the Author; Together with Sketches of Some of the Largest Stockholders, and Most Liberal Aiders and Advisers, of the Road.* 1872. Ebony Classics; Chicago: Johnson Publishing Co., 1970.

Stocking, George W., Jr. "From Chronology to Ethnology: James Cowles Prichard and British Anthropology, 1800–1850." In *Researches into the Physical History of Man,* by

James Cowles Prichard, edited by George W. Stocking Jr., ix–cx. Chicago: University of Chicago Press, 1973.

Stokes, Claudia. *Writers in Retrospect: The Rise of American Literary History, 1875–1910.* Chapel Hill: University of North Carolina Press, 2006.

Stokes, Mason. *The Color of Sex: Whiteness, Heterosexuality, and the Fictions of White Supremacy.* Durham: Duke University Press, 2001.

Stowe, Harriet Beecher. *A Key to Uncle Tom's Cabin: Presenting the Original Facts and Documents upon Which the Story Is Founded: Together with Corroborative Statements Verifying the Truth of the Work.* 1853. Bedford, Mass.: Applewood Books, 1998.

———. Preface to *Truth Stranger than Fiction: Father Henson's Story of His Own Life.* 1858. Williamstown, Mass.: Corner House, 1973.

———. *Uncle Tom's Cabin; or, Life among the Lowly.* 1852. New York: Vintage Books/ Library of America, 1991.

Stowe, William W. *European Travel in Nineteenth-Century American Culture.* Princeton: Princeton University Press, 1994.

Stroud, George M. *Stroud's Slave Laws: A Sketch of the Laws Relating to Slavery in the Several States of the United States of America.* 1856. Baltimore: Imprint Editions, 2005.

Stroup, William F., II. "Webs of Chaos: Implications for Research Designs." In *Chaos, Complexity, and Sociology: Myths, Models, and Theories,* edited by Raymond A. Eve, Sara Horsfall, and Mary E. Lee, 125–40. Thousand Oaks, Calif.: Sage, 1997.

Stuckey, Sterling. *Going through the Storm: The Influence of African American Art in History.* New York: Oxford University Press, 1994.

———. *Slave Culture: Nationalist Theory and the Foundations of Black America.* New York: Oxford University Press, 1987.

Suggs, Jon-Christian. *Whispered Consolations: Law and Narrative in African American Life.* Ann Arbor: University of Michigan Press, 2000.

Sullivan, Shannon. *Revealing Whiteness: The Unconscious Habits of Racial Privilege.* Bloomington: Indiana University Press, 2006.

Sundquist, Eric J. *To Wake the Nations: Race in the Making of American Literature.* Cambridge: Belknap Press of Harvard University Press, 1993.

Sweet, Timothy. *Traces of War: Poetry, Photography, and the Crisis of the Union.* Baltimore: Johns Hopkins University Press, 1990.

Takaki, Ronald. *Iron Cages: Race and Culture in Nineteenth-Century America.* New York: Oxford University Press, 1990.

Tate, Claudia. *Domestic Allegories of Political Desire: The Black Heroine's Text at the Turn of the Century.* New York: Oxford University Press, 1992.

Tate, Greg, ed. *Everything but the Burden: What White People Are Taking from Black Culture.* New York: Harlem Moon, 2003.

Taylor, Clare. *British and American Abolitionists.* Edinburgh: Edinburgh University Press, 1974.

Thoreau, Henry David. "Slavery in Massachusetts." 1854. In *The Norton Anthology of American Literature, Seventh Edition, Volume B: 1820–1865,* edited by Robert S. Levine and Arnold Krupat, 2046–56. New York: W. W. Norton, 2007.

"To Our Patrons." *Freedom's Journal,* March 16, 1827.

Trollope, Anthony. *North America*. 3rd ed. 2 vols. 1862. New York: St. Martin's Press, 1986.

Trumbull, Henry. *Life and Adventures of Robert, the Hermit of Massachusetts, Who Has Lived 14 Years in a Cave, Secluded from Human Society: Comprising, an Account of His Birth, Parentage, Sufferings, and Providential Escape from Unjust and Cruel Bondage in Early Life—and His Reasons for Becoming a Recluse: Taken from His Own Mouth, and Published for His Benefit*. Providence, R.I., 1829.

Turner, Frederick. "Foreword: Chaos and Social Science." In *Chaos, Complexity, and Sociology: Myths, Models, and Theories*, edited by Raymond A. Eve, Sara Horsfall, and Mary E. Lee, xi–xxvii. Thousand Oaks, Calif.: Sage, 1997.

Turner, Stephen. *Brains/Practices/Relativism: Social Theory after Cognitive Science*. Chicago: University of Chicago Press, 2002.

*The Uncle Tom's Cabin Almanack or Abolitionist Memento*. London, 1853.

Upchurch, Thomas Adams. *Legislating Racism: The Billion Dollar Congress and the Birth of Jim Crow*. Lexington: University Press of Kentucky, 2004.

Valelly, Richard M. *The Two Reconstructions: The Struggle for Black Enfranchisement*. Chicago: University of Chicago Press, 2004.

Van Deburg, William L. *Hoodlums: Black Villains and Social Bandits in American Life*. Chicago: University of Chicago Press, 2004.

Van Evrie, J. H. *White Supremacy and Negro Subordination; or, Negroes a Subordinate Race, and (So-called) Slavery Its Normal Condition, with an Appendix Showing the Past and Present Condition of the Countries South of Us*. New York, 1868.

Vlach, John Michael. *Back of the Big House: The Architecture of Plantation Slavery*. Chapel Hill: University of Chapel Hill Press, 1993.

Vogel, Todd. *ReWriting White: Race, Class, and Cultural Capital in Nineteenth-Century America*. New Brunswick, N.J.: Rutgers University Press, 2004.

Wald, Priscilla. *Constituting Americans: Cultural Anxiety and Narrative Form*. Durham: Duke University Press, 1995.

Walker, David. *David Walker's Appeal to the Coloured Citizens of the World*. 1830. Edited by Peter P. Hinks. University Park: Pennsylvania State University Press, 2000.

Wall, Cheryl, ed. *Changing Our Own Words: Essays on Criticism, Theory, and Writing by Black Women*. New Brunswick, N.J.: Rutgers University Press, 1989.

Ward, Samuel Ringgold. *Autobiography of a Fugitive Negro: His Anti-Slavery Labors in the United States, Canada, and England*. 1855. Chicago: Johnson Publishing Co., 1970.

Warren, Joyce W. *Women, Money, and the Law: Nineteenth-Century Fiction, Gender, and the Courts*. Iowa City: University of Iowa Press, 2005.

Warren, Kenneth W. *Black and White Strangers: Race and American Literary Realism*. Chicago: University of Chicago Press, 1993.

———. "From the Superscript: A Response to Michael Awkward." *American Literary History* 4 (Spring 1992): 97–103.

Washington, Robert E. *The Ideologies of African American Literature: From the Harlem Renaissance to the Black Nationalist Revolt*. Lanham, Md.: Rowman and Littlefield, 2001.

Watkins, William. *Address Delivered before the Moral Reform Society, in Philadelphia,*

*August 8, 1836.* In *Early Negro Writing, 1760–1837,* edited by Dorothy Porter, 155–66. Baltimore: Black Classic Press, 1994.

Webb, Frank J. *The Garies and Their Friends.* 1857. Baltimore: Johns Hopkins University Press, 1997.

Weierman, Karen Woods. *One Nation, One Blood; Interracial Marriage in American Fiction, Scandal, and Law, 1820–1870.* Amherst: University of Massachusetts Press, 2005.

Weinauer, Ellen M. "'A Most Respectable Looking Gentleman': Passing, Possession, and Transgression in *Running a Thousand Miles for Freedom.*" In *Passing and the Fictions of Identity,* edited by Elaine K. Ginsberg, 37–56. Durham: Duke University Press, 1996.

Weiner, Mark S. *Black Trials: Citizenship from the Beginnings of Slavery to the End of Caste.* New York: Knopf, 2004.

Weixlmann, Joe, and Chester J. Fontenot, eds. *Studies in Black American Literature, Volume II: Belief vs. Theory in Black American Literary Criticism.* Greenwood, Fla.: Penkevill Publishing Co., 1986.

Weld, Theodore Dwight. *American Slavery as It Is: Testimony of a Thousand Witnesses.* 1839. New York: Arno Press and the New York Times, 1968.

White, Barbara A. "'Our Nig' and the She-Devil: New Information about Harriet Wilson and the 'Bellmont' Family." *American Literature* 65, no. 1 (March 1993): 19–52.

White, Hayden. *Metahistory: The Historical Imagination in Nineteenth-Century Europe.* Baltimore: Johns Hopkins University Press, 1973.

Williams, George Washington. *History of the Negro Race in America from 1619 to 1880: Negroes as Slaves, as Soldiers, and as Citizens; Together with a Preliminary Consideration of the Unity of the Human Family, an Historical Sketch of Africa, and an Account of the Negro Governments of Sierra Leone and Liberia.* 2 vols. 1883. Salem, N.H.: Ayer, 1989.

———. *A History of the Negro Troops in the War of the Rebellion, 1861–1865, Preceded by a Review of the Military Services of Negroes in Ancient and Modern Times.* 1888. New York: Negro Universities Press, 1969.

"William Wells Brown at Philadelphia." *Liberator,* January 26, 1855, 14.

Willson, Joseph. *Sketches of the Higher Classes of Colored Society in Philadelphia: The Elite of Our People: Joseph Wilson's Sketches of Black Upper-Class Life in Antebellum Philadelphia.* 1841. University Park: Pennsylvania State University Press, 2000.

Wilson, Edmund. *Patriotic Gore: Studies in the Literature of the American Civil War.* New York: Oxford University Press, 1962.

Wilson, Harriet E. *Our Nig; or, Sketches from the Life of a Free Black, in a Two-Story White House, North, Showing That Slavery's Shadows Fall Even There, by "Our Nig."* 1859. New York: Penguin, 2005.

Wilson, Joseph T. *The Black Phalanx: African American Soldiers in the War of Independence, the War of 1812 and the Civil War.* 1887. New York: Da Capo Press, 1994.

Wilson, William J. "Afric-American Picture Gallery." In *The Anglo-African Magazine, Volume 1—1859,* edited by William Loren Katz, 52–55, 87–90, 100–103, 173–77, 216–19, 243–47, 321–24. New York: Arno Press and the New York Times, 1968.

Winks, Robin W. General Introduction to *Four Fugitive Slave Narratives,* edited by Robin W. Winks et al., v–vii. Reading, Mass.: Addison-Wesley, 1969.

———. Introduction to *An Autobiography of the Reverend Josiah Henson.* In *Four Fugitive*

*Slave Narratives*, edited by Robin W. Winks et al., v–xxxiv. Reading, Mass.: Addison-Wesley, 1969.

Wolf, Eva Sheppard. *Race and Liberty in the New Nation: Emancipation in Virginia from the Revolution to Nat Turner's Rebellion*. Baton Rouge: Louisiana State University Press, 2006.

Wonham, Henry B. *Playing the Races: Ethnic Caricature and American Literary Realism*. Oxford: Oxford University Press, 2004.

Wood, Forrest G. *Black Scare: The Racist Response to Emancipation and Reconstruction*. Berkeley: University of California Press, 1970.

Wood, Marcus. *Blind Memory: Visual Representations of Slavery in England and America, 1780–1865*. New York: Routledge, 2000.

Worley, Sam. "Solomon Northup and the Sly Philosophy of the Slave Pen." *Callaloo* 20, no. 1 (Winter 1997): 243–59.

Wyatt-Brown, Bertram. *Hearts of Darkness: Wellsprings of a Southern Literary Tradition*. Baton Rouge: Louisiana State University Press, 2003.

Yellin, Jean Fagan. *Harriet Jacobs: A Life*. Basic Books, 2004.

———. *The Intricate Knot: Black Figures in American Literature, 1776–1863*. New York: New York University Press, 1972.

Young, Elizabeth. *Disarming the Nation: Women's Writing and the American Civil War*. Chicago: University of Chicago Press, 1999.

Young, John K. *Black Writers, White Publishers: Marketplace Politics in Twentieth-Century African American Literature*. Jackson: University Press of Mississippi, 2006.

Zackodnik, Teresa C. *The Mulatta and the Politics of Race*. Jackson: University Press of Mississippi, 2004.

Zafar, Rafia. "Over-Exposed, Under-Exposed: Harriet Jacobs and *Incidents in the Life of a Slave Girl*." In *Harriet Jacobs and* Incidents in the Life of a Slave Girl: *New Critical Essays*, edited by Deborah M. Garfield and Rafia Zafar, 1–10. Cambridge: Cambridge University Press, 1996.

———. *We Wear the Mask: African Americans Write American Literature, 1760–1870*. New York: Columbia University Press, 1997.

# INDEX

Delany, Martin R., 31, 166, 195, 206
—works: *Blake*, 146, 164; *The Condition*, 209
Deleuze, Gilles, 63
Democratic Party, 206
Democratic State Convention (1860 Charleston, S.C.), 229, 231
Dimock, Wai-Chee, 154, 156, 160
Dixon, Thomas, Jr., 117, 199, 200, 205
Dorr, David F.: *A Colored Man Round the World*, 161–63, 182
Doughton, Thomas, 80
Douglass, Frederick, 31, 32, 79, 80, 89–90, 91, 95–96, 102, 116, 120–22, 124, 131–32, 151, 163, 164, 165, 166, 177, 178–80, 181, 205, 215, 241, 245
—works: *The Heroic Slave*, 12, 121; "Introduction to the Reason Why the Colored American is Not in the World's Columbian Exposition," 206–7; *Life and Times*, 193–95, 205; *My Bondage and My Freedom*, 103, 145–46, 194; *Narrative*, 116, 151, 205, 206; "Oration in Memory of Abraham Lincoln," 178–79
Douglass Institute (Baltimore, Md.), 124, 180
*Dred Scott* decision, 38, 47, 83, 119, 163, 174, 187
Du Bois, W. E. B., 24, 35, 203, 208
Duke University, 44
Duster, Troy, 56
Dyson, F. J., 38

Easton, Hosea, 107
Eglash, Ron, 74
Egypt, 162
Elaw, Zilpha, 81, 95, 102
Eliot, Samuel A., 92
Ellison, Ralph, 214
Emancipation Proclamation, 229, 232
Emerson, Ralph Waldo, 61
England, 93, 97, 167, 184, 206
Episcopalianism, 234
Ervin, Hazel Arnett, 23, 247

Europe, 163
Eusebius, 156
Eve, Raymond A., 64, 72, 73

Fabre, Geneviève, 214
Fahey, David M., 230
Fahs, Alice, 203–4
Farmer, William, 75
Federal Housing Administration, 41
Fisch, Audrey, 145
Fisher, William W., 39
Fontenot, Chester J., 246
Foote, Julia A. J., 95
Foreman, P. Gabrielle, 81
Foster, Frances Smith, 19, 78, 103–4, 123–24, 175
Foster, Stephen, 140
Fourth of July, 188
Fox, William Johnson, 168
Fractal geometry, 36–37, 38
Fractals, 21, 68, 63, 74
France, 182
*Frank Leslie's Illustrated Paper*, 126
Franklin, John Hope, 56
Fredrickson, George M., 56, 236
Freedmen's Bank, 194, 195
Freedmen's Monument, 178
*Freedom's Journal*, 123, 172, 197
Freemasons, 230
Fugitive Slave Law, 38, 163, 186, 187
Fulton, Alice, 21, 214

Gage, Frances Dana, 126, 128, 223
Gaines, Wesley J.: *African Methodism in the South*, 208
Gardner, Eric, 81, 104
Garner, Margaret, 91
Garnet, Henry Highland, 166
Garrison, William Lloyd, 146, 169
Garvey, Marcus, 11
Gates, Henry Louis, Jr., 12, 15, 19–22, 81, 87, 205, 246, 253–54
Gayle, Addison, Jr., 23, 246
Geertz, Clifford, 28
Georgia, 206, 184, 212